A SOLDIER AND A WOMAN

WOMEN AND MEN IN HISTORY

This series, published for students, scholars and interested general readers, will tackle themes in gender history from the early medieval period through to the present day. Gender issues are now an integral part of all history courses and yet many traditional texts do not reflect this change. Much exciting work is now being done to redress the gender imbalances of the past, and we hope that these books will make their own substantial contribution to that process. This is an open-ended series, which means that many new titles can be included. We hope that these will both synthesise and shape future developments in gender studies.

The General Editors of the series are *Patricia Skinner* (University of Southampton) for the medieval period; *Pamela Sharpe* (University of Bristol) for the early modern period; and *Penny Summerfield* (University of Lancaster) for the modern period. *Margaret Walsh* (University of Nottingham) was the Founding Editor of the series.

Published books:

A SOLDIER AND A WOMAN

Sexual Integration in the Military

edited by

Gerard J. DeGroot and
Corinna Peniston-Bird

Longman

An imprint of **Pearson Education**

Harlow, England · London · New York · Reading, Massachusetts · San Francisco
Toronto · Don Mills, Ontario · Sydney · Tokyo · Singapore · Hong Kong · Seoul
Taipei · Cape Town · Madrid · Mexico City · Amsterdam · Munich · Paris · Milan

Pearson Education Limited
Edinburgh Gate
Harlow
Essex CM20 2JE
England

and Associated Companies throughout the world

Visit us on the world wide web at:
http://www.pearsoneduc.com

First published 2000

ISBN 0 582 41439 3 CSD
ISBN 0 582 41438 5 PPR

British Library Cataloguing-in-Publication Data
A catalogue record for this book is available from the British Library

Library of Congress Cataloging-in-Publication Data
A soldier and a woman : sexual integration in the military / edited by Gerard J. DeGroot
and C.M. Peniston-Bird.
     p. cm. — (Women and men in history)
  Includes bibliographical references and index.
    ISBN 0–582–41439–3 (alk. paper) — ISBN 0–582–41438–5 (pbk.: alk. paper)
    1. Women soldiers—History. I. De Groot, Gerard J., 1955– II. Peniston-Bird,
C.M. III. Series.

  UB416.S65   2000
  355′.0082—dc21   00–021675

Typeset by 35 in 11/13pt Baskerville MT
Produced by Pearson Education Asia Pte Ltd.
Printed in Singapore

TO

LIEUTENANT-COLONEL
JANET ANN BORCH,
US ARMY

in every sense a soldier and a woman

AND

NICOLA F. PENISTON-BIRD

AMANDA C. PENISTON-BIRD

for their example and resolution

CONTENTS

CONTENTS

This book represents a labour of love. It is a subject of subtle nuance and cruel irony which inspires endless fascination, not to mention considerable frustration. During the course of writing and editing we have come to understand more deeply the role of women in society, the connection between service and citizenship, and the way that gender distinctions constrain both men and women.

We are aware that this is an ever-developing topic – that, in fact, provides much of its fascination. But we are also aware that, though great strides have been made in the sexual integration of some militaries, many of the problems which women soldiers face today are no different from those they have always faced. While military experience has changed women, women have not had great success in changing the military.

Progress is nevertheless evident, and that progress inspired the decision to divide the book into two distinct sections. Although 1945 is not by any means an identifiable watershed, it does nevertheless seem that the experiences of women in the military have changed more significantly since the Second World War than in the centuries before it. Before 1945 women's participation in the military was usually seen as a regrettable necessity brought about by wartime demands for labour. Because the participation of women in the military was often seen as unfortunate and sometimes as embarrassing, societies were keen to forget their contribution.

Since 1945, female military participation has been grafted onto a powerful feminist ethic. Though women have still contributed to wars out of necessity, there has in addition arisen a significant 'right to fight' movement which seeks to break down the barriers to service. That service has, in addition, proved a great deal more difficult to camouflage. Women are demanding expanded opportunities within the military and more recognition of their contribution. Recognition has not only come in the usual forms of medals and pensions, but also in a greater awareness of the special problems which women encounter in their service within what remains a distinctly masculine institution.

Some may judge this an overtly feminist book. That was never our intention. We set out to analyse the participation of women in the military in a way which would be accessible to the general reader but still challenging to the specialist in this new and growing field. We had no feminist agenda and urged our contributors to avoid imposing such an agenda on the reader. But the chapters in this book do reveal how women have been manipulated and exploited for particular purposes in wartime and how their important contributions to war have been discounted or ignored. In other words, the feminist message arises quite naturally out of the subject matter itself rather than as a dialectic imposed by the authors.

The project remained a labour of love because of the cooperation and diligence of the authors. They deserve congratulation for putting up with our editorial intervention with consummate graciousness. One of the great benefits of a project of this sort is the chance to meet (if only by e-mail) a talented and dynamic group of scholars scattered all over the world. We are deeply grateful for the opportunity to work with them. We are also grateful to Penny Summerfield for her constructive and timely advice, and to Julian Crowe for bearing our computer and e-mail problems with patience and grace.

Gerard J. DeGroot and
Corinna Peniston-Bird

St Andrews, November 1999

ACKNOWLEDGEMENTS

We would like to thank Lynda Van Devanter and Joan A. Furey for permission to cite the following poets from their anthology, *Visions of War, Dreams of Peace*, (New York: Time Warner Books, 1991):

Joan A. Furey, Norma J. Griffiths, Diane C. Jaeger, Diane Carlson Evans, Sara J. McVicker, Dana Schuster, Marilyn McMahon, Lily Lee Adams, Dusty, Mary Lu Ostergren Brunner, Penny Kettlewell, Sharon Grant, and Mary O'Brien Tyrell.

PART ONE

Sexual Integration in the Military
before 1945

INTRODUCTION

Arms and the Woman

GERARD J. DEGROOT

During the First World War, the British poet Nora Bomford expressed her frustration at being unable to fight for her country:

> *Sex, nothing more, constituent no greater*
> *Than those which make an eyebrow's slant or fall,*
> *In origin, sheer accident, which, later,*
> *Decides the biggest differences of all.*
> *And, through a war, involves the chance of death*
> *Against a life of physical normality –*
> *So dreadfully safe! O, damn the shibboleth*
> *Of sex! God knows we've equal personality.*
> *Why should men face the dark while women stay*
> *To live and laugh and meet the sun each day.*[1]

The Bomford poem expresses a number of themes central to this book. It is not an overtly feminist statement, though some feminists find her sentiments admirable. Rather, Bomford's desire to fight arises out of her love of country and her feeling of injustice at the fact that men should suffer war's horrors while women remain the protected ones. She also seems fully confident of the ability of women to fight, sensing that the obstacles to their participation in combat are arbitrarily determined gender distinctions – the shibboleth of sex. This book is about women who attempted to defy those distinctions, in the process challenging the essentially masculine nature of war. It is about revolution, but also counter-revolution – the way societies have contained the threat posed by women's participation in the military and how gender norms are powerfully reasserted when peace returns.

---

1. Nora Bomford, 'Drafts', in Catherine Reilly, ed., *Scars Upon My Heart* (London, 1981), p. 12.

Since the early 1970s, military service, and particularly participation in combat, has been seen by some feminists as one of the most important bastions of patriarchy. To knock it down, it seems, would leave the entire edifice of male domination fatally weakened. These 'right to fight' feminists have challenged governments and the military establishment to allow women into areas of combat from which they have heretofore been excluded. But for most feminists the issue is symbolic; few actually aspire to drive a tank or fire a machine gun in anger. Thus, the real battles have been fought by proxies: women who want to serve because they love their country or because they are attracted by the thrill of landing a fighter on an aircraft carrier in choppy seas. In fact, those women who want to fight very seldom express their demands in feminist terms or seek overtly to advance the cause of women. This is partly because the naturally conservative military is not a very comfortable home for a woman keen to rebel against social conventions. The woman who aspires to an active military career often wants only to change a few of the rules regarding where and in what capacity she herself might serve. She otherwise supports the military's role as a guardian of tradition. She wants to fight because she is proud of and seeks to preserve the society in which she lives.

As the chapters in this book demonstrate, those women who served in the military before 1945 did so for sublime patriotic reasons. They might have been empowered as a result of this service and made more aware of the injustices of patriarchy, but that was not the motivation for service in the first place. For instance, as Christopher Schmitz shows, British women who volunteered for service as nurses during the Boer War were very often members of suffrage societies, but their motivation for going was to relieve the suffering of soldiers and to play their small part in the defence of the British Empire. The benefit which their service brought to the cause of votes for women was incidental. Likewise, those who joined the 1st Russian Women's Battalion of Death during the First World War, as Laurie Stoff shows in her chapter, did so for overtly conservative purposes, namely because they wanted to win the war and preserve the political *status quo*. They opposed the Bolsheviks, even though, if propaganda was to be believed, the Bolsheviks offered the better hope for women's emancipation. One is reminded of the response the militant suffragette Emmeline Pankhurst gave to critics who questioned her willingness to serve the 'oppressive' British state after war broke out in 1914: 'What would be the good of a vote without a country to vote in?'[2] The story is the same in almost every chapter of this book: women are motivated by deeply patriotic feelings but are often frustrated in their attempts to express their patriotism actively.

---

2. Christabel Pankhurst, *Unshackled* (London, 1959), p. 288.

Service is sometimes seen as a way to achieve female empowerment, not through demonstrating the contribution women can make, but rather because the cause itself seems to offer the best hope for women. As Helen Young reveals in her chapter, Chinese women were motivated to participate in the Long March because of a desire to play a part in the Communist revolution, but also because Communism seemed to offer a better life for women.

This is significant because women have not traditionally been given an opportunity – through political or military service – to demonstrate their patriotism or devotion to a cause, and as a result have not been seen as real patriots. Lacking the opportunity to demonstrate their citizenship, they have been unable to prove that they are fully fledged citizens, deserving of the basic rights automatically accorded men. The testimony of women who served in the auxiliary forces in Britain during the Second World War reveals a deep sense of pride (not to mention delight) at being given the opportunity to bear the burdens of citizenship. Through service, a sense of belonging emerged. This process of realizing national identity is perhaps most evident amongst women (because they have seldom been given the opportunity to serve), but not peculiar to them. What the women felt was, for instance, hardly different from the emotions of British working-class males in the First World War, who flooded to recruiting offices when the Secretary of State for War, Herbert Kitchener, pointed at them from posters and told them they were needed. Never before had anyone in high authority expressed a need for them.

It is only by understanding the sense of importance felt by heretofore marginalized groups during wartime that one can understand the frustration felt when participation was denied. As Penny Summerfield demonstrates, the disappointment felt by women who wanted to join the Home Guard in Britain in the Second World War was deep because the very existence of the Home Guard seemed to demonstrate that the need was urgent. Men deemed unfit for regular military service (or those in reserved occupations) were being organized into local defence units because the threat of German invasion seemed real. The very fact that old or infirm males were granted such a symbolically important role made the denial of this expression of citizenship to able-bodied women seem all the more galling. The women concerned wondered why the preservation of certain gender roles seemed more important to the government than national survival.

Women who aspired to join the Home Guard argued that their member-ship was perfectly compatible with 'women's traditional role as guardian of the home'.[3] This was a powerful argument, as it played upon a culturally

3. Penny Summerfield, ' "She wants a gun not a dishcloth!": gender, service and citizenship in Britain in the Second World War', p. 124.

acceptable form of female violence common to many societies. For instance, in Vietnamese society, an ancient proverb holds that 'When pirates enter the home, even the women must fight'. At various times, in order to secure the services of women, Vietnamese nationalists defined the home in broad terms as the nation. But in Britain during the Second World War the argument – as it applied to membership in the Home Guard – was either rejected or simply ignored by the government. Nevertheless, at exactly the same time, the idea that women should defend their homes was used to justify their participation in the auxiliary forces, particularly when this participation came perilously close to actual combat. For instance, the disruption to gender roles which the mixed-sex anti-aircraft batteries represented was cushioned some-what by frequent reference to the idea that the women were protecting their homes from a very visible German invader. The theme arose again when the government proposed that some auxiliaries (including some gunners) might be sent to the continent after June 1944. Critics objected that this deploy-ment would transform the women from defenders to invaders. 'Any woman will defend her home', the Labour MP Mrs A. Hardie argued, 'but it is very different when you send her away to other countries. . . . It is a nice new world that some . . . picture for the rising generation of women, who now not only have to produce innumerable children but fight wars as well.'[4]

For many women, service to the cause was often an extension of what were seen as natural womanly duties. At the heart of the separate spheres argument was the contention that men and women each had unique talents which predetermined their social roles. Thus, Frederick Treves, surgeon to Queen Victoria and Edward VII, who favoured the employment of women in the Boer War, argued that 'the perfect nurse . . . is versed in the elaborate ritual of her art, she has tact and sound judgement, she can give strength to the weak . . . and she is possessed of those exquisite, intangible, most human sympathies which, in the fullest degree, belong alone to her sex'.[5] Those pressing for women's involvement in war argued that these uniquely female talents had application in a theatre of war. Mabel Stobart, who formed the Women's National Service League in Britain after the declaration of war in 1914, did so with the goal of 'forming Women's Units to do women's work of relieving the suffering of sick and wounded'.[6] It is interesting that Stobart came to her decision immediately following a peace demonstration in which she felt moved to take part. When, during the course of the demonstration, news of the declaration of war reached her, she immediately began to think

---

4. Hansard, 24 January 1945.
5. See Christopher Schmitz, 'We too were soldiers: the experiences of British nurses in the Anglo-Boer War', pp. 60–1.
6. Yvonne M. Klein, ed., *Beyond the Home Front* (London, 1997), p. 20.

about the contribution she could make to the war effort. She considered it her womanly duty to campaign against war while peace still seemed possible and to relieve the suffering of war once it emerged that a conflict was inevitable.

As the chapters in this book demonstrate, the qualities Stobart had in mind had wide application. British women who volunteered as nurses during the South African War were needed because the male nurses had so obviously proved incompetent, thus causing the sick and wounded to suffer unnecessarily. Likewise, women were needed on the Long March because they were especially well-suited to the liaison and propaganda tasks essential to that particular campaign. For the march to succeed, it was necessary to obtain the cooperation of the population in the areas through which the force travelled. Because women seemed less threatening than men, they found it easier to obtain the trust of the locals. Their apparently benign countenance rendered women particularly well-suited to insurgency campaigns. As Margaret Collins Weitz demonstrates in her chapter on the French Resistance, women made effective spies and assassins for the very reason that they were not expected to play such a role. But what was galling to those women eager to perform 'women's work' was that skills so self-evident often went unrecognized by male leaders. The qualities which made women valuable to a cause – namely their nurturing nature or innocent inconspicuousness – also impeded their recognition by the cause. Because war is brutal, those who appeared ingenuous and unthreatening seemed inappropriate to the struggle. In South Africa, China and France, women had first to convince male authorities that they were qualified for 'womanly' roles.

The participation of women in the military and in war is nothing new. While formal auxiliary units composed of women are largely a twentieth-century phenomenon, women have been performing auxiliary functions throughout the history of warfare. As Brian Crim has discovered in his investigation of women's role in warfare in early modern Europe, armies often depended upon women to perform these functions without which military campaigns could not succeed. The camp follower, heretofore seen as a parasite on the military body, was in fact an essential component in the logistical chain. Poorly paid soldiers, who could not afford to leave their wives and children behind when they went on campaign, took their families with them. In 1776, the Berlin garrison of Frederick the Great consisted of 17,056 men, 5,526 women and 6,622 children. Since these women and children lived in the camps or barracks with the soldiers, they were directly subjected to, and a part of, the martial culture.[7] They were relied upon to

---

7. See Scott Hendrix, 'In the army: women, camp followers and gender roles in the British Army in the French and Indian Wars, 1755–1765', p. 40.

perform functions essential to the unit's well-being, functions which, if not for the camp followers, would otherwise have been performed by male soldiers, thus removing them from their soldiering. Again, these duties – nursing, cooking, carrying water, removing the wounded, etc. – were natural extensions of the women's domestic chores and therefore ones which seemed better performed by women. But they were no less essential for being traditionally female tasks. There is some speculation that Molly Pitcher, who supposedly manned a cannon during the American Revolutionary War, was in fact not a real individual but a mythical archetype who represents those women who serviced the needs of male soldiers. Her name may have been an expression of the function she performed, namely carrying water to the troops.[8]

The female camp followers certainly did not see themselves as parasites. That they felt an essential part of the military machine is evident from a letter which Martha May wrote to Lieutenant-Colonel Henry Bouquet during the French and Indian Wars. May, pleading for leniency from Bouquet after an unknown act of insubordination, wrote: 'I have been a Wife 22 years and have Traveld with my Husband every Place or Country the Company Marcht too and have workt very hard ever since I was in the Army'.[9] As Scott Hendrix argues, what is interesting about the incident is the overt indicators of May's sense of belonging to the unit. Like any male soldier, she was subject to military discipline, but she also felt that her long record of devoted service to the unit entitled her to lenient treatment. She felt herself to be 'in the Army' and the authorities certainly treated her as if she was.

The chapters by Crim and Hendrix demonstrate that the exclusion of women from the military is a relatively modern phenomenon, while those by Young and Collins Weitz show that it is typical only of conventional militaries. The professionalization of the military in the nineteenth and twentieth centuries meant that women came increasingly to be excluded and the support functions they performed were taken over by men. But professionalization did not mean improvement in all areas; the exclusion of women from military nursing meant, for instance, that British soldiers died unnecessarily in South Africa. As the Long March and the French Resistance demonstrate, where this professionalization was less pronounced, due to the unconventional nature of the warfare, the exclusion of women was less prevalent.

As support functions were taken over by men they were also given a legitimacy never accorded them when they were performed by women. A

---

8. See Linda Grant DePauw, *Battle Cries and Lullabies: Women in War from Prehistory to the Present* (Norman, OK, 1988), pp. 126–31, for a discussion of the myth of Molly Pitcher.
9. Hendrix, 'In the army', p. 39.

man who carried ammunition, nursed soldiers, or cooked for an army in the First or Second World War was still considered a soldier, in a way that a woman who once performed these functions never was. What gave the man this legitimacy and soldierly identity was his masculinity. Because he was a man, he had a theoretic eligibility for combat, even though he might never actually have fought. Because men could kill, they were soldiers. Because women were not supposed to kill, they could never be soldiers. This distinction has continued to the present day: the man who serves as an entertainment officer for a military unit far from the front lines has little difficulty demonstrating his legitimate right to be called a soldier, whereas the woman who serves as a nurse at a casualty clearing station has continually to suffer doubts about her soldierly identity. She is, at best, merely a woman attached to the army, a professionalized camp follower.

It is, therefore, the potential to kill which determines real soldierly identity and is the qualification for the status and social capital which accrue from that identity. Back when physical strength was a prime determinant of military prowess, that potential seemed exclusive to men, even though women were still expected to play a role in defence of their home. With the passage of time and the development of increasingly powerful weapons which do not require brute strength to operate, that distinction has become ever more arbitrary and contrived. But it has not lost its power. It has been retained because, in patriarchal societies, it remains a convenient justification for excluding full citizenship to women. Thus, early in the twentieth century, many Western societies denied the franchise to women on the grounds that they could not fight for their country. This overlooked the fact that, at the very same time, up to one-third of the male population of military age were unfit for military service on the grounds of infirmity.[10]

Women did, occasionally, seize the opportunity to demonstrate that they too could perform in combat. Some found themselves thrust into the fray by odd circumstance, while others gained entry by subterfuge, often by disguising themselves as men. But because these exceptions were both rare and bizarre, they could be dismissed as unrepresentative. They did not therefore threaten gender distinctions which stemmed from the combat shibboleth. Some of these women were fascinating, others admirable, but all seemed freaks. Neither Joan of Arc nor the fabled women who dressed as men in order to fight in the American Civil War were considered sufficiently normal to overturn patriarchal precedents. And, as Hendrix persuasively argues, the fact that a few women disguised themselves as men in order to fight

---

10. Granted, many of the men rejected for service during the South African War, for instance, were not enfranchised either. But their disenfranchisement came as a result of their social class, not their gender.

merely demonstrates how gendered the military was. Participation in combat was closed to women unless they could become men.

Feminist historians have often bought into this arbitrary distinction by paying homage to these anomalies, apparently unaware of the fact that, by doing so, they have merely demonstrated that the exception proves the rule. Because these extraordinary women were considered 'freaks', they have not made a convincing case for granting status to the multitude of 'normal' women who show no such inclination to challenge gender boundaries in such spectacular fashion. For instance, Trieu Thi Trinh, a 9-foot-tall Vietnamese giantess who rode into battle against the Chinese in the third century AD upon a massive elephant with her pendulous breasts slung over her shoulders, is a safe heroic icon precisely because few women share her physiognomy. Boudicca, a favourite feminist hero, may have demonstrated that a woman can lead an army, but because she was so clearly an exception she has not done much to convince misogynists that women as a whole deserve full rights of citizenship.

In other words, there is great danger in eulogizing women who became men. The key to attacking the combat-based standard of social capital lies in disputing the system of measurement, not in placing disproportionate emphasis upon the odd exceptions who, by strange circumstance, have managed to satisfy it. It is true that, in the past, few women ever fought. But it is also true that few men did. The proportion of males in any society who actually serve is tiny, as is the proportion of soldiers in any army who actually fight.[11] Yet all males enjoy the status which combat accords. Clearly, the definition of service has to be widened if women are to be given full credit for their contribution. Napoleon recognized that an army runs on its stomach, that the key to a unit's effectiveness is its logistics system. Throughout history women have played enormously important roles in looking after logistical functions, but have not been recognized for doing so. The problem lies not in the contribution women have made, but in the standard by which that contribution has been measured. The great tragedy of Molly Pitcher is that she has been remembered because she might once have fired a cannon, not because she was probably a camp follower who carried much-needed water to thirsty troops. Yet, under the circumstances, the latter function was far more important to the survival of her unit than the former.

When provided with the opportunity, women have demonstrated that they can fight very effectively. But because women are not supposed to fight, the instances when they have done so have been discounted or carefully

---

11. In recent times, the proportion of combat soldiers in an army at war can be as low as 10 per cent, as was the case with the American force during the Vietnam War.

camouflaged. Female members of mixed-sex anti-aircraft batteries in Second World War Britain participated actively in combat, came under fire, and suffered wounds and fatalities as a result of enemy action. But, because this service threatened the combat taboo, a clever distinction was made so that women could remain, at least in theory, non-combatants. They were prevented from loading or firing the weapons (they merely aimed them) in order to maintain the illusion that they were not actually killing. Strange anomalies resulted: if the battery came under fire a man might subsequently be awarded a medal for bravery, but the woman who stood next to him was not eligible. Since she had not been in combat, she could not show bravery.[12]

In Russia, the combat taboo has proved an unaffordable luxury on two occasions during the twentieth century. During the First World War, women were formed into all-female battalions as a last ditch effort to stave off defeat by the Germans and to buttress the Provisional Government in its struggle against the Bolsheviks. The participation of women in combat was deemed necessary not only because of the desperate situation, but also because it was thought that their presence would lift the morale of male soldiers. Men, it was hoped, would either feel strengthened by the injection of new troops or shamed into extra effort by the threat of being upstaged by women. The eagerness of women to serve turned out to be of an order neither anticipated nor welcomed by the Provisional Government. Before long, 'unofficial' women's battalions were formed without government sanction. That women could perform adequately in combat was demonstrated by the action of the 1st Russian Women's Battalion of Death on 9 July 1917. The battalion impressed senior male commanders and embarrassed German troops forced to surrender to them. But, as Stoff has revealed, the main purpose of the plan backfired. Instead of inspiring regular Russian troops to greater efforts, the women's battalions caused a decline in morale, since male soldiers concluded that the situation must indeed be desperate if the country had been forced to turn to women. Nor did the experience have a measurable effect upon the future policies of the Soviet government toward the employment of women in combat. It was, instead, conveniently forgotten or derided as a desperate measure by a bankrupt government.

Nevertheless, in the Second World War, the Soviet government was forced to turn in desperation to women after the Germans invaded in June 1942. Women served in a number of different combat capacities in every branch of service, but most noticeably as fighter pilots. Despite being deployed in

---

12. See Gerard DeGroot, 'Whose finger on the trigger?: Mixed anti-aircraft batteries and the female combat taboo', *War in History* 4 (1997), p. 437.

antiquated aeroplanes, they performed with great distinction. According to Reina Pennington, an objective assessment reveals no difference in their standard of performance in comparison with all-male units. The women displayed the requisite ruthlessness and bravery in dogfights and, as with any such unit, suffered terrible casualties. But, after the war, the nation seemed determined to forget the experiment, which became an embarrassment. Women who wanted to continue in military aviation after the war were, by a variety of means, prevented from doing so. The status of Soviet women did not benefit measurably from their wartime combat contribution. They were encouraged instead to return to the home and to concentrate on having children in order to replenish the population depleted by war. Giving birth was presented as a more important and natural service to the state than that of combat.

It would seem that the best hope for female empowerment through military service might lie in unconventional wars or insurgent units, where the apparatus for their exclusion is not well-established and the pragmatism borne of desperation might offer them greater opportunity to defy the combat taboo. On the surface this seems to be the case. Women of the French Resistance and the Long March occasionally entered the forbidden zone of combat. But when they did so, they were seen as exceptions and the practice itself was not encouraged. Male soldiers (and quite a few women) still felt a profound sense of unease about the idea that women might kill. Nor did the status of the women concerned improve accordingly. In the case of the French Resistance, this is in part because insurgency operations often value women as women. In other words, womanly stereotypes are used to mask a sinister intent, a subterfuge which allows women to make a valuable, often deadly, contribution. Thus, the apparently pure-as-snow virgin tapes ammunition to the inside of her thighs and walks innocently past a guard, or the 'harlot' lures an enemy soldier with promises of carnal delights, then slits his throat. Both tasks require great bravery, but both merely confirm that the 'soldier' is in fact a woman, since neither could be performed by a man. Likewise, the Chinese women who eased the path of the Long March by liaising with the local population performed a task essential to the success of the operation, but that task merely confirmed that they were gentle women who did not stimulate fear. In all these cases, the women's contribution did not inspire a reconsideration of patriarchal social order because they did not threaten masculine stereotypes or contradict feminine ones.

An example of the way images of women warriors have been manipulated so as to maintain traditional gender divisions can be derived from the experience of Britain in the First World War. Only two women, Mairi Chisholm and Elsie Knocker, were allowed to serve within range of German guns. They were drawn to the idea of being men – in other words, doing what women were expressly forbidden from doing. Yet to the public they were attractive because they were either angelic or erotic, according to the taste of the observer. For most, they were the Angels of Pervyse – the masculinity of their motorcycle riding subsumed by their femininity as angels of mercy. But there were undoubtedly some observers who derived erotic satisfaction from photos of the comely young women attired in leather with a powerful motorcyle between their legs. According to either image, they were heroic but still essentially feminine. In contrast, the public felt deep unease about Flora Sandes, who actually fought with the Serbian Army and thus squandered her femininity. Photos of and comment about Sandes implied that she was not really a woman. She was attractive only to those who like their women butch.

The Sandes episode reveals how women who have trespassed into the military domain have been redefined and placed in an uncomfortable limbo where they have lost the most admired aspects of femininity but are denied the status accorded male heroes. Their service has not inspired a redefinition of the qualities of women as a whole or of the masculine nature of war. They are changed by their military service, but their service does not change the military. All this demonstrates that the ability to kill is a very odd sort of distinction by which status in society has been determined: women do not earn coveted political status when they demonstrate that they can kill, while men do not have to prove their ability to take another's life in order to earn that status. Just how important the symbols and gender distinctions are can be seen from the fact that opposition to women in the Home Guard was denied long after the threat of invasion had passed. Even though the Guard had no reasonable prospect of ever seeing combat, women were not allowed to join it. Likewise, women anti-aircraft gunners were forbidden from 'killing' the unmanned V-1 flying bombs.

The experience of Russian women demonstrates how difficult it is to break down gender distinctions. Maria Bochkarëva, who commanded the 1st Russian Women's Battalion of Death, sought to remove all traces of femininity among the women she commanded, in the mistaken belief that this would make them better soldiers and, at the very least, would render them more acceptable to the male military establishment. Items of personal hygiene like toothbrushes and make-up were confiscated, while the women were given crew-cuts, and were encouraged to smoke and swear. Giggling was strictly forbidden. Bochkarëva seemed to think that, through dressing and acting like men, women might become men, at least as far as the military establishment was concerned. Yet the disguise did not allow women entry into the exclusive masculine warrior culture; it only served to emphasize their alienation from feminine culture. In trying to be like men, they merely succeeded in being unlike women. Though one can see the fallacy in Bochkaréva's tactics, one can understand her motivation. The experiences of British servicewomen during the Second World War seems to suggest that proximity to an overtly masculine culture made women more concerned about asserting their femininity. Evidence suggests that the women became even more obsessed with make-up and frilly undergarments than they ever were during their civilian lives. Thus, forced to join the military, many women sought to assert their femininity, perhaps in fear that the institution might otherwise render them more masculine. But, in so doing, they merely underlined the fact that they were intruders in a male domain.

Fighting a war encompasses myriad tasks, not all of which involve cold-blooded killing. Because participation in war is accorded great prestige within society, women's participation has been either inhibited by arbitrary means or discounted when it plainly occurs. When women have contributed to the logistical apparatus of war, their contribution has not been recognized. When those contributions were eventually formally recognized through actual incorporation into the military apparatus, the women concerned were nevertheless marginalized as auxiliaries, in order to emphasize the difference between combatants and non-combatants. Auxiliaries did not enlist, they were enrolled; they were supervised, not commanded; and they were subject to an entirely different code of conduct from that which applied to men. All this underlined their inferior, semi-detached status within the military. When, on rare occasions, women were deployed in a combat capacity, no great precedents were set. Women who killed did not destroy the combat taboo. Their contribution has been subsequently discounted either by reference to the exceptional circumstances (desperate measures), or by downplaying the actual contribution, or by presenting the women themselves as freakish exceptions who are not identifiable as 'normal' women. Thus, David Robertson MP, one of the most outspoken critics of the campaign for women to be included in the British Home Guard, argued that 'a woman's duty is to give life not to take it'. To train women to kill was, in his mind, 'abhorrent'.[13]

The veterans of Soviet aviation studied by Pennington reveal how deeply embedded gender stereotypes are. Despite themselves demonstrating that women could be effective fighters, an astonishing number of them felt that war was simply not the business of women. They believed that women, as the givers of life, should not kill. 'War is not for women; women shouldn't participate. In a way it's against their nature, because women's first purpose is to preserve peace', one woman argued. Another female veteran felt that 'the very nature of a woman rejects the idea of fighting. A woman is born to

---

13. See Summerfield, '"She wants a gun not a dishcloth!" ...', p. 128.

give birth to children, to nurture. Flying combat missions is against our nature.' 'Was the war a woman's business?', a former pilot asked herself. 'Of course not . . . To be in the army in crucial periods is one thing, but to want to be in the military is not quite natural for a woman.'[14] Thus, they signalled an agreement with the widely held opinion that their service was an aberration – an unavoidable necessity of no relevance to the structure of normal life.

Nevertheless, many women were empowered (in a personal sense) by their experiences in the military, and the closer to combat they got, the more significant the transformation they underwent. For women, service to a cause inevitably meant dying for it, even when special efforts were made to protect them. The enormous significance of being able to die for one's country was not lost on the women themselves. Theodosia Bagot described the burial of a nurse who had died of typhoid in Bloemfontein, South Africa: '[If] the thought of a soldier's funeral is sad, what would the reader have felt had he passed one, wrapped like a soldier in the nation's colours, borne by soldiers to a soldier's grave, who was receiving the only earthly honour that could be done to a noble woman – a soldier's funeral!'[15]

Female martyrs and heroes proved useful during a war, but seemed a dangerous threat to the social order after it. Those interested in preserving the *status quo* (not all of them men) took steps to reassert feminine standards in order to curb any consequent improvement of women's status. For instance, as has been discussed, Soviet women pilots were prevented from continuing their commissions after the war ended. During the war, they were often presented in such a way as to stress their femininity. Thus they were shown in suggestive, vampish poses outside their aeroplanes, or, alternatively, were photographed knitting between flying sorties – a symbolic reassertion of motherhood, their natural domain. Posters depicting auxiliaries in Britain in the Second World War almost always showed them in clean, neat, well-pressed dresses and almost never depicted them doing tasks which involved using their muscles or getting dirty. During the last year of the war, these women were given time off for mothercraft lessons, in order to prepare them for and remind them of their peacetime role. This practice brings to mind the Amazons of Greek mythology who, according to Ilse Kirk, were transformed into proper women through marriage. In becoming wives and mothers, they were disarmed and made normal.[16]

---

14. See Reina Pennington, '"Do not speak of the services you rendered": women veterans of aviation in the Soviet Union', p. 164.
15. See Schmitz, '"We too were soldiers"', p. 164.
16. Ilse Kirk, 'Images of Amazons: marriage and matriarchy', in Sharon MacDonald, ed., *Images of Women in Peace and War* (London, 1987), p. 31.

One effective way of discounting the contribution of women to the military and thus to limit their empowerment was to present them as dangerous sexual predators, or else to imply that biological determinism (pregnancies, menstruation, and lower physical strength) rendered them ill-suited to warfare. The fact that camp followers have traditionally been seen as prostitutes rather than as useful adjuncts to early modern militaries might be seen as a calculated attempt to discount the contribution of women to war. According to this myth, they preyed upon male soldiers, sapping their strength. British and American auxiliaries during the Second World War had to endure a vicious whispering campaign which cast them as promiscuous adventurers who spread venereal disease and corrupted noble warriors. This had the added effect of emphasizing that women who went into the military were not normal women, and therefore their accomplishments had no relevance to the status of women as a whole. One widely publicized study of British auxiliaries praised the women's performance and capacity for hard work, but nevertheless found cause to mention that camp toilets often overflowed because sanitary towels were flushed down the drain. The implied message was that an exclusively male military would never have to suffer such a problem.

Barring women from service also allowed the 'sentimental difficulty' to be sidestepped: no women, no romance.[17] The soldier who falls in love is distracted from his primary function, which is to kill. Romance between military personnel has also been seen as destructive of unit cohesion, encouraging jealousy between comrades who should otherwise fight as a band of brothers. It is nevertheless generally accepted within the military establishment that male soldiers' sexual needs must be satisfied, which explains why brothels have often been officially sanctioned. Brothels also allow a measure of official control not possible with respect to freelance prostitutes or camp followers.

Clearly, when women entered the military before 1945, it was because there was no alternative. Desperate situations merited desperate means. Because their service seemed an aberration, minds were closed to the possibility that women might actually demonstrate that they were better suited to tasks long performed exclusively by men. The most important point about female service was that it freed men for more important tasks, namely combat. 'We are here to relieve men for more important jobs, and we therefore have to work like men',[18] one British woman proudly announced during the Second World War. As Summerfield shows, when women were

---

17. See Schmitz, '"We too were soldiers"', p. 63.
18. Frederick Pile, *Ack-Ack* (London, 1949), p. 193.

eventually allowed to join the British Home Guard, it was 'to perform non-combatant duties such as clerical work, cooking and driving'[19] and thus to allow the limited pool of combat-qualified men to be stretched further. This also conveniently opened service to women while still denying them the status which combat accords.

Women's contribution, and therefore women's status, has remained inferior even though the nature of what they do during war has evolved. Female service, be it combatant or non-combatant, was not seen as positive social good but rather as a make-do measure which had to be processed and presented in such a way as to limit the harm it caused to the social fabric. Just as war was an intrusion into peaceful harmony, so too women were seen as an intrusion into war. Thus, the military service of women had little effect upon their status within society or their perceived viability as professional soldiers.

When, after 1945, great strides were made in certain countries toward the integration of women into the military, this was usually motivated by advances in gender equality in other areas or by that traditional culprit – sheer necessity. For the most part, societies (men and women) did not want to know about the wartime exploits of military women. When Joseph Stalin praised the work of women in his speech of 6 November 1944, he did not mention that they had assumed a combat role. 'Do not speak of the services you rendered,' the Soviet women veterans were advised by a senior commander at the end of the Second World War. The choice of words seems intentional: women, as always, were serving men, even when they were actually killing the enemy. The unpalatable is easily ignored. When it comes to the contribution of women to the military, collective amnesia is official policy.

---

19.   See Sumerfield, 'She wants a gun not a dishcloth!', p. 131.

CHAPTER ONE

Silent Partners: Women and Warfare in Early Modern Europe

BRIAN CRIM

But Fate is a thing that no man born of woman, coward or hero, can escape. Go home now, and attend to your own work, the loom and the spindle, and see that the maidservants get on with theirs. War is men's business; and this war is the business of every man in Ilium, myself above all. (Hector to Andromache in Homer's *Iliad*)

The exchange between Hector and Andromache in Homer's classic epic poem about the siege of Troy is an excellent metaphor for Western civilization's attitude towards women and warfare. Safe behind the castle walls, Andromache exhorts her husband Hector to fight bravely as he pursues glory on the battlefield. As Homer's epic poems reveal, women's role in war was strictly defined as either 'holding the fort' when the battle was beyond the city gates, or as war's most vulnerable victims when the walls were breached. While the notion of war as 'men's business' is as old as Antiquity, equally ancient was the frequency with which women participated in war despite their officially sanctioned exclusion from the ultimate sphere of male activity. This chapter explains how gender in early modern Europe relates to war, how military authority sometimes devolved to powerful noblewomen, and, finally, how women from the lower classes managed to play a significant role in the mass armies of the sixteenth and seventeenth centuries. The writings of Christine de Pisan are examined in depth, to demonstrate both the roles which noblewomen could play and the restrictions which society imposed upon them. Although there is a wealth of information on women and warfare in the modern age, there is relatively little scholarship on women's participation in early modern European warfare. This chapter maintains that while war was men's business in early modern Europe, women were silent partners.

Most historians date early modern Europe from about 1350 to 1650. Because the relevant gender constructions originated before this period and numerous noblewomen who acted as warriors existed during the medieval era, this chapter will cover a broader period of time than the usual three centuries. The two most important developments in early modern Europe were the Renaissance and the Reformation. Both occurred in a violent setting, especially the Reformation, which was marked by dreadful religious wars throughout Europe. During times of instability, social constructions like gender were temporarily weakened and women took advantage of the new flexibility. In the midst of the social crises of the seventeenth century many women found themselves with opportunities that would have been unthinkable in a stable Europe unified under one religion. Social strife and civil wars, often with the potential to become international wars, were constants in early modern Europe.

Another constant was the living legacy of Antiquity. Beginning in the early fifteenth century in Italy, and spreading northwards across Europe over the next decades, a rediscovery of the classics from the Greco-Roman world took place. Art, philosophy, politics and even warfare were reinvigorated by the injection of classical learning. It is within this environment of chaos and intellectual dynamism that women's involvement in war was at its zenith, but by the close of the seventeenth century women's freedom of action with regard to war, not to mention a host of other issues, was gradually confined. The stability that had eluded Europe between the Black Death (1350–70) and the conclusion of the bloody Thirty Years War (1648) signified the end of European women's temporary freedom. The irony is that the closer Europe came to anarchy and degeneration, the more women were valued as social partners. Once the storm had been weathered, however, the gender hierarchy was re-established.

According to the ancient Greeks, women were considered to be biologic-ally inferior, and therefore deserving of a subordinate status. Plato believed that those who were cowardly and immoral were punished by being reborn as women in the next life. Aristotle, the source of European knowledge for nearly a thousand years, considered women imperfect men. He called women 'monstrous', and a 'deformity, but one that occurs in the ordinary course of nature'.[1] In a world where heroism was valued highly and violence celebrated, to be associated with women was an insult. Violence committed by women was not only unnatural, but upsetting to the social order. The violently unstable women in mythology, like Medea, who murdered her own children,

---

1. Aristotle quoted in Merry E. Wiesner, *Women and Gender in Early Modern Europe* (New York, 1993), p. 13.

or Clytemnestra, the murderer of the warrior-king Agamemnon, suggest that from the beginning of Western civilization's historical memory the relationship between women and violence was entirely negative.

The enduring image of the Amazon in mythology symbolizes Western civilization's fantasies and fears with regards to armed women. Scholars debate the actual existence of the Amazons, a tribe of women warriors said to border Greece along the Mediterranean coast, but their presence in the Greek imagination was very real. The Amazon state was described as a female Sparta, the warrior state that competed with Athens for dominance in Greece. In Amazon culture the gender roles were reversed so that men were treated as breeders and servants while women held the reins of power. Amazons were ferocious warriors who supposedly cut off their right breast so they could handle a bow unobstructed. The word 'Amazon' originates from the Greek phrase 'a mazos', or 'without breast'. The symbolic signific-ance of the Amazons was the threat they represented to Greek patriarchal society. Defeating the Amazons in battle, which by all accounts the Greeks did, ensured the preservation of a male-dominated civilization.

The great Athenian statesman Pericles argued that 'women are . . . to be neither seen, heard, nor spoken, yet they reproduce the generations of warriors who constituted Athens'.[2] In a proper society women were dutiful mothers for future soldiers. Even though Athenians viewed Spartans as rivals, the notion of the 'Spartan mother' was an admirable figure. Mothers not only produced sons for battle, they nurtured them to be patriotic war-riors willing to sacrifice their lives for Sparta's greater glory. The Greek poet Plutarch recounted the story of such a mother who appeared to show no remorse about burying her son: 'I bore him that he might die for Sparta, and this is the very thing that has come to pass for me'.[3] Greek culture celebrated the Spartan mother and feared the spectre of the Amazons, yet there were figures in Greek mythology which suggest a more ambiguous relationship between women and war. Athena was both a goddess of wisdom and a warrior, but this apparent anomaly is explained away by the fact that Athena was born from the skull of Zeus. In other words, she had no mother; she was the product of her father and was valued for her manliness. Another indication of women's proximity to war in the classical mind was the marriage between the Goddess of Love, Aphrodite, and Ares, the God of War. This combination should not be surprising to the modern reader given the number of wars in mythology started over women, the Trojan War being the most famous. European commentators in the early

---

2. Pericles quoted in Sharon Macdonald *et al.*, eds, *Images of Women in Peace and War: Cross-Cultural and Historical Perspectives* (London, 1987), p. 30.
3. Plutarch quoted in Jean Bethke Elshtain, *Women and War* (New York, 1987), p. 62.

modern period invoked the images of the Spartan mother, the Amazon, and the subversive relationship between women and war as a way to justify established gender constructions.

Despite the constant rhetoric against women, the realities of early modern life allowed them ample opportunity to transgress gender boundaries and play a substantial role in warfare. The earliest examples of women warriors were barbarians that confronted and eventually repulsed the mighty Roman Empire. The presence of women in combat startled Roman observers. One Roman general stationed in Britain admired the Celts' martial spirit, noting that 'In a fight any one of them can resist several strangers at a time with no other help than his wife's who is even more formidable, neck veins swollen with rage, swinging their robust and snow-white arms, using their feet and their fists and landing blows that seem triggered off by a catapult'.[4] The most famous woman warrior in British history was the Celtic Queen Boudicca (sometimes known as Boadicea). Assuming command of her tribe after her husband's death, she was said to have driven the Romans from her territory in the first century AD. Her story was recounted and immortalized by the Roman historian Tacitus. Although largely the product of legend, Boudicca is still regarded as a British national hero. There is no doubt, however, that women warriors were common among the barbarian tribes. Archaeologists have unearthed the graves of women buried with their dowries, expecting to find such items as utensils and pottery. Instead, they found suits of armour and a wide range of weaponry.

The collapse of the Roman Empire in the fifth century AD resulted in the establishment of the barbarian kingdoms which later became the principal European monarchies of the early modern era. These kingdoms were ruled by family dynasties that proved themselves in battle. The nobility, or the warrior class, was inextricably linked to the ruling family by military obligation. In exchange for military service, the monarch granted the nobles land and power over its inhabitants. This system of feudalism allowed families to acquire extraordinary power over other families and over the massive peasantry. Usually, kings succeeded each other, but it was not unusual for women to rule in place of a male heir. The queen was more than the king's wife; she was a partner in all royal matters, including war. Lesser noblewomen were also influential in maintaining the castle while noblemen fulfilled their military obligation to the king. Left in such a vulnerable position, these noblewomen often found themselves defending their property and practising diplomacy in the place of their husbands. Many gender historians agree that blood mattered more than gender restrictions when it came to the

---

4. Quoted in David E. Jones, *Women Warriors: A History* (London, 1997), p. 51.

power dynamics of the nobility. As long as the nobility was prominent, so too were women in warfare.

Powerful noblewomen interested in military affairs were often derided for imitating men. Such a criticism may not have been an exaggeration; many noblewomen consciously cultivated a masculine image because they recognized the value of masculine qualities for legitimizing their authority. Eleanor of Aquitaine (1122–1204), the most significant French noblewoman of the Middle Ages, was a strong personality dedicated to protecting her vast inherited kingdom in south-western France. After her marriage to Henry II of England, Eleanor helped rule a large part of Europe. She also heeded the call of the Crusades, travelling as a warrior among warriors to liberate the Holy Land in 1140. One Greek observer described the procession of knights on their way to Jerusalem that included Eleanor and her first husband, King Louis VI of France:

> Females were among them, riding horseback in the manner of men, not
> . . . sidesaddle, but unashamedly astride, bearing lances and weapons as
> men do. Dressed in masculine garb, they conveyed a wholly martial
> appearance, more mannish than the Amazons. One [Eleanor] stood out
> from the rest . . . and from the embroidered gold which ran around the
> hem and fringes of her garments was called the Gold Foot.[5]

Eleanor's obvious ambition and skill as a ruler made her an easy target for a culture which harboured misgivings about powerful women, but her exploits endeared her to her subjects, and her political ability, not to mention two strategic marriages, greatly expanded the territory of a future France.

One of Europe's greatest scholars and humanists was the Italian noblewoman Christine de Pisan (1390–1429). Trained in the classics and encouraged by her father and husband to pursue her intellectual interests, she wrote a number of important works extolling the virtues of women not only in her own age, but throughout European history. Among her many interests was instructing noblewomen in military affairs. Pisan's interest in warfare was not the result of a vested interest in seeing women transgress gender boundaries, as some scholars suggest, but a practical consideration for noblewomen left to maintain the household in their husbands' absence or death. Her influence on European political thought rivals more familiar intellectual counsellors like her fellow Italian, Niccoló Machiavelli (1469–1527). Pisan is valued today for her writings on women, but she also produced instructional texts for several noble families in France. She is an unusual figure in early modern Europe because she was a woman who was asked by

---

5. Quoted in Tim Newark, *Women Warriors* (London, 1989), pp. 107–8.

leading power brokers in Europe to write about distinctly masculine topics. Given her excellent intellectual background in the classics, and her strategic social position among the French nobility, her writings on war, diplomacy and court culture were not as anachronistic as they might at first seem. Pisan, like Machiavelli a hundred years later, wrote a manual for future princes, but she recognized the importance of giving political and military advice to women forced into similar situations.

Institutional misogyny was an obstacle to Pisan's desire to elevate women to the status of partners in the realm of politics. In 1404, she wrote her most famous work, *The City of Ladies*, to demonstrate women's contribution to civilization, especially warfare. She constructed the book as a dialogue between herself and the three virtues of Reason, Rectitude and Justice. Pisan designed her *City of Ladies* so that 'all women – whether noble, bourgeois, or lower-class – be well informed in all things and cautious in defending your honor and chastity against your enemies'.[6] It is no accident that her fictional city was surrounded by high walls capable of protecting women against attacks on feminine virtue. Pisan believed in gender differences, but she did not consider the differences between men and women to warrant value judgements as to which gender was more significant. Despite having written books on military subjects for women, she freely admitted that war was naturally a male sphere. Some of the heroic women Pisan presents in the dialogue concealed their femininity during battle. The barbarian Queen Fredegund, in a speech to her warriors, promised to 'abandon all feminine fear and arm my heart with a man's boldness in order to increase your courage and that of the soldiers in the army'.[7] This tactic was popular among powerful women: in 1588, as the Spanish Armada threatened England, Queen Elizabeth I made a similar comment to her assembled counsellors: 'I know I have the body of a weak and feeble woman, but I have the heart and stomach of a king'.[8] Pisan did not advocate that women take up arms for the sake of gender equality; she considered instruction in the martial arts a practical matter for a population of women who were likely to find themselves in a vulnerable position during the course of their marriage and widowhood. She suggested that, under normal circumstances, women should take advantage of their natural strengths:

> The proper role of a good, wise queen or princess is to maintain peace and concord and to avoid wars and their resulting disasters. Women

---

6. Christine de Pisan, *The Book of the City of Ladies*, in *The Writings of Christine de Pizan*, ed. Charity Cannon Willard (New York, 1994), p. 207.
7. Christine de Pisan quoting Queen Fredegund in *ibid.*, pp. 121, 119.
8. Elizabeth I quoted in Wiesner, *Women and Gender*, p. 242.

particularly should concern themselves with peace because men by nature are more foolhardy and headstrong, and that overwhelming desire to avenge themselves prevents them from foreseeing the resulting danger of terrors of war. But woman by nature is more gentle and circumspect.[9]

In 1410, Pisan wrote *The Book of the Deeds of Arms and Chivalry* for the future rulers of the powerful House of Burgundy. She advised the future princes to dedicate themselves to war not for personal glory, but for the good of the state. Fearing that noble youth was too materialistic, she laid great stress upon the Spartan example of training young men to be physically and mentally strong so that the rulers would command honour and respect from underlings. In her section on warfare, Pisan demonstrated a superior knowledge of specific armaments and outlined complex strategies for withstanding a siege. She also looked to the chivalric code to mediate what she believed were unnecessary horrors of war. Much of her thoughts on chivalry foreshadowed the writings of Hugo Grotius, the Dutch scholar considered to be the father of international law. In the *Book of Deeds*, she outlined the justifiable reasons for going to war, which she limited to the defence of the Church, feudal responsibility, and defending the honour of the family. She strictly condemned wars of conquest and revenge: 'For according to God's law it is not proper for man either to seize or usurp anything belonging to another, nor even to covet it'.[10]

Pisan wrote at a time when her adopted France was embroiled in the Hundred Years War with England. Consequently, many of her observations in *The Book of Deeds* are coloured by contemporary events. For example, she roundly condemned the massacre of prisoners of war as a result of Henry V's slaughter of captured French soldiers at the Battle of Agincourt (1415). She also condemned the abuses of poorly paid soldiers and greedy mercenaries, arguing that 'it is a great evil and a perverse practice that those who are established to defend the people should themselves pillage and rob them'.[11] Pisan, like the absolutist monarchies two centuries later, understood that the best way to prevent unruly armies was for the state to assume financial responsibility for the military class.

Pisan was painfully aware of her gender and of the credibility issues which arose when a woman scholar wrote about masculine subjects. She overcame many prejudices by virtue of her training in the classics. Her knowledge of warfare came from the ancients, and like a true humanist she quoted from them liberally. *The Book of Deeds* was presented as a wedding gift to Henry

---

9. Christine de Pisan, *The Treasury of the City of Ladies*, in *Writings*, ed. Willard, p. 215.
10. Christine de Pisan, *The Book of the Deeds of Arms and of Chivalry*, in *ibid.*, p. 293.
11. Christine de Pisan, *The Book of the Body of Polity*, in *ibid.*, p. 288.

VI of England and the French noblewoman Margaret of Anjou in 1445 by
an English nobleman. Ironically, Pisan's manual for French rulers fighting
the English turned out to be more popular in English than in French.
Apparently, her translators were also worried about convincing readers that
a woman could be an authority on war; over half of the known copies of
The Book of Deeds claimed male authorship.[12] Because Pisan was so exceptional
as a female expert on war, her accomplishments were concealed by a patriarchal culture unwilling to accept female authority in a male sphere.

Pisan's last piece before her death was a poem celebrating the conquest
of Rouen by Joan of Arc (1412–31) in 1429. Like Pisan herself, Joan of Arc
was a unique figure. She claimed that, as an adolescent, she had a vision
in which Saint Michael instructed her to help rid France of the English invaders. Incredulous, French noblemen dismissed Joan until she predicted
the outcome of a battle. Joan was sent to meet Charles VII and convinced
him that she was worthy of a command. Some scholars suggest that Charles's
decision is proof that a true warrior tradition for women existed in early
modern Europe. This argument appears more valid than the notion that
Joan convinced the most powerful men in France that she was chosen by
God to liberate France. By all verifiable accounts, Joan was a superb military commander, retaking territory lost to England earlier in the Hundred
Years War. She was so effective that a cabal of French nobles, concerned
that Joan's influence over Charles was too great, betrayed her to the English. The martyrdom of Joan of Arc made her far more significant in death
than while she was alive. Like Boudicca for the British, Joan of Arc remains
a French national hero. Pisan regarded Joan as validation for her lifetime of
celebrating women. Upon hearing of Joan's exploits, she wrote:

> *What honor for the female sex!*
> *God's love for it appears quite clear*
> *Because the kingdom laid to waste*
> *By all those wretched people now*
> *Stands safe, a woman rescued it*
> *(A hundred thousand men could not*
> *Do that) and killed the hostile foe!*
> *A thing beyond belief before!*[13]

What Pisan could not know was that the official reason Joan was burned
at the stake was not because she routed the English or threatened French

---

12. Glenda K. McLeod, ed., *The Reception of Christine de Pizan from the Fifteenth through the Nineteenth Centuries* (Lewiston, NY, 1991), p. 32.

13. Christine de Pisan, *The Poem of Joan of Arc*, in *Writings*, ed. Willard, p. 358.

nobles, but because she was supposedly a heretic for communicating with angels. She was also tried for breaking the prohibition against women wearing armour. Despite Pisan's best efforts, women were still not accepted as partners in warfare.

Pisan is the subject of strident debate between various disciplines. Feminists claim her as an early rebel against gender constrictions, which seems to misrepresent her intentions. She challenged misogyny without abandoning commonly held views on gender. Even in the *City of Ladies*, her conversation with the three muses reveals that women should be proud of being women. She nevertheless advised that, in time of war, women should behave like men because war was itself an aberration – a failure of diplomacy, law and religious faith. She considered noblewomen partners with their husbands in all enterprises, including defence. Women's role, as she demonstrated in her advice to future queens and princesses, was to influence their husbands to behave properly and act decisively. Women were the antidote to men's more aggressive nature. While it is tempting to judge Pisan as an important woman in the early modern era, it is more appropriate to judge her a significant political and military thinker independent of her relevance to gender history. Her body of work was diverse and rivals that of more famous minds from the Renaissance.

Concentrating on noblewomen and their relationship to war excludes the vast majority of women. This is not a deliberate omission, but the result of the nobility's dominance over military institutions for much of the Middle Ages. A few decades after Pisan's death, warfare changed considerably with the mass introduction of gunpowder weapons to the battlefield. Warfare was simply too expensive before gunpowder to be a profession for the masses. The mounted knight, replete with armour, a vast collection of steel weapons, and servants to carry the equipment, required money and considerable training. Artillery, and, later, hand-held gunpowder weapons, in the words of a noted military historian, 'put the noble man-at-arms at the mercy of the vile and base born'.[14] In a few hours, the simplest peasant could master the firearm and, once in battle, kill the most adorned and well-trained knight. Suddenly, warfare became a profession for young men and women seeking money, adventure and travel. Europe's monarchs, once dependent on the nobility, eliminated the monopoly of the ancient warrior class and looked to the cheaper alternative of mercenaries. Monarchs sought both to save money and to extend royal control over increasingly unruly nobles. Gunpowder may have displaced the nobility, but it hardly saved money, and the consequences for the population at large were devastating.

---

14.   Michael Howard, *War in European History* (Oxford, 1976), p. 14.

The development of mercenary armies, nominally controlled by monarchs, princes or anyone with enough money, caused warfare to affect the masses on an unprecedented scale. Since the expanded military class survived from the spoils of war, it did not hesitate to initiate conflict. Poorly paid mercenaries, often numbering in the tens of thousands, descended upon civilian centres for sustenance. 'They crawled with their crowds of camp followers over the face of the land like locusts', as historian Michael Howard describes, 'destroying any community luckless enough to find itself in their path.'[15] This sort of warfare thrived during the sixteenth and seventeenth centuries because much of Europe was embroiled in a civil war sparked by the Reformation. Mercenaries, royal armies paid by and loyal to the monarch, citizen militias, and entire cities unfortunate enough to be caught in a siege were amongst the combatants in Europe's 150-year cycle of self-destruction. As stated earlier, during times of social crisis, gender boundaries are susceptible to transgression. The women who entered the forbidden zone of masculine war included 'camp followers' who accompanied early modern armies, and religious zealots who fought, both directly and indirectly, in Europe's numerous religious wars. At no time in European history were so many women engaged in warfare – as spies, foragers, artillery personnel, or soldiers – than between 1500 and 1650. Naturally, most people were not pleased with this involvement because women's presence on the battlefield symbolized social chaos. The fact that women were actively involved in war seemed to suggest that society was on the brink of disaster because the gender hierarchy was unstable. After the gunpowder revolution, the need to reform military institutions and remove the inherent instability of the mercenary army dominated European debates about warfare for the next two centuries. Not surprisingly, some of the most convincing arguments in favour of state centralization of warfare invoked gender differences. By the conclusion of the eighteenth century, women were effectively removed from the battlefield and stripped of their traditional occupations.

The term 'camp follower' is falsely confused with 'prostitute'. Women in early modern armies provided invaluable functions necessary for an army's survival. The mercenary army was a travelling city, and women were as integral to this city as they were in every other. They scavenged for food, managed the field hospitals, carried artillery and ammunition, established camps, and occasionally fought alongside men. The nature of early modern warfare was such that the battlefield was ill-defined and the fighting fluid. It was impossible for women not to be caught up in battles. Some sly mercenary captains dressed women in men's clothes to fool prospective clients

---

15. *Ibid.*, p. 29.

about the actual number of troops being financed. Likewise, some women who desperately wanted to fight dressed like men on their own accord and fought. Most military historians have either ignored or condemned the women who accompanied early modern armies. The nineteenth-century German historian Hans Delbrück attested to the value of women in their capacity as nurses, but quickly dismissed the majority as a nuisance: 'All of the evils of the lack of discipline were multiplied as a result of the train [women] that was attached to the lansqunets [riflemen]'. Delbrück cited several examples where women proved to be 'great obstacles' to armies, but managed to contradict himself by quoting an anonymous soldier who took a more favourable view:

> How very helpful the German women in Hungary were to the soldiers in carrying necessities and in their care in sickness. Seldom is one found who does not carry at least 50 or 60 pounds. Since the soldier carries provisions or other materials, he loads straw and wood on her, to say nothing of the fact that many of them carry one, two, or more children on their back. Normally, however, aside from the clothing they are wearing, they carry for the man one pair of breeches, one pair of stockings, one pair of shoes, two Hemmeter, one pan, one pot, one or two spoons, one sheet, one overcoat, one tent, and three poles. They receive no wood for cooking in their billets, so they pick it up on the way. And to add to their fatigue, they normally lead a small dog on a rope or even carry them in bad weather.[16]

One unfamiliar with ordinary life in early modern Europe might regard this passage as evidence that women were used as simple pack mules. Most daily tasks required back-breaking labour, but women attached to early modern armies earned income that exceeded that available from other occupations. The women described in the above passage were entrepreneurs; they made their living, like the mercenary, from war. Single women in particular were always assured labour as long as there was war.

One of the most vocal critics of mercenary armies and camp followers was Machiavelli. His treatise *The Art of War* reiterated the theories of military organization from the Roman Empire. He assumed that all women within an army were prostitutes, who pursued 'those vile avocations which commonly make soldiers idle and seditious'.[17] Women, he argued, undermined discipline and were responsible for every conceivable vice. Discipline and patriotism were, in his opinion, the Roman army's greatest attributes. Contemporary

---

16. Hans Delbrück, *The Dawn of Modern Warfare, History of the Art of War*, Vol. IV, trans. Walter J. Renfroe, Jr. (Lincoln, NE, 1985), p. 65.
17. Niccoló Machiavelli, *The Art of War*, trans. Neal Wood (New York, 1965), p. 165.

Europe should, therefore, emulate Rome and not allow women on campaigns. In his prescriptions for waging war, Machiavelli thought in terms of the masculine *virtú* and the feminine *fortuna*. *Virtú* was boldness, bravery, aggression, resolution and decisiveness. *Fortuna*, on the other hand, opposed *virtú* at every turn as the source of faintheartedness, irresolution and hesitancy. Beyond describing the feminine as diametrically opposed to the superior masculine force, Machiavelli characterized *fortuna* as a fickle and destructive entity that needed controlling. In all fairness to Machiavelli, Pisan wrote of *fortuna* in similar terms, but not as harshly. Machiavelli counselled his students that 'it is better to try *fortuna* while she is still favorable than to try nothing and allow her surely to destroy you'.[18] In *The Prince*, Machiavelli was even more direct: 'I do not think, however, that it is better to be headstrong than cautious, for fortune [*fortuna*] is a lady. It is necessary, if you want to master her, to beat and strike her.'[19]

Machiavelli's ideal citizen was a self-sufficient armed man incorporated into a militia. He savaged the mercenary armies because they were independent of the states they were hired to serve and, therefore, wholly unreliable. While correct in his analysis, Machiavelli used gendered language both to assail the mercenary and to exclude women from the right to citizenship.[20] But it would be another 150 years at least before European war became the state enterprise envisaged by Machiavelli. The Protestant Reformation and the Catholic Counter-Reformation provided mercenaries and monarchs alike with ample opportunities to wage war for personal gain. The shock to European social, political and intellectual hegemony also allowed women to assume influential positions within both religions. As the religious wars ravaged the continent, women not only continued to follow mercenary armies in their traditional capacities, they also exploited opportunities unleashed by civil war.

The Protestant Reformation was as much about political ambition as genuine religious convictions. The pattern of conversion in France attests to the fact that certain families became Protestant to gain independence from the Catholic Crown. Women were usually the first to convert because religion belonged to the private sphere, in which they were prominent. Once the Reformation established itself, religion became a political issue and therefore a public matter. The blurring of spheres, and later the civil wars in France and elsewhere, opened up opportunities for women. Some scholars maintain

---

18. *Ibid.*, p. 122.
19. Niccoló Machiavelli, *The Prince*, ed. and trans. David Wooton (Indianapolis, IN, 1995), p. 76.
20. He even went so far as to write an essay titled 'How states are ruined on the account of women'. Niccoló Machiavello, *Discourses on Livy*, trans. Harvey C. Mansfield and Nathan Tarcov (Chicago, IL, 1996), pp. 272–3.

that Huguenot (French Protestant) noblewomen used religion specifically to gain more authority and independence. Since Protestantism required literacy, many more women were educated than ever before. As a protest movement, and one that encountered violent persecution, it is significant that so many women were at the vanguard of the new religion.[21] When persecution turned into a full-scale civil war in France, both Catholic and Protestant women not only remained aggressive leaders of their respective faiths, but also served as spies, military negotiators and city defenders, while also maintaining their more familiar role as the leader of the family during the husband's absence. Since women were generally excluded from persecution because they were considered unimportant in the public sphere, many men active in the civil war left women in control of the family and went into exile or joined a militia. For a brief period, the survival of the social order ironically depended on women subverting society's normal rules. Women entered the coveted guilds, managed property, and lived together and cared for each other during crises.

Between 1562 and 1598, France was racked by a series of bloody civil wars inspired by religion, but intensified by the political ambitions of nobles. The principal actors were the Huguenots and forces loyal to the Catholic monarchy. The Huguenots were a distinct minority, but they enjoyed the aid of friendly powers and a dynamic underground network of support. Even when Henry of Navarre, a Protestant who converted to Catholicism for the Crown, inherited the throne in 1589, disgruntled Catholics formed the Catholic League and continued the civil war. In the midst of sieges and occupation by enemy forces, women who lived through the French religious wars proved to be extremely valuable as informants and co-conspirators. Taking advantage of the gender stereotypes that assumed women were harmless, women moved freely within occupied cities and the countryside and conducted espionage on behalf of their faction. Beyond serving a military function, these women ran family businesses in men's absence. Women also occasionally acted as negotiators between hostile parties. It was not unusual, for instance, for wives to bargain for their husbands' freedom. Women were made emissaries because they could travel freely and were often the highest ranking member of a family if the men were at war.[22]

As the French religious wars drew to a close, a more dangerous conflict erupted in Germany, sparking what would become essentially a world war.

---

21. See Nancy L. Roelker, 'The appeal of Calvinism to French noblewomen in the sixteenth century', *Journal of Interdisciplinary History* 2 (1972), pp. 391–418.
22. A detailed example of women's involvement in the French religious wars is S. Annette Finley-Croswhite, 'Engendering the wars of religion: female agency during the Catholic League in Dijon', *French Historical Studies* 20 (1997) pp. 127–54.

The Thirty Years War (1618–48) began with a revolt in the province of Bohemia in 1618, and spread across Europe, eventually killing nearly one-third of the German population. The catastrophic conflict seemed to confirm Machiavelli's warnings about the dangers of mercenary armies. The costs of war, both monetary and human, spiralled out of control and left the European landscape and most state finances in shambles. The demands on the existing military infrastructure were so great that it became paramount for states not only to centralize bureaucracies responsible for managing war but also to control state finances in general. Between 1560 and 1660 states worked to form armies capable of combining firepower, mobility and defensive strength. Discipline and reliable payment of troops from a central source, not to mention loyalty to the Crown, were the most effective means of controlling war. This so-called 'Military Revolution', according to Howard, 'turned European armies from wolfpacks to performing poodles'.[23] The days of the travelling cities of mercenary armies laying waste to Europe were drawing to a close, and with them, the effective participation of women in warfare.

Once the job of supplying and providing medical care for armies became the state's responsibility, women lost their largest source of employment. The female entrepreneurs so effectively demonized by Machiavelli and others were displaced once the military establishment was 'democratized'. Scholars have traced the subordination of women and the artificial sexual division of labour to the monopolization of arms by men.[24] In addition to the state assuming control over the mechanics of war, states linked military service to citizenship. The logical outcome of the removal of women from the battlefield was their exclusion from the right to citizenship. The immediate crisis for women unlucky enough not to be born to privilege was the loss of one important source of economic viability. One anonymous woman at the conclusion of the Thirty Years War described her plight in these terms: 'I was born in war, I have no home, no country, and no friends; war is all my wealth and now whither shall I go?'[25] Just as women's roles in early modern Europe were prescribed in accordance with the prevailing interpretation of Antiquity, so too were women's roles in the early modern state related to the gender constructions of the Greco-Roman world.

---

23. Howard, *War in European History*, p. 73.
24. For an extended discussion of the economic dimensions of war, see Barton C. Hacker and Sally L. Hacker, 'Military institutions and the labor process: noneconomic sources of technological change, women's subordination, and the organization of work', *Technology and Culture* 28 (1987), pp. 743–75.
25. Quoted in Barton C. Hacker, 'Women and military institutions in early modern Europe: a reconnaissance', *Signs: Journal of Women in Culture and Society* 6 (1981), p. 654.

The philosopher Rousseau rediscovered the Spartan mother in his political writings when he recounted this ancient story:

> A Spartan woman had five sons in the army and was awaiting news of the battle. A Helot arrives; trembling, she asks him for news. 'Your five sons were killed.' 'Base slave, did I ask you that?' 'We won the victory.' The mother runs to the temple and gives thanks to the gods. This is the female citizen.[26]

Women's participation in warfare depended on class as well as on gender. Noblewomen were active partners within the family at a time when the family was the most powerful social unit in the state. A handful of these women were active in political and military affairs. For many women of lesser birth, early modern warfare, as the despondent woman mentioned above demonstrates, provided a living, family, friends, and a purpose. Theoretically, women were prohibited from entering the public sphere of war, but political turbulence enabled them regularly to transgress the artificial construct of gender and serve the military in various capacities. Women were silent partners in early modern warfare partly because their presence was an uncomfortable reminder of social disorder and partly because historians have not bothered to tell their complex story. Since military history involves more than chronicling battlefield events, it is important to recognize the contribution of women to logistics, medicine, espionage and, most dramatically, leadership in early modern Europe.

---

26. Rousseau quoted in Elshtain, *Women and War*, p. 70.

CHAPTER TWO

In the Army: Women, Camp Followers and Gender Roles in the British Army in the French and Indian Wars, 1755–1765[1]

SCOTT N. HENDRIX

In 1764, Henry Bouquet, a lieutenant-colonel in the British Army, led an expedition from western Pennsylvania to Ohio. Among the written orders for that expedition, one reads: 'One woman belonging to each corps and two nurses for the general hospital were all that were permitted to follow the army. The other women in the camp, and those unnecessary to the garrison were ordered immediately down the country into the settlement.'[2]

Bouquet (1719–65) was a Swiss soldier of fortune. He began his service as a volunteer in a Swiss regiment in the service of the Netherlands and later served in another Swiss regiment in the service of Sardinia in the War of the Austrian Succession, where he rose to the rank of lieutenant and the position of adjutant, and apparently impressed those around him with his soldierly prowess. After service with the Dutch Guard, where he fulfilled diplomatic as well as military duties, he finally took an appointment with the British Army in 1755, and came to North America as lieutenant-colonel of the 1st Battalion of the Royal American Regiment. There he is best remembered for his success at the Battle of Bushy Run against the Native Americans, during Pontiac's War in 1763, a victory said to have saved western Pennsylvania for the American colonists. Fortunately for posterity, he left an extensive set of papers which offers an interesting insight into the administration of the British Army during the French and Indian Wars.

---

1.   This chapter was made possible in part by a one-month Scholarship-in-Residence awarded by the Pennsylvania Historical and Museum Commission, in May of 1998, at the Bushy Run Battlefield Park.
2.   William Smith, *Historical Account of Bouquet's Expedition against the Ohio Indians in the Year 1764, Under the command of Henry Bouquet Esq.*, Philadelphia, Pennsylvania, 1756, facsimile reprint (Ann Arbor, MI, 1969), p. 39.

These papers allow a few passing glimpses of an often neglected subject, the eighteenth-century camp follower.

Camp followers, particularly women, are the forgotten stage hands of the great military dramas of the eighteenth century. Bouquet's order quoted above, as well as other excerpts from his papers, details the importance that they held for European armies of the period. The papers demonstrate that women camp followers were not, as has often been suggested, parasites who battened on to an army and progressively weakened it.[3] On the contrary, the women, children and non-combatant men who followed an army fulfilled many important functions. Either formally, on the ration strength or as private servants, or informally, as unsanctioned camp followers, they provided vital logistical support – cooking, cleaning, nursing, and generally maintaining the camps and quarters. At the same time they provided much of the social structure which helped make military life bearable. As Bouquet's order concerning 'unnecessary women' and the directions for the women who would be taken on the expedition demonstrate, women were indeed essential to the effective operation of the army.

Perhaps more importantly, the presence of large numbers of women and children, living intimately and closely with soldiers, created a military world which contrasts sharply with that of today. In particular, gender roles within eighteenth-century European military forces would have been quite different from those of armies of later periods. Furthermore, because of the presence of women and children living closely with the soldiers, methods for socializing and motivating male soldiers would have borne little resemblance to the techniques used in armies of the later nineteenth and twentieth centuries.

Women and camp followers

The armies of eighteenth-century Europe did not consist solely of soldiers. A long tail of putative non-combatants followed the wars and made up a large proportion of the military world. The largest portion of these were the women and children who were families of the soldiers, but there was also a large body of non-combatant men. These included artisans such as blacksmiths and carpenters, who provided auxiliary skills the army needed, in addition to officers' servants, sutlers and assorted others.

---

3. Cynthia Enloe, *Does Khaki Become You? The Militarization of Women's Lives* (Boston, MA, 1983), p. 2. Enloe argues that this view of women camp followers (the 'classic formulation') was partially created by military authority, and used to control women camp followers.

Sutlers were merchants licensed to follow the armies and sell to the soldiers. They and other merchants were vital to an army, for they provided certain foodstuffs and goods, such as fresh foods and vegetables, that the army did not generally stock. Bouquet was careful to organize and license them on the march to attack Fort DuQuesne in 1758.[4] His licence read in part:

> Whereas it is for the good of His Majesty's Service that a certain number of well regulated Merchants & Suttlers, be allowed to follow the Army on the Western Expedition.
>
> This is therefore to permit you to attend the Said Troops for this campaign, to furnish them with Dry Goods & Liquors. . . . And no soldier, or Women belonging to the Army, is to have any Spirits or other Strong Liquors from you, without Leave in writing from the Commanding Officer of the Regiment they belong to.[5]

The language used in the licence is very revealing. Women are described as 'belonging to the army'. This licence also hints at both the services camp followers provided and the problems they posed. Drunkenness constantly troubled commanders, yet alcohol (in moderation) was deemed necessary to the smooth functioning of an army. Camp followers often supplied the spirits, but became a problem if they themselves imbibed too much or encouraged soldiers to do so. From the point of view of authority, camp followers could be an attractive nuisance who tempted soldiers from their duty and led them into disorder.

Many of the sutlers were in fact women, who often had a reputation for being formidable characters. A famous literary example is the character of Mother Courage from Bertolt Brecht's play *Mother Courage and her Children*, which pertains to the period of the Thirty Years War, 1618–48. In the mid-eighteenth century, at a review at Potsdam, Frederick the Great is said to have ridden up a nearby hill to view his soldiers. At the top he found that two *Marketenderinen* (women sutlers) had set up their stalls. They informed Frederick that this location was perfect for their pitch, while he could watch his toy soldiers anywhere. Frederick is said to have beat a hasty retreat.[6]

There was also usually a large and assorted group of wives, mistresses and prostitutes, as well as entertainers and other miscellaneous followers, who trailed an army to entertain soldiers and extract most of their spare cash. Prostitution and other forms of sexual misconduct were perhaps not

---

4. Henry Bouquet, *The Papers of Henry Bouquet*, ed. Donald H. Kent *et al.* (Harrisburg, PA, 1951), Vol. II, pp. 112–13.
5. *Ibid.*, p. 114.
6. Christopher Duffy, *The Army of Frederick the Great* (New York, 1974), p. 134.

as common as horrified commentators imagined, but a certain percentage of women camp followers, as well as male soldiers, misbehaved. According to a letter which Lieutenant-Colonel Stephens wrote to Bouquet in 1759:

> I saw your direction to Co. Armstrong about the fair, I may say the foul Sex. I informed Him that I would advise you of his Conduct, who would have thought it? He has brought up a mere Seraglio [harem] with him and among the Rest, three of our Cast offs, Sent down some time ago.
>
> If a person of his rank and Gravity, a person whose example is so much respected, Connive at these things I fancy the thing will soon gain ground.
>
> All the women I wanted to get rid off, claim his patronage, and I have been obliged to Confine a Groupe of them, for pretending to go down, and then fetching a compass and Returning in the night to the Suburbs of Ligonier again.[7]

It should be noted that one probable reason for the commonly held view that most camp followers were prostitutes was the fact that marriage customs were much more informal and unregulated among the 'lower orders' that made up the rank and file in eighteenth-century European armies. As a result many marriages, which were probably considered valid by the parties concerned, were often judged unsanctioned and immoral by outside observers. Moreover, it was customary for a woman of the army whose husband died to take another husband almost immediately. This horrified more refined observers.

Many women doubled up on their duties. In Francis Grosse's famous (and satirical) *Advice to Officers of the British Army*, which offered humorous suggestions to all ranks of the British Army on how to better their lot, sergeants are advised:

> In order to turn the penny, contrive, when in camp, to let your wife keep a hut in the rear, and sell ale and gin. The standing orders only say, *you* shall not do it, but they do not prohibit *her*. Here you may settle with your men; and if they spend the greatest part of their pay in liquour, it is no more than they would do elsewhere, and you may as well have their money as another.[8]

One suspects that this was quite common practice. Many women camp followers were ingenious, and always on the lookout for a chance to make a little money. For example, on the sultry morning of the Battle of Köln,

---

7. Bouquet, *Papers*, Vol. IV (1978), p. 114.
8. Francis Grosse, *Advice to the Officers of the British Army: A Facsimile Reprint of the 6th London Edition with Introduction and Notes* (New York, 1867), p. 107.

18 June 1757, wives of the Prussian Regiment of Bevern broke into an ice-house and sold the chunks of ice, at high prices, to the soldiers who were sweltering in the ranks.[9]

Occasionally, some 'ladies' (a description usually reserved for officers' wives) would also come to follow the armies. While some followed the armies full-time, many more came only for a short visit. Occasionally a lady also gained official status with an army. Charlotte Brown was assigned as Matron to the General Hospital for Braddock's Army in North America in 1754. Her status as a lady is evidenced by the fact that she came with a maidservant, and the army assigned her a wagon to use as shelter and horses, certainly better than the lot of the average camp follower.[10]

Since ladies usually had more genteel manners than the wives of the en-listed men, they tended to escape the derision directed at most camp followers, who, on the whole, had an unsavoury reputation.[11] They were in particular often accused of looting.[12] In truth, many, perhaps most, members of eighteenth-century armies looted. But the problem of looting, in the eyes of military authority, was incidental to the fact that the tail of non-combatants provided much of the logistical functions of the army, as well as contribut-ing to the social fabric.

Although some camp followers stayed in quarters when armies went on campaign, others accompanied the army.[13] The numbers who did so in Europe would have been far larger than in North America, due to the smaller distances involved, and the lack of a need to be transported over-seas by ship. Sylvia Frey nevertheless estimated that 5,000 women followed the British armies in America during the Revolutionary War.[14] In this con-text, 'followed' is the operative verb. Women and children travelled by liter-ally following, walking behind, the army as it marched. In 1757 Bouquet directed that: '[n]o Women or Children are allowed to set upon the Waggons; & they shall follow upon the March the direction of that Officer [in charge of the baggage]'.[15] In the Prussian Army, camp followers observed the same custom, as they did in the Austrian and indeed all European

9. Duffy, *Frederick the Great*, pp. 59–60.
10. 'The Journal of Charlotte Brown, Matron of the General Hospital with the English Forces in America, 1754–1756', in Isabel M. Calder, ed., *Colonial Captivities, Marches and Journeys* (Port Washington, NY, 1935, 1967), pp. 169, 177–8.
11. Holly Mayer, *Belonging to the Army: Camp Followers and Community during the American Revolution* (Columbia, SC, 1996), pp. 146–7.
12. Sylvia R. Frey, *The British Soldier in America: A Social History of Military Life in the Revolutionary Period* (Austin, TX, 1981), pp. 76–7.
13. Frey, *British Soldier*, p. 20.
14. *Ibid.*, p. 17.
15. Bouquet, *Papers*, Vol. I (1972), p. 58.

armies.[16] Following the army could be an exhausting business. Brown's *Journal* details the effort that was involved in keeping up, and the hardships that bad roads and poor weather could cause. When the road was so bad that her wagon was unable to proceed, Brown 'walked till my [feet] were blister'd'. This must certainly have been a common occurrence for many camp followers. Her brother died on the march, and the rigours of campaigning eventually broke down her health as well.[17]

Camp followers performed many different functions. They cooked, nursed the ill and wounded, sewed, did laundry, acted as servants to officers, and performed many other necessary daily tasks. Some were customarily allowed rations in return for doing the cooking and cleaning for a company, but usually there were far more women following the army than were on the ration strength.[18] As Bouquet's above order demonstrates, some women followed the army into the field and indeed sometimes even into action. They commonly carried water into the ranks during battles and sometimes served as baggage guard. Frey reports that during the American Revolution, the wife of a grenadier was killed in the action leading up to the occupation of Philadelphia. During the fighting at Fort Ann a woman who kept close by her husband's side during the engagement was mortally wounded.[19] Indeed, stories of women found among the dead seem to be a staple of eighteenth- and early nineteenth-century battle reporting.

Camp followers were subjected to military discipline when necessary. One of the most illuminating documents in the Bouquet papers reads:

Carlisle 4th June 1759

Honoured S[r]/
Please to hear the Petition of your Poor unfortunate Servant Martha May now confined in Carlisle Gaol. Please your Hon[r] as my husband is an Old Soldier and Seeing him taken out of the Ranks to be Confined Put me in Such a Passion that I was almost beside myself but being informed, after that I abused Y[r] Honour, to a High degree for which I ask Y[r] Honour a Thousand Pardons, and am Really Sorrow for what I have said&done; Knowing Y[r] Honour to be a Compationate, and Merciful Man, I beg and hope you'll take it into Consideration that it was the Love I had for my Poor husband; and no —— hill will to Y[r] Honour, which was the cause of abusing so good a Colonel as you are. Please to Sett me at Liberty this time & I never will dis-oblige y[r] Honour nor any other Officer belonging to

---

16. Duffy, *Frederick the Great*, p. 59; and Duffy, *The Army of Maria Theresa: The Armed Forces of Imperial Austria, 1740–1780* (New York, 1977), p. 57.
17. Brown, 'Journal', pp. 178–88.
18. Frey, *British Soldier*, p. 20.
19. *Ibid.*

the Army for the future as I have been a Wife 22 years and have Traveld with my Husband every Place or Country the Company Marcht too and have workt very hard ever since I was in the Army I hope y^r honour will be so Good as to pardon me this [onct (stricken out)] time that I may go with my Poor Husband one time more to carry him and my good officers water in ye hottest Battles as I have done before.

I am

Y^r unfortunate petitioner and Hum:^{ble} Servant

Mar^a May

[Endorsed]   Petition of Martha May to carry Water to the Soldiers in the heat of Battle.

[Addressed]   To the Right Honble Colonel Bouquet These[20]

Martha May did not seem to have regarded it as exceptional that she had carried water in the 'hottest Battles', though she did view her self-proclaimed good service record as a sufficient reason to be released from jail. Nor did she seem to find it unusual that her husband's colonel had locked her up, though she certainly wanted to be released. As this document shows, some women considered themselves to be 'in the Army', and adopted attitudes appropriate to actual military service. Martha May had made an emotional and ideological commitment to the values of the army, and essentially identified herself as a member of it. She was angry not just that her husband was arrested, but because 'my husband is an Old Soldier and Seeing him taken out of the Ranks to be Confined Put me in Such a Passion that I was almost beside myself'.

This level of commitment was certainly not unique to Martha May. Matthew Bishop, who served in the British Army during the War of the Spanish Succession, tells of a sergeant in 'my Lord Hartford's Regiment' who 'had a sister in the French Service'. The sergeant arranged to have his sister cross the lines and meet him in the British camp.[21] In the course of a joyous reunion, livened with the brandy the sister had brought, the sergeant tried to convince his sister that she should join the British Army. The regiment's officers got into the act and 'boasted of our Provisions being far better than the French Army's, that we had good Beef, Bacon, and extremely fine Geneva [Gin], good bread, and above all, the English Pay was double that of the French'. She replied that she 'thought the French Provisions were preferable to ours, that all the world would allow their Bread to be better that that of any other nation; they had fine juicy Beef, none better to her Palate; and Brandy enough, which revived her soul; what could a Woman

20. Bouquet, *Papers*, Vol. II, p. 30.
21. Matthew Bishop, 'Life and Adventures', in *The Oxford Book of Military Anecdotes* (New York, 1985), pp. 148–9.

desire more?' Undaunted, the sergeant's sister maintained her allegiance to the French Army, eventually returning to the French camp. After which, 'the poor Sergeant's Joy was turned to Mourning, for he took on greatly when he saw himself disappointed of getting his sister into our Army'.[22] The language used is again significant and illuminating: the sergeant 'had a sister in the French Service' and was intent upon 'getting his sister into our Army'. In essence, the woman concerned was 'in the army'.

The families of soldiers were also caught up in, and part of, eighteenth-century European martial culture. With so many women following the drum, there were, of course, also a vast number of children. Frey estimates that the average British company had eight births annually, or a total of about 50 births per regiment per year. She postulates that during the American Revolution, with a British troop strength of 39,196, there were about 12,000 children with the army; yet this was in wartime, when military birthrates customarily dropped and many woman and children would have found it difficult to follow their regiment across the Atlantic.[23] In 1776, the Berlin garrison of Frederick the Great consisted of 17,056 men, 5,526 women and 6,622 children.[24] Since these women and children lived in the camps or barracks with the soldiers, they were directly subjected to, and a part of, the army and of martial culture.

Children were often raised to be soldiers, or soldiers' women, and many a soldier or camp follower was probably literally born into the army. The well-known opera *La Fille du regiment* (The Daughter of the Regiment), composed by Gaetano Donizetti in 1840, is a romanticized account of this common situation. In France in the eighteenth century, as was probably the case everywhere in Europe, it was customarily understood that boys who grew up following the army were intended to become soldiers as soon as they reached the necessary height. In 1766, Etienne-Francois de Choiseul, the French Minister of War, granted boys half pay from the age of six.[25]

One of the earliest efforts in public education in Europe occurred in Austria. There, after the Seven Years War, Maria Theresa made vigorous efforts to extend primary education to her subjects. The army seized on this project with great enthusiasm, expanding upon existing efforts to educate affiliated children. In most armies the regimental chaplain was expected to educate the children, an obligation that in practice was often ignored. The Austrian Army enlarged upon these arrangements with soldier-schoolmasters.

---

22. *Ibid.*
23. Frey, *British Soldier*, p. 60.
24. Duffy, *Frederick the Great*, p. 60.
25. John Childs, 'Families, Military', in *A Dictionary of Military History and the Art of War*, ed. Andre Corvisier (Oxford, 1994), p. 236.

It was felt that better education for the regiment's children would have many benefits. It would prevent the regiment's children from running wild, and would eventually provide a ready supply of literate non-commissioned officers.[26] In short, the eighteenth-century European military world was often a cradle-to-grave proposition. One was born into it, educated by it, and quite possibly died in it.

The eighteenth-century European military world, then, embraced far more than soldiers, including within it a horde of non-combatants – men, women and children. That military world was, in fact, a martial culture; it moved beyond the business of soldiering, extending into and affecting the private and social lives of all its members, military and civilian. This martial culture was pan-European in that it encompassed all the armies of western and central Europe to a greater or lesser extent, and the people who comprised those armies. These armies had far more similarities than differences, in terms of their weapons, organization and conditions of service.[27] As the case of Bouquet illustrates, the armies of the various states of eighteenth-century Europe often made no effort to restrict recruiting to their own nation; members of the European military world moved relatively freely from army to army. For instance, Bouquet's friend Frederick Haldimand, after serving with Swiss regiments and the Prussian Army, also joined the British Army and eventually gained a knighthood, the rank of lieutenant-general, and served as Commander-in-Chief in North America and Governor of Quebec. Examples of this type of movement were very common. As a result, the armies of Europe formed what was in many ways a unified culture, and one that was to a large degree separate from that of the civilian world.

When an eighteenth-century camp follower joined an army she joined a new world. As Martha May indicated, she might well have 'Traveld with my Husband every Place or Country the Company Marcht . . . and . . . workt very hard'. There was a real possibility that the vicissitudes of war might have led her into the army of a nation other than her own. For example, after the Saxon Army surrendered to Frederick the Great at Pirna on 17 October 1757, all of the Irish soldiers in the Saxon Army were forcibly impressed into a Prussian infantry regiment.[28] Over time a camp follower might well find that she had more in common with her fellow camp followers than she had with the home she had left behind. As one camp follower from the Thirty Years War remarked: 'I was born in war; I have no home, no

---

26. Duffy, *Maria Theresa*, pp. 57–8.
27. For instance when Bouquet joined the British Army, after having previously served with Swiss and Dutch regiments, there is no indication that the British felt that their new officer needed any retraining, or orientation; he was simply sent straight to his new command.
28. Duffy, *Frederick the Great*, p. 240.

country no friends; war is all my wealth and now whither will I go'.[29] In fact her home was war, the pan-European martial culture. While those involved in eighteenth-century military life were not completely isolated from the larger world, they were cocooned in a martial culture which affected most aspects of their lives.

Soldiers, camp followers and gender roles

The presence of large numbers of women and children in Bouquet's army, living in close proximity with male soldiers, would have produced a social atmosphere much different from that prevalent in late nineteenth- and twentieth-century armies. Quite clearly, eighteenth-century soldiers did not live in the isolated military environment experienced by soldiers in more recent times. A vast change began to occur in Western armies in roughly the second half of the nineteenth century when many of the duties of the camp followers were militarized and taken over by soldiers. The camp follower, and especially the women, vanished from Western military life. From the late nineteenth century until very recently, not only was soldiering a gendered occupation (that is, one which could only be filled by a male), but armies themselves were gendered (that is, they were all-male societies, where women were only occasionally found as wives or nurses).

The two world wars brought some change with the development of women's auxiliaries in many Western armies; nonetheless there were also very strong efforts, in most armies, to maintain a considerable degree of separation between men and women. For example, women serving with the US Army's Women's Army Corps in the Pacific in the Second World War lived in 'barbed wire compounds . . . which were thought necessary to protect them from the thousands of sex starved GIs nearby'.[30] Granted, not all women who served in the world wars experienced this isolation from combat and from men. Some saw combat with the Russian Army, and with partisan forces. In Britain some served with anti-aircraft units. Moreover, many women, whose roles were theoretically non-combatant and auxiliary, came very close to the war indeed. However, broadly speaking, male-dominated armies saw these developments as exceptions, and the end of wartime emergencies saw most women removed from combat roles, and usually from close interaction with male soldiers.

---

29. Enloe, *Khaki*, p. 4.
30. Ronald H. Spector, *Eagle Against the Sun: The American War with Japan* (New York, 1985), p. 395.

Retired Lieutenant-Colonel David Hackworth, writing about married life in the US Army in the 1950s and 1960s, described the lot of women married to army officers:

> all things considered theirs was a pretty empty lot. . . . We men just never stopped. . . . Having such a tight group of officers did wonders for the morale of the whole outfit but it took a hell of a toll on the home front. . . . None of us consciously decided to lock the girls out, but there was a certain perverse pleasure in speaking in the silent shorthand we'd developed over many a beer . . . while our wives, oblivious, chatted away by our sides.[31]

Likewise, in the modern French Foreign Legion, admittedly an extreme example of the gendered military, 'The real woman does not exist. The Foreign Legion is a unit without women. For starters it is too virile for them. . . . Outside the barracks, it is physical sexuality, mechanical, in pleasure spots. Inside the woman remains in the idealized imagination.'[32]

While this model of a gendered army has been changing in the 50 years since the Second World War, change has been slow, and there is still a strong tendency to view a male-gendered army as the norm. These expectations about gendered roles in a military setting have caused modern Western armies to adopt means of motivating male soldiers which are based upon this gendered conception of military life. Since women and children were far more present in the eighteenth century European military world, efforts to motivate male soldiers in the eighteenth century would have had to have been different.

Western armies, during the later nineteenth century and for much of the twentieth century, have used what Craig M. Cameron has described as a particularly 'hypermasculine' and sexually isolated environment to motivate male soldiers and make them aggressive.[33] A key part of this process is that male soldiers are separated from women, and the qualities that the army desires from them (discipline, physical toughness and aggression, among others) are identified as masculine and are praised, while undesired traits are scorned as feminine and undesirable.[34] Enloe argues that '[m]en are taught to have a stake in the military's essence-combat; it is supposedly a validation of their own male "essence". This is matched by the military's own institutional investment in being represented as society's bastion of

31. David Hackworth and Julie Sherman, *About Face: The Odyssey of an American Warrior* (New York, 1989), p. 368.
32. Douglas Porch, *The French Foreign Legion: A Complete History of the Legendary Fighting Force* (New York, 1991), p. 426.
33. Craig M. Cameron, *American Samurai: Myth, Imagination and the Conduct of Battle in the First Marine Division, 1941–1951* (New York, 1994), pp. 49–88.
34. Enloe, *Khaki*, pp. 14–15.

male identitiy.'[35] Soldiers who do not meet accepted standards in physical fitness tests or those who show cowardice are derided as 'faggots', 'girls', 'sissies' or 'women'. Since modern soldiers have typically been isolated in all-male settings, it has been possible to change their values, or alter their behaviour, using this method. Moreover, and less subtly, opportunities to visit the civilian world, and interact with women, could be manipulated very blatantly by authority as a tool to control soldiers. For example, Hackworth describes how, as a young corporal commanding a squad of soldiers in 1948, he motivated them by withholding their passes, and thus their ability to visit the civilian world and women.[36]

In the twentieth century, roughly since the First World War, this process was further concentrated and ritualized in basic training. Typically in basic training, new recruits were completely isolated from civilian influences, and not coincidentally, were also segregated from women. Until quite recently this segregated basic training was the norm in Western armies.[37] The single-sex, all-male barracks, also common in Western armies until comparatively recent times, helped to continue this segregation after basic training, and so helped maintain the values that were encouraged by basic training. In fact, this method of motivating male soldiers has been so common that it often seems the norm.

These were certainly not the norms in the military world of Bouquet, and in other armies of eighteenth-century Europe. Their very different practices pose certain questions. What effect would the non-isolated, sexually integrated environment of Bouquet's time have had on gender roles, and on efforts to motivate soldiers for battle?

Obviously, eighteenth-century armies did not isolate their soldiers from either women or the larger civilian world, and therefore they could not use interaction, or the denial of interaction, with women as a motivational tool. Nor did they have a long period of quarantined and ritualized basic training to inculcate martial values into their soldiers. Since soldiers were not isolated from women, they could not be motivated by isolation to behave more aggressively, and otherwise act in accordance with military values. Armies reflected the larger eighteenth-century world, with men, women and children all present.

It does, however, seem possible that the presence of women, children and non-combatant male camp followers might have been used in other and different ways, to bolster the male identification of the combatants. Instead of the absence of women being used to heighten aggression, and so make men more effective soldiers, perhaps their presence might have served

---

35. *Ibid.*, p. 15.
36. Hackworth, *About Face*, pp. 42–3, 215.
37. John Hockey, *Squaddies: Portrait of a Subculture* (Exeter, 1986), pp. 33–5.

to heighten the protective instincts of the soldier, and strengthen his identity as an arms-bearing male, with a duty to protect others. The close proximity of women, children and non-combatant men with whom the male soldiers had emotional ties would have been a powerful motivating force. In effect the soldiers would have been fighting directly to protect the lives of their loved ones, and to prevent their possessions from being looted. This was certainly not the only motivational force working on the eighteenth-century soldier. It might not even have been the primary one. Certainly, however, it must have had an important effect.

Traditionally, masculinity has been identified with bearing arms and defending women.[38] The immediate presence of women, children and non-combatant men, who did not for the most part use weapons, would have helped to highlight this element of masculinity in the soldiers who did bear arms. Bearing arms would also have clearly signified, and helped to reinforce, their status as soldiers.[39] For instance, most eighteenth-century soldiers carried a sword, even though those in the infantry and artillery had little expectation of using them in combat. In the Prussian service it was noted that: 'the soldier came to associate this weapon with a certain concept of honour, and he would consider it shameful to have carried no sword'.[40] This sword was clearly intended to mark a special status, and the honour was carefully guarded, and denied to those camp followers who were not actually soldiers. For example, in the French Army during the Napoleonic wars, officers' servants were forbidden to carry swords, except when actually in the field.[41]

There is evidence to suggest that women did sometimes directly encourage the soldiers to fight. During the massacre of the army of the new United States under the command of Arthur St Clair in Ohio in 1791, it is reported that the women camp followers shamed the cowards among the men.[42] This sort of encouragement is seen as one of the traditional roles for women in warfare.[43] Eighteenth-century armies simply made it possible to apply this sort of encouragement directly and unsubtly.[44] It is not hard to imagine that Martha May's husband might well have received some strong additional motivation to fight by the sight of his wife coming through the ranks bearing water.

---

38. Jean Bethke Elshtain, *Women and War* (Chicago, 1995), p. 5.
39. I am indebted to my colleague Jennifer Belden-England of the Department of History at the University of Pittsburgh for suggesting this possibility.
40. Duffy, *Frederick the Great*, p. 80.
41. John R. Elting, *Swords Around a Throne: Napoleon's Grande Armée* (New York, 1988), p. 177.
42. Edward Coffman, *The Old Army: A Portrait of the American Army in Peacetime, 1784–1898* (New York, 1986), p. 26.
43. Enloe, *Khaki*, p. 5.
44. Linda Grant De Pauw, *Battle Cries and Lullabies: Women in War from Prehistory to the Present* (Norman, OK, 1998), p. 19 and *passim*.

This military atmosphere, however, probably also served to reinforce many traditional gender roles for women. It has been argued that masculinization and feminization are ideas which emerge in tandem. They feed off one another.[45] This suggests that the effort which eighteenth-century armies would have expended to produce male soldiers proud of bearing arms, and of the status which that implies, would also have tended to restrict women to designated feminine occupations. So, by and large, women camp followers were confined to traditional women's activities. They cooked, sewed, washed clothes, nursed, tended children and so on. They did not normally bear or use weapons, or actively participate in the fighting. The well-known, and perhaps legendary story of Molly Pitcher manning an American cannon is an exception that helps prove the rule. Generally, women camp followers seemed to have performed every possible task to aid soldiers up to the point of using weapons and fighting the enemy.

More commonly, a women wishing to fight as a soldier would disguise herself as a man and enlist. While fairly uncommon, there nevertheless seems to have been a relatively large number of these cases in eighteenth-century armies. One Englishman joked in 1762 that there were so many women serving in disguise as soldiers that they should have their own regiment.[46] An English ballad entitled 'The Gallant She-Soldier' describes one:

> *With musket on her shoulder, her part she acted then,*
> *And every-one supposed that she had been a man;*
> *Her bandeleers about her neck, and sword hang'd by her side,*
> *In many brave adventures her valor have been tried.*

> *For exercising of her arms, good skill indeed had she,*
> *And known to be as active as any one could be,*
> *For firing of a musket, or beating of a drum,*
> *She might compare assuredly with any one that come.*

> *For other manly practices she gain'd the love of all,*
> *For leaping and for running or wrestling for a fall,*
> *For cudgels or for cuffing, if that occasion were,*
> *There's hardly one of ten that might with her compare.*

> *Yet civill in her carriage and modest stil was she,*
> *But with her fellow souldiers she oft would merry be;*
> *She would drink and take tobacco, and spend her money too*
> *When an occasion served, that she had nothing else to do.*[47]

---

45. Elshtain, *Women and War*, p. 258.
46. *Ibid.*, p. 105.
47. Victor Neuburg, *Gone for a Soldier: A History of Life in the British Ranks from 1642* (London, 1989), p. 86.

The relative abundance of women disguised as men serving as soldiers in the eighteenth century was certainly a complex phenomenon, with many different causes, and many implications beyond the scope of this essay. However, one way to explain this phenomenon would be to describe it as a tribute to the strength of eighteenth-century military gender roles. (This might explain the emphasis on the effectiveness of the woman's disguise, and her physical strength and skill at arms, in the ballad quoted above.) It suggests that the role of soldier was so firmly gendered as male, that any woman who wished to be a soldier had therefore to make herself a male.

Paradoxically, then, the presence of women disguised as men serving as soldiers suggests, among other things, the importance of the eighteenth-century gender identification of some, but not all men, as arms-bearing soldiers, and women as non-combatants. The transvestite women warrior can be seen as both supporting and subverting gender roles, and modern scholars debate this issue.[48] However, their numerous appearances in contemporary ballads, which, as the above example indicates, were generally approving in tone, and the lack of any evidence of a concerted effort to root them out, would seem to argue that they did not seriously threaten the identification of the soldier as primarily male. The 'she-soldier' according to Diane Dugaw was usually searching for love and glory, and many ballads ended with her returning to her feminine identity and marrying.[49] She highlighted the different worlds which men and women occupied in the martial culture; she did not seriously threaten them.

Conclusion

Camp followers have tended to leave little in the way of historical records. About Colonel Bouquet, who died in Florida in 1765, we know a great deal, recorded in six well-edited volumes. About Martha May, to our regret, we know little more than what has been recounted here.

The eighteenth-century European military world was, unsurprisingly, very different from that of today. The presence of a large numbers of camp followers, the majority of whom were the families of the soldiers, was perhaps the greatest of those differences. They were not, as some later commentators would suggest, parasites who trailed after the army, and milched the soldiers of their pay. Women camp followers identified themselves with

---

48. Diane Dugaw, *Warrior Women and Popular Balladry, 1650–1850* (Chicago, 1996), pp. 3–5, fn. 8, 215.
49. *Ibid.*

and as a part of the army. They felt that they were 'in the army'. They provided a large and diverse range of goods and services to the armies. To a large degree they were an army's logistical system. In fact, as Colonel Bouquet himself demonstrated, commanders would often take care to ensure that camp followers were present because they were often 'necessary'.

Most importantly, it seems reasonable to suggest that camp followers provided a social structure for the army that helped make eighteenth-century European military life tolerable. This martial social structure could in fact be described, in many ways, as family-like. From the point of view of the army concerned, it also provided an important component of the soldiers' motivation to fight. Military authority found that creating a family atmosphere could be very important for maintaining the morale of soldiers, and for this purpose women, unsurprisingly, were very useful.[50] The soldier fought for many reasons, but one of them was that he was often fighting directly for his family, who travelled with him, in the army.

---

50. See Enloe, *Khaki*, p. 5.

CHAPTER THREE

'We Too Were Soldiers': The Experiences of British Nurses in the Anglo-Boer War, 1899–1902

CHRISTOPHER SCHMITZ

October, 1899 – I received my appointment . . . to go out with the Canadian contingent then called to active service in South Africa . . . Upon our arrival at Cape Town we found our troops had orders to proceed up country immediately. We reported to the principal medical officer, making every effort to be allowed to accompany them to the front; but this we were told was impossible, as no nursing sisters could be accommodated in the field hospitals. So with very disconsolate feelings we . . . came to realise at that early date what served us in good stead later, viz. that we too were soldiers, to do as we were told and go where we were sent. (Georgina Fane Pope, 'Nursing in South Africa during the Boer War', *British Journal of Nursing*, 20 September 1902, p. 232)

For the 1,300 or more British and British Empire nurses who served in the Anglo-Boer War, most as members of the Army Nursing Service Reserve, the common experience was one of widespread prejudice from male doctors and hospital orderlies, as well as from the army establishment. Only as thousands of soldiers began to die of typhoid and dysentery were women allowed to serve in hospitals near the front. Through their service, they inspired much-needed reforms in the military medical system and also stimulated a considerable refining of their own professional identity.

The distinct gender divide and the struggle for professional status within army nursing were particularly pronounced in the war's earlier stages. As Pope observed, on arrival at Cape Town in November 1899, many nurses found that they were denied permission to join hospitals near the front. The comment 'we too were soldiers . . . to do as we were told and go where we were sent' superficially suggests compliance with gender divisions within the army medical service. However, an equally powerful implicit theme is that women nurses regarded themselves as 'soldiers', and wanted to be regarded on a basis of equality with male medical staff. The war also caused many prior assumptions to be questioned: the notion of 'the front', for example, became increasingly hard to define in a conflict that started with large numbers of non-combatants becoming besieged, and later developed into a fluid guerrilla war.

Nurses' letters and diaries suggest the extent of the gender prejudice they encountered during the war, as well as their frequently critical view of bureaucratic torpor and ineptitude within the Royal Army Medical Corps (RAMC). These accounts also illuminate their motivation to volunteer for war service, often from distant parts of the empire; their perceptions of the environment in which they worked; their (often maternal) relationship with patients; notions of comradeship between nurses, as well as problematic romances with male officers; and, perhaps most significant, the way war experiences influenced paradigms of probity and professionalism, which in turn complemented the long-term struggle for state registration of nurses, and the campaign for women's suffrage.

The British government and its army bureaucracy were clearly unprepared for the scale and length of the military commitment in South Africa. In mid-October 1899, when hostilities commenced, the British had around 20,000 troops garrisoned in Cape Colony and Natal. By January 1900, a series of military setbacks had led to the deployment of 130,000 troops in South Africa, rising to around 230,000 by July 1900. Battlefield casualties placed an enormous strain on the RAMC, especially during the first few months, but even worse were the catastrophic epidemics of typhoid (enteric) and dysentery, which caused escalating fatalities among soldiers and an unbearable strain on medical services. Ultimately, of the 448,000 British and imperial troops who served during the war, around 14,000 died of disease (9,000 from typhoid), compared with about 7,600 combat-related fatalities.[1] Additionally, some 30,000 fever victims were invalided home during the war. This not only posed major questions about the RAMC's ability to care for the sick and wounded, it also hinted at major deficiencies in Britain's military capabilities. In April–May 1900, when Commander-in-Chief Lord Roberts's force of around 35,000 troops at Bloemfontein was poised to strike northwards at Johannesburg and Pretoria, some 9,000 were in hospital with fever.

This crisis at the front was converted into a scandal at home, in part through highly critical reports by William Burdett-Coutts MP, who visited military hospitals early in 1900.[2] The government responded by setting up

---

1. R.J.S. Simpson, *The Medical History of the War in South Africa: An Epidemiological Essay* (London, 1911).
2. W. Burdett-Coutts, *The Sick and the Wounded in South Africa* (London, 1900).

a Royal Commission, which reported in January 1901.[3] The commission confirmed a widespread view that there had been insufficient female nurses in South Africa, and that matters were made worse by overcrowded hospitals and a bureaucratic and technically backward army medical system. The typhoid disaster, Pakenham argues, seemed avoidable: 'The disease feeds on poor hygiene and overcrowding . . . But by the end of the nineteenth century [it] was largely tamed. To prevent typhoid, you needed careful sanitation; to treat it, you needed careful nursing and a careful diet.'[4] Unfortunate soldiers caught up in besieged Ladysmith, or tarrying with Roberts in Bloemfontein, had little of either. The nurses, striving to comfort the sick and wounded, were fully aware of the obstacles they faced. Eloquent and perceptive comments in diaries, letters and official testimony provide clear evidence of the red tape, lack of medical supplies and fresh food, as well as the appallingly overcrowded hospital wards.

The number of female nurses employed during the war is uncertain. The British Army Nursing Service had just 75 full-time members when war began, while the Army Nursing Reserve had 101.[5] Only 12 women army nurses were stationed in South Africa at that time, together with a thousand male orderlies, a ratio which reflects prevailing RAMC wisdom that the former's function should be limited to supervising orderlies, who were responsible for general nursing and cleaning duties in wards.[6] The army's belated acceptance that more direct patient care should be undertaken by women led to a rapid increase in the numbers of female nurses who enlisted for service in South Africa, primarily from civilian hospitals. By March 1900 approximately 900 nurses were serving alongside 7,000 male orderlies and 800 doctors.[7] Ultimately perhaps as many as 1,300 to 1,400 women nursed in this theatre of war.[8] According to incomplete official records, at least 24 died (mostly of typhoid) while serving there.[9]

---

3. *Royal Commission Appointed to Consider and Report upon the Care and Treatment of the Sick and Wounded During the South African Campaign*, Sessional Papers, House of Commons, XXIX (1901); Report, Cd. 453; Minutes of evidence, Cd. 454.
4. Thomas Pakenham, *The Boer War* (London, 1979), pp. 381–2.
5. Leo Amery, ed., *The Times History of the War in South Africa*, Vol. VI (London, 1909), pp. 504–5.
6. Charlotte Searle, *The History of the Development of Nursing in South Africa 1652–1960: A Socio-Historical Survey* (Cape Town, 1965), p. 191; Anne Summers, *Angels and Citizens: British Women as Military Nurses 1854–1914* (London, 1988), p. 210.
7. Summers, *Angels and Citizens*, p. 207; Searle, *Nursing in South Africa*, p. 189.
8. Jan Bassett, *Guns and Brooches: Australian Army Nursing from the Boer War to the Gulf War* (Melbourne, 1992), p. 9. About 800–900 nurses went out from Britain, 400 were recruited locally in South Africa and just over 100 from the British Empire (Australia 60, New Zealand 25, Canada 18); Searle, *Nursing in South Africa*, p. 193; Joan Rattray, *Great Days in New Zealand Nursing* (London, 1961), p. 127; Brian Reid, *Our Little Army in the Field: The Canadians in South Africa 1899–1902* (St Catharines, Ontario, 1997), p. 152.
9. Public Record Office, London: WO 108/338, List of Casualties in the South African Field Force.

It is difficult to generalize about their motives for volunteering. Summers and Bassett both stress strong imperial loyalties, combined with a desire to promote the professional status of nursing. The nurses, who frequently had strong suffragist convictions, saw highly visible (though unquestioningly non-combatant) military service as a means to establishing equality with men. Summers and Bassett also highlight a less focused desire to 'participate in great events', as well as a simple sense of adventure, evident in many contemporary accounts.[10] On arriving at Cape Town with a New Zealand contingent on 14 April 1900, Nurse D.L. Harris found it hard to contain her excitement: 'This will be a memorable Easter, as tomorrow we begin an entirely new kind of life'.[11] The aristocratic Theodosia Bagot, accompanying the privately funded Portland Hospital from London in December 1899, declared that she and Lady Henry Bentinck had gone out 'in no official capacity, merely because we loved the cause, and enjoyed watching the results of what we had helped bring about . . . In going out to a war . . . I have fulfilled a dream of twenty years' standing.'[12] The nurses at times acted like tourists: many collected prized souvenirs (such as shrapnel) and took charabanc rides to the battlefields, enthusiastically recording their sightseeing. 'Mr Gardiner took me to the Basuto location', Harris wrote. 'I only got a few bangles and some nice knob kerrie sticks . . . Some of them were dancing.'[13] 'For most nurses', Summers feels, 'the war was . . . a once-in-a-lifetime experience, of which every exotic detail was to be relished.'[14]

Many of the obstructions placed in the way of the women volunteers in the early months of the war sprang from official suspicion that an element of naïve or meddlesome feminine curiosity was responsible for this sudden enthusiasm to follow the troops. Even long-serving nurses found their sense of professional pride wounded by this rush: 'During the height of the nursing-fever which seized women at that period, much discretionary power was needed to repel the unfit. The self-made testimonials laid before the [selection] committee were often amusing.'[15] As late as 3 April 1900, the Colonial Secretary, Joseph Chamberlain, was prompted to cable Sir Alfred Milner in Cape Town that 'The Queen regrets to observe the large number of ladies now visiting and remaining in South Africa . . . and strongly disapproves of

10. Bassett, *Guns and Brooches*, pp. 9, 13–14; Summers, *Angels and Citizens*, pp. 181, 189, 203–4, 272.
11. MS diary, Nurse D.L. Harris, National Army Museum (NAM), London, 7611–17, entry for 14 April 1900.
12. Dosia Bagot, *Shadows of the War* (London, 1901), pp. xiv–xv.
13. Harris, NAM 7611–17, 13 September 1900.
14. Summers, *Angels and Citizens*, p. 203.
15. Sarah Tooley, *The History of Nursing in the British Empire* (London, 1906), p. 185.

the hysterical spirit which seems to have influenced some of them to go where they are not wanted'.[16]

More serious, however, was a fundamental War Office objection, particularly pronounced early in the conflict, to the notion of women serving in any capacity within the army system, an objection reinforced by the RAMC's deep antipathy to women in any role other than as supervisory sisters within base hospitals, far removed from the seat of war. Fired by first-hand experience of soldiers' suffering and maladministration in army hospitals, Burdett-Coutts told the Commons on 27 July 1900 that 'one of my great complaints has been that, starting from a theoretical and very obstinate objection to female nurses in the [War] Department at home, there has not been anything like a sufficient supply of nurses to meet the cause of sickness and enteric fever'.[17] Even the Hospitals Commission was forced to concede that

> Before this war, the employment of nurses was but slightly recognised in the army . . . but as the war went on and it became obvious that the deficiency of trained orderlies could not be satisfactorily made good it became evident that nurses must be largely employed . . . In this war, at any rate at its commencement, some members of the Royal Army Medical Corps appear to have had a difficulty in divesting themselves of the old traditions of the Service, which are undoubtedly antagonistic to the employment of nurses in military hospitals.[18]

There was also bias against colonial and locally recruited nurses.[19] The net result was that civilian nurses' offers of help were taken up far too slowly during the crisis months of February–May 1900. As Francis Fremantle, who served as a civilian surgeon in the war, caustically remarked: '"No," replied Red-Tape last October, when the matron of Guy's wrote and offered the services of half the Guy's nurses; "It is not anticipated that the services of any nurses, other than those of the Army Nursing Service or Army Nursing Service Reserve, will, under any circumstances, be required"'.[20] Eleanor Laurence, matron in the Pinetown Hospital, near Durban, complained in June 1900: 'It seems sad that when there are so many fully-trained nurses in England longing to come out, these poor fellows should not be getting the best nursing they might have'.[21]

---

16. George Buckle, ed., *The Letters of Queen Victoria*, 3rd series, III. 1896–1901 (London, 1932), pp. 520–1.
17. Burdett-Coutts, *Sick and Wounded*, pp. 127–8.
18. *Royal Commission*, Cd. 453, p. 7.
19. Bassett, *Guns and Brooches*, pp. 21–3; Searle, *Nursing in South Africa*, p. 193.
20. Francis E. Fremantle, *Impressions of a Doctor in Khaki* (London, 1901), pp. 73–4.
21. Eleanor C. Laurence, *A Nurse's Life in War and Peace* (London, 1912), pp. 171–2.

Nurses' recollections tell of wards and tents overflowing with desperately ill patients, lack of food and equipment, uncooperative male orderlies, and ceaseless battles with filth, flies, heat and dust, all met with immense stoicism. Conditions within besieged Ladysmith were especially bad, as Natal-born nurse Kate Driver testified:[22]

> It was now well into December [1899] and our nurses were beginning to break down . . . The rations for all were decreasing . . . The heat had become nearly unbearable and the storms were many. The whole camp reeked of dysentery and enteric . . . The flies were black on the canvas of the tents. Over our heads from daylight till dark the continual roar of the big guns was exhausting to all.

Even after the siege was lifted, conditions remained awful. In April 1900, another nurse in Ladysmith (who felt driven to protect her anonymity) wrote:

> The real condition of the wards and the men was appalling . . . There was no linen of any sort, no pillows, except flat straw bolsters . . . and the poor patients' heads sinking in the holes . . . they were just off the floor. Most distressing of all was the condition of the men themselves. Rows of white and yellow-boned, hollow-eyed men were lying or sitting up in their beds, and a few were crawling about with their clothes literally hanging on bones, waiting on one another. The orderlies on our approach had hastily entered their wards concealing their pipes – smoking as usual. The heat was intense, and those with fever were lying panting and saturated with perspiration, loaded with blankets, their poor mouths all clogged together, with the flies swarming round them in thousands with their horrid buzzing noise.[23]

Conditions in Bloemfontein were equally desperate. 'The flies were the worst enemies', Bagot remarked. 'Field hospitals were the paradise of flies . . . The roof of the tent was literally black with them.'[24]

Overcrowding, the dust storms, the plight of the fever victims – all burnt deeply into recollections. Harris, serving at No. 8 General Hospital, Bloemfontein, recorded on 14 May 1900:

> This hospital is terribly over-crowded. It is equipped for 500 men, and once had nearly 1700 cases – almost all enteric, and nearly all very bad. The orderlies are terribly over-worked, and only have about one night a week in bed, so of course they are often found asleep on duty.[25]

---

22. Kate Driver, *Experiences of a Siege: A Nurse Looks Back on Ladysmith*, rev. edn (Ladysmith, 1994), p. 20.
23. Sister X, *The Tragedy and Comedy of War Hospitals* (London, 1906), pp. 82–3.
24. Bagot, *Shadows of the War*, pp. 164, 166.
25. Harris, NAM 7611–17, 14 May 1900.

Though typhoid was endemic throughout southern Africa and dysentery had been the scourge of the military camp for centuries, poor supervision of the sanitary system and fresh water supply was clearly a major cause of the epidemics, exacerbated by the ubiquitous flies which spread the diseases.[26] Recovery was known to depend upon close and careful nursing and a strictly controlled diet, including plenty of fresh milk and eggs. But the latter were often impossible to obtain.[27] In May 1900, Pope wrote: 'Fresh milk was very hard to get – an officer's servant was shot dead by the Boers in his effort to get some at a farm near by – but of condensed milk, beef-tea, champagne, and jelly we had plenty'.[28] Another nurse, at Ladysmith in April 1900, painted a harrowing picture:

> These half-starved men died very gradually, and each day it is truly haunting to see living skeletons, with hollow eyes, gaunt cheek-bones, sitting or lying up in bed, eagerly trying to get down as much food as they can . . . They have turned against the tinned milk utterly, and there is not enough fresh – only forty pints of it amongst eleven hundred![29]

Basic items of equipment were lacking. In Ladysmith, in May 1900, one nurse complained: 'the equipment of the ward consisted of one feeding-cup (broken spout), a few cups, no shirts or pyjamas, no sheets, two mackintoshes, and the mattresses in such a condition as to be causing bed sores'.[30] In Kimberley, after the siege had been lifted, Sister Henrietta, struggling to nurse the wounded from Roberts's columns, bemoaned 'The difficulty we had in getting washing done for a thousand sick in our worn-out town, with scarcely a bar of soap within 500 miles'.[31] The cause of these supply problems was inadequate War Office logistical planning, in particular the much-discussed transportation difficulties suffered by Roberts in his advance along the tenuous railway line running northwards to Johannesburg.

The army's logistical problems were just one manifestation of a general institutional torpor which nurses encountered. RAMC red tape was often the bane of their lives. 'Sister X', secure behind her cloak of anonymity, was especially scathing:

26. Simpson, *Medical History*, pp. 2, 67; Searle, *Nursing in South Africa*, p. 188.
27. See Superintendent Sister S.E. Webb, evidence, *Royal Commission*, Cd. 454, p. 252.
28. Georgina Fane Pope, 'Nursing in South Africa during the Boer War', *British Journal of Nursing*, 20 September 1902, p. 233.
29. Sister X, *Tragedy and Comedy*, p. 93.
30. *Ibid.*, p. 120.
31. Sister Henrietta, 'War nursing in South Africa, 1901', *British Journal of Nursing*, 27 September 1902, p. 256.

The R.A.M.C. system is a very complicated one. Even the ward cannot be scrubbed without the signature of the medical officer . . . 'Why aren't there any sheets?' we ask from time to time. 'Couldn't get none till I had your signature, Sister,' replies an orderly . . . To ask for a syringe of any sort creates a panic. The dispenser comes up to see if you really want this, and can you wait until tomorrow? . . . This system of hospital work will take ten years off our lives . . . I can't imagine how the Army Sisters put up with it.[32]

The continual struggle against red tape, she concluded, 'tended to blunt all one's interest in one's work and patients, and crush any enthusiasm. I was beginning to see why the orderlies took so little interest in their work.'[33]

Undoubtedly the most contentious problem the nurses encountered involved the male orderlies. Even Laurence, an otherwise even-handed commentator, admitted that 'orderlies (though very willing) had everything to learn of ward duties; they could not even undress these men when they had been lifted on to their beds, much less any idea of washing them; a delirious man was a new experience to them'.[34] Criticisms of the system and of individual orderlies were frequently much more vitriolic. For instance, Driver wrote:

some of our orderlies did their utmost to be of service, but there were not enough of them. Of the rest it is hard to speak. They did such vile and brutal things; they stole the food and stimulants, they treated the patients with utter callousness and often with cruelty; and their language to the nurses when we asked them to do things was unspeakable. I used to think that if I were a man I would have given many of them the biggest hiding they had ever had.[35]

Sister Henrietta thought the orderlies 'do not appear to me to be the right class of men. They are above half the work, and not up to the other half . . . They are too often rough to the patients, greedy, lazy, and, I fear, dishonest.'[36] Harris, then at Green Point Hospital, Cape Town, noted with some relief on 3 May 1900 that 'Major Trevor was on the warpath this morning . . . [and] gave the orderlies a good talking to, for wh. I was thankful, for they are a stupid lot of men and don't know how to work'.[37] Most trenchant of all, 'Sister X' described a catalogue of sins:

---

32. Sister X, *Tragedy and Comedy*, pp. 39–42.
33. *Ibid.*, p. 126.
34. Laurence, letter, May 1900; *A Nurse's Life*, pp. 162–3.
35. Driver, *Experiences of a Siege*, p. 28.
36. Sister Henrietta, 'War nursing', p. 256.
37. Harris, NAM 7611–17, 3 May 1900.

Pay Day was a day of thirst riots! . . . there had been regular brawls, even open fights, and one orderly . . . had nearly had his eye knocked out. Meanwhile another had tried to remove a splint off the shattered arm of one of the patients, thinking he was doing him a good turn. 'All right, old chappie, won't 'urt you more than I can 'elp!' he had spluttered over the unfortunate individual, who . . . was trying to struggle up. . . . he was dragged off by the afflicted Sister, and conveyed by two *fairly* sober orderlies outside the ward and deposited on the ground.

The ward I was to have in my charge . . . I can truthfully say [was] quite the filthiest I have ever been into . . . There were three orderlies, so there was no excuse . . . The floor was a sickening spectacle, the men having expectorated all over it . . . the bedside tables were caked with spills of milk and beef tea . . . I saw the men I had to deal with by their demeanour, and what I was to expect. They were outside, as usual, smoking. I called one in. The R.A.M.C. one came in, with a threatening attitude . . . I set the orderlies about cleaning the ward. 'Don't see much the matter with it myself,' said the senior orderly defiantly . . . Such is one instance of how the poor patients were faring, and the dire necessity of a nurse.[38]

Such heat was generated over this issue, fanned by similar accusations from Burdett-Coutts,[39] that the Hospitals Commission made an examination of the orderly question a central part of their inquiry. Of 462 witnesses examined, 25 were nurses or nursing auxiliaries. Yet when questioned about the competence of orderlies, only one expressed openly negative feelings, while six gave a mixed response. Among the latter, Sister Whiteman at Fort Napier Hospital suggested that some were good, some bad, and a few often intoxicated. On balance, the commissioners took heart from this evidence, concluding that 'the way in which the orderlies as a body discharged their duties has deservedly been the subject of high praise from many witnesses', but that 'complaints . . . undoubtedly in some cases . . . are well founded. Some orderlies have been inattentive, and some rough.' The commissioners recommended even greater use of female nurses.[40] A dissatisfied Burdett-Coutts judged these findings inconclusive and equivocal, and suggested that many witnesses, including patients, had been afraid to speak frankly.[41]

At the heart of the tension between nurses and orderlies lay the established RAMC system of war hospitals. There were three types: general hospitals theoretically had 520 beds; stationary hospitals 100 beds; and field

38. Sister X, *Tragedy and Comedy*, pp. 28–9, 119–21.
39. Burdett-Coutts, *Sick and Wounded*, pp. 66–7.
40. *Royal Commission*, Cd. 454, pp. 201–2, 455; Cd. 453, pp. 7–10, 14.
41. William Burdett-Coutts, *The Hospitals Commission: Comments on the Inquiry and the Report* (London, 1901), pp. 1–13.

hospitals with stretchers for about 100 men. Stationary hospitals were the link between field hospitals at the front and general hospitals at the base. As Fremantle put it, stationary hospitals were supposed 'to be ready . . . to enter a captured town before a General Hospital can be brought up country'.[42] In other words, they were often quite mobile. At the start of the war, the official female nursing establishment for general hospitals was one matron and eight sisters, while it was not anticipated they would serve at all in stationary or field hospitals, due to their proximity to the front. However, the pressures of war caused great upheavals in all these precepts. Female nurses were soon employed in greater numbers in the general hospitals, and were also engaged in stationary hospitals. Although they were still officially barred from field hospitals, in a few instances exceptions were made out of necessity. Nevertheless, the principle that they might serve in field hospitals was not conceded by the RAMC, even after the war.[43]

The growing acceptance of expanded female nursing, in both general and stationary hospitals, followed from a re-evaluation of two key issues: the function of male orderlies within the RAMC, and women's allowable proximity to the front. In the wake of the Burdett-Coutts revelations, and the Hospitals Commission report, nurses' organizations urged that orderlies should be better trained and placed under the direct control of matrons, while a greatly expanded and better organized system of army nursing should assume most of the actual care of patients in general and stationary hospitals.[44] Leading medical figures who had experienced war service supported this move, among them Sir Frederick Treves, surgeon to Queen Victoria and Edward VII, who recommended that because the good orderly was a 'rare bird', and since 'a very liberal employment of nurses in fixed hospitals has proved in the present campaign to be in every way eminently satisfactory', it followed that 'Orderlies should be reserved for the field hospitals, in which the employment of nurses is impossible. There is no doubt that all nursing should be in the hands of properly trained women whenever and wherever the employment of women is possible.'[45] Such recommendations regarding the respective roles of nurses and orderlies were implemented for all practical purposes by the later stages of the war, and the suggested reform of army nursing came into effect in March 1902,

42. Fremantle, *Doctor in Khaki*, pp. 58, 547.
43. *Royal Commission*, Cd. 453, pp. 5–7; Searle, *Nursing in South Africa*, p. 191; Juliet Piggott, *Queen Alexandra's Royal Army Nursing Corps* (London, 1975), p. 32.
44. Ethel McCaul, 'Some suggestions for army reform: III. Army nursing', *Nineteenth Century* 49 (April 1901), pp. 583–4; 'The Matrons' Council, Army Nursing Reform', *Nursing Record*, 6 April 1901, p. 270; *Nursing Record*, 27 April 1901, pp. 331–5.
45. Frederick Treves, 'The South African Hospitals Commission', *Nineteenth Century* 49 (March 1901), p. 405.

with the formation of the Queen Alexandra's Imperial Military Nursing Service (QAIMNS).[46]

The related issue – the proximity of women to combat zones – was, as Treves's comment suggests, less straightforward to resolve, since nurses' ambitions clashed awkwardly with deep-seated Victorian inhibitions about exposing feminine virtue to the brutalities of war. Difficulty arose in part because the war had thrown into confusion the concept of the front. Nurses caught up in sieges found themselves under fire, often relishing the experience. Within encircled Ladysmith, Driver strolled one morning, with some fellow nurses, 'up Convent Hill to see where all [the] shells were coming from . . . [and] walked among the soldiers, going as far as [we] were allowed to go'.[47] In besieged Mafeking, Sister Craufurd and other nurses frequently had to run the gauntlet of Boer rifle and shell fire.[48]

Such well-publicized accounts underlined the ability of women to cope with sieges and enemy attack. The status of stationary hospitals was also ambiguous; many were thought of as field hospitals and, with the ebb and flow of conflict, some could be suddenly transformed into casualty clearing stations. Treves clearly thought of his unit, in which he employed four nurses, in these terms, referring to it (incorrectly) as 'No. 4 Stationary Field Hospital'.[49] A few nurses, among them Bagot, briefly assisted in genuine field hospitals,[50] while many others, in general or stationary hospitals, sometimes found themselves dangerously close to the fighting.[51] These experiences fed demands for women nurses to be allowed nearer to combat. Sister Ethel McCaul, one of Treves's Natal contingent, argued that 'if it were recognised that two or four Army sisters could always follow the column, as we did, there would be no difficulty in selecting suitable women for this really grand service'.[52] The *Nursing Record*, like Burdett-Coutts, saw no difficulty in female nurses serving in field hospitals.[53]

Burdett-Coutts had, indeed, injected an important new dimension into discourse about the role of women nurses in the war. In the House of Commons, on 27 July 1900, he argued:

46. *The Times*, 12 March 1902, p. 4, 28 March 1902, p. 8; Piggott, *Queen Alexandra's Corps*, pp. 37–40; Tooley, *History of Nursing*, pp. 178–86; Summers, *Angels and Citizens*, pp. 220–31.
47. Driver, *Experiences of a Siege*, pp. 8–9.
48. Tim Jeal, *Baden-Powell* (London, 1989), p. 292.
49. Frederick Treves, *The Tale of a Field Hospital* (London, 1900), pp. 1, 12. He obtained permission to take the nurses with this hospital only on condition that no precedent was set. However, with expressions of approval from periodicals like the *Nursing Record* (21 July 1900), it was inevitably seen as an important milestone; Summers, *Angels and Citizens*, p. 212.
50. Bagot, *Shadows of the War*, pp. 162–3.
51. Pope, 'Nursing in South Africa', p. 233; Laurence, *Nurse's Life*, pp. 263–6.
52. McCaul, 'Suggestions for army reform', p. 584.
53. *Nursing Record*, 11 August 1900, p. 113.

We ought to accept at once, in any campaign carried on in a civilized country such as South Africa, where women are respected in every way, the principle of having a very large number of female nurses certainly at the base and stationary hospitals. The Boers themselves have female nurses in their field hospitals and very admirable they seemed. I do not, however, insist on female nurses going with field hospitals, but I do think they ought to be with field hospitals when they become stationary hospitals.[54]

Burdett-Coutts, like Treves and McCaul, recognized that the distinction between field and stationary hospitals was becoming blurred but, more significantly, suggested a distinction between 'savage' and 'civilized' arenas of war. While the RAMC might hesitate to send women to nurse in Asante or the Sudan, there was presumed to be no physical or moral danger if nurses were captured by the Boers. This variation on 'white man's war' or 'gentlemen's war' mythology was increasingly prominent in the debate. One nurse argued that 'in future white wars both hospitals and women nurses must be carried nearer the front . . . The women would not be murdered or ill-treated – in a white man's land, at any rate – any more than the sick and wounded are.'[55] Notions of the relationship between feminine identity and military endeavour were clearly being recast in the crucible of war.

Such debates and proposed reform were shaped by prevailing paradigms of feminine virtue. For nursing in general, professional values had developed within a distinctly female framework; hospital sisters were seen as paragons of womanhood, of probity and efficiency, who nevertheless maintained a modest respect for male superiority in well-defined traditional areas. Summers suggests, in respect of military nursing, that:

[A] new conception of female heroism . . . had been developing in England . . . Men's superior strength and aptitudes were to remain uncontested; firearms training and rough living in camps were to remain largely male preserves. Above all, the battlefield itself was to stay out of bounds. It was for woman to maintain her philanthropic persona: to support her nation at war at a discreet distance, carrying out the work of healing . . . To look war full in the face would be a 'degradation to woman's nature, which should revolt at the idea of taking the lives of others'.[56]

From a male perspective, the desirable qualities in military nurses seemed clear. For Frederick Treves, 'the perfect nurse . . . is versed in the elaborate ritual of her art, she has tact and sound judgement, she can give strength to

---

54. Burdett-Coutts, *Sick and Wounded*, pp. 127–8.
55. *Nursing Record*, 18 August 1900; cited in Summers, *Angels and Citizens*, p. 215.
56. Summers, *Angels and Citizens*, p. 189.

the weak . . . and she is possessed of those exquisite, intangible, most human sympathies which, in the fullest degree, belong alone to her sex'.[57] Of their service with him in Natal, he wrote, 'They brought to many of the wounded and dying that comfort which men are little able to evolve, or are uncouth in bestowing . . . the tender, undefined and undefinable ministrations of women'.[58] Burdett-Coutts echoed this in July 1900: 'Any man who has been seriously ill knows the difference between an orderly with horny hands and creaking boots, smelling of tobacco . . . and the real ministering angel – the female nurse'.[59]

The nurses themselves occasionally refer in correspondence and diaries to these ministering virtues and a strange symbiosis with their patients: a comforting quasi-maternal relationship, both offered and sought. Writing in 1906, Sarah Tooley recounted that:

> the suffering man leans on a woman's sympathy, her voice soothes, her hand calms and comforts. 'Sister, won't you dress me?' is the frequent request of the soldier who has struggled back to life . . . And when the shadows deepen, and the hour of passing approaches, it is to the sister that Tommy confides his farewells.[60]

'I believe, Nurse, if you would let me put my head on your lap, I'd go to sleep', a patient in the Intombi Camp hospital, Ladysmith, told Driver in late November 1899. '[I] calmly lifted his head onto my lap, and before long he was sleeping calmly.'[61] Five months later, Sister X recorded: 'We had a sad case of poor Captain G., in the Inniskilling Fusiliers, being brought in with dysentery . . . He passed away like a little child; the most beautiful death I have ever seen.'[62]

Nurses were expected to be gentle comforters, proficient dispensers of complex modern medical procedures, and models of self-discipline and punctuality. But as products of an age in which gender roles were being redefined, if rather slowly, they also wanted to be soldiers, as Pope had implied, insofar as they might take a non-combatant role alongside the men. A keen sense of this redefinition is also apparent in Tooley's claim that 'No place is too remote, no climate too deadly, for the nurse to ply her ministrations. Like the soldier she obeys the call of duty, and, if need be, gives her life in the cause. In field hospital in time of war . . . or on the

57. Preface to Laurence, *A Nurse's Life*, p. vi.
58. Treves, *Tale of a Field Hospital*, p. 35.
59. Burdett-Coutts, *Sick and Wounded*, p. 201.
60. Tooley, *History of Nursing*, pp. 176–7.
61. Driver, *Experiences of a Siege*, p. 17.
62. Sister X, *Tragedy and Comedy*, p. 102.

South African veldt . . . the trained nurse is to be found.'[63] Death alongside the combatants was, naturally, the ultimate symbol of this brave new role. Bagot described the burial of a nurse who had died of typhoid in Bloemfontein: '[If] the thought of a soldier's funeral is sad, what would the reader have felt had he passed one, wrapped like a soldier in the nation's colours, borne by soldiers to a soldier's grave, who was receiving the only earthly honour that could be done to a noble woman – a soldier's funeral!'[64] The soldiering symbolism is powerful. As Summers comments, 'By the turn of the century, it was as if femininity itself, and with it much of feminism, had been militarised, and provided with a new uniform: a nurse's dress'.[65]

Claims to professionalism, and pressure for greater responsibility and status within the army medical system, were reinforced by the perceived probity of the nurses employed. The British Army had long recruited nurses of what it conceived the right social calibre, effectively limiting enlistment to single women from middle-class and upper middle-class backgrounds, with a preference for daughters of military personnel, doctors and clerics. This not only ensured that they had an appropriate education and sense of decorum, but also addressed long-standing anxieties about the dangers of flirtation within the rough environment of military hospital wards. Social distance was thought to be the best barrier to unwanted assaults from ordinary soldiers.[66] However, as nursing recruitment for South Africa escalated, the ability to monitor enrolment was weakened, with a consequent rise in concern about the character of some nurses, especially those engaged locally. Laurence, while posted in Durban, in February 1901, complained that 'some of the sisters now . . . seem to think that they have come out to South Africa only to enjoy themselves, and that they are setting about it in a way in which no lady would care to emulate'.[67] Three months later, stationed at No. 18 General Hospital at Charlestown, her complaints had become more focused:[68]

> Some of the sisters . . . talk about very little else except the men they have been dancing with, and so on . . . I am glad I am not Lady Superintendent up here: I should find it hard to know where to draw the line with the present lot of sisters; at first they were given every liberty, and were rather encouraged to go to dances and riding picnics, etc., with the men; then,

---

63. Tooley, *History of Nursing*, pp. v–vi.
64. Bagot, *Shadows of the War*, p. 155.
65. Summers, *Angels and Citizens*, p. 204.
66. Romantic entanglements between nurses and officers, a very different matter, are discussed below.
67. Laurence, *A Nurse's Life*, p. 250.
68. *Ibid.*, pp. 272, 282.

when their behaviour began to be talked about, the authorities put up notices in our mess-room of rules referring to conduct . . . which we cannot say are unnecessary, because there are just a few sisters who don't care what they do – one of them was seen at a hotel at the next station smoking cigarettes with a most undesirable companion! . . . the sooner sisters of that sort are weeded out the better.

Sister Henrietta, long-serving supervisor of a nurses' residence in Kimberley, suggested that women newly recruited from Britain should be closely supervised by experienced sisters, to prevent imprudent behaviour.[69] Burdett-Coutts also thought that 'the sentimental difficulty' (flirtation) was best solved by rigorous selection and supervision of recruits.[70]

Laurence was probably complaining about nurses fraternizing with officers, rather than enlisted men. Officer–nurse relationships are seldom mentioned, either at an official level or in private papers. Summers suggests that long-standing reservations within the army medical service about bringing nurses into contact with invalid officers diminished during the war, and that with the army medical reorganization after the war 'questions as to the propriety of allowing ladies to minister bed cases of their own social class appear to have been laid to rest'.[71] Valuable light is thrown on the problem of wartime romantic relationships, and nurses' concerns about professional probity, by correspondence written in 1901 by Sister Katharine Nisbet to her future husband, Major James Watson. She was matron at the Imperial Yeomanry Hospital, Pretoria, and seems to have met Watson when he was visiting his wounded brother. The letters reveal a deep anxiety about their friendship and 'those who would give anything to catch me'. On 11 February 1901 she warned: 'you must not come specially to see me when you visit the hospital nor must you send your orderly up with notes etc. My pedestal is high enough to be in good view of everyone here & I simply must live up to every letter of the high tone and standard I have tried to set & maintain here.' The friendship continued, causing her feelings of vulnerability and confusion to worsen. Again, on 6 March, she described the difficulties of balancing her personal and professional life: 'It is easy for a man to find friends . . . The Matron's frock is not always comfortable. It makes one long to throw it away.' Nisbet also provides clear evidence of the close bonds of affection forged between women nurses, often, perhaps, precisely because they were impeded from forming relationships with men. On 13 March,

---

69. Sister Henrietta, 'War nursing in South Africa', p. 256.
70. Burdett-Coutts, *Sick and Wounded*, pp. 202, 205–6; interview with *'The Hospital' Nursing Mirror*, July 1900.
71. Summers, *Angels and Citizens*, pp. 293–4.

she told Watson of her closeness to her colleague Evelyn Leggatt: 'No one will ever know all she has been to me & how much she loves me & how much I love her'. A month earlier, she had written: 'I am not one who has had many men friends. I am not that sort & my work & therefore my life has been spent more amongst women, & they interest me far more than men do.'[72]

The Army Nursing Service was permanently altered as a result of the Anglo-Boer War. The chorus of criticism from civilian doctors and nurses about antiquated and cumbersome RAMC procedures, echoed by other influential voices, prompted a major re-evaluation during the war. Criticisms of the system came not only from Burdett-Coutts, the Hospitals Commission, and establishment figures like Treves, but also from one of the latter's nurses in Natal, Ethel McCaul. After a series of scathing articles for the *Daily Chronicle*, she provided a more measured list of suggestions for reform, published in the *Nineteenth Century*. The organization and status of army nursing, she argued, should accord with that in the best civilian hospitals, with the Matron-in-Chief's salary being raised to at least £300 a year, and with more rigorous control over admission to the reserve and training of orderlies.[73] At the same time, in April 1901, the Matron's Council, on behalf of the profession at large, was urging Lord Raglan at the War Office to initiate a wholesale reform of army nursing.[74]

Under such pressure, an interlocking series of reforms was soon set in train. An Army Nursing Reorganization Committee was set up in June 1901 by St John Brodrick, the Secretary for War. This, in conjunction with initiatives arising from Queen Alexandra, led to the formation of the QAIMNS in March 1902. By 1906 there were 271 female nurses in the Service, 70 of these in South Africa.[75] For Summers, the South African War, unlike the Crimea, brought 'a major and irreversible policy shift on the employment of female nurses in wartime'.[76] It could also be argued that the general campaign for nursing professionalization was accelerated by the war and consequent developments in military nursing. After many years' unsuccessful campaigning, the first truly broad-based coalition of interests promoting state registration for nurses was formed in 1902, and four years later the British Medical Association voted almost unanimously in favour of state registration.[77]

---

72. MS letters, Sister Katharine Watson (nee Nisbet), NAM 5412–4–45/132.
73. McCaul, 'Suggestions for army reform', pp. 580–7. During the war, starting salaries for army nursing sisters were £40 p.a., for matrons £60, and for the Matron-in-Chief £200; compared with £200 or more for RAMC lieutenants, and £36 to £91 for sergeants.
74. *Nursing Record and Hospital World*, 6 April 1901, p. 270; 27 April 1901, pp. 331–5.
75. Fremantle, *Doctor in Khaki*, pp. 474–90; Summers, *Angels and Citizens*, pp. 220–7.
76. Summers, *Angels and Citizens*, pp. 205–6.
77. Tooley, *History of Nursing*, pp. 386, 392.

It is somewhat harder to assess how the careers and sense of professional identity of individual nurses were transformed by their service in South Africa, let alone more fundamental questions about whether this or any other war contributed to the emancipation of the women involved. In the context of British women's general experience of twentieth-century conflict, Penny Summerfield argues that while it is difficult to assess the impact for them collectively, in terms of either a narrowing or a widening of gender identities and opportunities, there is abundant evidence in the accounts of individual women that they found war a profoundly transforming experience.[78] As far as the Anglo-Boer War is concerned, it seems clear that collective as well as individual perceptions of changing career options for nurses were taking place. Quite apart from material changes in the organization of army nursing and in the terms of pay and promotion, numerous nurses experienced an enhanced sense of their own professional competence. Indeed, their collective critique of male orderlies (who did not always deserve such attacks) may have been an unconscious reflection of a rising tide of gender-specific professional identity. In relation to the raising of feminist consciousness, Summers convincingly suggests that, after 1902, 'Adventures which before the war had been confined to a few individuals in exceptional circumstances were now the experience of hundreds of British women volunteers'.[79]

78. Penny Summerfield, 'Women and war in the twentieth century', in June Purvis, ed., *Women's History: Britain, 1850–1945* (London, 1995), p. 326.
79. Summers, *Angels and Citizens*, p. 215.

CHAPTER FOUR

They Fought for Russia: Female Soldiers of the First World War

LAURIE STOFF

In the early morning of 9 July 1917, the soldiers of the 525th Kiurug-Dar'inskii Infantry Regiment crouched in their trenches outside of the town of Smorgon, in south-eastern Lithuania. The Russian troops had spent the last two days enduring heavy German artillery fire. At 3:00 a.m., the soldiers were ordered to attack. But no one moved. Officers begged the hesitant rank and file to act, to no avail. Instead, the troops convened their soldiers' committee and began to debate the necessity of engaging in such a dangerous manoeuvre. The futile debates went on for hours; the opportune time for attack was quickly passing. Shortly before dawn, a single volunteer unit of less than 300 troops decided to seize the initiative and attack, with or without the support of their hesitant compatriots. This virgin unit had been waiting more than a month for an opportunity to prove itself in battle. A few hundred committed volunteers joined this detachment of zealous soldiers, and as the sun's first rays filtered into the trenches, they rushed over the top into no man's land. They went with the hope that the waverers would be inspired by their example and would follow them into battle.

The Russian troops managed to advance across the battlefield with few casualties, despite intense German artillery. Their success inspired some of the reluctant soldiers, who began to come out of the trenches. Eventually, more than half of the corps joined the advance, and the Russians were able to take the first and second line of German trenches. But the success proved short-lived. Some Russian soldiers found stores of alcohol left behind by the retreating Germans. Weary of war, they found this temptation too great to resist. The volunteers beseeched their conscripted comrades to continue attacking, but these entreaties had little effect on the troops greedily gulping the abandoned spirits. The original group attempted to carry on, but upon reaching the third line were forced to retreat in the face of a fierce German counter-attack. The Russian troops lost all the ground they had gained, but managed to capture nearly 200 Germans. In the midst of the chaos of battle, some of the prisoners could be heard crying out: 'Good God! Women!' 'Damn! What disgrace! Captured by women! Damn!'[1] The astonished Germans had been captured by members of the 1st Russian Women's Battalion of Death.[2]

During the First World War, thousands of Russian women donned military uniforms and set out to defend their nation in battle. In the first years of the war, hundreds joined the fighting; by 1917 the numbers of female soldiers had reached approximately 6,000. Their experience was unprecedented. The Great War fostered an explosion of Russian female participation in combat, far surpassing previous or contemporary examples of women soldiers. More significantly, Russia was the only country among the belligerents to employ women systematically in sexually segregated military formations. Russia's female soldiers have largely been forgotten, despite the obviously striking nature of the phenomenon. But contemporary observers did not miss the salience of women in combat. Those who encountered the female soldiers were fascinated by them. The women became momentary media stars as domestic and foreign presses printed numerous accounts of their feats. They were pushed aside by subsequent historiography for a number of reasons, the most prominent being that they ended up on the losing side of the upheavals of 1917. Organized under the auspices of the Provisional Government, the women's military units were associated with the 'bourgeois' elements the victorious Bolsheviks were determined to crush. In fact, a sub-company of one of the women's battalions was involved in the defence of the Winter Palace during the October Revolution. As a result, the women were ridiculed, maligned and ignored. But they are important. Their stories must be told if we are to understand more fully the war, the Revolution, and the roles and experiences of women, inside and outside Russia.

The women warriors

The magnitude and scope of the First World War required belligerent governments to mobilize vast numbers of citizens to meet wartime needs.

---

1. Boris Solonevich, *Zhenshchina s vintovkoi: Istoricheskii Roman* (Buenos Aires, 1955), p. 129; Rheta Childe Dorr, *Inside the Russian Revolution* (New York, 1917), p. 74.
2. See Maria Botchkareva, *Yashka: My Life as Peasant, Officer and Exile*, as set down by Isaac Don Levine (New York, 1919), pp. 209–17; Solonevich, *Zhenshchina s vintovkoi*, pp. 120–33; as well as Documents of the 1st Siberian Army Corps, in *Rossiiskii Gosudarstvenyi Voenno-Istoricheskii Arkhiv* (Russian State Military-Historical Archives) documents in *fond* (collection) 2277, *opis* (index) 1, *delo* (file) 368. Subsequently RGVIA, f./op./d./ 1.

This included millions of Russian women who went to work, replacing men sent to the battlefields. Many also went directly to the front to serve their country. The majority served as nurses and other medical personnel. Officially, female nurses were supposed to remain three or four miles from the front line in mobile field hospitals, but many did work close to the fighting, sometimes even in the trenches. Women also served in other front-line capacities such as drivers, mechanics, ditch-diggers, and other non-combat auxiliary functions.[3] A few even became pilots, such as E.P. Samsonova and Princess E.M. Shakhovskaia.[4] Hundreds of Russian women were unsatisfied with auxiliary work and entered the fighting itself. Since Imperial Russian law forbade women's enlistment in the active army, these women frequently disguised themselves as men. Lack of standardized recruitment regulations, lax bureaucratic procedures, and superficial or non-existent medical examinations allowed women in disguise to remain undetected. A few were even accepted as women, as enlistment often depended on the personal prerogative of the commanding officer. Most of the records which document the existence of these female combatants pertain to those whose true sexual identity was discovered only after they were wounded and examined by medical personnel. One can only assume that there may have been many more women who fought and perhaps died in male units but were never exposed.

Individual women who entered the ranks of the army as combatants were of various social backgrounds, education levels, ages, and geographical origins. Some were as young as 14. A number of students from *gymnasiia* (high schools) and the women's higher courses (the Russian equivalent of universities for women) went into combat. Women in higher social positions used influence and connections to enter the ranks of the active army to fight alongside their husbands, fathers and brothers. It was not uncommon for women soldiers in Russia to be the wives or, more often, the daughters of officers. Aristocratic and noble women fought alongside those from the peasantry and working classes. While most served in the rank and file, some even became officers. They not only proved capable of withstanding the grisly conditions of trench warfare, but many also demonstrated courage in the face of great danger.

In investigating these female warriors some remarkable portraits emerge. Command personnel frequently used high praise in describing their female soldiers. While men hesitated, women often volunteered for dangerous reconnaissance missions and in many instances were the first to rush from

---

3. Tikhon Polner, *Russian Local Government During the War and the Union of the Zemstvos* (New Haven, CT, 1930), p. 255.
4. 'E. Samsonova', *Zhenshchina i Voina*, 1 (5 March 1915), pp. 5–7; Nikolai Ardashev, *Velikaia Voina i zhenshchiny russkiia* (Moscow, 1915), p. 13.

trenches during attacks. Russia's women soldiers often proved more enthusiastic, better disciplined, more courageous and more self-sacrificing than
their male compatriots. Many were even awarded high military honours
like the St George's Cross for their courage. The desire to avoid detection
of their true sexual identity undoubtedly inspired the women to perform
well. They may also have wanted (consciously or unconsciously) to demonstrate that they could successfully fulfil this traditionally male role. In order
to escape criticism based on gender, those whose true sex was known were
careful not to err or malinger in their duties. Even more significant to their
performance is the fact that all women combatants were volunteers. They
willingly chose to give their lives in the war, unlike the vast majority of conscripted males who lacked the same zeal for the cause.

For many of these individual women soldiers, the motivation for joining
the fight was to defend their nation against an enemy that had been made
to appear demonic by early war propaganda.[5] Patriotic fervour was at its
height in the first few months of the conflict, and it seems that the greatest
number of individual women went to the battlefields during this period.
Aside from patriotic sentiments and fear of German domination, many had
a religious impetus to fight. After all, the army was fighting for God as well
as Tsar and Fatherland. A number cited faith as their source of strength
and determination. Another motivating force behind female participation
in combat was a desire for adventure. For some young girls who had spent
very sheltered lives in their parents' homes and in all-female institutions,
going to war provided a chance to see the world. Some were bored with
their restricted lives and felt the need to be useful to their country. Others
used the war as an opportunity to forget about personal misfortune or
tragedy. Still others sought to avenge the death of a loved one or family
member. All shared a basic patriotic devotion to the homeland.

The all-female military units

By the spring of 1917, the phenomenon of individual women joining male
units would give way (though not completely) to separate, all-female military
formations. The organization of all-female units can be partly attributed to
the tradition of Russian women warriors in this and previous wars. Indeed,
a number of the units were created by female veterans. More important,
however, were the particular political and social conditions created after the

---

5.   Hubertus Jahn, *Patriotic Culture in Russia During World War I* (Ithaca, NY, 1995), *passim*.

fall of the Imperial government and during the attempts to reconstruct Russia. The newly established Provisional Government confronted a multitude of difficulties, including horrendous inflation, food shortages, and an increasingly bitter struggle for power with the Petrograd Soviet of Workers' and Soldiers' Deputies. Aside from these serious internal problems, the country's involvement in the international war was relentlessly draining the country's resources, both human and material. Despite these difficulties, Russia's new ruling order remained convinced that Russia had to remain in the war. The situation at the front was not promising, however. The majority of Russia's soldiers retained an essentially defensive stance immediately following the February Revolution, unwilling to abandon their positions and allow the enemy to break through the front, an act perceived by some as a 'betrayal of the Revolution'.[6] The army hoped to hold the line until the new government could negotiate peace with the Central Powers. But peace did not come in a timely fashion.

In March the Petrograd Soviet issued Order No. 1. This decree gave the rank-and-file soldiers rights as citizens, allowed them to create committees to represent their interests, outlawed corporal and capital punishment for insubordination and desertion, and thereby 'democratized' the army. The dissemination of Order No. 1 significantly changed the balance of power between soldier and officer. Highly mistrustful of their officers, who tended to come from the upper classes, many soldiers were quick to condemn their commanders for sympathy with the old regime. The slightest suspicion of counter-revolutionary attitudes was justification for arrest, beating and even murder. Order and discipline became increasingly difficult to maintain among war-weary peasant soldiers eager to return home and exercise their new-found freedom and take part in the widespread land-grabbing going on in the countryside. By mid-April the situation had begun to deteriorate significantly in certain regions. Desertion, declining discipline and morale, collapse of authority, fraternization with the enemy, defeatist sentiment and agitation, and the overwhelming desire for peace, were all on the rise. Mutinies became frequent in some units, and increasingly took on a violent character. As General Mikhail Alekseev, Commander-in-Chief of the Russian Army, commented shortly before his dismissal in mid-May 1917: 'the internal rot has reached its limit . . . The troops are no longer a threat to the enemy, but to their own fatherland.'[7]

In spite of these tremendous problems, the government and the high command of the army resolved to undertake a final offensive in order to

---

6. Alan Wildman, *The End of the Russian Imperial Army. Vol. 1: The Old Army and the Soldiers' Revolt (March–April 1917)* (Princeton, NJ, 1980), p. 236.
7. *Ibid.*, p. 74.

achieve the decisive victory they believed was necessary to end the war 'honourably'. They planned the attack to begin in the summer of 1917, coordinated with the offensive to be launched by the Allies in the west. The entire effort, they realized, would be a failure unless they could rebuild the morale of the troops and restore the army's battle competence. Thus, in the spring of 1917, they embarked on a campaign to raise the fallen spirits of the soldiers and ready the army for the attack. The Provisional Government sent emissaries to the front for the purpose of inspiring the troops; they implored the soldiers to obey their commanders and continue the struggle for victory. Although the men often responded positively to the patriotic orations and impassioned pleadings of those such as Prime Minister Alexander Kerensky, they could not be sufficiently motivated to engage in sustained fighting.

Witnessing the failure of their efforts, the government and military authorities grew increasingly willing to resort to more unconventional methods. The new government called upon every citizen to aid the homeland. Even the Soviet of Workers' and Soldiers' Deputies appealed to the nation to mobilize all available resources to repel the enemy.[8] In response, a number of volunteer organizations were created in an effort to revive the army and strengthen the morale and resolve of the troops at the front. In May, General Aleksei Brusilov, Commander-in-Chief of the South-western Front, proposed the formation of 'revolutionary' units, including special 'shock' detachments and 'battalions of death'. These units were to be composed of the most dedicated and patriotic volunteers.[9] Brusilov had successfully used such units to break through enemy lines during the 1916 offensive on the South-western Front. The shock troops were to be organized into battalions bearing their own insignia: black and red chevrons on their sleeves and skull-and-crossbones on their caps, symbolizing dedication to the revolution and a willingness to die for the homeland. Strictly disciplined, highly trained, and intensely loyal to superiors, such revolutionary battalions were sworn to fight to the death.[10] The aim of these formations was to lead attacks in order to 'arouse the revolutionary, offensive spirit in the Army . . . by giving [the soldiers] faith that the entire Russian people stand behind them' and to 'carry along the wavering elements inspired by their example'.[11]

8. 'Resolution of the All-Russian Conference of the Soviet of Workers' and Soldiers' Deputies', in Frank Golder, ed., *Documents of Russian History, 1914–1917*, trans. Emmanual Aronsberg (New York, 1927), p. 332.
9. 'Telegram from General Brusilov to Supreme High Command', in N.E. Karakurin and Ia.A. Iakovleva, eds, *Razlozhenie Armii v 1917 godu* (Moscow, 1925), p. 64.
10. *Razlozhenie Armii*, pp. 68–9.
11. General Brusilov's directive of 22 May 1917, in Wildman, *End of the Russian Imperial Army*, p. 79.

When Brusilov became Supreme Commander-in-Chief of the Russian Army in late May, he introduced revolutionary formations throughout the army. A Central Executive Committee for the Formation of Revolutionary Battalions was established under Supreme High Command (Stavka), and all command personnel were requested to create 'committees for the organization of revolutionary battalions' both at the front and in the rear.[12] Other quasi-military and private volunteer groups were formed to augment Brusilov's efforts by recruiting and organizing 'everyone who holds dear the fate of our motherland'.[13] Escaped prisoners of war, wounded veterans, holders of the St George's Cross, and other such associations began forming their own volunteer units. The 'League of Personal Example' aimed its recruitment efforts at workers, soldiers, students, cadets, officers and officials, and even actively sought to enlist women. 'The Military League' intended to create a Women's Volunteer Committee, which would be charged with the formation of Women's War-Work Detachments to employ women in specialized auxiliary military functions such as telephonists, telegraphists, drivers, electrical technicians, clerks, topographers and medics.

The extension of various rights and freedoms to the general populace and to the army after the February Revolution was another condition important for the creation of all-female combat units. The new Provisional Government was proclaimed a social democracy, and equality of all citizens was to be guaranteed. Russia became the first great power to grant women the right to vote on 20 July 1917. Numerous progressive women pressed the government to extend female participation in the public sphere to include military service. This established a political basis, at least in theory, for the inclusion of women in combat. The February Revolution had also precipitated a revitalization of women's organizations, which pressed the government to allow greater involvement in every aspect of the war effort, including combat. Many women were caught up in the renewed dedication to the war effort. Some felt sincerely that female activity should extend beyond mere auxiliary functions. There was a widespread feeling that with the death of autocracy and the proclamation of social democracy, women would finally be given the equality to which they had long aspired. War work, they hoped, would be rewarded with political and legal rights. Some had become disillusioned by the inability of men to end the conflict. They were distressed by what they perceived to be cowardice and irresponsibility on the part of male soldiers who refused to fight. In a metaphor reflective of their traditional roles as caring nurturers, many women perceived the army as 'sick',

---

12. Correspondence to the Minister of War, Extract from a report by 'The Military League', RGVIA 366/1/90/50.
13. *Razlozhenie Armii*, p. 69.

in need of a strong dose of morale to recover its fighting prowess. They believed that wavering men needed to be reminded of their duty as soldiers, and that the presence of women in combat would serve to 'heal' the troops, i.e. to jolt them out of their complacency and shame them into fighting again. Thus, the idea of all-female military formations began to circulate in Russian society at this time.

In May 1917, the Ministry of War began receiving a number of petitions from individuals and women's groups requesting permission to organize female military units.[14] However, it was Maria Bochkarëva, a peasant from Siberia, who is credited with obtaining official permission for the formation of the first women's combat unit. Bochkarëva had fought with the Russian army from the very beginning of the war, earning two medals for bravery and achieving the rank of a non-commissioned officer. She envisaged a separate all-female military formation as a solution to the army's problems, and managed to enlist the support of Duma President Mikhail Rodzianko and Commander-in-Chief General Brusilov, who immediately recognized her propaganda value. At the end of May 1917 she, along with her influential sponsors, presented the idea to Kerensky, now Minister of War.[15] Despite some initial reservations about possible 'moral' problems, the minister eventually gave his approval for the formation of the 1st Russian Women's Battalion of Death under Bochkarëva's command. Bochkarëva wasted no time, and began publicizing for recruits immediately, placing posters around the city.[16] The results were promising. Initially, approximately 2,000 women enlisted.[17] The minimum age for acceptance was 18, and those under 21 had to have parental permission. All volunteers underwent complete medical examinations performed by a commission of female doctors. The Petrograd Military District issued them necessary equipment, supplies, and uniforms complete with the special insignia of the battalions of death. The members swore an oath of loyalty to the Provisional Government. The Kolomensk (Smolny) Women's Institute became their barracks and training grounds. Bochkarëva, who was promoted to sub-lieutenant, and 25 male instructors from the Volynskii Regiment began an intensive training programme to prepare the women for combat. The recruits rose at 5:00 a.m., drilled until

---

14. 'Letter of a Woman-Volunteer to the Minister of War', in *Razlozhenie Armii*, p. 70; Records of the Main Directorate of the General Staff, Department of Organization and Service of Troops, RGVIA 2000/2/1557/3, 4; and Correspondence to the Minister of War from Maria Bochkarëva, RGVIA 366/1/90/4.
15. Botchkareva, *Yashka*, pp. 156–61. The only official record located pertaining to Kerensky's involvement is a letter addressed to the Minister of War, dated 28 May 1917, from Bochkarëva. RGVIA 366/1/90/4.
16. Botchkareva, *Yashka*, p. 161; Solonevich, *Zhenshchina s vintovkoi*, p. 34.
17. Botchkareva, *Yashka*, p. 164; Solonevich, *Zhenshchina s vintovkoi*, p. 54.

11:00 a.m., were fed a sparse meal, and continued training well into the evening. The women engaged in strenuous physical exercises, marching drills, hand-to-hand combat, and most importantly learned how to use rifles and bayonets.

Bochkarëva was extremely hard on the volunteers. She instituted the strictest discipline and severely punished the most minor transgressions. All volunteers were given crew-cuts and dispossessed of all personal hygiene items, including toothbrushes. Bochkarëva was determined to remove all traces of femininity from the women and transform them into soldiers able to withstand all the hardships of war. Moreover, she insisted that the unit adhere to old army discipline, despite the changes implemented following the February Revolution. Each woman signed a waiver of their rights as soldiers guaranteed by Order No. 1. The women were denied leave and subject to corporal punishment. Emphasizing quality over quantity, the commander used the first weeks of instruction to weed out those she felt would be unable to perform in combat. The slightest hint of femininity was considered frivolity and grounds for dismissal. Giggling was strictly forbidden. Bochkarëva encouraged (and she herself practised) distinctly male behaviour such as smoking and swearing in her quest to make 'real' (i.e. male) soldiers out of the women. Those who could not or would not accept her iron regime were dismissed; 700 'unreliable' elements were purged.[18]

The social composition of the battalion spanned class levels from peasantry and working class to aristocracy, with a significant proportion from the upper and middle strata. One of the women who left a record of her involvement with the battalion, Nina Krylova, contended that most volunteers were literate and urban, with 50 per cent having at least gymnasium-level education, and 25 per cent educated to university or *kursistki* (women's higher courses) level. There were even a few women from the highest levels of Petrograd society, including Princess Tatuieva and Maria Skrydlova, daughter of a Baltic fleet admiral. Bochkarëva chose those from military families and with higher education to command companies and platoons within the battalion. There were a number of professional women in the ranks, including several doctors, and many more were clerks, stenographers and other office employees. There were also a considerable number of dressmakers, domestic servants, peasants and factory workers. The majority were ethnically Russian, but several were Polish and Jewish, and there was one Japanese and one Estonian woman. Most recruits were single and childless.[19]

---

18. Botchkareva, *Yashka*, pp. 160–5, Solonevich, *Zhenshchina s vintovkoi*, pp. 47–65, 72.
19. Dorr, *Inside the Russian Revolution*, pp. 56–7; Bessie Beatty, *The Red Heart of Russia* (New Yark, 1918), pp. 100–1; Botchkareva, *Yashka*, pp. 164–77; and Solonevich, *Zhenshchina s vintovkoi*, p. 65.

During the month of training in June, the battalion suffered from a number of internal and external difficulties. The women met much resistance from Petrograd society. There were those who thought it disgraceful for women to be soldiers and did not hide their distaste. The most caustic derision, however, came from the Bolsheviks, who regularly taunted the women with threats and even violence. Critics on the left were not ideologically opposed to the idea of women soldiers, but they attacked the pro-war and pro-government position of the battalion. The harsh methods of the commander also drew much criticism from within and without. Bochkarëva's refusal to allow soldiers' committees caused considerable disquiet. Some women began to agitate for greater representation and voice in the battalion, as well as less stringent punishment. Bochkarëva would not give in to these demands and summarily dismissed all the 'rebels', which included most of the more educated and upper-class volunteers.[20] The unit was left with only about 300 mostly working-class and peasant women by mid-June and was reconstituted a detachment.[21]

The women finished training at the end of the month. The Metropolitan blessed their colours at a large public ceremony at St Isaac's Cathedral. Thousands turned out to see the world's first all-female combat unit march down the streets of Petrograd. The women soldiers were dispatched to the front to participate in the coming offensive. Their baptism in battle (on 9 July at Smorgon, as described in the beginning of this paper) proved decisively that women could serve in combat as well as, if not better than, men. All of the command personnel who were involved in the campaign commented that the women carried out their duties extremely well. Reports from the front enthusiastically lauded their bravery, discipline and composure, as well as their initial success in inspiring the hesitant men to attack.[22] Ten of the women soldiers were awarded St George's Crosses for their courage, and 20 others received other medals. Despite the proof provided by this event, Russia's military authorities continued to doubt the value of women as soldiers.

Meanwhile, many individuals and women's groups from all over the country, inspired by the example of the 1st Russian Women's Battalion of Death, sent requests to the Ministry of War for permission to form units in their localities. A number of private women's organizations took their own

---

20. Some educated women, like Krylova and her friend Leila, Tatuieva, and Skrydlova, remained loyal to Bochkarëva.
21. Petr A. Polovtsoff, *Glory and Downfall: Reminiscences of a Russian General Staff Officer* (London, 1935), pp. 220–2; Solonevich, *Zhenshchina s vintovkoi*, pp. 57–8, Botchkareva, *Yashka*, pp. 174–81.
22. Reports of the Commander of the 525th Regiment and the Commander of the 172nd Infantry Division to the Chief of Staff of the I Siberian Army Corps, RGVIA 2277/1/368/1, 66.

initiative to create all-female military units. The presence of hundreds of individual women in the ranks of the active army from the very beginning of the war undoubtedly contributed to and facilitated this process, for several of them played essential roles in the promotion and organization of the new women's units. Public demand, coupled with the attention the women's combat unit was receiving both at home and abroad, meant that the authorities could not ignore the women's military movement. The Provisional Government, particularly the Ministry of War, regarded Bochkarëva and her women's battalion largely as an instrument of propaganda. The new leadership believed that the women could have a positive effect on the war-weary army. But the government could not tolerate the formation of armed bands of women over which it did not have direct control.

The commotion that sporadic grass-roots women's combat formations generated in military circles convinced the Ministry of War that it was necessary to establish a consistent policy regarding the women's military movement. On 1 June 1917, Kerensky authorized the organization of further combat units composed of women volunteers.[23] The Main Directorate of the General Staff, the central executive planning apparatus of the Ministry of War (hereafter referred to as GUGSh from the acronym of its Russian title *Glavnoe Upravlenie Generalnago Shtaba*), was to oversee the formation of such units. GUGSh was given authority over all of the private groups involved in the formation of women's military units. No units were to be created without official sanction. The army administration decided that women should be designated for three types of military service: combat, communications, and medical aid. Originally, two all-female infantry battalions were to be formed, the 1st Petrograd Women's Battalion and the 2nd Moscow Women's Battalion of Death, in addition to the one already established by Bochkarëva. Some of the women who had been rejected by Bochkarëva joined these units. The women's battalions were to consist of between 1,000 and 1,400 members and include supporting sub-units such as machine-gun, communications, cavalry scout and sapper detachments. Four separate communications detachments would be organized, two in Moscow and two in Petrograd. The district military headquarters were charged with supervising and assisting the organization and training of the units in their respective cities. The local women's associations were also to aid in the recruitment and registration process.[24]

Despite the directives of the army administration, private women's quasi-military organizations continued to function outside official control.

23. Correspondence of the Ministry of War, RGVIA 2000/2/1557/29.
24. Documents pertaining to government policy on the formation of women's military units are located in RGVIA 2000/2/1557.

Throughout the summer of 1917 the women's military movement continued to grow in the private sphere, with more independent female units created. Petitions from women requesting permission to join the active army continued to flow into the War Ministry. In an attempt to control these efforts and to compensate popular demands, GUGSh resolved to expand the number of women's military formations. In mid-July, the agency approved a petition from a privately organized women's combat unit in Ekaterinodar to join the ranks of the active army as the 3rd Kuban Women's Shock Battalion. Similarly, the administration decided to create seven additional communications units, five in Kiev and two in Saratov. In both of these cities women's military units had already been formed by private initiatives.[25] The staff of the headquarters of the Western Front also proposed the creation of a women's unit, the Minsk Separate Guard Militia.[26]

Dissatisfied with official efforts, women in the private sector continued their impromptu efforts to aid the military and to seek employment in various functions at the front. Local women's groups organized female volunteers in Poltava, Ekaterinburg, Tashkent, Baku, Viatka, Minsk, Mogilëv, Perm, Mariupol', Odessa, Kiev, Saratov and Ekaterinodar.[27] The numbers involved in combat and combat-related activities had grown so significantly that in August 1917 a Women's Military Congress was convened in Petrograd with the goal of coordinating the efforts of the various women's military units around the country. The government was unable to bring these grass-roots efforts under control. The uncertain and unmanageable nature of independent formations made the task of formulating a consistent policy virtually impossible. Furthermore, the women's units were given inadequate attention and assistance from the military administration, which was beset by a myriad of other problems and shortages. Many within official military circles were unwilling to make a commitment to the idea of all-female military formations. Some, such as General Anton Denikin (Stavka Chief of Staff), wanted proof that women soldiers could withstand the conditions of war and perform satisfactorily in combat. The participation of Bochkarëva's battalion in the battle at Smorgon provided this sort of proof, so much so that even Denikin praised their accomplishments. But this still did not convince military authorities that women's combat units were a good idea. There were those who thought this commendable performance in battle was an anomaly, and doubted that it could be repeated. More importantly, the positive influence of the women's unit on the male soldiers was perceived (correctly) as limited

---

25. *Ibid.*
26. Correspondence of the Main Directorate of the General Staff to the Chief of Staff of the Western Front, RGVIA 2003/2/349/44, 46.
27. Correspondence of the Ministry of War, RGVIA 2000/2/1557.

and ephemeral. Like all Provisional Government attempts to inspire the men to continue fighting, female soldiers failed to provide sufficient and sustained impetus to men who desired peace more than anything else. And, as anti-war sentiment grew, many male soldiers became increasingly hostile towards women who wanted to continue fighting.

As a result of these misgivings, as early as August there was a growing inclination in the military establishment to discontinue the organization of women volunteers for combat. Increasingly, such activities were regarded as draining badly needed resources away from other military endeavours. GUGSh decided to cease the formation of communications detachments composed of female soldiers, since efforts to organize such units had not met with success.[28] The military authorities also began to have second thoughts about deploying women's units in battle. A shift of focus, therefore, occurred in September towards the use of women in auxiliary functions. GUGSh desired that those women's units originally designated for combat participation should be assigned to the defence of railways.[29] The order was never implemented, however, because it met so much opposition from the male soldiers assigned to this task.[30]

Unofficial grass-roots women's units continued to spring up well into the autumn of 1917. The army was frustrated with its inability to control such formations. Moreover, the idea of independent bands of armed women was quite unsettling to many men. GUGSh now considered the problems caused by the women's units to be greater than the advantages derived from them. The administration concluded that the significance of the women's military movement had been 'strongly exaggerated by the press' and by individual women and organizations pressuring the government. Convinced that the women's military formations could no longer have a positive impact, especially once it became clear that the summer offensive had failed, the military authorities questioned the value of their continued existence. The Ministry of War now began to withdraw official support, leaving the battalions essentially to run themselves.[31]

As a result, the Moscow Women's Battalion of Death experienced numerous problems in organization and training. Neighbouring male units expressed open hostility to the presence of women in the ranks. Supplies and equipment

---

28. Correspondence of the Ministry of War, RGVIA 2000/2/1557/136.
29. Correspondence of the Main Directorate of the General Staff, Department of Organization and Service of Troops, RGVIA 2003/2/349/34.
30. Correspondence of the Ministry of War, RGVIA 2000/2/1557/206; A.S. Senin, 'Zhenskie batal'ony i voennye komandy v 1917 godu', *Voprosi Istorii* 10 (1987), p. 179.
31. Correspondence of the Minstry of War, Report from the Department of Organization and Service of Troops, RGVIA 2000/2/1557/190.

provided by the district military authorities were inadequate, and their uniforms were ill-fitting, since, of course, they had been designed for men. The lack of proper footwear was particularly troublesome, aggravated by a leather shortage. Many of the women had become disillusioned because of the difficulties they faced and the loss of support from the military establishment. Nearly 350 members left the unit in September after GUGSh allowed the commanders to dismiss those who desired to be released from service. In late September the commanders of the Moscow Women's Battalion of Death decided to disband the unit completely, as it now seemed impossible to retain any kind of internal cohesion. Just prior to official disbanding, approximately 500 volunteers from the Moscow battalion requested to be dispatched to the front. Without GUGSh's knowledge, they were sent to various positions along the Romanian, South-western and Western Fronts. It is not known whether these women ever saw combat. Twenty-five members of the Moscow battalion were accepted into the Aleksandrovskii Military School in June, and, after receiving the appropriate training, all graduated and were promoted to officer rank. They were slated to take command of the various women's military formations, replacing male officers who had temporarily commanded the units until the women completed their necessary military instruction.[32] However, the Bolshevik seizure of power in October ensured that these women would never take their posts. The Kuban Women's Shock Battalion faced serious organizational problems as well, and never participated in any combat activity.[33] The Minsk Separate Guard Militia never even got past the organizational stages.[34]

Undoubtedly, the most well-known and controversial event in the history of the all-women's combat units is the so-called 'storming of the Winter Palace', during which some women soldiers found themselves in the midst of one of the key battles during the Bolshevik seizure of power. In the weeks preceding the October Revolution, the 1st Petrograd Women's Battalion was in camp outside the capital, near the Levashevo station on the Finland road. The women had completed their training and were awaiting orders to be sent to the front. On 24 October, the commander of the battalion received orders for the women to report to the square in front of the Winter Palace. The women believed that there was to be a parade and that Kerensky would review the unit prior to its departure for the front. After arriving in the city, the Petrograd Military District ordered the women to take up position on

---

32. Documents on the 2nd Moscow Women's Battalion of Death, RGVIA 3474/2/1–14; Senin, 'Zhenskie batal'ony', p. 181.
33. Documents on the Formation of the 3rd Kuban Women's Battalion, RGVIA 1300/1/239.
34. Correspondence of the Main Directorate of the General Staff, Department of Organization and Service of Troops, RGVIA 2003/2/349/46.

the Palace Square to defend the Provisional Government. Members of the battalion were distraught. Their goal was to fight Russia's external enemies; they had no desire to become embroiled in the political struggle. In keeping with these sentiments, the battalion commander marched the majority back to their encampment. He had, however, been persuaded to leave a subdivision of his 2nd Company, comprising 137 women, on the square for the purpose of assisting the delivery of benzene. When the Red Guards and other Bolshevik supporters arrived, these women did their best to defend the Palace, remaining faithful to the oath they had sworn to the Provisional Government. It was this activity which has given fame, or perhaps infamy, to the Russian woman soldier. The women and their fellow defenders, a handful of young cadets, were no match for the Bolshevik forces and were defeated and captured. Some of the women suffered verbal, physical and sexual abuse at the hands of Red Guards and soldiers. After being held for several days, the small unit was released and sent to rejoin the remainder of the battalion at the Levashevo camp. Many had nowhere to go, however, so they remained in camp even after the Military Revolutionary Committee ordered the official dissolution of the battalion on 21 November 1917.[35]

When the Bolsheviks seized Petrograd on 25 October 1917, Bochkarëva's unit was still at the front. There the antagonism with which the majority of male soldiers regarded the women had grown so hostile that the commander realized she had no other alternative but to disband the battalion and allow the women to leave the front. The danger from fellow Russian soldiers had become as great, if not greater, than that from the enemy. Of the 15 women's military formations designated by the Ministry of War, this small detachment was the only unit known to have fulfilled the intent of the women's military movement: to defend the homeland against the external enemy.

With the Bolsheviks in power and an armistice with the Central Powers in the works, the new government had little use for what were perceived to be 'bourgeois' women with guns. Therefore, on 30 November 1917 GUGSh issued the final decree ordering any remaining women's military units to disband.[36] Although this signified the close of the women's military movement begun under the auspices of the Provisional Government, it is not the end of the story of female participation in military functions. Thousands of female soldiers went on to fight on both sides during the Civil War. And during the Second World War, Russian women again entered the armed

35. Maria Bochkarnikova, 'Boi v Zimnem Dvortse', *Novyi Zhurnal* 68 (1982), pp. 215–27; 'Oktiabr'skoe Vooruzhennoe Vosstanie v Petrograd', *Velikaia Oktiabr'skaia Sotsialisticheskaia Revoliutsia* (Moscow, 1957), p. 281.
36. Miscellaneous Correspondence of the War Ministry, RGVIA 2000/2/1557/211–12.

forces in significant numbers serving in a variety of capacities, including combat.

The participation of Russia's women in the First World War is truly remarkable. Not only were their numbers unparalleled, but never before had a government of men organized women for active combat in a theatre of war. Yet the actions of these women had little effect upon post-war society. Russia's women soldiers proved definitively that women could participate in even such an exclusively male activity as combat. Such evidence could have shattered notions of biological inferiority and opened the door to female participation in a variety of male-dominated areas, including the military. But this did not happen. The circumstances in which women became soldiers were generally regarded as exceptional. After the conclusion of hostilities, women were expected to return to their traditional roles in society. By officially sanctioning, organizing and sending women soldiers into battle, both the Provisional and Soviet governments made explicit statements about acceptable gender roles. Yet neither carried through the broader implications of this statement. In fact, both governments, as well as the majority of society, seemed to overlook, or even consciously ignore and reject, the sociological meaning of this action, regarding it as a necessary, but unfortunate measure dictated by the exigencies of war and national survival.

The creation of the women's units in Russia during the First World War can be distinguished as a consistent social movement, for it was not only carried out by the military establishment, but also by women with a conscious social and political agenda. There is a clear link between female participation in combat during the Great War and the early twentieth-century women's movement, both in Russia and in the West. Feminists and progressive women tended to be very supportive of the all-female military units, as the women soldiers were explicitly dismissing arguments used to exclude women from involvement in the affairs of the nation. But the influence of the Russian women's military movement was limited in this sphere as well. Even the most militant suffragettes were made uncomfortable by the emulation of such violent and destructive male behaviour by women, who were still supposed to be the caring, nurturing members of society. They found it very difficult to accept such a radical change in women's gender roles.

The Russian Provisional Government employed these women not for their abilities on the battlefield, but specifically because they were women and, as such, useful propaganda in the campaign to continue the war. The women soldiers were intended to act as inspirational symbols for male soldiers, to motivate and even shame them into resuming their military duties. In this context, the women's units are quite revealing of Russian concepts of patriotism and its myths, and they demonstrate how out of touch the elites were with the mass of war-weary, conscripted peasants in the army. Appeals to 'masculine', chivalrous and patriotic duty to defend their country fell flat with the majority of draftees, who little understood the complexities of geopolitics. Using women to remind men of these obligations was ineffectual. In fact, the entire idea was based on an internal paradox. Most peasant-soldiers fought because they were ordered to do so and because as men they were socialized as defenders of the weaker sex. When women appeared at the front in uniforms and with guns, many men no longer understood what they were defending. As a result, many were content to have women do the task they were unwilling to do themselves, abandoning the women on the battlefield. Moreover, many were hostile to the women soldiers, who represented the desire to continue fighting when the majority of men now wanted nothing else but to return home. Thus, while the women proved competent in battle, they could not inspire the mass of war-weary troops. Despite their limited success, we should not overlook the significance of Russia's women soldiers. Their activities were unprecedented. But they are important as much for the way they were received as for what they achieved. Their reception within Russian society and by subsequent historians reveals the deep unease about the idea of women in combat and the pitfalls which lay ahead for those women who might want to fight for their country.

CHAPTER FIVE

Women at Work: Chinese Soldiers on the Long March, 1934–1936

HELEN PRAEGER YOUNG

In 1934, the Chinese Communist Army bases on provincial borders in central and south China were blockaded and under constant attack by Chiang Kai-shek's Nationalist army. The Communist forces began to withdraw from their base areas, marching west and north. This retreat, which became a symbol of victory, is known as the 20,000-*li* Long March.[1]

The military and political history of the journey has been written in many languages, but in the West there is little available about the women soldiers who made the arduous journey.[2] In many reports of the now legendary Long March, there has been only an occasional paragraph or chapter about the surprisingly large number of young women who walked some 10,000 kilometres or more with a fighting army. More than 2,000 of the women who joined the Red Army in the 1920s and early 1930s participated in the Long March.

These women were born and raised during the turbulent early twentieth century. Sun Yat-sen's new Republic replaced the Qing dynasty in 1911, not without difficulty. New ideas of democracy and socialism were capturing the minds of the young in the May 4th Movement, which took its name from student demonstrations in Beijing on 4 May 1919 against the terms of the Versailles Treaty at the end of the First World War.[3] This movement

---

1. One *li* equals approximately half a kilometre.
2. Standard accounts of the Long March include Edgar Snow, *Red Star Over China* (New York, 1938), pp. 171–96; Dick Wilson, *The Long March 1935* (London, 1971); Harrison Salisbury, *The Long March, the Untold Story* (New York, 1985); Benjamin Yang, *From Revolution to Politics* (Boulder, CO, 1990), and an English-language publication, *The Long March, Eyewitness Accounts* (Beijing, 1950).
3. The Versailles Treaty awarded German concessions in China to Japan, even though China was also an ally. This provision was later rescinded.

was the crystallization of far-reaching political, cultural and social changes which had been fermenting in China. The Chinese Communist Party was founded in 1921.

Radical young teachers, men and women, infuriated by the Chinese government's appeasement in the face of Japanese aggression and incursions into Chinese territory by other nations, returned to their home provinces to teach. They electrified young students with their patriotic, revolutionary fervour. They called into question many traditional ideas, advocating, among many other things, equality between men and women.

During the 1920s, rampaging warlord armies impoverished the people in many areas, hitting hard the tenant farmers who already lived on the brink of starvation. By 1925, the young Nationalist government, in coalition with the Communists, organized an army to fight the warlords and unify the country. As disagreements between the two parties increased, the Nationalists turned on their former allies in 1927. They destroyed Communist Party organizations in the cities and arrested, tortured and executed many young men and women suspected of Communist affiliations. Both men and women revolutionaries fled to the mountains in several provinces to join the Red Army at one of the several Chinese Soviet base areas which had been established. The Nationalist forces surrounded the base areas, besieging the Communist forces until the Red Army forces broke through the Nationalist lines in an effort to reach troops in other base areas. These were the troop movements we know as the Long March.

The following stories about the work done by women during the Long March are drawn from translations of a series of interviews by the author between 1986 and 1989, in an oral history fund-raising project for the Chinese Children's Fund. The 23 women who were interviewed represent a fair selection of Long March veterans. When they began the Long March, their ages ranged from 12 to 32; 14 were 17 years old or younger when they joined Chinese Communist Party organizations and the Red Army. They came from seven different provinces and quite varied backgrounds: 11 were sold or given to other families as infants or small children; 12 were illiterate when the Long March began and the others had some kind of schooling, although only one had gone beyond junior middle school. Three of the interviewees were married to generals, others to political commissars, some to lesser leaders; the rest were unmarried or had left their husbands to join the revolution. Three gave birth to babies on the march, and one carried her infant daughter with her.

The interviewed group, although representative of the women who made the Long March, were not representative of Chinese women generally. Because there was so much regional variation in the way women were treated in China at that time, as well as wide variation in both class and individual family attitudes, it is difficult to generalize about the status of women, except to say that women generally were in an inferior position. Those families who followed the hierarchical Confucian ethic – emperor above subject, father above son, husband above wife, and upon husband's death, eldest son above mother – also ascribed to *zhongnan, qingnu,* putting a high value on boys and a lower value on girls. There was also an economic basis for this saying: girls married into other families, which then claimed their labour and allegiance, while the sons stayed with their parents, assuring them of support in old age. In the early part of the twentieth century, foot binding was still prevalent in some areas and some levels of society, although there was governmental effort to change this practice. None of the women interviewed had bound feet, although several had had their feet slightly crippled before they rebelled against the practice when they were young girls. There was one woman with bound feet who accompanied her husband on the Long March with the 1st Front Army; she was an army dependent, however, rather than a soldier, and did not work.

What work women soldiers did on the Long March reflected the nature of the political and military leaders with whom they travelled. There were about 30 women with the strictly disciplined 1st Front Army, which included the top political leadership of the Chinese Communist Party. The 1st Front Army left the Central Soviet base in Jiangxi Province in October 1934. The 4th Front Army, which had approximately 2,000 women and was constantly moving and fighting, included support services similar to those in a small city. The 4th left the base area in north-central Sichuan in March 1935. The 2nd and 6th Army groups, which were reorganized as the 2nd Front Army during the Long March, included about 25 women. They left the Chinese Soviet base they had established in the mountains, where the borders of Hunan, Hubei, Sichuan and Guizhou provinces converge, in November 1935, almost one year after the 1st Front Army ended its march.

When the 1st Front Army left the Jiangxi Soviet base area, many of the women who had been students at the party school were grouped together as a work team. In their first encounter with a physical examination, they were checked to ensure they did not have tuberculosis or other ailments which would prevent their making an arduous journey. They were also tested for colour blindness, night blindness, as well as sharpness of vision and hearing. The women who had the exam were not wives of high leaders, although many later married men of importance. They had previously demonstrated their leadership qualities as political workers known as 'cadres', usually in the Women's Department of the Communist Youth League or the Communist Party in their home villages. The base areas had both a civilian government structure and a military one. Communist government organizations in the base areas operated at the village, county, district, provincial and central, or 'national', levels. Most of the women who participated in the Long March worked at the provincial or central level.

In addition to the work team, there were women who were attached to a special unit within the Health Department in the 1st Front Army. Some were high-level leaders' wives, who were brought along not only because of their husbands but also because they themselves held high-ranking jobs. Several were ill. Deng Yingchao, Zhou Enlai's wife, had an active case of tuberculosis and travelled much of the time on a stretcher. Some of the women were pregnant when they began the march; others became pregnant during the year they were on the move.

Before the army left the Jiangxi Soviet, the decision was made to leave all children behind. Those who were mothers had the job of finding local families willing to adopt their children. Those who were pregnant knew they would not be able to keep their babies once they were born.

The women in the 1st Front Army travelled with the top leadership, well-protected by the fighting soldiers. The tasks they fulfilled on the march varied from situation to situation and from person to person. The illiterate peasant women in the work team, accustomed to heavy work in the fields, carried boxes of medicines and sometimes stretchers, while also performing the ongoing job of recruitment and replenishment of supplies. Educated women had the responsibility for changing the minds and attitudes of the peasants concerning their opinions of Communists, of soldiers in general, of the national government, and of landlords. They created propaganda material in the form of posters and drama and supervised women and men soldiers to shout slogans, sing songs, put on plays, and make speeches to the people in the towns and villages they travelled through. They went into village homes to talk with the peasant women, to persuade them to sell or contribute grain to the Red Army. They also recruited soldiers and transport workers by obtaining the consent of the women to let their husbands and sons go.

Zhong Yuelin, the youngest of the 1st Front Army women, was an illiterate teenager when the Long March began not far from her home in Jiangxi Province. When she was eight years old, her father became ill with jaundice and was not expected to recover. At that time, farm families in China who did not own land were barely able to subsist. Losing adult labour due to illness or death of a parent was so devastating that most families could not survive intact. Thus Zhong Yuelin's mother, fearing she could not raise all of her children alone, sold her daughters into other families, keeping her son with her. Zhong was in her teens when the Red Army came to the village into which she had been sold. Touched by the rhetoric promising land to the poor and equality between men and women, she joined a young women's organization. At the first meeting, she was asked to introduce herself but could not: she had never been given a name of her own! Heretofore known only as her father's daughter or her brother's sister, she chose her name and began her work with local Communist organizations, becoming one of the youngest leaders in the Women's Department. Just before the 1st Front Army left on the Long March, she and other cadres were sent out to recruit soldiers from the surrounding towns and villages.

Recruitment continued after the Long March began, and was complicated by the negative ideas the peasants held about the Red Army. They had heard about 'Zhumao', a contraction of the surnames of the Red Army leaders, Zhu De and Mao Zedong. 'Zhu' has the same pronunciation as the word for 'pig' and the word for 'red'. 'Mao' can be understood as both 'sword' and 'hairy'. Thus the Nationalists used visual images of hairy red pigs wielding swords in their anti-Communist propaganda.

Zhong Yuelin described the work she did on the Long March:

> Our main job was still to recruit for the Red Army. Another job was to find transport workers to help us, and to do propaganda work with the civilians. The route we were taking had been occupied by the Nationalists. The civilians had been deeply influenced by the Nationalist reactionary propaganda which said that the Communist Party shared property and wives, telling how bad Zhumao was. The Red Army had never been along this road and these civilians didn't have any idea what [kind of army] we were. In many places, when we arrived the civilians had run way. The road we took was in the mountains, where the houses were isolated and there weren't any large villages.
>
> We marched every day. When we arrived at a place, we immediately went out to find transport workers. Do you know what I mean? They were the people who carried things. When we first started out we had stretchers and documents in iron boxes. [Our group] didn't carry the boxes, just the stretchers.

The young women in the work team with Zhong Yuelin marched at night across Jiangxi Province with the Red Army, breaking out of the Nationalist blockade of the base area. When they reached Hunan Province, night marches continued, for they had been spotted by the Nationalists and daylight bombing raids began. As they fought their way across Hunan and into Guizhou, they worked at four principal tasks. First, they constantly sought out civilians willing to be hired as short-term transport workers who travelled with the army several days before returning home. Since the Red Army had no motor vehicles and was short of pack animals, transport workers played a crucial role during the early part of the Long March. The second task of the women's work team was to counteract the Nationalist propaganda with their own, to persuade local peasants to support the Red

Army, often using what we would now term 'street drama' to help the peasants understand the nature of their own oppression by the landlords. Third, they investigated the areas they marched through in order to locate homes of landlords and confiscate grain, which was both shared with the peasants and used to feed the troops. Their fourth task, to care for the ill and wounded, became increasingly important as casualties mounted. They not only found transport workers to carry wounded soldiers but also shouldered the stretchers themselves if carriers were not to be found. When they stopped to rest, the women fed their charges and dressed their wounds before they themselves could eat and rest. They also had the difficult job of locating village families with whom they could leave the severely wounded whom they could not carry along.

Healthy women who were not part of the work team did similar work. Xie Fei, allowed to attend school by an indulgent father, had become a revolutionary when she was a 13-year-old student on Hainan Island. After her entire family became involved in revolutionary activities, they were exiled. She became a Communist underground worker in Hong Kong and Singapore before returning to China and going into the Jiangxi base area. Although attached to the Security Bureau, she travelled with the other women in the Health Department and participated in recruitment and propaganda.

Kang Keqing, wife of Commander-in-Chief Zhu De, marched with the Military Headquarters as Political Instructor. She not only did the same tasks as the other women, she also carried a weapon and may have actually been in battle on one occasion.

Liu Ying, who defied her father by going to a tuition-free school established by young socialists and communists, was the most educated of the women interviewed, having studied at the college level in Moscow before returning to China and joining the Red Army in Jiangxi. She worked directly under the Political Commissar of the 1st Front Army in the Logistics Department. Explaining the nature of her work, she said:

> The Logistics Department was in charge of things like money, guns and ammunition, uniforms, machines, printing presses – all the things that we moved [from the base area]. A great many of the soldiers we recruited had to carry those things. As a leader in the Political Department, I managed things in the transport team. When we didn't have any transport workers, I had to go out to recruit them. When they were unwilling, we had to do some political work. When there wasn't any food, I had to scrounge some. There were many other cadres in the Political Department besides me who also did this kind of thing, but I was the leader.
>
> When we stopped at a campsite where ordinary people and local tyrants were nearby, we separated the rich and the poor very clearly. We divided

what we gathered [from the wealthy] among everyone because we couldn't carry a lot of things. If we took some things from a poor family when they were not at home, we wrote a note and left some money. When the ordinary people came back home and found it, they believed we were truly the army of the poor people. Later on when we came to a place to stop, the people didn't run away. They helped us and gave us food. We gave them money, silver. I kept doing this on the Long March until we got to Zunyi.

The 1st Front Army was fluid not only in troop movements but also in organization and in leadership. The deep schisms within the party over military tactics also reflected political disagreements. Leaders who had been educated in Moscow and adhered to the instructions of the Communist International (Comintern) were in opposition to Mao Zedong and Zhu De, who advocated guerrilla warfare. Mao and Zhu believed their tactics, which earlier had been successful in establishing and maintaining the Chinese Soviet base areas, should not have been abandoned, as the Comintern agent had directed.

In addition, the Red Army efforts to move north in Hunan province and join Communist troops in the Hunan–Guizhou–Sichuan base area were thwarted by the local Hunan and Nationalist troops. With the route north blocked, they were forced to continue west into Guizhou Province. By the time the 1st Front Army had been travelling three months, it had lost more than one-third of its forces. It stopped in the area around Zunyi, the second largest city in Guizhou Province, to regroup, reorganize and replenish supplies. During this time, the Political Bureau (Politburo) leaders met in what has become known as the Zunyi Conference, where Mao Zedong regained power.

Most of the women had little understanding of what the leaders were doing, unless they were married to high-level people. Even then, they had their own work to do. Kang Keqing said she knew something was going on because the place where she and Zhu De stayed was being used for meetings, but she was busy collecting grain in another part of the city and knew none of the details. Qian Xijun, on the other hand, reported that she was aware of the divisions in the leadership. As the wife of Mao Zedong's brother, she had been travelling with wives whose husbands held high positions and she listened to their discussions about the conflicting policies. Most of the women, however, although they were cadres, knew only what the ordinary soldiers knew: that the army was taking time to rest and to gather supplies while the leaders were holding meetings. Only later, as the information about the decisions at the Zunyi Conference was reported to lower levels in the military and political hierarchy, did they learn that Mao Zedong's policies had been adopted and that there had been a shift in power away from the group supporting the Comintern. Liu Ying continued:

After the Zunyi meeting, we jettisoned many things, because it had been a mistake to try to carry so many things. When the enemy attacked, we couldn't fight. We weren't 'moving house', we had to travel lightly. The people who could walk were sent to the front. I was sent to the Centre. Three people were in charge of the Central unit: Chairman Mao, Zhang Wentian, Wang Jiaxiang. This team was equal to the Central Government. Because of the reorganization, many soldiers were freed to fight at the front, making the army more effective. Chairman Mao thought the women could do the work: manage the everyday living, raise the morale of the bodyguards, take notes during meetings. I was General Party Secretary for a while.

For the next two months, the 1st Front Army moved and fought in Guizhou and Yunnan in a futile effort to reach the 4th Front Army in Sichuan. It was during these months that the first two babies were born on the Long March, and another dimension was added to the work the women performed. In this case alone, their work was gender-specific: men did not assist at childbirth. The first baby was born to Liao Siguang and the second to He Zizhen, Mao Zedong's wife.

Liao Siguang's story is translated from a written account of her recollections of the Long March, since she became ill immediately before our scheduled interview. She wrote:

I had a premature birth when we entered the minority nationality area of Guizhou. I remember on that day we plunged through two or three lines of the enemy blockade and continually ran more than 100 *li*. Just before reaching the camp area, I began to have stomach pains. My back was aching, and perspiration was rolling off me like peas. The Company Commander and the doctor recognized the symptoms and gave me their horse to ride. [The pains] still didn't ease up. Deng Dajie[4] understood the situation. She quickly got off her stretcher and gave it to me. During that time, relations between women comrades were closer than hand and feet. When we reached camp, my seventh-month baby was born. It was a male baby, and cried loudly as if he wanted to announce his arrival. Deng Dajie happily said, 'He is a future Red Army soldier who should be carried on a stretcher to the people's area to be raised'.

Liao Siguang, of course, did not actually have the option of carrying the baby with her, since the 1st Front Army had decided to leave the children behind. She wrapped the baby in a towel, wrote a note in which she included his birth date, the fact that he had been born when the Red Army was travelling

---

4. Deng Yingchao, Zhou Enlai's wife. 'Dajie', literally meaning 'older sister', is a term of affection and respect.

through the area, and her hopes that the baby would be well cared for. When she left her baby in an empty farmhouse and continued marching, she did not know that she would never be able to find her child again.

After the 1st Front Army traversed Yunnan Province and crossed the upper reaches of the Yangtze River, they were in the foothills of the Himalayas, in areas where many Tibetans lived. As they moved from north-western Yunnan into western Sichuan Province, they finally joined troops from the 4th Front Army. They crossed several snow-capped mountain ranges at altitudes around 3,000 metres, and at this time the nature of their work again changed. Although the local Tibetans were often hostile to the Han Chinese Red Army, the greatest enemy had become the terrain itself. The principal task for the women became finding food for themselves and others in their unit. While part of the work team was foraging for food in the mountains, Zeng Yu began labour. The inexperienced young women with her delivered her baby, before leaving the child in an abandoned Tibetan house.

Again there were political conflicts at the top, this time between the 1st and 4th Front Army leaders. Some of the women were detached from the 1st Front Army and transferred to the 4th. In Kang Keqing's case, it was because her husband was kept with the 4th Front Army. She was demoted from her position as Political Instructor at Headquarters and was sent to the Party School to be Party Secretary there. Wang Quanyuan and Wu Fulian worked with women in the 4th Front Army to buy grain from the Tibetans and were unable to rejoin the 1st Front Army before it moved north and east, towards Shaanxi Province.

Because of the conflict between the leaders of the two front armies, the 1st Front Army slipped away after it crossed the grasslands. The grasslands in northern Sichuan are high-altitude prairies, some dry and some marshy, requiring at least a week to traverse. The 1st Front women had a single purpose: to survive the grasslands crossing. They prepared grain for the crossing, shared ground cover and blankets and took turns carrying cooking pots and basins as they trudged across the vast expanses. Exhausted, their clothing in tatters, barefoot or wearing makeshift shoes made of pieces of leather, they did little other work until they reached their comrades in Shaanxi Province in October 1935.

When the Long March had ended for them, they had little perception of the heroic aspect of their ordeal. They resumed working at many of the same tasks they had been doing before and during the Long March. Zhong Yuelin, who was married in December after the end of the Long March, explained: 'One day I got married and the next day I went to the country-side to recruit for the Red Army'.

The women in the 4th Front Army also perceived little difference between the kind of work they did before, during and after the Long March. In fact,

Lin Yueqin believed that the Long March actually began for her in 1931 or 1932 when the 4th Front Army left the Soviet base area on the borders of Hubei, Anhui and Henan provinces to move and fight its way to the border of central Sichuan and Shaanxi, where another base area was established.

Lin Yueqin was 15 in 1929 when the Red Army guerrillas came to her hometown in Anhui Province. Daughter of a shop owner, she had been to school for a year or two, and was facing a future which included being married into another family. 'Every girl in our small town was wandering around the town talking all day long about joining the Red Army', she said. Her relatives gathered to talk her out of it, but she cut off her pigtails, joined the Communist Youth League and left home. She became a bureau leader in the Children's Corps, a Communist Party organization. Then, she said, 'Spring 1932, the blow came'. The Communist Party was waging a campaign to drive out members whose class status was 'bad'. It was assumed that those who had some schooling could not have come from poor families, and therefore must belong to the landlord class. Lin Yueqin, who was literate, was among those dismissed from her job. 'That was called being "combed out". I couldn't work in the Children's Corps. Where could I go?'

Before a decision could be made about the disposition of those being 'combed out', the Nationalist encirclement forced the army to abandon the Soviet base area and move on. Lin and the others followed the army, refusing to return home for several reasons. Most important was the fact that the Nationalists had retaken their hometowns and, as Communists, they would be subject to imprisonment and execution. Even if they were kept safe from the Nationalists, their reputations would be ruined because they had run away and joined the Red Army. Additionally important was the fact that they were committed to the Communist Party, and even though they were under suspicion in the Red Army they did not want to leave. Therefore, they helped with whatever needed doing in the army, although not in a leadership capacity. They mimeographed notices, parched rice for field rations, changed bandages for wounded soldiers. Finally, by the end of 1932 they were accepted into the propaganda team. 'To be a member of the propaganda team meant that you had joined the Red Army', Lin Yueqin explained.

> Each of us was given a lime pail and with a brush we wrote slogans on boulders: 'Overthrow the local tyrants and divide the fields. Workers and poor people, don't run away, don't be afraid. We are the Red Army. [We] overthrow the rich and help the poor.' Wherever we went we had the lime pail with us.
>
> When we came to a campsite where there was a big village, we would investigate the landlords. We would look at their homes to see whether the family had many places for grain storage, whether they collected rent.

Then we would ask the masses if this family was rich or not. When the masses would nod their head, saying they were [wealthy], we would open the grain storage places and confiscate the grain.

The 4th Front Army set up a base area in north central Sichuan on the border with Shaanxi Province in an area where opium was flourishing. Lin Yueqin said almost all the heavy labour was done by the women, since many of the men were opium addicts. The men stayed home, cooking and caring for children. 'There were fewer males [available] to be recruited, so we had to recruit women.' Men and women in the 4th Front Army then helped the husbands give up opium. They broke opium pipes, prohibited the peasants from growing opium, and promoted raising larger crops of food.[5]

Lin Yueqin was transferred out of the propaganda team and assigned to logistics in charge of a women's clothing factory which, after induction into the army, became a Women's Engineering Battalion. When Lin was made battalion commander, her class status was resolved positively, on the basis of her continued devotion to the army even after she had been combed out. The battalion was composed entirely of women, with the single exception of a man 'who kept the accounts and was in charge of the mess'. She continued:

When there was cloth we made clothes. When there was no cloth and there were battles at the front, we went to the front to help with the transport. When we had nothing else to do, we usually had some training, including military training and literacy lessons. At that time, Women's Engineering Battalion didn't mean engineers at the front who built bridges, paved roads, set up ambushes. We didn't do this kind of work. The women mainly remained in the rear, helping with logistics. We were soldiers from the clothing factory, so we were [also] called the Women's Factory Battalion. In the 4th Front Army there were many others [women's units] besides the Women's Factory Battalion: Women's Independent Battalion, [later, the] Independent Regiment. Different counties had Women's Independent Battalions. There were an especially large number of women working in the rear doing logistics, including those working in the local soviet governments, those working in the post offices, hospitals – especially hospitals. Nurses and doctors in hospitals [were] all women.

Zhang Wen was one of the young women who worked in a clothing factory. When she was a child, her parents were tenant farmers in debt to the landlord. To ensure she had food to eat, they sent her to work for the landlord. Badly beaten after being unfairly accused of stealing flour, she

---

5.   See the article by Wang Dingguo, 'The fight to ban opium in the Soviet areas of Sichuan', *Women of China* (October 1997), pp. 43–4.

returned home and began working in the factory when she was 13. Her story continues:

> The factory was very simple. We worked with our hands and needles – there were no machines. The clothes we produced were [the kind of] clothes worn by ordinary people, sleeves and body all in one piece. The work was hard. We were each supposed to produce one set of clothes a day. If a person was quick, it was possible, but a slower person couldn't do it. What I described was the situation in the ordinary times.
>
> I was fourteen when I joined the Logistics Department of the 4th Army Group of the 4th Front Army, with the quilt and clothing factory. The woman who was head of the Group went to my home to ask my mother if she would be willing to let her daughter join the Red Army. My mother said she couldn't oppose it because men and women were equal now, and because I wanted to. My mother let me go.

Zhang Wen's mother probably did not object to her daughter's joining the Red Army for a variety of reasons. The fact that almost everybody who worked in the factory was joining must have been important in that collective society. Also, the knowledge that Zhang Wen was approaching marriageable age and was soon to leave the family anyway would have made it easier for her mother to let her go. Additionally, if she were still in the army when she became old enough to marry, it would be the army's responsibility to find a husband for her, relieving her parents of the task. Zhong Wen described her early work in the army:

> When the army moved, the factory moved. When there was a battle at the front, and quilts were needed at the battlefield, we sometimes worked until mid-night. The work was hard, but when we worked, everyone was in high spirits. We sang revolutionary songs while we worked. We felt happy in this way. Our entertainment was what we made for ourselves because there was no other entertainment at that time.

Li Yanfa, also from the same county, was in a far more desperate situation than Zhang Wen, since both her parents were addicted to opium. Her mother died and her brothers left home, leaving her alone with her addicted father. When she was 12, she decided to join the Red Army, explaining, 'I said I would go join the revolution to get food to eat. I had no other purpose. [I was] just a starving teenager.' Her father, who threatened to pull the tendons from her legs if she joined, sent her to the family to whom she had been affianced before she was born. She ran away when she was 13. Under-age, she talked her way into a nearby army unit and was assigned to do propaganda work until she became ill with typhoid and was sent to the hospital. 'They didn't let me leave and I started working in the hospital as a nurse', she said. Her tasks included medicating wounds, dressing wounds and giving injections. 'The doctor told us what injections [to give]. I never went to school. The doctor taught us.' She rolled bandages of gauze, or any other available cloth and sterilized cotton for dressings. 'The cotton came from quilts we got from the local tyrants. [We] put the cotton in a basin, boiled it and sterilized it. We used that to dress the wounds.'

When Li Yanfa was asked if she knew when the 4th Front Army began the Long March, she explained that they were simply told they would be going a long distance. In preparation, they returned the slightly wounded soldiers to their units and carried the severely wounded soldiers on stretchers. About her work on the Long March, she said:

> The thing I remember most was burying the dead. There were a lot of
> dead people, because we were in the general hospital. Every day we carried
> the dead out. At first, we could find some soil to cover the face. When we
> went farther [into the Snow Mountains], we couldn't even find any soil.
> We'd use a piece of a woven mat and roll the body up in that, bind it and
> bury it. Later on, [in the grasslands] we couldn't even find any woven
> mats, so we just used grass to bind up the corpse.

After marching for several months, the 4th Front Army met the 1st Front Army. When the 1st continued north, the 4th turned south, re-crossing the grasslands and the snow mountain range. Liu Jian, who was a cadre working in the headquarters of the 4th Front Army, had known hardship intimately. Her father had been a member of the Farmers' Alliance, an organization with the reputation of banditry and allied with the Communists. When his work took him away from the family too often, Liu Jian's parents entrusted her to her aunt and uncle to raise, not knowing that the uncle was an opium addict. He promptly sold her for several ounces of opium. She was so badly mistreated by her owner that she contemplated suicide before her father found her and helped her join the Red Army. When the 4th Front Army was climbing the glacial mountain range, Liu Jian said, they were ill-prepared.

> We were having a hard time. We didn't have any grain because we hadn't
> made any preparations when we went through places where we could have
> gotten grain. Women comrades carried guns, bullets, stretchers, whether
> they were leaders or not. I carried stretchers, too. It was very hard to walk
> carrying stretchers. There were rocks on the road, high piles of rocks. If
> there were only a twisted, narrow path, how could the stretchers go? Some
> would go in front crawling down the rocks with the stretcher on their
> backs. Those behind pulled back on it. We did this over and over again.

Kang Keqing, who had been transferred from the 1st Front Army by this time, was with Liu Jian's unit when it spent three days crossing a glacier mountain range in the foothills of the Himalayas. She became ill and Liu Jian's group was instructed to leave her behind in a ditch. Unwilling to participate in an action which would undoubtedly cause the death of the wife of the army supreme commander, they improvised a stretcher made of saplings and their own leggings and brought her safely down the mountain. They eventually settled in Ganzi, where they met the 2nd and 6th Army Groups in July 1936. Liu Jian continued:

> Our squad went to find the minority people and to do ideological work with the lamas. If we'd done our work well, they'd sell wool to us. We gave them money for it. Some of the money was paper money, some was silver coins. In the places where there were no people, we took the wool and left a note with some money. We did our ideological work very slowly and carefully.
>
> We rested there for three months. We were preparing to cross the grasslands the third time. After we bought the wool, we washed it in the river, then we used a stick to beat it until it was soft. We spun the wool so we could make clothes. Since we didn't have any knitting needles to make sweaters, we used the ribs from umbrellas for needles or we would get the thin branches from trees. If we wanted to make a sweater this long, we'd need several dozens of those twigs because they broke very easily. If they were rough, they couldn't go through [the yarn]. We not only made sweaters for ourselves, but also for people in the 2nd Front Army who had also come to cross the grassland. Each of us made one for ourselves and one for them. If you don't have anything to wear, how can you cross the grassland? That would be too much!

While they were in Ganzi, He Manqiu, who at 14 had run away to the 4th Front Army in Sichuan 'before my grandmother could find a mother-in-law for me', embarked on a new career. Deeply upset by the general lack of medical knowledge of women's physiology and diseases, she trained as a nurse in the general hospital. When the 4th Front Army was resting and regrouping in Ganzi in western Sichuan, the doctors, each of whom had been allowed to bring one medical text with them on the march, established a medical school. Since she had some schooling before she joined the army, she easily passed the exam. She entered medical school and eventually became an army doctor.[6]

---

6. He Manqiu's story, 'From soldier to doctor: a Chinese woman's story of the Long March', appears in *Science and Society* 56 (Winter 1995–96), pp. 531–47; republished in *China Review* 20 (Fall 1996), pp. 16–23.

The 2nd and 6th Army Groups had left the Guizhou–Hunan border in November 1935, with about 25 women. Two sisters, Jian Xianren and Jian Xianfo, were married to the generals of the army groups, General He Long and General Xiao Ke. The older sister brought her infant daughter, He Jiesheng, with her on the march; her younger sister gave birth to a baby in the grasslands. The two army groups followed parallel routes, rarely converging along the way. After the two groups met the 4th Front Army, they reorganized to become the 2nd Front Army.

There were four women from the 2nd Front Army who were interviewed. In addition to the two Jian sisters, Chen Zongying, married to Ren Bishi, the highest political leader, worked as a telegraph decoder. She had been chosen for this work because she had demonstrated her ability to stand up under interrogation in a Nationalist prison in the early 1930s, and because she was illiterate. If captured, she would not be able to reveal the content of the telegrams she decoded. The fourth, Ma Yixiang, was 11 or 12 when she begged the Red Army to allow her to join a hospital unit as a laundress. She believed the family she had been sold to would beat her to death. As the Red Army marched along, her duties expanded to include simple nursing, recruiting and propaganda work.

Jian Xianren, who brought her newborn baby with her on the Long March, did propaganda work when she was not caring for her child. Her sister, Jian Xianfo, had been trained as an art teacher before she joined the army. Her primary job in the propaganda team was painting posters. All the women who worked in propaganda spoke of the need to convince the peasants that the situation they lived under was neither acceptable nor necessary. Her paintings illustrated the nature and extent of landlord exploitation of the peasants who worked their land.

Both the artist and the telegraph decoder became pregnant just before they left the Hunan–Guizhou–Sichuan base area on the Long March. They delivered their babies in the summer of 1936, when the 2nd Front Army was in the grasslands. In both cases, a male doctor was in attendance, but during the actual deliveries the doctor and husbands stayed outside the shelters the women had found, while women assisted at the birth. They each got on horseback and continued the Long March within a day or two of delivery. Unlike the women under the strict discipline in the 1st Front Army, they did not leave their babies behind but were able to carry them along.

The 4th Front Army had crossed grasslands three times. The first time was with the 1st Front Army. When the two front armies disagreed about destination, the 4th turned south, re-crossing the grasslands. After the 4th joined with the 2nd Front Army, it again turned north to rejoin the 1st. Liu Jian could not remember whether it took two weeks or nearly three before they were out of the grasslands:

There was sand and rock to walk on, but you can sink into the quicksand. As you walk along, you just get pulled in. Pools of water here, pools of water there. The road was so narrow. You could walk one way, but not another. If you'd try to run, you'd fall down. If you fell into the muddy quicksand, and someone tried to pull you out, you would sink in deeper. It was like paste, pulling you down. From a distance it looked like wheat, yellow. The grass wasn't very tall. When you looked in the distance, you could see the edge, but actually after you'd walked three days in it, you still haven't come to the end. Even if there were water, you didn't dare drink it. The water stank.

Walking in the grasslands was like walking on a blanket – one foot goes down and the other goes up. Really soft. We didn't have any more grass shoes by then. The grass was bent down to the ground, so it was slippery to walk on. If you couldn't walk right, you'd fall on your butt! It was like that all around. There were muddy bogs of quicksand, some big and others not as big. If you walked into a quicksand bog you couldn't walk out. There would be one on this side, one on that. No order to it.

None of us thought about whether we would be alive tomorrow if we were alive today. We only thought about getting to a place where we could get some food and have a good sleep. This was our highest hope, because at the end, we didn't have any grain.

Safely out of the grasslands, Jian Xianfo's husband was transferred to the West Route Army, while the others in the 2nd and 4th Front Armies continued to the Shaanbei base area, where the 1st Front Army was headquartered. She, her baby, and two male soldiers who helped her, followed her husband's unit, until the fighting became so intense that they struck out on their own to find the 1st Front Army in the adjacent province.

Difficult as bearing and caring for children while travelling with a fighting army was, the women all considered themselves far more fortunate than women who did not join the army. They felt that the party and the Red Army were their extended family, assigning work (and sometimes husbands), requiring discipline while nurturing them, providing education and experience far beyond anything they could have imagined when they were young. Their opportunities for a richer life were far greater than those of their friends who continued living in their hometowns, subject to the male-dominated family hierarchy and often to poverty as well.

In standard Western histories about the Long March, there are few or no index listings for propaganda, recruitment, collecting grain, or taking care of the wounded or babies. In other words, the logistical support work that women and men performed is assumed necessary, but worth little mention, in military or political histories. The usual focus of standard histories is the suffering of the women. The women interviewed, however, did not view themselves as victims, but believed their work on the Long March was essential. The work they did was the meat of their own stories, a substantial part of the broader history.

Much of the work the Red Army women soldiers did was of a nurturing nature, defined in most societies as 'women's work', although it was being performed in far from traditional circumstances. They procured food, hired help, sewed clothing, gave routine medical care, delivered babies. Other work, however, cannot be as comfortably placed in the category of nurturing. Even though Red Army women could interact with village women more easily than male soldiers could, they basically did the same work as men in the propaganda team. The women did transport work, shouldering packs and stretchers as needed. And in some circumstances they shouldered guns as well. Both men and women decoded telegrams, wrote slogans and painted posters, took notes in meetings, recruited soldiers.

The lives of the veterans of the Long March, especially those with the 1st and 2nd Front Armies, have been significantly different from those of their family and friends in their villages who did not participate in the Long March. Many of the veterans ended in Beijing or provincial capitals, retired from positions of prestige, if not power. A large number of them married prominent men, and while it can be argued that they held their positions because of their husbands, this was not true of all. One, with no important husband, held the most powerful position: General Secretary of the Communist Party in Guangdong Province. Many of the others were members of the Chinese People's Political Consultative Conference at the national or provincial level. The large number of women in the 4th Front Army who were captured by Ma Bufeng's troops after the Long March did not fare as well. However, beginning in the early 1980s, there has been a concerted effort to identify these women, many of whom were given as concubines to their captors, and reinstate them as honoured veterans of the Red Army. While most of the Long March participants did not 'hold up half the sky' in the country's decision-making positions, they are still considered 'national treasures' and treated with great respect and, though not empowered, are greatly honoured. Perhaps we should not ask to what extent were the women able to achieve what the men did, but rather ask what were the women actually doing? In other words, questions such as 'Did the women achieve high political positions after the Long March was over?' would instead become 'What was it that the women achieved politically?'

CHAPTER SIX

Lipstick on her Nipples, Cordite in her Hair: Sex and Romance among British Servicewomen during the Second World War

GERARD J. DEGROOT

It is widely assumed that war is erotic.[1] The precariousness of wartime life renders morality irrelevant. Young women, removed from parental control, and aroused by a range of erotic stimuli (danger, uniforms, guns, alcohol), offer themselves willingly to randy warriors. Or so it seems. With respect to Britain during the Second World War, actual evidence reveals much more restraint than myths suggest. Within the women's auxiliary services, where rampant promiscuity was allegedly the norm, there was in fact no great loosening of morals. Granted, some women had sex at an earlier age and in different circumstances than would otherwise have been expected. But servicewomen were not transformed into insatiable harlots, as lurid rumours suggested. Romance blossomed more than passion exploded.

Awakenings

Nine out of ten single women and eight out of ten married women were employed in the forces or industry by the end of the war. For many women this meant leaving family or locale for reasons of employment, an unaccustomed

I would like to thank Elizabeth Conder, Nicholas Evans, Ian Kirby, Corinna Peniston-Bird and Lena Troth for their assistance with the research for this article. I would also like to thank Norma Porter for transcribing the interviews and the Carnegie Trust for providing financial assistance with research costs.

1. See, for instance, Paul Fussell, *Wartime* (New York, 1989), pp. 96–114; and John Costello, *Love, Sex and War* (London, 1985).

degree of female labour mobility. The jobs women performed were also distinctly different, no more so than in the military. Though women had staffed the machinery of war during the Great War, their amalgamation into the military was much more profound two decades later, and their range of tasks widened significantly. The combined strength of women's services in mid-1944 was 467,000, of which 207,492 were in the Auxiliary Territorial Service (ATS), 176,800 in the Women's Auxiliary Air Force (WAAF) and 75,000 in the Women's Royal Naval Service (WRNS). This represented 12 per cent of British military strength.[2]

Socially mobile females, removed from parental restraint and with money in their purses, alarmed society's self-appointed moral guardians. It was widely assumed that venereal disease and illegitimacy were on the increase, although few actually bothered to check the figures. In *The Spectator*, an 'expert' wrote:

> We have here . . . multitudes of reckless, unstable girls who drink far too much and are determined to have a good time come what may. . . . Venereal diseases are, of course, spread by promiscuity, and this is promoted principally by absence from home with only remote prospects of returning there; reaction from mental strain; boredom; the possession of money to burn; 'gold-digging'; [and] indulgence in alcohol in dosage a little higher than is customary.[3]

Popular prejudice echoed expert opinion. Every 'respectable' person had a story to tell about a disgraceful woman who had discarded her inhibitions and taken to drink and sex. The pub was headquarters of the fallen. 'Girls in there . . . lose all self-control. That's where the trouble starts – this disease and everything else', one opinionated punter told a Mass Observation representative.[4]

Behind the myth there was a core of truth. Young and inexperienced women were thrown into a strange and turbulent world full of temptations. 'I thought I was worldly wise, but I was barely "street-smart" enough to cross one, let alone deal with the wolves on the other side', Winifred Lane recalled. 'I can only conclude that such innocence was itself protection of a kind.'[5] Beatrice Carter confessed that 'My sex education was my Mum

---

2. Dorothy Sheridan, 'ATS Women 1939–45: challenge and containment in women's lives in the military during the Second World War' (unpublished M. Litt. dissertation, University of Sussex, 1988), pp. 12–13.

3. 'The War Disease', in Fiona Glass and Philip Marsden-Smedley, eds, *Articles of War* (London, 1990), pp. 263–7.

4. From 'Women in public houses', in Dorothy Sheridan, ed., *Wartime Women* (London, 1991), pp. 195–205.

5. Winifred Lane, unpublished reminiscences, Imperial War Museum (hereafter IWM) 89/19/1, p. 1.

saying when I menstruated at 12, showing me pads, etc, "now you mustn't play with boys". I knew nothing of babies or how they appeared, knew nothing of lesbians or homosexuals, or condoms.'[6]

For many women military life brought sexual awakening. 'Army life made me grow up for I was very naïve (I realise now)', Pauline Mills wrote.[7] The barrack room was a great melting pot; the experienced and the innocent mixed in a sometimes volatile dynamic. A sense of sisterhood led to a sharing of experiences between individuals whose paths might otherwise never have crossed. G. Morgan found herself billeted with an ex-prostitute who 'delicately explained the facts of life'.[8] One woman in her unit applied lipstick to her nipples before going off camp. 'I can only conjecture her reasons for this, but at the time it seemed to me to be an awful waste of a scarce commodity.'[9]

Therese Roberts felt that life in the army 'made me grow up a little quicker I think than I might have done'.[10] While this did not necessarily mean a faster pace towards sexual maturity, that was sometimes a side effect. This was particularly true in sexually integrated units. But almost all of the women interviewed for this study professed that the actual level of sexual activity was greatly exaggerated. The women may have felt more comfortable in the company of men, and therefore more inclined to form intimate relationships, but they still felt constrained by taboos against pre-marital sex. 'It was not so different from anywhere else regarding people being thrown together', Marjorie Hugget thought; 'lots of flirtation, but mostly light-hearted.'[11] 'Immorality in those days was a lot less immoral than it would be today', another woman remarked. 'We were all much more innocent.'[12]

One prominent factor limiting sexual activity was the strictly controlled ATS environment. It was far easier for a woman factory worker to lead a life of promiscuous adventure than a driver or cook attached to the navy. Opportunities for misbehaviour were also limited by the low income in the services, generally much lower than a woman could make in a civilian, war-related industry. Low pay limited entertainment, and especially restricted opportunities to get drunk. 'Drunkenness was difficult on 2/- a day with cigarettes and cosmetics to buy', Morgan felt.[13] Though wartime scare stories about working-class women who shed their inhibitions as they downed

---

6. Beatrice Carter, interview with the author, 5 March 1995.
7. Pauline Mills, correspondence with the author, 17 March 1995.
8. G. Morgan, personal memoir, IWM pp/MCR/115, pp. 1–2.
9. *Ibid.*, p. 17.
10. Therese Roberts, transcript of oral interview, IWM ref. 11786/1, p. 16.
11. Marjorie Huggett, correspondence with the author, 29 August 1995.
12. Sheridan, 'ATS women', p. 65.
13. Morgan memoir, p. 18.

their drink were undoubtedly exaggerated, it is likely that the level of sexual activity was proportionate to the incidence of intoxication.

The writer Freya Stark felt that the 'chief virtue for the semi-military female services' was to service soldiers' sexual needs. 'It is, I think, an ungenerous heart that does not give itself in wartime, when men's mere physical hunger for women is so great.'[14] While this was not a widely held opinion, quite a few male soldiers undoubtedly agreed with Stark. 'I did come across the attitude from some of our soldiers', Ellen Roper recalled, 'that we were there for their pleasure.'[15] After hearing that she was to be posted overseas, V.C. Cole received a panicked letter from a protective brother who feared for her safety in the supposedly looser sexual morality on the continent:

> He begged me not to volunteer . . . as I would only land up as a ground sheet for the officers. These were his exact words and he gave me one or two incidents about life out there. Little did he know that a lot of the male personnel at home were no better and one found it very hard at times to keep them at arm's length.[16]

L. Goosens confirmed that dances at a nearby marine base were often 'more like a wrestling match'.[17] Some women took to arming themselves with hatpins to ward off overly aggressive males. But very few women complained of what would today be called sexual harassment. This is perhaps more an indication of the standards of the time than the actual behaviour of the men. Midge Baylen felt that most of the men acted like 'big brothers' who liked to tease the women, but only a few 'seemed somewhat too persistent and a bit overt in the way they expressed affection.'[18] Jean Wallace, a WAAF, described the men as 'predatory' (married men being the worst) but claimed that she 'never heard of rape or sexual harassment of WAAFs'.[19] Goosens told how men would regularly spy on them while they were dressing, conduct generally tolerated by the authorities, who took a 'boys will be boys' attitude.[20] Occasionally, however, a persistent harasser was prosecuted, in part to reassure the women and their parents. An example was, for instance, made of a Captain E.A. Alterskye, who was 'severely reprimanded' for 'improper conversations' with ATS women and for attempting to kiss them.[21]

14. Jenny Hartley, ed., *Hearts Undefeated* (London, 1994), p. 210.
15. Ellen Roper, correspondence with the author, 31 August 1995.
16. V.C. Cole, AA Command Memoir, IWM, ref. 86/6/1, p. 47.
17. L. Goosens, personal memoir, IWM, 92/30/1, n.p.
18. Mrs J.O. Baylen, letter to the author, 22 February 1999.
19. Jean Wallace, personal memoir, IWM 91/36/1, p. 18.
20. Goosens memoir.
21. *Daily Mirror*, 13 October 1941.

The awakening was not always of a heterosexual nature. The circumstances of military life, with segregated barracks and tight supervision, meant that affairs with other women were much easier to engineer than those with men. Morgan recalled some relationships between women that 'went beyond the bounds of normal friendship', but she did not feel that lesbians were more prevalent than in any other communal setting. Only one case that she could recall attracted official attention, when an ATS officer and private deserted and set up house together.[22] For some women, the mere existence of lesbians was a shock:

> It was [during training] that I found out what a lesbian was. . . . two girls were pointed out to me as being about to be thrown out of the army because 'they had been found in bed together'. Now I, the oldest of five children at home, could not understand why two girls should want to share a bed when they could enjoy the luxury of a bed to themselves. To me a single bed was paradise. That's how innocent I was.[23]

Middle-class officers sometimes reacted in alarm at what appeared to be lesbianism but in fact had an innocent explanation. As the above testimony indicates, many young women from poor backgrounds were used to sharing a bed with other siblings at home. These women sometimes found nights in the barracks unsettling. K.P. Mannock, one of the more sensitive ATS officers, recalls trying to persuade them 'that they need not be frightened of sleeping alone since there were no fewer than twenty others in the same barrack room, yet . . . when the lights were out, they would double up if not treble up for coziness sake; a deadly ATS sin'.[24] An extraordinary number of women also complained about the terrible cold of the barracks, which might explain the occasional tendency to share beds.

Romance

During the war, Lieutenant E.S. Turner, an officer on a mixed anti-aircraft battery, regularly contributed poems to *Punch* that played upon relationships between male and female soldiers. A typical example was 'Gun-site Good Night', which included the following lines:

---

22. Morgan memoir, pp. 18–19.
23. Miscellaneous material deposited in IWM, p. A38.
24. K.P. Mannock, unpublished memoir, IWM, no ref., p. 47.

The shoot is done, the rounds are spent,
Goodnight my sweet. I swear
I worship you. I love the scent
Of cordite in your hair.[25]

Turner's light-hearted poems probably accurately reflected the wartime atmosphere. The evidence suggests that, far from encouraging promiscuity, military life and war in general inspired nothing more significant than a thirst for romance. The times were exciting and dangerous, and men in smart uniforms were doing heroic things, or at least claiming to do so. Romance certainly seems to have been the predominant desire among the women, rather than sexual adventure. Quite a few formed lasting relationships with male colleagues that sometimes led to marriage. For most, purity remained important and marriage sacred. But, it has to be understood that this was romance of a very precarious kind. 'No matter how much they wanted it, no relationship could be permanent', Jean Wallace commented. She admitted that this occasionally 'bred desperation and recklessness'.[26] In other words, while the transience of life sometimes led to erosion of restraint, it probably more often meant that relationships were not allowed to develop long enough (and to sufficient intensity) for moral conditioning to be worn away.

In her diary A. Laws confirmed that mild flirtation was more common than rampant licentiousness: 'Our girls may go out dancing and what not, but they do know where to draw the line'.[27] Joy Harwood, who served in the WAAF, expressed a similar opinion:

Most of the men we met, young and fit for military service, would at some stage pose the question, 'Do you?', but usually they were willing to accept 'No' for an answer . . . Fear of The Consequences meant for most of us that we carried our virtue around like albatrosses, longing to shift the burden if only we could be sure it were safe to do so, hovering in a half light of indecision. . . .

As far as I was concerned, passion was bound in any case to fight a losing battle in the face of the extreme discomfort of it all; the back seat of a car was the wrong shape, a cornfield prickly and alive with small black insects, the weather always too hot or too cold, and the boy friend too hasty or too casual. Then again, we had to be back in billets by midnight, or else we had to report for duty just as the big film was coming on, and one way and another it was surprising there was any romance in our lives at all.[28]

---

25. Lieutenant E.S. Turner, 'Gun-site Good Night', *Punch*, 4 August 1943.
26. Jean Wallace, unpublished memoir, IWM 91/36/1, p. 17.
27. Diary of A. Laws, 29 January 1945, IWM, P347.
28. Joy Harwood, 'Green 232', unpublished memoir, IWM 88/53/1, pp. 24–5.

'I can only recall four cases where a girl was discharged under what was known as paragraph 11 [illegitimate pregnancy] . . . and one of those girls told me herself she was plied with drink by a Yank at a dance when on leave', commented Frank Reeves, a gunner on a mixed battery.[29] Likewise, Morgan remembers only one woman among the 200 in her battery who became pregnant outside marriage during her two years with the unit.[30]

The desire for romance seems to have encouraged an enhanced femininity among servicewomen. Diaries, memoirs and interviews reveal an obsession with clothes and cosmetics. Feminine images even figured large in deciding which branch of the military to join; Goosens, for instance, confessed that her interviewing officer's 'smart uniform . . . went some way to our decision to join'.[31] The WRNS had an easier time attracting recruits than the ATS in part because the former had the smarter uniform. Mrs E. McMurdo, whose family had always served in the army, confessed to 'an entirely feminine preference for naval uniform. For the chance to wear one of those cute little sailor hats I was more than willing to give family tradition and my military ancestors the bird.'[32] The drab khaki colour of ATS garb was universally despised, in particular the standard issue khaki underwear – dubbed 'passion-killers' or 'come to Jesus knickers' by the women. Desperate ATS recruiters boasted that 'You are not required to wear the issue underclothing . . . but you will want to when you try them!'[33] But, in truth, they found themselves on a losing wicket. 'I'll never forget the loathing on seeing my legs clad in khaki lisle stockings', Iris Bryce wrote. 'I felt like my Gran.'[34] McMurdo was hauled before the military authorities accused of 'mutilation of kit' after she took a pair of scissors to her underwear in an attempt to improve their allure.[35]

An enterprising manufacturer played to the universal loathing of the ATS uniform by encouraging women to feel that, even if they could not look feminine on the outside, they could at least feel feminine underneath:

> *Said a sparkling young thing in the ATS*
> *'Without Wolsey I think I'd go BATS. For*
> *their undies and stockings and marvelous*
> *frockings I give them my hearty CONGRATS!'*[36]

---

29.   Frank Reeves, correspondence with the author, 26 April 1995.
30.   Morgan memoir, p. 18.
31.   Goosens memoir.
32.   E.M. McMurdo, 'One girl's war', unpublished memoir, IWM 85/18/1, p. 2.
33.   Sheridan, 'ATS women', following p. 17.
34.   Papers of Iris Bryce, IWM 96/4/1.
35.   McMurdo, 'One girl's war', p. 9.
36.   Sheridan, 'ATS women', following p. 60.

The easy explanation for this heightened interest in dress and cosmetics is that wartime shortages made women covet these commodities more than usual. B.J. Wright noticed how, when her unit was posted abroad, an unaccustomed availability of cosmetics 'gave us a chance to enjoy the delights of femininity again'.[37] Morale rose accordingly. But it is also possible that the essentially masculine environment in which these women lived made them ever more keen to assert their femininity. This would certainly accord with evidence that the war encouraged romance more than promiscuity: the women were keen to look pretty, not necessarily sexy. Cosmetics and underwear made them feel good about themselves. 'And now, for a whole fortnight, I can continue to be as female as I like', Maureen Bolster wrote to her husband Eric at the beginning of her leave. 'I can wear what I choose, paint my nails, do a little experimental cooking, lie in the sun with as little on as I please, and wear new nice things for your benefit.'[38] Even women who had not ordinarily paid much attention to these matters found themselves caught in the feminine whirl. Mannock recalled how the regulation stipulating that ATS women must be in military dress at all times encouraged an unaccustomed rebelliousness: 'Sometimes I felt that the world had indeed gone crazy when I, a woman of nearly fifty, would cram a khaki skirt and shirt over a civilian dress and rush down stairs to a waiting car where the offending uniform would be slipped off'.[39]

Promiscuity obviously worried military authorities. Both venereal disease and pregnancy removed a woman from service and tarnished the image of the service. But romance, even if chaste, was considered a distraction which reduced the effectiveness of auxiliaries and adversely affected the cohesiveness of a unit. Behaviour was therefore constantly monitored, and love affairs positively discouraged. One important function of ATS officers was to do their best to make sure that romances did not take hold: 'if you were caught with a fellow more than twice they'd think something was going on and post you'.[40] If, despite all the restraints, marriage resulted, one of the individuals (usually the woman) would quickly be posted elsewhere after the statutory one-week leave for a honeymoon. As Turner wrote in 'Epithalamium':

> My Number Four (so rapt with life)
> Has wed my Number Four (a bore).
> I pray her days run free from strife –
> My Number Four!

---

37. B.J. Wright, 'The adventures of a nobody in the WAAF', unpublished memoir, IWM 83/46/1.
38. Maureen Bolster to 'Eric', 23 May 1944, IWM 78/38/1.
39. Mannock memoir, p. 120.
40. Shelley Saywell, *Women in War* (Wellingborough, 1988), p. 29.

The rules, which frankly I deplore,
Are adamant that man and wife
May not live here as heretofore.

Hush, hush the clarion, mute the fife!
For him the tent, for her the door.
I hate to wield the cruel knife —
My Number Four![41]

Because there was a war on and labour was in short supply, the women's services could not afford to be too condemning of misbehaviour. The regime was rigid, but most women who went astray were generally treated leniently and often with admirable compassion. Lesbian love affairs did not automatically lead to dismissal from service; instead the women in question were given separate postings. Cases of venereal diseases were treated in such a way as to ensure 'utmost secrecy'. After hospital treatment was completed, the woman would be posted to another unit where her condition would be monitored. Pregnant women (even if unmarried) were released six months before the birth but were allowed to return six months after the birth if a vacancy existed. Great care was taken to make sure that unmarried pregnant women were not simply thrown onto the streets. Commanding officers were advised to liaise with welfare bodies like the Salvation Army or the Church of England.[42]

The whispering campaign

In December 1941, Henderson Stewart, MP for East Fife, told the House of Commons that the ATS had a 'thoroughly bad reputation' and was 'not the sort of service to which a nice girl goes'. Canon Headley Burrows of Bournemouth weighed in with stories of an 'appalling tendency to drunkenness' among servicewomen, evidence which reached him from no less reliable a source than his maid, who relayed stories told by her sister, who was in the ATS.[43] In making these allegations, Burrows and Stewart were giving voice to rumours that had been circulating virtually since the beginning of the war. Vee Robinson recalled how, shortly after volunteering, she was walking down the street, feeling proud of herself in her new uniform. She passed two young girls loitering in a doorway.

---

41. E.S. Turner, 'Epithalamium', *Punch*, 10 January 1945.
42. 'Notes for the guidance of WAAF administrative officers on hygiene and health of WAAF personnel', n.d., Public Record Office (hereafter PRO) AIR 2/6402.
43. *Sunday Express*, 18 January 1942.

They sniggered and one said loudly 'OGS'.
'What's that?' asked the other.
'Don't you know?', answered the first, 'it means officers' groundsheet' and they laughed. I was furious. . . . That was the first time I had heard the slur, but it wasn't the last.

All of the women's services attracted salacious rumour, but none more so than the ATS, most likely because of its largely working-class membership. (According to middle-class myth, workers were known to have insatiable sexual appetites.) One ATS member wrote:

Our attitude toward civilian opinion of us was that these were views expressed by self-righteous middle class ladies, who made damned sure that their daughters were in reserved occupations and who could thus stay at home. We felt that they thought of us girls in uniforms and away from home as promiscuous sluts.[44]

The ATS also inherited the poor image of the army as a whole, again a reflection of class bias. Joan Hill, who was 19 when she joined the ATS, encountered stiff resistance from her father, an army veteran who had no desire to see his daughter share his experiences.[45] Those who felt the effects of this whispering campaign most profoundly were the women posted to mixed anti-aircraft batteries. The range of erotic stimuli which the mixed battery presented was a potent catalyst to fantasy. One can easily imagine how those susceptible to erotic suggestion would have reacted to the idea of six women and two men in the heat of battle sweating in the dark to the pumping rhythm of an ack-ack gun.

Many of those interviewed blamed the popular press for spreading the rumours, in particular papers from the Beaverbrook stable. Yet, however logical such an allegation may seem, it is ill-founded. Perusal of the Beaverbrook papers reveals no consistent effort to besmirch the ATS. In fact, like all papers, they tended to print responsible articles praising ATS women for their heroic contribution to the war effort and castigating those who slandered servicewomen.[46] Instead, the rumours grew out of prejudices against the type of women who joined the ATS and, even more importantly, from the public's taste for salacious gossip. It does not seem reckless to conclude that many people wanted to believe the worst about a group of women perceived

44. Jean Wallace, unpublished memoir, IWM 91/36/1, pp. 15–16.
45. Joan Hill, correspondence with the author, 16 April 1995.
46. A cynic might argue that this was a clever way of having cake and eating it: the rumours could be reported at the same time that gossip-mongers were censured.

as threatening. Many felt a profound unease about the idea of women in uniform, as Zelma Katin, a mere bus conductress, discovered:

> To many people – perhaps because they suffer from sexual frustration – the sight of any girl in any kind of uniform, even Salvation Army uniform, at once suggests immorality. . . . Numbers of passengers believe that the last act of a conductress and her driver or motorman each night before going home is the exercise of sexual intercourse. . . . I have noticed the suspicion on women's faces when, passing me while the tram is waiting at a terminus, they observe me enjoying a cigarette with the motorman.[47]

When the women in question not only dressed like men, but began to act like them – in some cases to the point of actual combat – the threat was magnified. One good way to deal with this threat was to paint it scarlet. A similar process occurred in the United States, where malicious gossip caused a severe decline in recruitment to the Women's Army Corps (WAC). A WAC liaison officer remarked in disgust that 'men have for centuries used slander against morals to keep women out of public life'.[48]

For the women's services, the whispering campaign and Henderson Stewart's ill-informed remarks had serious implications for recruitment. Burchill recalled that 'malicious rumours . . . about the moral qualities of the ATS' made her feel 'very apprehensive'. Upon arrival at her training camp, she found herself 'in the company of many other young women all of whom, it seemed, were having the same feelings of apprehension about joining'.[49] Parents ordered their daughters not to join the women's services. (Ironically the other options were to join the Land Army or to enter a war-related industry, where the temptations and risks were arguably greater.) When women did not join the auxiliary services men were not released for combat. A panicked Captain David Margesson, the War Minister, told the Commons on 16 December that 'there is absolutely no foundation whatsoever for this whispering campaign, which I regret very much indeed, as they are a fine body of women who are doing a fine job of work'.[50]

The ATS reacted by forming its own public relations unit, which responded to each salacious rumour by releasing 'an inspiring photograph of some smart, sturdy ATS in military postures'.[51] Much publicity was given to Private Nora Caveney, an anti-aircraft predictor in the 148th regiment,

---

47. Hartley, ed., *Hearts Undefeated*, p. 207.
48. Costello, *Love, Sex and War*, p. 87.
49. I. Burchell, personal memoir, IWM ref. 88/50/1, p. 2.
50. Hansard, 16 December 1941.
51. Frederick Pile, *Ack-Ack* (London, 1949), p. 193.

who, after being hit by a bomb splinter, held the target until she collapsed and died. Strategically timed articles in the national press sought to reassure parents:

> The jibes one has heard about the behaviour of the ATS are so false as to be ludicrous. No mother need be afraid of entrusting her daughter to a gunner unit; she will be very well provided for. Most of the officers, and all the junior ones, have been through the ranks and know well the special needs and problems.[52]

In order to demonstrate that moral issues were taken seriously, service officials released reports of punishments meted out to officers convicted at courts-martial for seducing servicewomen. This was, however, a double-edged sword since it effectively reminded parents of the hazards that might await their daughters. Protecting the image of the women's services was a difficult job, since a single piece of bad publicity could upset months of careful spin doctoring. Margaret June Philips caused considerable controversy and embarrassment when, during a disciplinary hearing, she claimed she had gone absent without leave (AWOL) because she was frightened in camp: 'We are not allowed to lock the doors – even the bedroom doors – and civilian men get into our huts at night'.[53] The hearing decided that Philips was merely playing to public concerns and that her allegations had no foundation. But the damage was done.

The worried government immediately commissioned a formal investigation into the welfare of servicewomen. The commission, which consisted of three men and five women, was chaired by Violet Markham. On the behaviour of servicewomen, it took a view later echoed by the women interviewed for this study:

> the Women's Services . . . to-day represent a cross section of the population and all types and standards are represented among them. The innocent and the experienced, girls from good and girls from bad homes, are all thrown together. If a woman has learnt loose habits in civilian life, she brings those habits with her into the Services.

'Allegations of general immorality', the Commission discovered, 'have . . . resolved themselves into one or two cases which, in the course of gossip, have been multiplied times over.' Furthermore, 'loose behaviour' was not 'the product of service life' but was instead introduced from outside. 'Service

---

52. Major D. Rees Williams, 'The gunner-girls', *The Spectator*, 24 April 1942, p. 396.
53. *The Times*, 24 February 1942.

life, with its discipline, work and good comradeship, generally speaking puts the relation of men and women on a healthy and normal basis. It is a corrective rather than an incitement to bad conduct.' As for the whispering campaign, the report offered a plausible explanation, but one which left a great deal unsaid:

> The British . . . are not a military race. They cherish a deep-rooted prejudice against uniforms, consequently a women in uniform may rouse a special sense of hostility, conscious and sub-conscious, among certain people who would never give two thoughts to her conduct if she were a private citizen.[54]

Guardians of morality

The women's services, aware of the need to maintain an image of moral purity in order to avoid public criticism, relied upon strict disciplinary procedures to control behaviour and punish offenders. But whereas discipline in an all-male unit had the predominant aim of making men into efficient soldiers, in the women's auxiliaries the regime was designed also to protect feminine virtue. As the Markham Report argued, 'the auxiliaries of to-day are the wives and mothers of the future and satisfactory as is the standard of health in the services, no one desires to apply a wholesale hardening process to the young women who are serving their country effectively and well'.[55] Protection of this type implied better amenities, shorter hours, and less rigorous training than were experienced by men in the regular army. It also implied monitoring of personal relationships. The women were to be protected from men, from other women and from the temptations of wartime life.

The main purpose of ATS officers was to oversee the welfare and behaviour of servicewomen, since training and operational command were the exclusive remit of male regular army officers. Servicewomen were encouraged to see in their commanding officer a 'guide, philosopher and friend'.[56] As a public relations article in the *Journal of the Royal Artillery* made clear, the regime was quite intrusive:

---

54. Report of the Committee on Amenities and Welfare Conditions in the Three Women's Services, August 1942 (hereafter: Markham Report), paras 200, 207–8, pp. 49–51.
55. Markham Report, para. 25, p. 8.
56. 'Notes for the guidance of WAAF administrative officers on hygiene and health of WAAF personnel', n.d., PRO AIR 2/6402.

ATS officers . . . are responsible for the administration and discipline of the women. They pay their women, conduct their physical training, give them certain talks and lectures applicable to women, look after their welfare, hold their own Orderly Room and Office Hour, do their health and hygiene inspections, and arrange the girls' recreational training and games.[57]

Though intrusive, this protection was genuinely well-intentioned and as such a manifestation of that common middle-class assumption that the working classes could not be trusted to look after themselves. For instance, a WAAF memo addressed the problem of drunkenness:

The habitual taking of alcohol should be discouraged. While it should be appreciated that many women in the Services have been accustomed in the past to temperate indulgence in alcohol without undesirable repercussions, a danger arises in the case of the young recruit who is a stranger to alcohol, but who may be led astray by older and more sophisticated companions. The officer should be on the lookout for this and can often, by changing hours of work and barrack huts, break up undesirable associations.[58]

Laws recorded in her diary a section meeting in January 1945 when an ATS officer announced that enlisted women would be 'allowed out in twos [but] must behave properly and not sing in the street and drink too much wine'.[59] Goosens recalled how the women in her unit were not allowed to make their own way to dances, but were instead escorted by a certain Corporal Trodd, who 'would have made an ideal prison wardress'. After the dance 'Trodd . . . had the cheek to make us form fours on the dancefloor, and she marched us all off back to the Castle. We were furious and dreadfully embarrassed in front of all the men.'[60] Descriptions of the regime bring to mind the Girl Guides, except for the fact that the women in question were much older. Not surprisingly, experience in the Guides was advantageous for middle-class women who sought commissions.

Officers were very concerned that their 'girls' should project the right image. In October 1941 Chief Commander the Honourable Mrs Gilmour withdrew six ATS women from an army revue because she felt that the costume, which included a three-inch 'skin belt' at the midriff, was indecent.[61] In March 1944, Leslie Whateley, Director of the ATS, issued an order

---

57. J.W. Naylor, 'Mixed batteries', *Journal of the Royal Artillery* 69 (1942), p. 204.
58. 'Notes for the guidance of WAAF administrative officers on hygiene and health of WAAF personnel', n.d., PRO AIR 2/6402.
59. Laws diary, 3 January 1945.
60. Goosens memoir.
61. *Daily Mirror*, 24 October 1941.

prohibiting auxiliaries from smoking 'while walking in the street, sitting in a bus or standing on a station platform'. She thought that 'such habits looked unattractive and unfeminine in civilian clothes, and in uniform worse'.[62] This ruling caused some consternation in the Commons among liberal-minded MPs, who felt that an unfair double standard was being applied, but the War Minister refused to reverse the prohibition.[63]

Sex education had to be approached with enormous care, since the military preferred a naïve woman to a knowledgeable one. Male soldiers were freely given condoms, but women soldiers were not. The Markham Committee saw the military experience as an opportunity for social engineering:

> there should be in all three Services a lecture to auxiliaries on the wider implications of sex behaviour explaining the value to both the community and to the individual of stable family relationships based on the permanent physical, emotional and intellectual partnership of a man and a woman; not because the sex morals of the Forces are more precarious than those of civilians but because . . . life in the Forces presents new educational opportunities.[64]

The committee hoped that 'carefully planned lectures and discussions on personal relationships, the psychology of sex and the sociological implications of the family should be introduced into officers' training and refresher courses'.[65]

In practice, sex education fell short of this ideal. Euphemistically entitled 'hygiene' lectures scratched the surface of sex issues, often leaving the naïve even more confused:

> The War Department thought of many things but [sex education] was not one of them. There certainly were no contraceptives made available to the girls, so our fate was in the hands of our men. All we had were myths and old wives' stories which we had brought into the forces with us, like the popular one that if you had sex standing up, you could not get pregnant. No consideration was shown for the private dilemmas we faced.[66]

Experience differed from unit to unit, according to the enthusiasm of the welfare officer for the issue. 'Even in the ATS we girls were told nothing of contraception', Carter recalled, 'only in a plummy voice the lady officer,

---

62. Hartley, ed., *Hearts Undefeated*, p. 113.
63. Hansard, 4 April 1944.
64. Markham Report, para. 118, p. 30.
65. *Ibid.*, para. 120, p. 30.
66. Wallace memoir, p. 17.

saying now girls, wash up as far as possible and down as far as possible, but girls, never never forget possible. . . . Like lambs to the slaughter we were.'[67] On the other hand, one woman found lectures on venereal disease a bit too enthusiastic:

> We were examined for venereal disease when we joined the army, and every month at the medical inspection. Great moral emphasis was laid on not having affairs with men, which sort of filtered through – although nobody paid much attention. Yet at the same time girls . . . became obsessed with the whole VD thing . . . it was drummed into you so much. Most of us had never heard of VD or knew what it was, but like many others I developed a discharge out of pure psychosomatic terror.[68]

Behind the regulations and discipline there lurked an elaborate public relations exercise. The Markham Committee recognized that 'The woman in uniform becomes an easy target for gossip and careless talk. To be seen drinking a glass of beer in a public-house is to provide a text for fluent remarks about the low standards of the Services.'[69] Worried parents had to be reassured that service would not mean the ruin of their daughters. 'There is no doubt in my mind', a War Office internal memo stated, 'that the health and welfare of young women working away from home in very unfamiliar conditions should be carefully attended to by experienced women forming a branch of the ATS Directorate. Parents will be far more ready to let their daughters join up if this is provided for.'[70]

Military law provided a useful tool for controlling behaviour, though most officers (of both sexes) felt that it could have been applied more aggressively. The regulations governing male and female soldiers were very similar, but the way they were applied was far different. For instance, a woman was far more likely to be punished severely for 'conduct unbecoming', but if she went AWOL the punishment was lighter. Prison was deemed decidedly unwomanly and it was feared that the prospect of it might dissuade the right type of women from volunteering. Therefore, except in the most severe cases, detention and other minor punishments were used instead. Yet conscription drew into the services many women who had a cavalier attitude towards authority and who exploited the impotence of the legal system. One ATS report told how 'defaulters . . . escaped from camps and barracks clothed in shirts and knickers and without their shoes; they squeezed

---

67. Carter interview.
68. Costello, *Love, Sex and War*, p. 81.
69. Markham Report, para. 200, p. 49.
70. War Office internal memo, 20 July 1940, PRO WO 32/10040.

through lavatory windows which appeared small enough to preclude the passage of anything bigger than a cat; they scaled walls and dodged guards'.[71]

Great care was given to counselling and education of problem cases, as opposed to punishment, but this proved inadequate when it came to the most incorrigible offenders. In the interests of protecting the rest of the women, those deemed unsuitable were combed out. A WAAF memo complained that 'Some of these delinquents are of a very bad moral character and . . . to retain them amongst airwomen from decent homes and of high moral character is most unsatisfactory not to say dangerous'.[72] Problem women in the WAAF were put into three groups: 'mentally sub-normal types', 'irresponsible high-spirited types' and 'delinquent types'. While the first two categories might be brought round through counselling, education and discipline (special schools were established), the third was deemed 'useless and should be discharged from the Service'.[73] The predominant concern was the effect that the 'really bad hat' might have upon the rest of the women. One ATS memo recommended that a particular servicewoman should be 'discharged . . . [because] she seems a person entirely irresponsible . . . her morals are far from good, and she would not, in my opinion, be a good influence in any Company'.[74]

Women were intentionally deployed in areas that would limit opportunities for misbehaviour. Thus, for instance, it was decided early in the war that women gunners would not be deployed on mobile anti-aircraft units, since the accommodation was not as secure. In other words, a woman in a tent was more likely to fall victim to a marauding male than one in a locked barracks. Their deployment as searchlight operators was curtailed after it was realized that each unit would need one strong male to start the electric generator and to handle the rifle issued for defensive purposes (women were not allowed to handle weapons). As Frederick Pile, commander of Britain's ground anti-aircraft defences, remarked, 'It can be imagined what play could have been made by the more prurient sections of the Press with the fact that among these unchaperoned young women lurked a solitary male soldier'.[75] When, later in the war, women had to be posted overseas, new concerns arose about their susceptibility to sexual temptations in cultures assumed to be of a lower moral standard. A great deal of attention was therefore devoted to protecting these women from the advances of foreign

---

71. J.M. Cowper, 'The Auxiliary Territorial Service' (War Office, 1949), p. 76.
72. G. Baker to D[irector]WAAF, 5 October 1942, PRO AIR 2/4090, Memo 141.
73. 'WAAF memo, 'Special school of instruction', n.d., PRO AIR 2/4090.
74. DATS confidential memo, n.d., PRO WO 32/10662.
75. Pile, Ack-Ack, p. 227. Only one female searchlight unit was therefore commissioned.

males, including an insistence that 'Women should be quartered in Nissan huts or empty houses and should not be billeted on French families'.[76]

Brick walls?

After the war, Jenny Nicholson, a one-time WAAF public relations officer whose remit was to deal with the whispering campaign, argued that

> Naturally with such a vast cross-section of British womanhood as there was in each of the services there were bound to be individuals whose standard of behaviour wasn't up to the average scratch. But service life didn't breed them. They arrived like that. Happily, behaving well was a good deal more contagious than the other thing, so once a brazen hussy found herself separated from her hometown gang of brazen hussies and among a number of sensible people, the tendency was for her to grow noticeably more subdued as time dragged on. It was certainly true to say that the women who entered the service like driven snow and turned cheap and nasty by it were exceptional.[77]

Evidence supports this view. Rates of illegitimacy and venereal disease were significantly lower within the women's services than among civilian women.[78] 'It can be said with assurance that no woman runs an extra risk of becoming pregnant by joining a Service', the Markham Report stated.[79] While this is not necessarily an indicator of lower sexual activity (it may simply show that servicewomen took better care of themselves), it does suggest that the women services did not deserve the opprobrium heaped upon them.[80]

Almost all of the women interviewed for this project agreed with Nicholson. Joyce Truman dismissed talk of licentiousness within the ATS, as 'ABSOLUTE NONSENSE!!'[81] The most any woman would confess to was the odd romance or innocent flirtation. A few mentioned vague memories of women who 'got into trouble' but insisted that they were the exception. Most regretted how the bad behaviour of a few tarnished the reputation of the entire service. 'I feel that not just ack ack girls but girls in all the services were much maligned', Patterson commented. 'You'll always get the few

---

76. 'ATS for service overseas', 12–15 December War Office Conference, PRO WO 32/9402.
77. Hartley, ed., *Hearts Undefeated*, p. 209.
78. Markham Report, paras 125–7, pp. 31–2.
79. *Ibid.*, para. 126, p. 31.
80. See memorandum by Director General, Medical Services (Air Ministry), 1942, PRO AIR 2/6402.
81. Joyce Truman, correspondence with the author, 18 April 1995.

who spoil it for the others. One thing in our favour, we hadn't been brought up to think that sex was the be all in life.'[82]

On the other hand, it is certainly possible that witnesses were simply reluctant to talk about their sex lives to a male researcher of a younger generation. One struggles to see over a brick wall of reticence. Or, the scarcity of scandalous stories might simply be explained by the mechanics of finding contacts to interview. Much depends on where the researcher enters the chain of witnesses. Contacts suggest other contacts with whom they have maintained close contact for the past 50 years. Thus, they essentially clone themselves and their stories develop a familiar echo. The prostitutes and loose women who might once have raised havoc in barracks do not perhaps attend the ex-servicewomen's functions or Women's Institute fêtes where one-time auxiliaries meet and reminisce.

But virtually all of the women, while claiming that they behaved properly, also claimed that their fellow servicewomen did. They all described an atmosphere of upright moral behaviour and strict discipline in which the opportunities for adventure were actually rare. They may have been naïve, but they could not have been blind. One suspects, therefore, that this picture of restraint is closer to the truth than the licentiousness preferred by gossip-mongers. As the Markham Committee recognized, 'virtue has no gossip value'.[83] Perhaps there is some truth to the common refrain that it is wrong to go looking for 1990s behaviour in the 1940s. Running through the interviews a single statement echoes: 'there was not nearly so much pro-miscuity as there is today'.[84] And perhaps the myths of ATS promiscuity are yet another rebuttal of those who believe that war, that 'great locomotive of history', brought profound social dislocation. These women found war tragic, exciting, romantic, but also temporary. While adventures proved tempting, they understood that when peace came traditional morality would be revived and that the penalties for a momentary lapse might be a lifetime of woe.

The whispering campaign should not seem unfamiliar. Stories of sexual misbehaviour have always been valuable commodities in the scandal market. Voyeurism of this type – a potent mix of titillation and prudery – is soft-core porn which costs nothing to enjoy and need not be hidden in brown paper envelopes. It feeds on popular myth and prejudice, in this case of virile warriors and lusty working-class girls. Even if servicewomen were not promiscuous, there were those who derived enormous pleasure from imag-ining that they were. If war seems erotic it is because some people want it to be so. It is always tempting to make the past more exciting than it was.

---

82. Doris Patterson, correspondence with the author, 15 March 1995.
83. Markham Report, para. 199, p. 49.
84. Pat Gibson, correspondence with the author, 31 August 1995.

CHAPTER SEVEN

'She Wants a Gun not a Dishcloth!': Gender, Service and Citizenship in Britain in the Second World War

PENNY SUMMERFIELD

Citizenship was predicated upon military service in the minds of many nineteenth- and twentieth-century Britons. In the Second World War, mobilization of the British population was extensive. Nearly 5 million out of a working population of 15 million men, plus at least 1.5 million men from the colonies, were conscripted or volunteered for the armed forces. In addition nearly 500,000 women, out of a female working population of 7 million, joined the women's auxiliary forces, organized for the support of the male military. Some women volunteered; others were called up under National Service legislation which made war service compulsory for young single women from the end of 1941.[1]

This wartime militarization of British society made more than usually tenuous the claim on citizenship of those who refused or did not qualify for military service, and specifically for combatant status. Civilian identity in wartime was uncertain even though both regulation and cultural norms for specific groups justified the non-combatant position. Thus the Schedule of Reserved Occupations prevented people in particular categories of skilled work from being called up, and it was not considered appropriate (as we shall see) for women to have combatant roles.[2] In practice the distinction between combatant and non-combatant roles was hard to maintain because air attack, bombing and the threat of invasion dispersed the front line and brought it home. But the heroic status of the military citizen in wartime political rhetoric and popular culture polarized the two identities and increased the insecurity of the civilian.

---

1. H.M.D. Parker, *Manpower, A Study of War-time Policy and Administration* (London, 1957), pp. 113, 291–2.
2. P. Inman, *Labour in the Munitions Industries* (London, 1957), pp. 35, 52, 67, 135; Parker, *Manpower*, pp. 158–60.

In this context, many men and women who were excluded from military service sought quasi-military roles which they could combine with civilian forms of war work. This was easier for men to accomplish than women. One way in which men could do it was to join the Home Guard, first known as the Local Defence Volunteers. This volunteer, part-time citizens' army was formed in May 1940 in response to the apparent ease with which the German army overran France. It was renamed the Home Guard in July 1940 and became an adjunct of the army, subject to War Office regulation. Its members were provided with uniforms, ranks and some military equipment.

The non-regular, part-time status of the Home Guard, its chronic shortage of equipment and the absence of an invasion caused it to be commemorated as comic in popular culture. *Dad's Army*, the popular television series first broadcast from 1968 to 1977, portrayed Home Guards as incompetent if sincere civilian men, playing at war.[3] At the time, though, the Home Guard was seen as practically necessary and symbolically important. Home Guards were trained to resist invasion, to perform guard duties and to participate in the training of regular army units. According to Paul Mackenzie, the number and enthusiasm of male volunteers, and the inclination of some of them to use radical models of democratic military organization, went beyond the War Office's expectations and preferences.[4] The symbolic importance of the organization was expressed in its name: as Antonia Lant points out, wartime terms like Home Front, Home Security, Home Intelligence, the BBC Home Service and the Home Guard used the word 'home' to stand for both dwelling place and nation.[5]

However, in spite of uniting the domestic with the national in its title, and notwithstanding its democratic and inclusive origins, women were excluded from the Home Guard until 1943. The denial to women of any membership until 1943, and of full membership from that date until the stand down of the Home Guard at the end of 1944, meant that civilian women were refused an expression of citizenship available to civilian men. This chapter discusses this exclusion, and the campaign which women waged against it, as a specific case of a larger social and political process. The gender boundary between military masculinity and non-combatant femininity was destabilized nationally and internationally in wartime. The defence and ultimate preservation of that boundary in Britain in the Second World War is indicative of its cultural centrality to the maintenance of the social order.

---

3. J. Richards, '"Dad's Army" and the politics of nostalgia', in J. Richards, ed., *Films and British National Identity, from Dickens to Dad's Army* (Manchester, 1997), pp. 351–66.
4. S.P. Mackenzie, *The Home Guard. A Military and Political History* (Oxford, 1995), pp. 34–6 and 68–76.
5. A. Lant, *Blackout. Reinventing Women for Wartime British Cinema* (Princeton, NJ, 1991), p. 44.

The history of this exclusion and women's opposition to it can be told as a drama played out on the floor of the House of Commons, the dialogue structured by the formal conventions of Parliamentary Debates and Question Times. Developments were affected by events taking place offstage, both within the War Office and in localities across the country where women sought to participate in home defence. Parliament was the public forum in which protests could be voiced and the government pressed to make commitments, the fulcrum between the power of the military establishment on the one hand, and that of the women's rights lobby on the other. The main players on the government side were Sir Edward Grigg, Parliamentary Under-Secretary for War from 1940 to 1942, followed (confusingly) by another Grigg, Sir Percy James Grigg, Secretary of State for War from 1942 to 1945. The feminist opposition was led by one of the 14 wartime women Members of Parliament, Edith Summerskill, Labour MP for Fulham West. Also involved were various other government ministers and their underlings, and a heterogeneous but growing collection of male MPs and Home Guard commanders who supported Summerskill.

The specifics of the argument concerned whether women should be permitted to join the Home Guard, to wear its uniform and to use its weapons. The larger issues were whether it was appropriate for the military defence of home and nation to be a solely masculine task in total war, and thus for the concept of national identity to be divided by gender. Such a division would perpetuate the traditional dual construction of patriotism, polarized between masculine militarism epitomized by engagement in 'active service' and feminine passivity symbolized by watching and waiting for the returning heroes.

In the summer and autumn of 1940, pressure to include women as well as men in the concept of active patriotism was mounted by Summerskill with the support of other parliamentary feminists, including Eleanor Rathbone and Mavis Tate. They formed the same kind of cross-party alliance that Alison Oram has observed in the context of wartime campaigns for other equal rights objectives.[6] However, the questions asked by Summerskill and her colleagues about whether women would be allowed to join the Home Guard received simple negatives on the grounds of (unspecified) matters of principle and organization. All Summerskill could get from war ministers was that women could not be recruited because there were not enough uniforms for them. 'Perhaps', said Sir Edward Grigg in early November, 'later on it may be possible to do something.'[7] But 'later on' was a long time

---

6.   Alison Oram, '"Bombs don't discriminate!" Women's political activism in the Second World War', in C. Gledhill and G. Swanson, eds, *Nationalising Femininity. Culture, Sexuality and British Cinema in the Second World War* (Manchester, 1996), pp. 53–69.
7.   Hansard, 6 November 1940.

coming. In the meantime parliamentary discussion of the Home Guard was the occasion for presentations of British national identity which were exclusively masculine, and for women's protests against such constructions.

In the adjournment debate of 19 November 1940, for example, Sir Edward Grigg, opening the debate, gave a potted history of the Home Guard. It had been formed, he explained, by 'men of all ages in all parts of the country' who 'were eating their hearts out because for one reason or another they had no opportunity for offering military service'. Grigg described the Home Guard as a 'lusty infant'. Summerskill interjected 'it is of only one sex', to which Grigg replied crushingly, 'most infants are, I believe'. Grigg waxed lyrical about the Britishness of the all-male force: 'It is Britain incarnate, an epitome of British character in its gift for comradeship in trouble, its resourcefulness at need, its deep love of its own land, and its surging anger at the thought that any invader should set foot on our soil'. Grigg referred to St George, St Andrew, St David and St Crispin, the patron saints of England, Scotland and Wales, and the saint associated with Agincourt and the unmanliness of English gentlemen a-bed upon that day. All these saints, said Grigg, were 'alive and marching in its democratic ranks'. Summerskill, enraged by his casual and confident alignment of British democracy, patriotism and resourcefulness exclusively with men, threw in 'What about Boadicea?' This time Grigg could not, apparently, summon a riposte, but continued: 'The morale of this country was never low, but action raises morale. The Home Guard has thus enabled all sorts and conditions of patriotic men to express themselves in service, with tonic effect.'[8]

Summerskill bounced back in debate. She laid out her egalitarian approach: 'I want to make it clear', she said, 'that I am not asking for women to be included solely as cooks and clerks in the Home Guard but in the same capacity as men, with equal rights and no privileges.' She drew a parallel with women's demand for the vote 30 years earlier. The ability to serve the country in a military capacity had been used as a definition of citizenship and a reason for excluding women from the franchise before 1918. Summerskill was demanding that equal right, that access to full citizenship, now. She specifically rejected the 'watching and waiting' definition of feminine patriotism. The lingering male prejudice that women are 'still weak, gentle creatures who must be protected' had to go, she said. Women must be allowed, trained and equipped to defend themselves and their country.[9]

---

8. *Ibid.*, 19 November 1940.
9. *Ibid.*, 19 November 1940.

Summerskill's powerful speech provoked no response. In summing up the debate Anthony Eden, Secretary of State for War, ignored her contribution. He spoke of tin hats and badges, expenditure, machine guns, attendance at courses, and the relationship of the Home Guard to the army and its command structure, but he avoided any mention of women's membership. The only involvement of women suggested by any other participant in the debate was the proposal of Sir Thomas Moore, Conservative MP for Ayr Burghs, that the Home Guard should have a ladies' night every Saturday, to stimulate recruitment and maintain cohesion.[10]

A year later the government had not changed its mind about women's membership of the Home Guard, even though 1941 saw a huge intensification of the mobilization of women for industry, civil defence and the auxiliaries to the armed forces, as well as enormous military pressure on Britain. The contradictory character of the situation, in which women, like men, were in danger but were prevented from learning how to defend themselves, was becoming evident to a growing number of MPs. On 13 November 1941, Squadron-Leader Errington, MP for Bootle, urged that the implications of modern warfare were that everyone was involved. He said that women in Britain were asking 'what they should do if a German came to their door', to which another MP retorted 'shoot him'. 'But', replied Errington, 'they have nothing to shoot him with and the women are not to be trained and given information with which to protect themselves . . . why should not our women be taught the use of hand grenades and revolvers?' He received no answer except that there were still to be no women Home Guards.[11]

The determination with which the War Office kept women out of the Home Guard is all the more remarkable in view of two concurrent developments. First, the National Service No. 2 Act, passed in December 1941, made single women aged 20 to 30 liable for conscription to war industry, civil defence or the women's auxiliaries to the armed forces. Second, the same Act introduced the conscription of men to the Home Guard. Men aged 18 to 51, who were not in the armed forces, could henceforth be compelled to serve part-time in the Home Guard.[12] These moves had two implications. First, the labour shortage was so desperate in the regular armed forces that women as well as men had to be conscripted to them. (A gesture towards sustaining the division between combatant men and non-combatant women was nevertheless made, in the requirement that women's consent in writing must be obtained before they could be ordered to use lethal weapons.) Second, there was an equivalent labour shortage as

---

10. *Ibid.*, 19 November 1940.
11. *Ibid.*, 13 November 1941.
12. N. Longmate, *The Real Dad's Army: The Story of the Home Guard* (London, 1974), p. 58.

far as the Home Guard was concerned such that it could not rely on volunteers but required conscripts. Summerskill was quick to ask why, in that case, women as well as men could not be recruited to the Home Guard, and was told that there was simply no adequate place for them.[13]

In the Adjournment Debate of December 1941 Summerskill pushed the case in the context of growing support from male MPs.[14] While still claiming equal rights, she now endeavoured to minimize the threat to conventional gender relations presented by the prospect of women tending hearth and home while armed with hand grenades and revolvers. Membership of the Home Guard, she argued, was perfectly compatible with 'women's traditional role as guardian of the home'. She did not mean that they should wash up for the Home Guard, she hastened to add. Unfit men could do that! But she held up to ridicule the possibility that a woman would find herself sitting by an injured man in an invasion, forced to look on ineffectually while explaining 'it was not womanly for me to learn to use a rifle'.[15] Sir Edward Grigg, summing up the debate in December 1941 as Eden had done in November 1940, again opposed the recruitment of women to the Home Guard. He did at least refer to Summerskill's speech this time, but said 'I can give her very little hope'.[16]

Summerskill claimed during the debate of December 1941 that the official reluctance to allow women to use lethal weapons had greatly stimulated women's interest in them, and that, although formally barred from the Home Guard, women were taking action for themselves. There is indeed evidence that women were illicitly joining the Home Guard and training with its male members in the use of weapons. A report in the *Daily Mail* of 29 October 1941 stated that 50 women at a factory in Tolworth, Surrey, had been training with the factory's Home Guard unit for three months in drilling, marching and rifle-drill, and had provided their own uniforms. Sergeant-Major Leonard Stevens, in charge of the unit, said: 'Although the girls are not officially recognized as Home Guards, they go on manoeuvres and train the same as the men. Four nights a week they go on parade. Their keenness and spirit are magnificent.'[17]

Within the War Office there was disquiet about such developments. In the autumn of 1940 the War Office had had no policy towards women in the Home Guard beyond the assumption (given expression in Parliament) that they had no place in it. When, in response to feminist pressure, policy

---

13. Hansard, 18 December 1941.
14. *Ibid.*
15. *Ibid.*
16. *Ibid.*
17. *Daily Mail*, 29 October 1941.

was articulated, reasons for this dominant view were made explicit, at least within the private memoranda of the War Office, if not in public. Late in December 1940, Lieutenant-General Sir Ralph Eastwood, Director-General of the Home Guard, stated:

> Under no circumstances should women be enrolled in the Home Guard. I agree with C[ommander]-in-C[hief], H[ome] F[orces], that it is undesirable for women to bear arms in the H[ome] G[uard], and I do not think anyone should be enrolled in the HG who is not under an obligation to bear arms when called upon to do so.[18]

In October 1941 his successor Major-General Lord Bridgeman elaborated this argument in relation to men who might want to avoid military service. Everyone 'who enrols in the HG does so with the obligation to be trained in the use of arms'. This was necessary 'to prevent Conscientious Objectors and others being able to slide into the HG to get the protection of the uniform and yet decline to prepare themselves to fight the King's battles'. Since it was not possible to require the same thing of women, who could by virtue of their sex perform only non-combatant duties, they could not be admitted.[19] The approach was expressed in terms of gendered military recruitment strategy. Other officials discussed the matter of women's admission mostly in terms of pragmatics focused on resources. Since there were not enough trainers, rifles, uniforms or boots for men, none could be spared for women. But neither Eastwood nor any other official ever made explicit the principle behind their belief that women should not be armed and trained to fight.[20]

However, as the report in the *Daily Mail* suggests, War Office policy was being ignored not only by women who wished to join the Home Guard, but also by some Home Guard commanders who were happy to admit them. The reasons were mainly to do with labour supply. For example, Brigadier H.P. Currey, commanding the Sussex and Surrey area, wrote to his commanding officer on 3 September 1941, 'There is a growing tendency to rely on the employment of women as the HG loses men owing to call ups for the Services'. He did not advocate the integration suggested by Tolworth-style rifle drill for women, suggesting rather a women's auxiliary that would provide such services as clerking, storekeeping, driving and catering, with

---

18. Public Record Office (hereafter PRO) WO 32/9423, memorandum (memo) 27 December 1940.
19. *Ibid.*, DG HG to Sir Douglas Brownrigg, 1 October 1941.
20. G. DeGroot found the same evasion in relation to women firing anti-aircraft guns: 'Whose finger on the trigger? Mixed anti-aircraft batteries and the female combat taboo', *War in History* 4 (1997), pp. 434–53.

the same relationship to the Home Guard as that of the Auxiliary Territorial Service to the army.[21] Summerskill kept in close contact with commanding officers of Home Guard units who shared Currey's approach, as well as those who went further and agreed with her that women's training should include weaponry. She wrote to the Prime Minister, W.S. Churchill, on 31 October 1941, quoting at length from a letter by Major Gavin Jones, commander of Letchworth Home Guard. He had written: 'I want to raise a women's platoon in this town. My own Home Guard here are over-whelmingly in favour of the idea . . . I do not expect the women to do heavy work like route marching or fighting in open warfare in the field. I want them for static guards in the town.' Summerskill added that if women could serve on gun sites they could surely 'serve as guards for defence purposes'. Attached to the copy of her letter in the War Office file is a handwritten slip addressed to 'S of S for War' stating 'I favour the idea. WSC.'[22]

The War Office policy of excluding women from the Home Guard was not, however, going to change on the say-so of the Prime Minister, or as a result of pressure from commanders desperate for personnel. An order was issued which was intended to quell the subversive practice of female recruit-ment. It was published in *The Times* on 12 November 1941:

> The War Office has sent an order to all Home Guard units that the training of women as unofficial Home Guard units has not been authorized. Weapons and ammunition in the charge of the Army or of Home Guard units must not be used for the instruction of women and the use of the name Home Guard is not permitted.[23]

Undaunted, Summerskill continued to work to bring the influence of the Home Guard commanders with whom she had formed an alliance to bear on the War Office. Some were not in favour, as she was, of arming women, but all saw a role for women in the Home Guard, and Summerskill capital-ized on the support of the less, as well as the more, militant. She suggested on 5 December 1941 that the Secretary of State for War should receive a deputation of commanders 'who are anxious to ask you to consider allow-ing women to join the Home Guard; alternatively they wish the ban which prohibits men in the HG instructing women in the use of rifles to be ended'. Military protocol was used to turn down her suggestion. The Secretary of

---

21. *Ibid.*, memo by Brigadier H.P. Currey, Commander, Sussex and Surrey Area, 3 September 1941.
22. *Ibid.*, Summerskill to W.S. Churchill, Prime Minister, 31 October 1941.
23. *The Times*, 12 November 1941.

State could not see commanding officers of units over the heads of their superiors.[24]

Nevertheless the War Office took the contention that Home Guard commanders were keen on recruiting women sufficiently seriously to put it to their own, rather loaded, test a few months later. In September 1942 General Sir Bernard C.T. Paget, Commander-in-Chief Home Forces, wrote to army commanders throughout Britain requesting them to obtain the views of Home Guard commanders on the desirability of recruiting women. Paget's letter was far from dispassionate. He referred to help given informally to the Home Guard by the Women's Voluntary Service and continued, 'unless it is really necessary for the well being and efficiency of the Home Guard that this women's service should be put on an official basis, I should prefer to carry on with the present arrangement'. Paget was particularly hostile to giving armbands or badges to women helping the Home Guard. 'Experience shows that the grant of a brassard', he thundered, 'will lead inevitably to a demand for full enrolment with everything which it entails, namely free uniforms.'[25] In spite of his discouraging tone, however, several of the army commanders reported that women's assistance was important to the Home Guard and that formalization of the relationship should include the issue of a badge or armband.

Meanwhile, women who wished to participate in home defence had formed their own Home Guard, the Women's Home Defence Corps. The earliest move in this direction occurred in the summer of 1940 when, in a celebration of a feminine identity which (as we shall see) male politicians derided, a group was set up calling itself the Amazon Defence Corps.[26] In January 1942 *The Times* reported that women were learning to shoot in 30 Women's Home Defence Units and by December 1942 there were said to be 250 such units, mostly undertaking duties that would release men for active service.[27] A leaflet about the organization explained that its objective was 'To train every woman in the country to be of the maximum use in the event of an invasion' and listed the most important areas of training: musketry, bombing, the use of the tommy gun, unarmed combat and field craft.[28]

Women's Home Defence had some influential supporters. For example, Dame Helen Gwynne-Vaughan, a university professor and leader of the Women's Auxiliary Army Corps in the First World War as well as Director

24. PRO WO 32/9423, Summerskill to Rt Hon. Capt. Margesson, MP, 5 December 1941.
25. *Ibid.*, B.C.T. Paget to army commanders, 30 August 1942.
26. Fawcett Library, 355.244.2:396.5. Thanks to David Doughan for information about this organization.
27. Hansard, 8 December 1942.
28. PRO WO 32/9423, enclosed with a letter from Summerskill to P.J. Grigg, 29 March 1942.

from 1939 to 1941 of its Second World War equivalent, the Auxiliary Territorial Service, worked in parallel with Summerskill in pressing for recognition. Whenever the opportunity arose during 1942, Summerskill drew attention to the activities of Women's Home Defence. Her tactic was to force the government to give the women official recognition by demonstrating that women's combative part in organized Home Defence was already a *fait accompli*.

The campaign for recognition drew outspoken condemnation from members of the male establishment outside the parameters of policy-making. They framed their objections not in terms of recruitment strategy or the allocation of resources, but of fundamental differences between the sexes. For example, David Robertson MP was explicit about the damage which he felt Women's Home Defence was doing to gender identities, in his response to a constituent who wrote asking him to press for official recognition of her unit. He wrote: 'a woman's duty is to give life and not to take it, and the training which your Movement gives in unarmed combat, signalling, fieldcraft and musketry is abhorrent to me'.[29] We should not leave his expression of the popular understanding of women's duty without asking questions about the implications for masculinity of the bipolarity of gender identities central to it: if a woman's duty was to give life and not to take it, what was a man's, to take life and not to give it?

Robertson was not alone in finding Women's Home Defence 'abhorrent'. But the War Office did not suppress the organization, even though officials realized that they had grounds to do so. Membership was technically illegal, since Women's Home Defence was an armed organization outside the regulation of the Crown. In April 1942 the Deputy Under-Secretary for War wrote to the Vice-Chief of the Imperial General Staff: 'The training which is being given by the Women's Home Defence appears prima facie to be contrary to the law which prohibits "all meetings and assemblies of persons for the purpose of training or drilling themselves or being trained or drilled to the use of arms . . . without any lawful authority from His Majesty or the Lieutenant or two Justices of the Peace of any county"'. However, he and others within the War Office conceded that the strength of numbers in the organization, coupled with the head of steam built up by Summerskill, made it politically impossible to suppress the Women's Home Defence Corps. However much the War Office would have liked to quash it, legal proceedings were ruled out because 'If any steps are taken to stop the activities of the organization there will no doubt be a mass of protest'.[30]

---

29. *Ibid.*, David Robertson MP for Streatham to Miss B. Gooch, Women's Home Defence, Streatham, 2 October 1942.
30. *Ibid.*, Minute from Bovenschen, DUS, to VCIGS, 22 April 1942.

Summerskill's tactics had paid off thus far, but the War Office was a long way from capitulating to her demands. During 1942 internal War Office memoranda indicated that there were two issues at stake. On the one hand there was Summerskill's position, namely that women should 'be enlisted into the Home Guard as fully combatant members of it to man barricades, to go on reconnaissances etc after being trained in the use of the rifle and if necessary in automatic weapons'.[31] No one in the War Office would accept such a scheme (even though, as we have seen, some local Home Guard commanders and the Prime Minister himself did so). On the other hand, there was the possibility that women should form some sort of auxiliary to the Home Guard. This would put on an official basis a longstanding informal arrangement with the Women's Voluntary Service (WVS), under which WVS members provided services such as catering, and performed tasks such as 'garnishing camouflage nets' for the organization, but emphatically did not bear arms.[32] The WVS fitted into the polarization of wartime gender roles, while contributing to it a construction of feminine patriotism which went beyond the passivity of 'watching and waiting' and yet did not challenge the masculine combatant sphere. The WVS was the Home Guard's feminine counterpart. Like the Home Guard it was voluntary and part-time, but while the Home Guard developed military skills and assisted the regular armed forces, members of the Women's Voluntary Service mobilized their domestic skills. The WVS's main roles were to help local authorities cope with problems such as air raids, evacuation and salvage and to provide comforts for troops in transit. In the words of Herbert Morrison in 1943, its members 'were applying the principles of good housekeeping to the job of helping to run the country in its hour of need'.[33] Many members of the government could not understand why such a role did not satisfy Summerskill.

A scheme to supply the Home Guard with a limited number of women auxiliaries on the WVS pattern was drawn up by the Director-General of the Home Guard early in 1942. It was dogged for 12 months by fears within the War Office that it would 'burst its bonds in a very short time', leading to the full integration of women in the Home Guard, and by the objections of rival ministries that it would compete for dwindling supplies of women workers.[34] The campaigners upped the stakes. In January 1942

---

31. *Ibid.*, Minute of meeting between Edith Summerskill and Secretary of State for War, 27 February 1942.
32. *Ibid.*, minutes of 27 December 1940, 15 January 1941, 7 May 1941, 30 June 1941, 11 July 1941.
33. Louise Westwood, 'More than tea and sympathy', *History Today* 48 (1998), p. 3.
34. PRO WO 32/9423, Bovenschen, Permanent Under Secretary for War, 1 April 1942; Ministry of Home Security, 9 December 1941, 16 February 1942, 18 February 1942; Ministry of Labour, 11 March 1942.

Dame Helen Gwynne-Vaughan presented the War Office with a memorial advocating the enrolment of women in the Home Guard, signed by 20 men and women involved in distinguished military and public service (including six Home Guard officers and two leading members of the WVS).[35] Among the memorialists there was a split (just as there was amongst Home Guard commanders) between those who envisaged women contributing as members of an auxiliary, and those like Summerskill who wanted full integration. Summerskill held the two groups together. She kept up the pressure at Question Time in the House of Commons. She asked, for example, why the government was using boy members of the Home Guard, aged only 16, to take the place of ATS on daytime shifts at anti-aircraft sites, rather than using women, and whether the women who were spending their spare time helping the Home Guard would be exempt from compulsory firewatching duties introduced in 1942, as were Home Guard men. She did not receive direct answers, just the stonewalling one that these questions were irrelevant since women were not members of the Home Guard.[36] Summerskill wrote to Grigg in March 1942, on Women's Home Defence letterhead, asking whether in view of a recent appeal by the government to 'every individual to resist the invader if the need arose', Grigg 'would consider raising the ban on the musketry instruction of women by the Home Guard'. She followed this up with a resolution calling for recognition of the Women's Home Defence Corps, passed at a meeting held to celebrate the opening of its 150th unit.[37] In July 1942 the Inter-Parliamentary Home Guard Committee (on which Summerskill sat) voted in favour of women being admitted to the Home Guard for auxiliary duties.[38] Eventually in October 1942 Sir Percy James Grigg conceded that women were providing 'many useful services' to the Home Guard, and that their membership was now 'under discussion'.[39] But it was not until April 1943 that the scheme to admit women to the Home Guard as auxiliaries was implemented.

The context is important. In that month, the war appeared to be hastening forward the cause of the equality of the sexes. Women MPs won a two-year campaign for women to be granted equal compensation with men for war injuries, and the recruitment of women to industry and the forces, including anti-aircraft gunsites, was intensified. With the principle of equality established in one vital area, and such thorough-going involvement of women in the war effort, could objections to women joining the Home Guard really be sustained?

---

35. *Ibid.*, Dame Helen Gwynne-Vaughan to War Office, 21 January 1942.
36. Hansard, 22 October 1942.
37. PRO WO 32/9423, Summerskill to Grigg, 29 March 1942 and 20 April 1942.
38. *Ibid.*, Notes from a meeting of the Inter-Parliamentary Home Guard Committee, 21 July 1942.
39. Hansard, 13 October 1942.

It seemed not, but the concession Sir James Grigg announced was a limited one. It amounted to a watered-down version of the auxiliary scheme, favoured, as we have seen, by some of the commanders and petitioners whom Summerskill marshalled behind her. Summerskill's own preference, shared by others among her supporters, for full equality including the training of women in the use of weapons was not granted. A small number of specially nominated older women would be recruited 'to perform non-combatant duties such as clerical work, cooking and driving'. Women were to be helpers, WVS-style, not sisters in arms. They would not be defending their hearths with hand grenades and revolvers, but enabling men to do so.[40]

Summerskill was known to be critical of any such differentiation between men's and women's roles within the organization, and was jeered at for it in the corridors of power. In correspondence in December 1942 with Herbert Morrison, Minister for Home Security, about Summerskill's demands, Sir James Grigg wrote: 'Most of what you have read in the newspapers on the subject of women in the Home Guard is untrue, particularly that part (nearly the whole in fact) which emanates from our Amazonian colleague Summerskill'. The characterization of Summerskill not only as a liar but also as an 'Amazonian' derided her by analogy with the mythical women warriors from Scythia who cut off a breast the better to fire their arrows.[41] Early in 1943 Morrison (who was one of Summerskill's Labour Party colleagues) responded snidely to Grigg, 'Your critic referred to wants a gun, not a dishcloth. This proposal will appeal to her only if she sees in it a stepping stone to manlier things'.[42] His statement at the same time ridiculed Summerskill for stepping out of line as a woman in her desire for a gun, and communicated contempt for women in general who served in wartime with mere dishcloths.

One of the wartime symbols of active patriotism was military uniform. We have seen that women who joined Home Guard units during the period of prohibition made or bought their own, as did members of Women's Home Defence. We have also seen that opponents of women's entry to the Home Guard, such as Sir Bernard Paget, were particularly vitriolic about the likelihood of women demanding military clothing. The official Women Home Guard Auxiliaries of 1943 were not to be allowed uniforms. They were to be given a 'badge brooch' and that was all.[43]

The Home Guard Auxiliaries' 'badge brooch' became the focus of objections in 1943–44. In August 1943 Summerskill complained that, in the

---

40. *Ibid.*, 20 April 1943.
41. WO 32/9423 P.J. Grigg to Herbert Morrison, Minister of Home Security, 22 December 1942, marked SECRET.
42. *Ibid.*, Herbert Morrison to P.J. Grigg, 6 January 1943.
43. Hansard, 20 April 1943.

absence of a uniform, women Home Guards were driving lorries and going on night exercises in cretonne frocks and high-heeled shoes. She argued that women Home Guards needed uniforms for four reasons: practicality, discipline, to eliminate class distinctions and to bring them under the Geneva Convention, so they would not be shot on sight by the enemy as *francs tireurs*.[44] But Minister without Portfolio, Sir William Jowitt, said women Home Guards could not have uniforms because there wasn't enough cloth.[45] Sir Thomas Moore, the uncertain ally of the 'ladies' nights' suggestion, took up the cause on Summerskill's behalf, conjuring yet more colourful images of women doing masculine tasks in feminine garb. Women were not joining the Home Guard in large enough numbers because there was no uniform for them, not even a steel helmet, he said in March 1944. 'They are given one of the cheapest forms of plastic brooches, which breaks if you touch it . . . these girls would perhaps be driving lorries, taking ammunition to the front, while attired in flimsy chiffon frocks. This sort of thing is ridiculous.'[46] All the War Office would say was that women had all the protection they needed.[47]

In March 1944 a different issue concerning uniforms was raised. MPs became aware that women Home Guards had discarded cretonne and chiffon and were wearing uniforms of their own pattern and choice, and questioned whether this variety and individualism was appropriate. Grigg's response was 'I honestly think the best course is to turn the blind eye'.[48] MPs pressed the government on its refusal of official uniforms, when cloth was found for those of a wide variety of wartime women's organizations. Included in this list was the Women's Voluntary Service, which had provided the War Office with the model for the compromise on which it finally settled. But, having allowed women to become Home Guard Auxiliaries, the government seemed to want to forget they were there. Not only were they refused uniforms, they were not allowed to claim any subsistence allowances for their work (unlike the men they were doing it with) and, when the Home Guard was 'stood down' at the end of 1944, they were not to receive certificates like those of the men, signed by the King and thanking them for risking their lives.[49] Under pressure the War Office produced a less glorious certificate for women, signed by Sir James Grigg, the Secretary of State for War who had been so very reluctant to allow them an equal role, thanking them for their loyal service.

---

44. *Ibid.*, 3 August 1943.
45. *Ibid.*
46. *Ibid.*, 2 March 1944.
47. *Ibid.*, 9 May and 16 May 1944.
48. *Ibid.*, 28 March 1944.
49. *Ibid.*, 28 March, 31 October and 7 November 1944.

How can we interpret this story of resistance to women's membership of the Home Guard and refusal of recognition once their presence was permitted? Women Home Guards seem to have had a symbolic importance that far outstripped their numbers, which at the height of recruitment were just 32,000 compared with 1,750,000 men.[50]

The three ways of understanding gender suggested by Joan Scott are helpful.[51] Scott suggests, first, that gender is a vital part of social relationships: the two sexes are socially differentiated as groupings with different types and domains of power, such that, together with other constituents of social relations like 'race', class and age, gender plays a key role in the way people relate to each other, individually and collectively. Second, gender permeates thinking about the way society is organized, and hence culture is saturated with gendered meanings, norms and representations. Third, gender is central to the formation of identity, to the sense of self which it is possible for individuals to acquire.

In terms of wartime social relations, the material pressure of labour shortages in the context of the totality of war pointed to the inclusion of women in a voluntary defensive force. This development might have been simply another aspect of the wartime modifications of gender relations in Britain, caused by the recruitment of women to areas of industrial production and military organization that were usually predominantly male. The resulting instability might have been controlled and contained, as it was in other areas, by the designation of women as temporary substitutes for men (dilutees, auxiliaries). But enduring ways of thinking about gender relations led to implacable resistance to such changes within the Home Guard because, in the specific context of home defence, the logic of women's involvement moved particularly swiftly towards the goal of arming women. As Summerskill understood so clearly, if women were to defend themselves, their homes and their children against an invader, they needed to be trained and equipped with weapons even more than, say, women in the forces repairing aeroplanes or cooking for the troops. But weapons for women were unacceptable in national defence and offence, because the conjunction was incompatible with the dominant contemporary constructions of femininity and masculinity. Femininity meant giving service to combatant men, preferably of a domestic kind. Hence Morrison's gibe against Summerskill: 'she wants a gun not a dishcloth'. The meaning of masculinity in relation to weapons was even less explicitly rendered. No one said 'she wants a penis', but the references to Summerskill's Amazonian qualities and desire for 'manlier things', and the

---

50. Central Statistical Office, *Fighting with Figures* (London, 1995), Table 3.9.
51. J.W. Scott, 'Gender: a useful category of historical analysis', in J.W. Scott, ed., *Feminism and History* (Oxford, 1996).

blanket refusal even to debate whether women might use guns in certain circumstances, suggest that the association of the gun and the phallus lurked deep within the subconscious of the War Office. It seems that allowing women guns would have been tantamount to collective emasculation.[52]

So women were not trained and equipped in the use of weapons, in spite of the growing difficulties of distinguishing between combatants and non-combatants in the Second World War, and the glaring contradictions in terms of female vulnerability which the refusal exposed. Furthermore, eventual acceptance of women in the Home Guard stopped short of acknowledging them as warriors. That social identity could still be denied, above all by the refusal of a uniform, tantamount to an insistence on feminine dress, the cretonne or chiffon of wartime representations of civilian women and of MPs' fantasies.

The argument presented here is not intended to advance the cause of militarism by advocating that women should have an equal place with men in bearing and using ever more horrible weapons. The importance of this history lies in its salience as a wartime situation in which potential for change was resisted in the cause of maintaining, or salvaging, gender stability, and its revelations that, central to thinking about this stability was the maintenance of the masculinity of weaponry. As such the story acts as a case study of the wartime history of gender relations. In this 'case', the potential for a new role for women created by the logic of total war was more completely resisted by the requirement that conventional feminine and masculine identities be maintained, than in other cases.

The story can also be read as a case study of the more general processes by which gender inequalities are reproduced: the trivialization of the issue of equal rights; the denial to women of 'real' membership of the social organization in question and hence of qualifications for equal treatment; the contradictions inherent in the maintenance of gender difference. These are features common to numerous episodes in the history of women. Likewise, women's dual response in this instance is prevalent in women's history more generally. On the one hand women took the initiative in the face of exclusion, creating an unofficial organization with homemade uniforms and clandestine weapons training. On the other hand they complied with the eventual concessions, accepting the limited, non-combatant role reluctantly permitted them. Women's combination of self-help and self-denial in the history of their involvement with the Home Guard represents in microcosm the history of women's simultaneous resistance of and compliance with the gendered power structures that define their place as citizens.

---

52. On the equation of the gun and the phallus see S. Gubar ' "This is my rifle, this is my gun": World War II and the blitz on women', in M.R. Higonnet, J. Jensen *et al.*, eds, *Behind the Lines. Gender and the Two World Wars* (New Haven, CT, 1987), pp. 227–59.

CHAPTER EIGHT

Soldiers in the Shadows:
Women of the French Resistance

MARGARET COLLINS WEITZ

'Madame. If the French army had been composed of women and not men, we Germans would never have gotten to Paris.' Such were the German prosecutor's observations to Agnès Humbert at her trial. The young woman was arrested in spring 1941 for resistance activities. While she was sentenced to five years imprisonment, ten of her group received the death sentence, including three women.[1]

What women did in French resistance to German occupation and the Vichy regime during the Second World War has received little attention from historians. Yet women's participation in that war-within-a-war was considerably greater than their participation in French society at that time.[2] This situation is not unique to France. During recent D-Day commemorations, virtually no mention was made of the Allied women who participated in the campaign.

The comparative invisibility of women in French Resistance history may be attributed in part to the problems inherent in a definition of resistance and to the nature of women's contribution – primarily extensions of their everyday activities such as errands (liaison, transporting supplies and arms), secretarial work (typing clandestine papers and decoding) and hospitality (sheltering and feeding the pursued). Echoing Virginia Woolf we might ask: 'Who has heard of Jean Moulin's sister?' Laura Moulin spent her weekends typing, decoding, and running errands for her famed brother. But she – like

1. Agnès Humbert, *Notre guerre* (Paris, 1946), p. 136. The men were executed while the women had their sentence commuted to life imprisonment.
2. See Henri Noguères, *La vie quotidienne des Résistants: de l'armistice à la Libération* (Paris, 1984). Noguères is the author, with Marcel Degliame-Fouché, of an authoritative five-volume history of the Resistance, *Histoire de la Résistance en France* (Paris, 1967–81).

many women who participated in the French Resistance – does not figure in studies of the Resistance.

The secrecy entailed in clandestine operations made it difficult to grasp their scope and nature, and hindered post-war efforts to write the history of the French Resistance. A related problem was that, by definition, underground movements do not leave written records. It was imperative that only what was absolutely necessary be committed to paper. Even where archival materials on the Resistance exist, access has been a major problem. Moreover, this documentation must be utilized with caution. The prime source for information on women's roles in the Resistance is oral testimony. This remains true even though these accounts may contain errors. This essay is based upon archival research, secondary sources and approximately 80 in-depth interviews utilized for *Sisters in the Resistance: How Women Fought to Free France 1940–1945.*[3]

French Resistance started with the German invasion. Patriotic individuals who could not bear the sight of German soldiers on French soil reacted instinctively. Some also wanted to combat the Vichy regime of Marshal Pétain. For the first two years of the Occupation, the activities of resistance groups consisted largely in making contacts, meeting others to maintain morale and sharing ideas, printing tracts and papers, and laying foundations for future projects.

Although a fair number of French claimed to be members of the Resistance after victory, they were few and far between in the early days of the Occupation. The exact number can never be known, but 220,000 men and women were officially recognized by the post-war government. Among the difficulties inherent in any attempt to write a comprehensive history of the Resistance is that of the many unknown individuals involved. Some died, were overlooked, or just returned to their pre-war lives without their contribution being known – the latter was the case with most women. In addition to those who joined networks or movements, a far larger number helped the Resistance in other ways. Movements developed independently on French soil, while networks were structured and government-sponsored organizations formed to facilitate escapes, gather intelligence, and undertake action of a military nature.

Maquis (clandestine paramilitary groups) were formed on German-occupied French territory, generally in rugged, out-of-the-way locations. With the Allied landings the maquis rose up and joined regular troops. Few women were enrolled in maquis units, but it was largely women and young

---

3. For an extensive bibliography on the French Resistance see Margaret Collins Weitz, *Sisters in the French Resistance: How Women Fought to Free France, 1940–1945* (New York, 1996; paperback, 1998).

girls who supplied the men hidden in the countryside – at great risk to themselves. Without their support the maquis could not have existed. Yet, after the war, these women, like so many other French women involved in underground activities, did not seek official recognition for their voluntary participation, as did their male counterparts. They did not see themselves as veterans. They simply did 'what had to be done'. The theme of self-effacement runs through their testimony.

Women who wanted to work with the Resistance were not always readily accepted. Traditional, largely Catholic France placed much emphasis on the domestic role of women as housewives and mothers, preserving the family unit. That a significant number of French women subscribed to conservative views of women's place in society puts the activities of women in the Resistance in sharper relief. Though perhaps not always cognizant of the wider implications of their commitment, they broke with tradition. Because women in French society of that time were not fully fledged citizens, and hence were not active in a wide range of professions and public spheres, they had difficulty establishing their credentials. But ironically, once admitted, women operatives had a decided advantage in clandestine work because their activities were less subject to public scrutiny.

Few French women held leadership positions in Resistance movements and networks. Berty Albrecht seconded Henri Frenay in organizing the movement Combat. It was she who conceived of and produced the movement's first newsletter, which developed into *Combat*, the major clandestine paper in the southern or unoccupied zone. Lucie Aubrac helped found the movement Libération-Sud and worked on its paper, *Libération*. Marie-Madeleine Fourcade, the only woman to head a major network, served initially as the right hand of commandant Georges Loustaunau-Lacau in setting up the Alliance network sponsored by British Intelligence, which soon had over 3,000 members. When the British appointed Fourcade to replace the network's captured leader, she encountered problems in establishing her authority. French women who wanted to join military or paramilitary organizations also experienced discrimination.

Charles de Gaulle, a professional soldier, viewed resistance from a military perspective, underestimating *résistants'* accomplishments, capabilities and potential. It was not until March 1941 that de Gaulle's group, based in London, first mentioned the Resistance in France. In addition, de Gaulle refused to have any dealings with French groups working for the British and set about organizing networks (*réseaux*), as had the British. Furthermore, as a traditional military leader, de Gaulle had difficulty envisaging women in combat. When he did finally incorporate women into the French Army, it was to release men to fight. In whatever group, women had to deal with stereotypes of women's presumed weaknesses and shortcomings. Most were assigned traditional feminine support roles, for the customary view held that: 'War is a man's affair'.

In her study of *partisanes* and gender politics in Vichy France, historian Paula Schwartz holds that there were few *partisanes*, that is, full-time gun-carrying women fighters in France.[4] For the most part, women in combat or combat-supported positions were PCF (French Communist Party) members or women serving in party organizations, particularly the Francs-Tireurs-et-Partisans (FTP, consisting of irregulars and guerrillas). Communists participated in more unconventional forms of fighting – sabotage and guerrilla attacks – that women could help carry out. Nevertheless, a report at the 1975 Communist-sponsored conference on women in the French Resistance stated specifically that 'an infinitesimal number of women fought with weapons'.[5]

Scarcity of weapons was one factor. Maquis units trained with broom handles while waiting to acquire weapons. In contrast to the situation in Italy or Greece, there was strong prejudice against women bearing arms in France. The PCF did use women liaison agents to deliver weapons and hide them in places where attacks were scheduled. These women were instructed to retrieve the valuable weapons whenever possible. This meant that while the men armed with weapons had at least a plausible chance of defending themselves, the women who carried arms hidden in shopping bags and baby carriages were at greater risk. Women's presence in rural camps was unacceptable. They were assumed to undermine the legitimacy and safety of such groups because supposedly women gossip and cannot keep secrets. And they become intimately involved with the men. Orders were issued in late 1943 to phase out women in the FTP maquis; this was part of a larger effort to bring these groups into a single *professional* national military organization, with an all-male force.

Claude (Georgette) Gérard's background helps explain how she came to the unusual position of head of a maquis. Her father had been wounded fighting in the First World War and died in the post-war period from his war injuries. She notes that when she was young the themes of fatherland (*patrie*), the defence of one's country (*pays*), and the honour of serving one's native land were prominent. Like many from eastern France (in her case, Lorraine), she became convinced in the 1930s that war would soon break out. Deeply regretting that women were not admitted to the army, Gérard decided to study for a degree in engineering so that, even if she could not join the army, she could at least work in a war factory. She studied

---

4. Paula Schwartz, '*Partisanes* and Gender Politics in Vichy France', *French Historical Studies* 16 (1989), pp. 126–50.
5. *Les Femmes dans la Résistance* (Monaco, 1977), p. 245.

engineering while teaching mathematics courses to support herself. As soon as war was declared, Gérard found work as a technician in a metallurgical factory, heading south in the exodus of May 1940 as the French fled the advancing German *Blitzkrieg*.

Gérard's efforts to join the FFL (Free French; later Fighting France) were unsuccessful. By the end of 1940, she had managed to contact an Allied intelligence service and was scouting possible parachute landing spots and furnishing details on German troops for them. In late 1941 she joined Combat as assistant to the head of its paper. Gérard was responsible for printing and publishing a clandestine paper that rapidly reached a print run of 100,000 per month, and later double that. This led to her arrest by Vichy police after a printer had betrayed her. She was not held long, but three weeks later was arrested and released again. She realized she had to leave the area.

Combat assigned her to the Dordogne region to help organize the Secret Army (AS) there. She went from village to village setting up sections, assuring liaison, planning arms raids and sabotage. This was the first time she had visited that part of France.

> I tried to enlist reserve officers for the AS. They all refused. To inspire confidence I didn't let on that I was really in charge. I pretended to represent a male head. When the Resistance movements joined into MUR [Mouvements Unis de Résistance, MUR; *mur* means wall in French] in January 1943, I became regional head for the maquis in seven departments. Because of my experience, Combat offered me several assignments but I chose this one. Until August 1944 I was the only head; then co-head after that date. There was so much to do. Everything had to be organized. I was helped by a male military commander who took the name of *Pierette* [a woman's name; Gérard's resistance pseudonym Claude is unisex; such names were often selected by *résistantes* to conceal their sex]. He handled the military aspects. I was in charge of the organization. By November 1943 the total number in the maquis under me was close to 5,000; divided into camps of 120 at most; hidden in the forests. Arms were parachuted in by the English. We experienced more difficulty getting plastic explosives for sabotage.

Her responsibilities required Gérard to be on the move constantly; by now the Gestapo was hot on her trail. For her own safety she never spent more than one night in the same place. The Militia (the French equivalent of the SS) sent a few men to infiltrate their groups. There were many arrests among the AS and maquis in the region Gérard directed, including her assistant Pierette, who was arrested in December 1943. When the FFI (Free French Forces of the Interior) were formed early in 1944, maquis groups were incorporated into it. Because Gérard was too well known she was sent to head a French intelligence network. Germans arrested her in May 1944 and put her in a Limoges prison. She was recognized and arrested as a maquis leader – not as head of an intelligence network. 'The *least* I can say is that I was very badly treated. If I am alive today it is because of the Liberation. The FFI surrounded and attacked the prison before the departing Germans could massacre us.'

In the early summer of 1944 she went east on a Franco-American intelligence mission, linked to General George Patton's Third Army, headquartered in Luxembourg. As the camps were freed she helped repatriate deportees. Continuing her career with the military, Gérard was given the rank of major when women were integrated into the regular French Army. Although all her previous experience had been in commanding men, she ended up supervising women.[6]

As one of the few women known to have headed a maquis group (and hers was by far the largest) Commandant Gérard's experience was atypical. Since few – either men or women – sought to join de Gaulle in London in the early days, one would assume the welcome mat would have been out for those who wanted to sign on with his fledgling group. Such was not the case, however, for French women who wanted to join the FFL. And, once accepted, they had difficulty convincing their supervisors they could do something other than the usual women's tasks: secretarial and administrative work, nursing, or chauffeuring.

Imaginative improvisation: Jeanne Bohec

Jeanne Bohec of Brittany was trained as a chemist, and wanted to put this expertise at her country's service. She worked in a gunpowder factory in Brest. The workday was ten hours long and the salary very modest, but she was helping her country. When the Germans invaded France in late spring 1940, the lab was moved into a tunnel to escape the bombings. Bohec went to England by boat when she learned German forces were approaching. This was 18 June 1940, the day after Pétain announced that he was suing for an armistice. She was 21. It was a spur-of-the-moment decision; she had little money and not even a coat with her. Bohec was anxious to use her considerable knowledge of nitrates to help the Allied cause. But authorities did not know what to do with her, since the British women's auxiliary had

---

6. Testimony of Claude Gérard, 31 January 1950, from the personal archives of Marie Granet; see also Nicole Chatel, *Des femmes dans la Résistance* (Paris, 1971), pp. 17–18.

no policy on accepting refugees, and de Gaulle's FFL did not yet accept women. For some months she lived with an English family where she babysat and improved her English, all the while becoming more frustrated in her desire to 'do something'.

Having finally come to the realization that Frenchwomen also wanted to volunteer, de Gaulle authorized the formation of a women's corps toward the end of 1940.[7] Bohec was among the first five women accepted into the auxiliary on 6 January 1941. (By the end of the war there were about 4,000 women in the corps.) The French women's volunteer unit was modelled on the Auxiliary Territorial Service (ATS) of the British Army. The women in the FFL contingent ranged in age from 17 to over 50. They came from every social group, and from every French territory. From what she observed, Bohec was not certain that all her compatriots fully accepted the discipline of the corps. Several young women provoked gossip because they appeared overly interested in men. In addition, FFL women replaced the gas masks they were issued with personal effects – the canvas carrying bag became, in effect, a handbag. Some insisted upon wearing silk rather than regulation wool stockings and had their uniforms tailored to fit better. Upon completion of basic training, the women were assimilated into the French forces and assigned to secretarial duties or nursing.

For her part, Bohec was eventually allowed to undertake what the military then considered a man's job. But she had to insist. 'They tried to train me as a nurse's aid', she recalled. 'I hated it. I had chemistry and scientific training and had worked with gunpowder. I hadn't escaped France and joined up just to fold bandages.' She took stenographic lessons but continued to demand a job appropriate to her skills. At last, in 1942, she was promoted to corporal and assigned to a lab where she was the only woman. Her top secret assignment was to find the best ways of undertaking sabotage with chemicals that could be readily purchased in drug stores. To this day the formulas are still secret. The work was extremely dangerous; all the chemists working on the project were hospitalized for burns at one time or another. It was fascinating work, but hard, and still was not the active participation she sought.

Sometime later, she was asked to instruct French agents being dropped into France in the fundamentals of explosives. While the British were sending women agents, the French intelligence service, the BCRA, was not. When she questioned why it would not be possible for her to train men

---

7. Originally called the Corps Féminin, the name was changed within a year. *Corps* means body, as well as formation, and the possible meaning of 'Feminine Body' provoked unwanted humour. The name was changed to the Corps des Volontaires Françaises in November 1942 and then to the Auxilaires Féminins de l'Armée de Terre in 1944.

already in France, the BCRA adamantly maintained that women would not be accepted. But Bohec insisted. 'I kept banging my head against the wall. But then I am from Brittany and Bretons are stubborn. So I asked and asked, to the point where they finally said, all right. I was the first woman to be taken by the BCRA and sent to France.'

This was another top secret assignment, so training was intensive and rigorous. At Sabotage School there were seven in the class – Bohec and six men. They learned how to fire guns (including machine guns), how to become accomplished thieves, how to conduct sabotage. They were also trained in silent killing. The training left her sceptical about her chances against a strong, determined man, but it gave her confidence in her potential and inspired a combative spirit that would be essential. During parachute training Bohec again found herself the only woman in the group. As she was quite petite, she had to have specially made parachute boots and harness. On their first jump she led her classmates out of the plane. The English were fine, she observes. The only discrimination came from the men in the BCRA, who initially did not want women involved.

Bohec was promoted to second-lieutenant upon completion of her training, and placed on a mission to her native Brittany. Her equipment included a purse fitted with a secret compartment. Somehow it did not feel right so she crocheted one for herself. She was disappointed also with the diminutive handgun she was issued – apparently suited to a 'lady'. She threw away her cyanide capsule, deciding that God would help her keep quiet if tortured. Then it was off to France, where she finally was able to parachute on the third attempt. 'I was scared, but less than you might expect. There were so many things to think about that you didn't have time to be afraid.'

The maquis member who met her after she landed did not expect agent Rateau to be a woman – and a young one at that. 'What's going on? They're sending us childen now!' But this was hardly child's play. A male colleague who parachuted into France with her was arrested and shot three weeks later. At least seven female agents who had infiltrated by parachute were captured and executed in the course of the war.

Bohec bought a bicycle (*the* mode of transportation during the war) so she could circulate freely; she cycled to all the neighbouring villages to teach maquis units how to handle weapons and explosives. She also found time to have a suit and dress made. 'Dressing, sleeping, and eating properly, are also elements of clandestine life', she maintains. She worked with the FFI and gave courses in sabotage and clandestine warfare to maquis fighters. She also participated in sabotage missions.

In preparation for the Allied landings, Bohec was assigned to cut a major railway line – part of the Green Plan to disrupt as many railway lines in Normandy as possible. On one occasion, the detonator had been left out of the armament drop so she fashioned one herself. Bohec subsequently joined up with the major Breton maquis near Saint-Marcel and served as their decoder. When the BBC gave the signal for the general insurrection of the maquis, Bohec wanted to get a machine gun and join in the attack on the Germans. The local FFI agreed, but the team that had recently parachuted in did not. As she recalled, they insisted: 'No, this is not a woman's affair'. By this stage, her maquis companions felt differently. They considered her a comrade – one of them. The disagreement reveals the attitudinal differences between the more conventional professional soldiers in uniform, who could not accept the idea of women using guns, and the Resistance – the army of the shadows – which assumed a more pragmatic view, born of circumstances. The latter sometimes allowed women to fight if the situation warranted it.[8]

Finding a role in the Free French: Sonia Eloy

Bohec had specialized training that the resistance military forces eventually saw reason to use, yet she encountered major problems in trying to convince the Free French in London to make use of her training. It was even more difficult for young women without professional training to join the FFL. But they persisted. Sonia Eloy overcame many obstacles before becoming one of de Gaulle's *demoiselles*, or maids of honour. There was precedent in her family for serving the country. Her mother was an American who had been decorated by Marshal Pétain for work on the front in 1917–18. Eloy learned English as a young girl and had visited England and the United States. She was 17 when she took part in the student demonstration on Armistice day in 1940 and was briefly arrested with others. Bowing to family pressure, she left the capital with her mother in late January 1941 – on the last train for American citizens and their dependants.

Once in the United States she tried unsuccessfully to enlist in the FFL. She then tried to enhance her profile by taking political science courses at Smith College and, later, by doing volunteer work for the FFL delegation in New York. She also took flying lessons, but these were interrupted with the advent of the Japanese attack upon Pearl Harbor. Meanwhile, all her letters to the FFL in London went unanswered. She was angry with de Gaulle. At first, he invited the military, engineers, workers, sailors, and aviators to join

---

8. Jeanne Bohec, *La Plastiqueuse à bicyclette* (Paris, 1975) and 'Une femme dans la guerre: du 18 juin 1940 à la Libération', in *Les Femmes dans la Résistance*.

him – everyone, it seemed, but French women. Her desire to make a contribution to the war effort was further impeded by the fact that Great Britain forbade entry to non-essential people, and the United States refused exit visas to women under 25 who wanted to go to countries at war. Eloy was finally accepted into the FFL and in early August 1943 her orders arrived. 'I was to leave for England with four friends. The Liberty ship took 24 days to cross the Atlantic. German submarines attacked almost daily. Ten ships in our convoy were lost.'

In London at last, Eloy signed her formal engagement: 'for the duration of the war plus three months'. A sympathetic female captain allowed her to sign up for the entry exam for liaison officer. Her fondest hope was to be sent back to France on secret missions. Among her qualifications were an excellent memory and native command of English. She was sent for training with the British at Guildford Barracks. There they marched, drilled, and did military exercises. On her return to London she learned that she had been accepted to liaison officers' school.

Because she was young – and without relatives in London – Eloy had to stay at Moncorvo House barracks. She studied under very difficult conditions, with a schedule so tight that she bought a bike to travel between the dormitory and her classes.

> Like the other women candidates in our mixed group – I studied assiduously in order to succeed; memorizing all kinds of military details. We stuffed our heads with figures, acronyms and abbreviations. But my efforts paid off. I scored fifth out of our class of forty-two (and second on the military section). What a relief! Now I was a second-lieutenant.
>
> The practical sessions were varied and sometimes surprising. We worked in kindergardens, maternity clinics, and rehabilitation hospitals for children traumatized by the bombings; in soup kitchens and factories – and in a laundry. We had courses in childcare, first aid, nutrition. We visited a hospital that outfitted amputees. Finally we spent ten days at a large Ford factory where we learned how cars ran; how to care for them; and how to repair them. Each day when we returned to London we had gym sessions.

The women's section of the French liaison mission was now a coherent unit thanks to the efforts of its new head, Captain Claude de Rothschild, an energetic woman who knew how to command obedience and gain respect. Eloy was among the first group of French officers to attend the Civil Affairs Staff College at Wimbledon that trained British officers to work with local French civil authorities. Men and women followed the same programme – with a few exceptions. For instance, only the women were taught how to build outdoor kitchens and prepare meals for an entire school.

The BBC announced that women military would not be sent to France until two months after D-Day. We resigned ourselves for the wait. Then, to the amazement of all – and the consternation of our male colleagues – we women were ordered to prepare to leave for France. They needed us to help with the many civilians in refugee camps. The 28th of June, sixty of us left for France under Captain Rothschild. For security reasons we changed trucks and trains several times. When we got to Newhaven the activity was unbelievable. Ships of all sorts and sizes. Two by two we proceeded to the quay. On seeing us the Tommies whistled and waved. One shouted: 'The war's over boys; they're sending the girls'.

Back in their native land, the French women reported to a British officer. He was furious that the 60 liaison officers they sent him turned out to be 60 women. The British high command and de Gaulle, he concluded, had obviously gone mad. Captain Rothschild calmed him down and he finished by welcoming them. Nearby soldiers who approached soon left, disappointed, when they learned the women were neither canteen nor United Services Organization personnel. The group quickly started work in the town of Bayeux.

After organizing things at Bayeux we were split up and sent to different villages. When our mud-covered vehicle finally made it to our new destination, we once again found an officer angry that he had been sent some women – and young ones at that. He already had eight hundred refugees on his hands 'who didn't even speak English'. We set about organizing life in the camp.

Assignments to other refugee camps followed. At Cavigny near Saint-Lô, a brusque American officer was amazed to discover that the young French female officer spoke English – or rather American – so well. He questioned her further. Her response reveals the reason for many *résistantes'* commitment – a visceral patriotic reaction.

I told him I was nearly twenty-five – which was somewhat exaggerated. When he asked me why I joined the army, I told him that I was in France when the armistice was signed and the Germans marched in. I was revolted and heartsick to see German soldiers walking the streets of Paris – as conquerors. As if Paris belonged to them. To see their black and yellow posters everywhere. To hear them singing as they marched. In short; all that. I couldn't really explain it. It would take too much time. It was a reflex. They were there, *chez nous*, and that was unbearable. I wanted to do something, to serve. That was all.

When Paris was liberated there was a family reunion with many relatives. Eloy had come back after almost four years away. Her father was now a member of the Resistance Committee. The joy of Liberation was short-lived, however. What she describes as a 'hangover' ensued. Communist and non-Communist *résistants* disagreed over how the country should be governed. Eloy was pained to observe that the Parisians considered the war over now that the capital was free, although it went on for many difficult months elsewhere. Parisians seemed absorbed in their personal affairs. For Eloy and the other women liaison members, it was on to Germany to continue setting up camps. She received orders to report to the city of Weimar.

> Colonel Lewis called and asked me to meet him in the hotel bar. He ordered two scotch and sodas for us. I was amazed because I had never seen him drink, and there he was, swallowing his in one gulp. It was his first drink in thirty years he later told me. He needed courage. He had a very difficult assignment to propose. I could honourably refuse. The assignment was Buchenwald. Of course my girls and I will go, I answered. I knew virtually nothing about the camps except that people were mistreated there and dozens died. 'Thousands', he interrupted. 'There are about fifteen to twenty thousand prisoners still in the camp. The Germans kept very good records.' We made plans to visit the camp the next day. When he left I remembered that he didn't tell me about Buchenwald, as he said he would. Later I was to observe that those who had been to the camps did not talk about it.

This tour of inspection gave Eloy the distinction of being the first woman officer to enter Buchenwald. She and her team set about trying to organize the camp. Their primary concern was to save lives. It was a heroic task. When the war ended and the Russians took over the area, Eloy and her team returned to France.

> I left Germany for Paris, and demobilization, and serious things. I was only twenty-three years old yet I felt very *old* and very *wise*. My two years of military life coincided with the brief passage from youth to adulthood. Those two years taught me many things. Above all, to recognize what is important and what is not. I'm glad people are starting to become interested in what women did during that war. General de Gaulle grudgingly acknowledged that women helped 'a little'![9]

---

9. Interview with Sonia Vagliano Eloy, 1985; see also her *Les Demoiselles de Gaulle, 1943–1945* (Paris, 1982).

Conclusion: women as unsung heroes

The women's section of the FFL was organized along traditional military lines. Members were assigned women's work, as befitted their sex. To participate in missions and manoeuvres ran counter to traditional, patriarchal wisdom about women's place in the military. Even when they were assigned to run refugee camps – assignments men found 'beneath their masculine dignity' and did not perform as well – women's presence so close to the troops was not welcome.

Women in the Resistance undertook difficult assignments – from parachuting into enemy-held territory to saving concentration camp survivors. At the end of 1942 the French in Algeria initiated plans for women's sections in automobile transportation, headquarters personnel, and support and health services. An order dated 22 October 1943 authorized a military unit for women between 18 and 45 years of age. The women's auxiliary (Auxilaire Féminin de l'Armée de Terre, AFAT) was created by de Gaulle in January 1944. Thus women's presence in the French Army was institutionalized. Their role? To free men for combat.

Let us briefly consider women's roles in underground movements during the Second World War in several other countries. The presence of Italian women in that country's resistance (directed against Mussolini's regime as well as the Germans) was so pervasive that, as in the case with French women, it would be impossible to quantify it or describe it accurately. Their activities were similar to those of Frenchwomen: sheltering the persecuted, supplying the partisans, sabotaging products destined for Germany. As in France, liaison agents, *staffette*, became the vital link fusing all aspects of Italian resistance. A representative *stafetta* was Andreini Morandi-Michelozzi, a student at the University of Florence. Since she spoke English she was assigned to help British prisoners of war hiding in a nearby village. She visited captured partisans in jail and also distributed *La Libertà*, the journal of the Tuscan Party of Action. The Germans came to the Morandi home when her brother killed a German soldier who had discovered the hiding place of their group's clandestine radio. She was captured and subsequently imprisoned. In prison she was placed in a cell with Orsola Biasutti De Cristoforo, a woman who had worked extensively to help Jews and Allied prisoners.

In contrast to France, there were a considerable number of Italian women partisans. Of the 35,000 women so recognized, 5,000 were imprisoned, 650 were executed or died in combat, and approximately 3,000 were deported to Germany. The first detachment was formed in the mountainous Piedmont region. Ninety-nine women partisans died there. 'For the first time in Italian history large numbers of women were partners with men, fighting together as equals for a common cause', Maria de Blasio Wilhelm maintains.[10]

Resistance in Greece was against both the Germans and the puppet government they established. Repression was harsh. Among women in the Greek Resistance was Hélène Ahrweiler, later a specialist in Byzantine history and Rector of the University of Paris. During the German occupation of Greece she noted secret information on little slips of paper she could swallow if necessary. She learned to memorize or write only the essential points, to distinguish the essential from the superfluous – practices that served her in her professional career.[11]

Eleni Fourtouni's most powerful memories of her childhood in Greece are of women involved in both political action and combat. She saw regiments of women march through her village at dawn and return at night, battle-weary, carrying their dead and wounded. She also saw women executed, their bodies dragged through the village streets. These memories prompted her to write *Greek Women in Resistance* (1986). In the book she retells the experiences of demonstrators such as Maria Karra, a young girl active in the Resistance even though her uncle, with whom she lived in Athens, disapproved. She recounts the story of Levendokaterini from Crete, which the Germans had captured in May 1941, a few weeks after their occupation of Athens. Levendokaterini was a 21-year-old war widow with two children, whom she left to join the partisans. She borrowed a gun from a 75-year-old man, promising him that she would be 'worthy of it'. She kept her promise, helping to free her native land, but was later executed during the civil war that followed the defeat of the Germans.[12]

The resistance exploits of women in Italy and Greece, as throughout occupied Europe, were similar in certain respects to those of Frenchwomen. The major difference was that there were few French women partisans. One possible explanation is that both Italy and Greece attained nationhood in the preceding century, after considerable, non-traditional warfare. France, on the other hand, has a much longer history as a nation and therefore a much more established, and conventional, military tradition.

Historically, French women have helped defend their country and participated in revolutions – from Geneviève holding off Attila and his hordes, to Louise Michel fighting in the Paris Commune uprising, to the best-known

10. Maria de Blasio Wilhelm, *The Other Italy: Italian Resistance in World War II* (New York, 1988), p. 119. See also Lucia Chiavola Birnbaum, *Liberazione della donna: Feminism in Italy* (Middletown, CT, 1986). See also Claudio Pavone's authoritative *Una guerra civile* (Turin, 1992).
11. Hélène Ahrweiler interview, 1984.
12. Eleni Fourtouni, *Greek Women in Resistance* (New Haven, CT, 1986).

figure, Joan of Arc. During the Second World War, French women from all walks of life rendered indispensable services to their country, as they had in the past. There was no sphere of resistance work where women were not present, although the military and maquis did not readily welcome them and few held leadership positions. These volunteers had no weapons and often no relevant training; they had just their enthusiasm and their commitment. There were no precedents for what they did. Once involved, women proved to be extremely flexible and adapted readily. They organized as they went along, one agent frequently serving in different capacities. The problems they faced and the tasks they took on were comparable in many instances with what women face in their daily lives – a factor that made their interventions particularly efficacious. They played many roles.

A striking feature of the *résistantes'* narratives is the repeated use of the expression 'playing a role'. These women often had the opportunity to try out unsuspected acting skills as they changed identities. To escape capture and difficult situations – or just carry out missions – women assumed different personalities and different appearances. They experimented with different styles and make-up. As was mentioned above, feminine appearance remained a prominent concern among many *résistantes* and was important for morale. One woman agent usually not interested in fashionable clothes succumbed and invested in a good coat – without guilt or regret. The woollen coat was her armour, which would help her look better and resist. Another factor that helped was the stereotyped view of *la Française* the enemy held – at least in the early days of the war. Attractive young women were seldom suspected of working in the underground, sometimes even when caught *en flagrant délit*. The accepted view of women's presumed vanity provided cover for those undertaking decidedly non-traditional feminine roles. Some maintain that women adapted more readily and more quickly to illegality and clandestine life than did men, who are generally less flexible. Within French society, male conduct was more codified.

Women in the Resistance had significant obstacles to overcome. They had continually to prove themselves. Female stereotypes did not allow for women to embark upon non-traditional activities – chief among them, fighting the enemy. Once accepted, women did not necessarily find some of the 'men's clubs' to their liking. Marie-Madeleine Fourcade was upset by the infighting and bickering she found among the French groups de Gaulle brought together, but agreed to join them because she was a committed Gaullist (she had earlier worked for the British).[13] Disagreements among

---

13. Interviews with Marie-Madeleine Fourcade, 1983 and 1984. See also her *Noah's Arc* (London, 1973).

résistants, arising from the usual personality conflicts, were often exacerbated if politics was involved. Not having the vote proved an ironic advantage for French women. With the possible exception of some enrolled in the PCF or those committed Socialists, few women had a political agenda.

Living in permanent fear and anxiety required a new kind of courage – a daily heroism. Liaison agents faced possible arrest many times each day, while those who headed their units lived more protected lives. Thus, at the lower rungs of resistance, danger was greatest. Lucie Aubrac felt that farm women who hid parachuted arms had a much more dangerous assignment than she and the men who led hit squads. Her attacks were carefully planned, sudden and short-lived, while the farm women spent months knowing the enemy might discover their arms caches. They had to live daily with that fear.

Women's reactions to weapons varied. While a few became crack shots and experts in explosives, others were not interested in handling weapons. Few women undertook sabotage. It has been suggested that this is a psychological response: women do not like to destroy. Yet some women did volunteer to blow up bridges and factories. If, granted, they were few in number, that was partly because they were seldom given the opportunity. Weapons and explosives were in short supply. They were also unlikely to have the technical training necessary and wartime did not provide the spare time to train them. Jeanne Bohec's background in explosives was unusual.

Another apparent distinction between the sexes was their response to torture. According to network head Fourcade and others, women held up better under torture. None of her female agents broke under torture, while some men did. She believes that menstruation and childbirth condition women to deal with pain and blood. *Résistantes* did not condemn those who talked under torture, although Geneviève de Gaulle was not alone in observing that she did not know what she would have done if she had seen her child or grandchild tortured. There were instances where this occurred and the women remained silent. Some women viewed the German occupation of France in physical terms. It was rape, a violation of their country. They could not remain passive and joined the Resistance.

Young women in the Resistance had to confront problems their male colleagues did not. A serious one was trying to ascertain if the German soldier, policeman, or man eyeing or following them was displaying the *usual* male interest, or was he perhaps tracking them? Obviously this was not easy to discern. To avoid such problems some wore wedding rings, invented fiancés or used other ruses. Trying to explore the issue of sexual activity in the Resistance is difficult for the researcher because of the reticence, modesty and discretion of the women concerned. They were brought up at a time when such things were not discussed, and most are still uncomfortable with the subject, even though the Resistance was not composed of saints. There were serious relationships that led to post-war marriages, on occasion between couples of different social backgrounds who would not have met otherwise. There were also short-lived liaisons due to chance encounters, but it was widely realized that such encounters posed serious security dangers.

By and large, girls in pre-war France accepted the norms of a male-dominated society and its role assignments. But young women who chose to work for the Resistance did many things that were out of character for their milieu. A major discovery was that of self. Pursuing assignments, young *résistantes* found unexpected resources and aptitudes. During their wandering, gypsy-like existence, liaison agents undertook activities and savoured a freedom of movement not always possible previously. They enjoyed independence from their families and assumed new identities and occupations as they led new lives – lives that went against tradition. They helped disprove the contention of Vichy and the Church that Frenchwomen were 'spoiled'.

All the women who participated in the Resistance acknowledge that their lives were changed by that experience, although changes differ from one individual to another. For many the intense experience of the Resistance was the high point of their lives, as well as one of self-discovery. Yet, as noted Communist *résistante* Marie-Claude Vaillant-Couturier observes, these women were not predestined to be heroines: 'They were women and young girls like others who sought happiness and loved life. But they realized, some immediately, others, little by little, what made happiness impossible; oppression, their country humiliated under the Nazi boot, the loss of liberty.'[14]

---

14. Marie-Louise Coudert, with Paul Hélène, *Elles: La Résistance* (Paris, 1983), p. 18.

CHAPTER NINE

'Do Not Speak of the Services You Rendered': Women Veterans of Aviation in the Soviet Union

REINA PENNINGTON

'Warfare is . . . the one human activity from which women, with the most insignificant exceptions, have always and everywhere stood apart. . . . Women . . . do not fight . . . and they never, in any military sense, fight men.'[1] So writes the eminent military historian John Keegan. It has often been said that one of the first casualties of war is truth – as would appear to be the case here. Women are the 'invisible combatants' of military history in general, and of the Second World War in particular.[2] This chapter examines what happened to one important group of these invisible combatants after the war.

The Soviet Union was the first state to allow women pilots to fly in combat. In October 1941, less than four months after the German invasion, an all-female Aviation Group, No. 122, was formed under the command of the famous pilot Marina Raskova. The 122nd trained the entire personnel – pilots, navigators, mechanics and ground crews – for three new regiments: the 586th Fighter Aviation Regiment, the 587th Bomber Aviation Regiment (later the 125th Guards), and the 588th Night Bomber Aviation Regiment (later the 46th Guards).[3] The women's regiments carried no special designation; they were neither formally called 'women's' regiments, nor were they auxiliaries. The women used standard Soviet flying clothing and equipment; they did not receive uniforms designed for women until 1943. In general, these regiments seem to have been officially regarded as typical military regiments in all respects except their initial recruitment.

1. John Keegan, *A History of Warfare* (New York, 1993), p. 76.
2. D'Ann Campbell, 'Women in combat: the World War II experience in the United States, Great Britain, Germany, and the Soviet Union', *Journal of Military History* 57 (1993), p. 301.
3. A typical regiment consisted of three squadrons of ten aircraft each.

These combat regiments were activated in early 1942, and served until the end of the war. According to Soviet records, they flew a combined total of more than 30,000 combat sorties, produced at least 29 Heroes of the Soviet Union (of the 33 female aviators and 93 total women who received that medal) and included in their ranks at least three fighter aces (despite the fact that the women's fighter regiment was relegated to air defence duties).[4] Two of the regiments received the elite 'Guards' appellation. Despite solid records of combat performance, virtually all women in aviation were demobilized from the Soviet Air Force in 1945. Those who remained were often relegated to lower status jobs and often demoted in rank; some became air traffic controllers or parachute packers.

There is evidence that the performance of Soviet women in combat has been forgotten by the general Soviet public. Anne Griesse and Richard Stites noted that 'for the most part public recognition of women's sacrifices and experiences in war was not played up very much. What was stressed in the postwar years were the new crucial roles for women, for instance, motherhood and the labor force.'[5] This phenomenon of selective amnesia is not unique to the Soviets. Social anthropologist Sharon Macdonald points out that because war is traditionally defined as masculine, women in combat disrupt the social order by their very existence. They are outside the social framework of understanding, and when history is written after the war, their experiences are usually explained away or simply forgotten.[6]

A deeper examination reveals that other factors overrode any considera- tion of wartime performance in the decision to exclude women from the post-war military. This chapter will begin by evaluating the combat per- formance of Soviet women aviators and describing what happened to these women when the war ended. Next, the influence of several important factors on the government's decision to demobilize women and the women's own acquiescence will be discussed; these factors include cultural ideas of gender roles, social policies of pronatalism, and psychological effects of war- weariness. Finally, evidence will be presented that political decisions were made long before the end of the war to bar women from the post-war Soviet military.

---

4. An 'ace' is usually defined as a fighter pilot who has five or more kills.
5. Anne E. Griesse and Richard Stites, 'Russia: revolution and war', in Nancy Loring Goldman, ed., *Female Soldiers – Combatants or Noncombatants?: Historical and Contemporary Perspectives*, (Westport, CT, 1982), p. 79.
6. Sharon Macdonald, 'Drawing the lines – gender, peace and war: an introduction', in Sharon Macdonald *et al.*, eds, *Images of Women in Peace and War* (London, 1987), p. 6.

Combat performance

Before attempting to assess the combat performance of women in aviation, a brief review of the wartime activities of the three 'women's' regiments is in order.[7] The best known, the 46th, was nicknamed the 'night witches' by the Germans. This regiment had one commander throughout the war – Yevdokia Bershanskaia. It was the only one of the three regiments that remained all-female to the end of the war. The 46th flew night bombing missions in the Po-2 biplane – a wood and canvas, open-cockpit relic from the 1920s. These aircraft were not equipped with parachutes or self-defence machine guns until near the end of the war. One test pilot described what it was like to fly the Po-2 in combat: 'It means coming under fire from anti-aircraft weapons of every calibre . . . it means enemy night-fighters, blinding searchlights and often bad weather, too: low clouds, fog, snow, ice, and gales that throw a light aircraft from one wingtip to the other and wrench the controls from your hands. . . . And all this in a Po-2, which is small, slow and as easily set alight as a match.'[8]

The 46th changed airfields frequently, flying from rough, makeshift airstrips very near the front lines. On average nights, the regiment flew 100 sorties, with each crew making 5–10 flights. On occasion the regiment flew more than 300 sorties in a single night; some pilots and navigators completed as many as 17 flights on such nights. One pilot in the 46th ended the war with more than a thousand combat flights. The regiment as a whole completed more than 24,000 combat sorties between 1942 and 1945.[9] According to Polina Gelman, a navigator who earned the Hero of the Soviet Union (HSU) medal for her 860 combat flights, some men tried to get the women to slow down, telling them, 'the less you fly, the longer you'll live'.[10] Casualty rates were high, but normal for a Soviet night bomber regiment; the 46th lost about 27 per cent of its flying personnel.

The 125th Dive Bomber Regiment started the war with a catastrophe. In January 1943, on the way to their first combat base, Marina Raskova, the first commander of the 125th, was killed in a crash during a blizzard. The women feared their regiment would be disbanded and its members

---

7. For a detailed description, see Reina Pennington, 'Wings, women and war: Soviet women's military aviation regiments in the Great Patriotic War' (M.A. thesis, University of South Carolina, 1993), chapter 5: 'The women's combat aviation regiments at war'.

8. Svetlana Alexiyevich, *War's Unwomanly Face* (U voiny – ne zhenskoe litso . . .), trans. Keith Hammond and Lyudmila Lezhneva (Moscow, 1988), p. 153.

9. Irina Rakobolskaia, personal interview, 10 May 1993; Shelley Saywell, *Women in War* (Markham, Ontario, 1985), p. 144; Evgenia Zhigulenko, 'Those magnificent women in their flying machines', *Soviet Life* (May 1990), p. 13.

10. Polina Gelman, letter to author, 28 July 1992.

dispersed. Instead, at the beginning of February, they received a new commander: Valentin Markov. He was an unwilling commander, at first, and the women members of the regiment were resentful that Raskova was replaced by a man. Ultimately, trial by fire bonded them together. Like other dive bomber regiments, the 125th sustained heavy casualties, especially in the winter of 1943–44. To this day, Markov is greatly admired by the women veterans for bringing the regiment through the war. The 125th lost 22 per cent of its flying personnel in the war.[11]

The 586th Fighter Aviation Regiment began combat duty in April 1942, when it was assigned to the Air Defence Forces. It was most active in the middle part of the war, as was typical of air defence regiments.[12] The 586th flew Yak series fighters in varying models throughout the war. Its mission was to protect vital ground targets against enemy attacks, and to provide fighter escort for bombers and transports. The first commander of the 586th was replaced after only six months, apparently for incompetence. Major Alexander Gridnev, a newly released political prisoner, became the second commander of the 586th in October 1942. In the autumn of 1942, when Soviet fighter regiments were increased from two squadrons to three, the 586th received a squadron of male pilots. Very little information about these men has been published. Like Gridnev, they are almost invisible in the official histories.[13]

Altogether, the 586th made more than 9,000 flights, of which 4,419 were considered to be combat sorties. A total of 125 air battles occurred, during which 38 aircraft were shot down (12 fighters, 14 bombers, 1 transport and 11 reconnaissance). A variety of ground targets were also destroyed (including 2 Ju-52 aircraft on the ground, 4 tanks, 30 vehicles, 20 horses and several anti-aircraft sites).[14]

---

11. Casualties were estimated by counting personnel and deaths noted in regimental histories and other sources. For the 46th, my primary source was Evodokia Bershanskaia *et al.*, eds, *46 Gvardeiskii Tamanskii zhenskii aviatsionyi polk* (The 46th Guards Taman Women's Aviation Regiment) (n.p.: Tsentral'nyi Dom Sovetskoi Armii imeni M. v. Frunze, n.d.). Raisa Aronova quotes a figure of 33 casualties, *Nochnye ved'my*, 2nd edn (Moscow, 1980) p. 161. For the 125th, my primary source was V.F. Kravchenko, ed., *125 Gvardeiskii Bombardirovochnyi Aviatsionnyi Borisovskii ordenov Suvoroba i Kutuzova polk imeni Geroia Sovetskogo Soiuza Mariny Raskovoi* (Moscow, 1976).
12. M.A. Kazarinova *et al.*, *V nebe frontovom: sbornik vospominanii sovetskikh letchits-uchastnits Velikoi Otechestvennoi voiny* (In the Sky Above the Front: A Collection of Memoirs of Soviet Women Pilots/Who Participated in the Great Patriotic War), 1st edn (Moscow, 1962), 2nd edn (Moscow, 1971), p. 276; Vera Semenova Murmantseva, *Zhenshchiny v soldatskikh shineliakh* (Women in Soldiers' Overcoats) (Moscow, 1971), p. 49; 'Istrebitel'nogo aviastionnogo zhenskogo polka v Otechestvennoi voine', document in archives of 586th Fighter Aviation Regiment; Steven J. Zaloga, 'Soviet air defence radar in the Second World War', *Journal of Soviet Military Studies* 2 (1988), pp. 104–16.
13. Alexander Vasilevich Gridnev, letter to Klavdia Ivanovna Terekhova-Kasatkina.
14. 'Vypuska iz istoricheskogo formuliara 586 IAP', archives of 586th Fighter Aviation Regiment.

Available sources indicate little or no difference in the numbers and types of missions flown by the women's aviation regiments and other Soviet Air Force regiments. Chief of Staff Irina Rakobolskaia noted that 'nobody made any allowances for our youth or sex. They demanded from us nothing less than from a men's regiment.'[15] Vladimir Lavrinenkov, General-Colonel of Aviation and twice HSU, confirmed that the women flew the same types of missions and performed as well as the men:

> The women pilots served at the airfield on an equal footing with the men. And they even fought no worse than the men. . . . It wasn't easy for the girls at the front. Especially for women fighter-pilots: air combat demanded from them unusual physical strength and endurance. And the fact that the girls without complaining bore all the difficulties is a credit to them, and evoked tremendous respect from those around them.[16]

Markov believed that the women's regiments were treated the same as male regiments, and given the same sort of combat assignments. He even admits that 'there were times, though, when I wished the command would remember that they were women and not throw them into the inferno of fighting'.[17]

A number of women did not survive the war. The Soviets have not published precise figures on women's wartime casualties, but fairly accurate information can be determined from interviews and unit histories. According to a regimental album edited by former commander Bershanskaia, the 46th lost a total of 31 in the war, or approximately 27 per cent of the total flying personnel assigned during the war. Kravchenko's album for the 125th does not give a list of casualties, but mentions the deaths of 22 flying personnel, or about 22 per cent.[18] At least 10 women pilots of the 586th died during the war, or close to 30 per cent.

Awards and decorations also tell us something about combat performance. All personnel of all three regiments were decorated; 29 received the HSU, roughly equivalent to the American Medal of Honor. Although women aviators constituted only a fraction of total women in service, they accounted for nearly one-third of the 93 HSU medals given to women. However, Griesse and Stites made the interesting observation that 'women were congratulated collectively for their wartime efforts, both military and otherwise, while men received recognition as individuals'. Moreover, over half the HSU medals awarded to women were given posthumously (the majority of

---

15. Irina Rakobolskaia, letter to author, 10 August 1992.
16. Vladimir Dmitrievich Lavrinenkov, *Vozvrashchenie v nebo* (Return to the Sky), 2nd edn (Moscow, 1983), pp. 56–7.
17. V.V. Markov, 'Gorzhus' boevymi druz'iami', *V nebe frontovom*, p. 32.
18. Bershanskaia *et al.*, eds, *46 Gvardeiskii*; Kravchenko, ed., *125 Gvardeiskii.*

men who received the HSU were alive), and no woman received the medal more than once (many men were second- and third-time winners).[19]

Available sources indicate that unit cohesion was good to excellent in all three regiments. Another question is that of battle protection – the idea that some men might jeopardize the mission because of their attempts to over-protect women. The sources reveal no cases in which male pilots were more protective of women colleagues than of male pilots in similar situations. On the other hand, several women pilots died while defending a male colleague against attack. The question is difficult, since all pilots bear a mutual responsibility for one another in the air. But in Soviet tactics, leaders have primary responsibility for attacking, while wingmen have primary responsibility for protecting their leaders. When the women pilots flew with men, the men generally had more combat experience and flew as the leaders. Thus it was often the women who performed the role of protector, rather than the men.

In short, while conclusive statistics on combat performance have not been compiled, subjective indicators suggest that the performance of the women's regiments was at least as good as that of comparable male regiments.

Demobilization of women veterans

In autumn 1945, a decree was issued demobilizing all women from military service except for a few specialists.[20] For the most part, women were discharged from the Soviet military very quickly after the war, and were subsequently banned from service academies (virtually the only way to become a military pilot and/or officer in the Soviet Union). A tendency to revert to old hierarchies is common throughout history, and that is precisely what happened in the Soviet Union.[21] There was no change in the cultural perception that, except during emergencies, war (and therefore military service) was simply not women's work.

The rapid demobilization of women from military service and their virtual exclusion thereafter was due largely to pronatalist governmental policies and the need for workers in the civilian sector. Because of heavy wartime casualties and because women were already an essential portion of the workforce before the war, Soviet women had a dual obligation in 1945. While the government stressed that women were 'first and foremost wives

19. Griesse and Stites, 'Russia: revolution and war', p. 78.
20. *Ibid.*
21. Macdonald, 'Drawing the lines', p. 9.

and mothers,' they were also workers; in late 1945, even after many men had been demobilized from service, women made up 63 per cent of the workforce in Moscow.[22]

Information on the post-war fate of women veterans is difficult to obtain. References are scattered throughout memoirs, unit histories, and interviews, but there is no authoritative documentary source. Between 500 and 700 women served in the three 'women's' regiments, plus an undetermined number in the rest of the Soviet Air Force. In their regimental photo albums, the 46th listed 240 personnel and the 125th listed 289. The 586th would have been slightly smaller, since fighters were single-crew aircraft. Approximately one-third of the personnel in the 125th and 586th was male.[23] I compiled information on 77 women veterans of aviation (28 pilots, 15 navigators, 2 gunners, 2 engineers, 24 mechanics and armourers, and 6 staff officers). This group is a random sample, representing perhaps 18 per cent of women veterans of aviation who survived the war. Though not truly representative, it is at least indicative of what happened to the women veterans.[24]

The women veterans were a varied group with widely differing levels of education. Most of the pilots and many of the navigators had been involved in aviation before the war; most were airclub-qualified pilots and many were full-time or part-time instructor pilots in airclubs or at aviation schools. Most pilots and navigators, and some mechanics, had been university-level students at the outbreak of the war. Most of the mechanics were drawn from factories and technical schools. Nearly all these women hoped to return to their old jobs, or complete their education, once the war was over. Many also felt a strong desire to start families, as was usual for Soviet women in their early twenties.

The war took a toll on the health of all veterans, including the women. Health problems resulting from wounds and injuries, illness and stress accounted for many women being denied permission to continue in military service after the war. Pilot Maria Smirnova, who hoped to fly in civil aviation, failed the medical examination. 'I had undermined my physical and mental health at the front; I was completely exhausted by the four years of war and combat.'[25] There appear to be a number of women veterans who were allowed to continue flying in either military or civil aviation for only a year or two after the war, then were declared medically unfit.

---

22. Gregory Malloy Smith, 'The impact of World War II on women, family life, and mores in Moscow, 1941–1945' (Ph.D. dissertation, Stanford University, 1989), p. 333.
23. *Ibid.*
24. The distribution by regiment was as follows: 46th – 22; 125th – 29; 586th – 23; other –3.
25. Anne Noggle, *A Dance with Death: Soviet Airwomen in World War II* (College Station, TX, 1994), p. 37.

Only 12 veterans of the 77 studied remained in military service: nine pilots, one navigator, an engineer and a staff officer. Women who had the best chance of remaining in military service for long-term careers seem to be those who had pre-war service in non-flying positions. Of the flying personnel who continued in the military, half were discharged by 1950. Pilot and HSU Klavdiia Fomicheva stayed in the service after the war, telling her friends, 'I can't think of anything else I would rather do. I plan to stay with the regiment, but if and when it is disbanded – well, there are other units. I can't live without flying.'[26] Fomicheva apparently was sent to the Zhukovsky Academy, where she served as a flight instructor, until a serious illness caused her death.[27]

It was unusual for women to remain in the military; Galina Dzhunkovskaia described a 1949 reunion where she told Fomicheva, 'it seems that you and I are the last Mohicans'. At least five pilots from the 125th (Antonina Skoblikova, Tamara Rusakova, Elena Kulkova-Maliutina, Antonina Bondareva-Spitsina and Fomicheva) plus one navigator (Galina Dzhunkovskaia-Markova) remained in service for at least a few years after the war. At least two fighter pilots from the 586th remained in service (Zoya Pozhidaeva and Olga Yamshchikova). Yamshchikova remained in military aviation as a test pilot, and is often credited in Soviet sources as the first woman to fly a jet (Ann Baumgartner of the United States was actually the first). She is credited with flying more than 50 different aircraft types in over 30 years of flying.[28]

Many of the women veterans had held positions in civil aviation before the war, and many hoped to obtain post-war employment there. However, only a few managed to find positions – 10 out of the 77 in this survey (eight pilots, one navigator and one mechanic). There may have been a preference for women who flew aircraft most similar to those in civil aviation. At least two former fighter pilots found civil aviation jobs. Fighter pilot Klavdiia Pankratova echoed the common belief that fighter pilots were usually rejected by Aeroflot.[29]

A number of women who were unable to remain in the military or to find flying positions in civil aviation ended up in other sorts of aviation-related

---

26. Galina I. Markova, 'Youth under fire: the story of Klavdiya Fomicheva, a woman dive bomber pilot', in Jean Cottam, ed., *Soviet Airwomen in Combat in World War II* (Manhattan, KS, 1983), pp. 126–7.

27. Galina Dzhunkovskaia, 'Vyderzhka i khladnokrovie', *V nebe frontovom*, 1st edn, p. 75; Galina Dzhunkovskaia, 'Komesk', *V nebe frontovom*, 2nd edn, pp. 124–32.

28. Nina Slovokhotova, 'Ot motorista do letchika-ispytatelia', *V nebe frontovom*, 1st edn, p. 218; Alexei Flerovsky, 'Women flyers of fighter planes', *Soviet Life* (May 1975); Liudmila Zabavskaia, 'Women fighter pilots', *Soviet Military Review* (March 1977). See K. Jean Cottam, ed., *In the Sky Above the Front: A Collection of Memoirs of Soviet Air Women Participants in the Great Patriotic War* (Manhattan, KS, 1984), p. 270 note 28; Noggle, *Dance*, p. 170.

29. *Ibid.*, p. 184.

work. Since some of these women had been combat pilots during the war, it appears they loved aviation so much that they were willing to accept low-prestige, low-paying jobs rather than switch careers. Others, like mechanics, simply continued in the same line of work. Tamara Pamiatnykh apparently became an aircraft controller because it allowed her to remain connected with aviation while raising three children and following her husband's military career.[30]

Some of the women returned to university studies taking advanced degrees in science and engineering. Former 46th Guards Chief of Staff Rakobolskaia became a senior professor of physics at Moscow State University (MGU).[31] Former 586th armourer Nina Yermakova remained a mechanic of armament for an aviation plant after the war, she says, 'because I didn't want to give up aviation'. Although the work was 'very hard' and 'mostly manual labour', she worked for 50 years until her retirement.[32]

Of those women who entered professional fields and party work, Gelman returned to MGU, taking degrees in history and training as a military interpreter.[33] The former regimental navigator of the 586th, Azerbaijani Zuleika Seidmamedova, was demobilized after the war, even though she had been a military navigator before the war. Seidmamedova returned to Baku, became involved in party work, and in 1952 became Azerbaijan's Minister of Social Security.[34] Zina Vasil'eva went to a financial technical school and Anya Artem'eva became a pediatrician.[35] Former mechanic Olga Vorontsova became a legal investigator in Volgograd.[36]

Others went to work in factories. Former 586th armourer Anna Shibaeva returned to the medical equipment plant where she had worked before the war, and remained there until her retirement, while mechanic Galina Drobovich worked at a nuclear research institute, and later as a telephone station master.[37] Armourer Anna Kirilina returned to her pre-war occupation in textiles, saying 'as a pilot loves her aircraft, I loved my instrument very much, and when I returned to the plant, entered the room, and saw my textile instrument standing there, I rushed up to it. I was extremely happy that I had returned to peaceful labor.'[38]

30. Noggle, *Dance*, p. 162.
31. Irina Rakobolskaia, personal interview, 10 May 1993.
32. *Ibid.*, pp. 171–2.
33. Polina Vladimirovna Gelman, personal interview, 3 May 1993.
34. Valentina Endakova, 'Letchik-ministr', *V nebe frontovom*, 2nd edn, pp. 363–7.
35. Evgeniia Zapol'nova, 'Neziraia na trudnosti', *V nebe frontovom*, 1st edn, p. 87; L. Ya Eliseeva, 'Sila sovetskogo patriotizma', *V nebe frontovom*, 1st edn, p. 114.
36. Eliseeva, 'Sila sovetskogo patriotizma', p. 114.
37. Noggle, *Dance*, pp. 181, 190.
38. *Ibid.*, pp. 113, 125.

HSU and former 46th pilot Nadia Popova told one interviewer that she did not miss her flying days. 'How could I explain . . . that peace was the only thing we cared about? Not one girl in our regiment chose to remain in the forces. We just wanted to return to a normal life.'[39] Such generalizations must be taken as representative, not authoritative. Smirnova, also a veteran of the 46th, said that 'after the war our regiment was released, and we all wanted to fly in civil aviation'.[40] Some personnel from the 46th did stay in the service.[41] Some – particularly the pilots – clearly regret being forced to leave their flying careers after the war. As late as 1988, former fighter pilot Klavdia Terekhova said, 'My flying was the best thing I've had in life'.[42] Bomber pilot Bondareva-Spitsina, forced to quit flying in 1950, said in 1990: 'I often have dreams about aircraft – of flying. It is my favorite dream.'[43]

Cultural ideas of gender roles

One of the most important factors in the exclusion of women from the post-war military was the fact that gender roles had changed very little. Whatever the reasons for allowing women to fight, the Soviets did not see wartime integration of women into the military as a catalyst for fostering long-term changes in gender roles in society.

The women's aviation regiments received surprisingly little media attention during the war. The 'night witches' of the 46th garnered the most attention from the Soviet media, possibly because the 588th was the only one of the original three women's regiments to remain all-female throughout the war, and so was the only 'true' women's aviation unit. Furthermore, these women pilots were seen as more vulnerable than the others, and so better fitted traditional ideas of gender roles. The 46th flew the outmoded wooden biplane, the Po-2, while the other units flew modern fighters and bombers. The image of women flying this frail little plane into the jaws of death undoubtedly appealed to the press.[44] An American reporter would probably

39. Saywell, *Women in War*, pp. 157–8.
40. Noggle, *Dance*, p. 33.
41. Pilot Serafima Amosova-Taranenko stayed until she was medically retired in 1947. Pilot Mariia Tepikina-Popova flew in civil aviation but was medically discharged in 1948; Noggle, *Dance*, pp. 47, 63.
42. Alexiyevich, *War's Unwomanly Face*, p. 50.
43. Noggle, *Dance*, p. 109.
44. I owe thanks for this idea to the Canadian historian K. Jean Cottam; in her letter to me of 9 April 1991, she suggests that 'praise was heaped and still is almost exclusively on the Po-2 pilots. Is it because they flew more "feminine" aircraft?'

have described them as 'feisty' – an adjective that denotes someone who is full of spirit, but essentially powerless. That the Soviets held this sort of image of the 46th pilots is evident in the title of an *Ogonek* feature article about them: 'Eaglets'.[45] Male pilots also flew the Po-2 in combat, and were often described with the popular bird-of-prey monickers ('falcons', 'eagles') – but never with the diminutive form, which is generally used in situations of patronization.

The frequent use of the term 'girl-pilots' (*devushki-letchiki*) further supports the thesis that the women pilots were not regarded on equal terms with the men; most Soviet pilots during the war were quite young, but the men were never described as 'boy-pilots'. Griesse and Stites found that this distinction applied not just to women pilots but to all women. 'Women were rarely referred to in these wartime years by their functions alone; they were not specialists, fighters, or workers, but women-specialists, women-fighters, or women-workers.'[46] While there was probably no intentional denigration of the women pilots, the terminology is not consistent with the idea that Soviet propaganda tried to portray the women as equal to men.

Macdonald believes that society makes the experience of women warriors acceptable by 'recasting' their stories in one of two ways: either the women are portrayed as unnatural, 'manly' creatures, or else their femininity is stressed and their traditional female virtues are played up while their role in combat is explained as due strictly to exceptional circumstances.[47] The Soviets took the second approach. There was an overwhelming emphasis on how women remained women at the front; a number of the photographs, for example, were obviously staged to fit society's conceptions of how women at war would behave. One woman pilot is shown standing beside her plane in full flight gear, primping before a huge mirror; other photos show the women in dugouts decorated with plants, reading to one another and sewing.[48] While the women did sew in their off-duty time, there is no mention in the memoirs that pilots had mirrors brought to plane-side as part of their pre-flight routine.

The slanders they suffered are further proof of the lack of acceptance of military women, of their failure to change ingrained ideas about gender roles. Women who served in the military were still categorized in many Soviet minds as 'camp followers'. Many Soviet women have reported the stigma they faced as women at the front, both during and after the war. One woman recalled her post-war reception: 'I went [home] as a heroine, never thinking that a girl from the front line could be received the way I was . . . I

45. B. Tseilin, 'Orliata' ('Eaglets'), *Ogonek* 27 (840) (1943).
46. Griesse and Stites, 'Russia: revolution and war', p. 79.
47. Macdonald, 'Drawing the lines', p. 7.
48. Photographs in author's personal collection.

came to know insults, I heard offensive words.' She then recounted the reaction of her new in-laws to their son's front-line marriage: 'Who have you got married to? An army girl. Why, you have two younger sisters. Who will marry them now?'[49] The belief persisted that any woman who went to the front was looking for action in more ways than one.

Gender roles were firmly entrenched in Soviet culture. Many women recall prejudices they faced even before the war, when flying was widely seen as 'not a job for the women'. Bondareva of the 46th recalled that when she joined an airclub in 1936, her father was 'dead against it . . . Until then all the members of my family had been steelworkers . . . My father believed that a woman could be a steelworker but never a pilot.'[50] Marina Chechneva (later a pilot with the 46th and an HSU) described the manner in which her male flying club instructor actively discouraged her from seeking a career as a pilot as being typical of the 1930s:

> Not everyone believed that we would be able to work in this field on an equal basis with men. The example of the famous women pilots did not convince the skeptics. 'Aviation is not a woman's affair', they declared repeatedly, and tried in every way possible to dissuade young women from joining the aeroclub.[51]

If aviation was seen as outside the scope of acceptable women's work, then military aviation was even less acceptable. For example, despite her fame and influence, Raskova met strong resistance over forming the women's regiments. According to A. Skoptsineva:

> It was not easy for Raskova to convince those who came out against her idea for the creation of women's aviation regiments, who tried to prove that war was not a woman's affair. Coming forward on behalf of one thousand women and girls, who appealed to her at the beginning of the war with patriotic letters, Raskova stubbornly demonstrated that if the war had become a nationwide matter, then it was impossible not to reckon with the patriotic feelings of women. . . . Persistence won out.[52]

Many Soviets believed that women should serve in the military only in the most desperate circumstances. Even then, only the persistence of the women themselves forced a temporary expansion of gender roles, one that was almost doomed to snap back and even produce a post-war backlash.

---

49. Alexiyevich, *War's Unwomanly Face*, p. 244.
50. *Ibid.*, p. 29.
51. Marina Chechneva, *Nebo ostaetsia nashim* (The Sky Remains Ours) (Moscow, 1976), pp. 9–10.
52. A. Skopintseva, 'Knigi o ratnykh podvigakh sovetskikh zhenshchin' ('Books On the Feats of Arms of Soviet Women') *Vestnik protivovozdushnoi oborony* (March 1978), p. 89.

One can assume that the women who remained in military flying after the war supported the idea that women should continue to perform combat duties. The 586th pilot Petrochenkova noted that she was 'eager to fly more' but acceded to her husband's and family's demands.[53] Fighter pilot Pankratova, who flew in her husband's regiment during the war but was forced to retire afterwards, said, 'I have the strong belief that it doesn't matter whether it is a woman at the controls; a woman can be a military pilot, she can fulfill combat missions'.[54] In a speech in 1979, former 46th pilot HSU Nina Raspopova said, 'It is necessary to fight for peace not only with words. I also fight physically. I fight as a communist, as a mother of two sons, as a person who knows well what war is like.'[55]

Some women veterans (especially support and former enlisted personnel) nevertheless espouse essentialist arguments that it is simply not in 'women's nature' to participate in war. They often invoke women's role as child-bearer and 'nurturer' as contradictory to any soldiering role. Former mechanic Zoya Malkova, despite volunteering for service, claimed that 'at that time and now, my position is that war is not for women; women shouldn't participate. In a way it's against their nature, because women's first purpose is to preserve peace.'[56] Navigator Akimova of the 46th said that 'the very nature of a woman rejects the idea of fighting. A woman is born to give birth to children, to nurture. Flying combat missions is against our nature.'[57]

However, even those who hold such attitudes do not necessarily believe that women should never fight. Former 46th pilot and HSU Smirnova remarked in 1990, 'was the war a woman's business? Of course not.' On the other hand, she stressed that the 46th outperformed a male Po-2 regiment with which it was based, and she supported women's role in civil aviation. Akimova proudly pointed out that 'at the cornerstones of our history, women were together with men'. She objected primarily to the idea that women should *want* to fight: 'To be in the army in crucial periods is one thing, but to want to be in the military is not quite natural for a woman'.[58] Many veterans of the regiments believe that while women are perfectly capable of military duty, there is simply no necessity for their service in peacetime. 'I think that there is no need for women to serve in military aviation at the present time', said Rakobolskaia. 'Why would they want to? A passion to fly can be satisfied in sport aviation.'[59]

---

53. Noggle, *Dance*, p. 178.
54. *Ibid.*, p. 184.
55. Marina Chechnera *'Lastochki' nad frontom* ('Swallows' Over the Front) (Moscow, 1984), p. 72.
56. Noggle, *Dance*, p. 217.
57. *Ibid.*, pp. 147, 166, 201–2.
58. *Ibid.*, pp. 36–7, 94.
59. Rakobolskaia, letter to author, 10 August 1992.

These attitudes were of course shaped by the culture in which the women lived and by which they were educated. Performance was not the issue; none said women should not be in the military because they could not do the job. Most of the objections are practical. In the Soviet Union, military life was extremely difficult – more so than in many other countries. In a country where the men do notoriously little housework and rarely assist with childcare, the women might find it difficult to imagine combining a military career with a family. It was not enough for the women to change; men had to change too.

In her study of sexual equality in modern Soviet policy, Gail Lapidus found that despite legal and political equalities, there was no evidence that the Soviet government systematically sought to change the social status of women. Lapidus believed many people were misled by the authoritarian nature of the Soviet state into believing that all important developments in society were centrally planned. 'Soviet efforts to alter the position of women have lacked the centrality, coherence, and deliberateness that are often assumed by admirers. Particularly since the 1930s, the position of women in Soviet society has been shaped in fundamental ways by economic and political choices in which a concern for sexual equality has been negligible.'[60]

Pronatalism, family choices

One specific aspect of gender roles that affected women veterans was the traditional Russian stress upon motherhood. Stalin's pronatalist policies of the 1930s were evident in the reduced availability of abortion, virtual absence of birth control, and laws making divorce more difficult and costly. Pronatalist policies were even more pervasive in the post-war years, undoubtedly accelerated by the need to replace the tens of millions of people lost during collectivization, the purges and the war.

Moreover, traditional views of women's role in the family were always strong in the Soviet Union, and perhaps especially so among those who survived the war. Gregory Smith concluded that while the image of women was one of independence early in the war, it changed back to one stressing the importance of motherhood and family by 1944. Smith noted that 'the overwhelming sadness of the era is the most salient feature of the wartime psyche of the Soviet Union, and perhaps this is why people desperately

---

60. Gail Warshofsky Lapidus, 'Sexual equality in Soviet policy: a developmental perspective', in Dorothy Atkinson *et al.*, eds, *Women in Russia*, (Stanford, CA, 1977), p. 117.

clung to tradition, to something comfortable, to the desire to retreat into a solid world, a world of home, family, and personal comfort'.[61]

There was clearly a deliberate policy to downplay the role of women in combat and stress traditional female roles which was implemented long before the end of the war. Smith's analysis shows that the media image of Soviet women as strong and independent peaked in late 1941; as early as 1942, women were given decreasing press coverage every year, and the family was given increasing attention.[62] Olga Mishakova, a member of the editorial board of *Krestianka* and author of several wartime pamphlets about women in the war, wrote in March 1945: 'in the Red Army . . . women very energetically showed themselves as pilots, snipers, submachine gunners [etc.] . . . But they don't forget about their *primary duty* to nation and state, that of *motherhood*' (emphasis added).[63] This statement appeared in *Pravda* and carried the implied official weight of that publication. Mishakova's position was an omen of the pronatalist policies promulgated after the war's end. The August–September 1944 issue of *Rabotnitsa*, the magazine for working women, was dedicated to motherhood.[64] This sort of 'patriotic motherhood' is often associated with 'the determination of political leadership to preserve patriarchy'.[65]

Most Russians still believe that motherhood takes precedence over career, and precludes military work. Even Gridnev, who gave the highest assessment of the skills of the women fighter pilots of his regiment, told me that 'the main calling of a woman is the preservation and increase of the human race' and stated that this was 'obviously' the reason there were so few women in the Soviet military after the war.[66] Rakobolskaia commented, 'I think that during the war, when the fate of our country was being decided, the bringing in of women into aviation was justified. But in peacetime a woman can only fly for sport. That's how it seems to me. Otherwise how can one combine a career with a family and with maternal happiness?'[67] Rakobolskaia, a senior faculty member in physics at MGU for many years, did not seem to find an academic career incompatible with having a family.

In the 1940s, most Soviet men believed that women were morally obligated to give up a career when it came time to bear children. Some women, like Valentina Petrochenkova, were forced by their husbands to choose between family and career. In 1946, Petrochenkova's husband – a test pilot

---

61. Smith, 'Impact of World War II', pp. iv, 342.
62. *Ibid.*, pp. 133–4.
63. Olga Mishakova, 'Sovetskaia zhenshchina velikaia sila', *Pravda* 8 March 1945, p. 3.
64. Smith, 'Impact of World War II', p. 164.
65. Carol R. Berkin and Clara M. Lovett, eds, *Women, War and Revolution* (New York, 1980), p. 212.
66. Gridnev, letter to author, 19 August 1992.
67. Rakobolskaia, letter to author, 10 August 1992.

– gave her an ultimatum: give up flying, or get divorced.[68] Pankratova married another fighter pilot during the war, transferred to his regiment, and flew there for the last year of the war. But after the war, she says, 'it came to who should retire. It was not the men, of course; I was made to retire, and I didn't want to. Later I tried to go into civil aviation, but they hated fighter pilots, they didn't take me. So I had to quit flying.'[69]

Mechanic Nina Karaseva-Buzina married a military pilot and could not work because of frequent transfers. She also noted the concern that wartime work might affect her ability to bear children. 'There was some question as to whether we mechanics could bear children after the heavy work and the overstraining of our strength during the war, but it didn't affect us [even though] we had bad nutrition, never enough sleep, and very hard work.'[70]

Not all women believed that flying and family were mutually exclusive; many of those who continued flying also had children. A few of the women veterans, including Raskova herself, had started families before the war. Maria Akilina, a pilot in the 46th, married and had two children before the war. Her husband, a bomber pilot, was sent to the front the first day of the war; Akilina immediately volunteered and was eventually assigned to the 46th. She was not informed until after the war ended that both of her children and her husband had perished during the war.[71] Pilot Olga Lisikova flew in civil and military aviation since 1937; she flew many missions in sub-zero temperatures during the Soviet-Finnish War in 1939–40, stopping only when she was eight months pregnant. She then became a military pilot after the war began, and tells many proud stories of how she accomplished missions at which men had failed.[72]

Nevertheless, an overwhelming number of the women veterans believe that flying must stop when childbearing begins, and that a woman cannot remain in the military and have a family at the same time.

Planned exclusion of women from the post-war military

Some women wanted to continue flying but simply found it too difficult. If they had faced obstacles in their pursuit of aviation careers before the war,

---

68.   Valentina Petrochenkova-Neminushchaia, personal interview, 9 May 1993.
69.   Noggle, *Dance*, p. 184.
70.   *Ibid.*, p. 86.
71.   Noggle, *Dance*, pp. 97–8.
72.   *Ibid.*, pp. 236–45.

the impediments became entrenched after the war. More than a simple reversion to old societal structures, there seems to have been a retrenchment, even a backlash, against women who sought non-traditional careers. For example, while women had been discouraged from attending academies before the war, after the war they were officially prohibited from enrolling. Griesse and Stites note that Stalin's pre-war policies had already set the tone for the military's attitudes towards women. 'Along with the still officially held doctrine of equality of the sexes . . . arose a kind of conservative reaction in the Stalinist thirties to *actual* equality of the sexes . . . Pronatalist, sexist, and suspicious of spontaneity, Stalinism assured that the Soviet high command would have a deeply ambivalent attitude to the participation of women in the next war.'[73]

Even before the war ended, there were plans to dismantle the 'women's' regiments as soon as peace came, and policies within the military to oust most women from service. Medical reasons were frequently used to prevent otherwise highly qualified women from continuing in service. In March 1945, the regimental commander of the 46th Guards Night Bombers decided to send two pilots – Ekaterina Riabova and Maria Smirnova, both winners of the HSU – to the Zhukovsky Military Aviation Academy in Moscow. Upon their arrival, they were called in by the commanding general for a 'chat'. He told them:

> You are real heroes of our Motherland. You have already proved what Soviet women are capable of when their help is essential. But the conditions of study in a military academy take a heavy toll on the female body. You lost a lot of strength and health in the war. We must protect you. Enrol to study in a civilian university instead.

The girls understood, according to one author, that the friendly general was politely turning them away. Riabova's husband, an Il-2 pilot who won the HSU twice, was sent to the Zhukovsky Academy immediately after the war; apparently his health was not questioned.[74] One might 'logically' assume that the women's health had indeed been undermined by the hardships of war. Yet Riabova was strong enough to complete her undergraduate studies, travel to Italy, Finland, Germany, Korea and Bulgaria on speaking engagements, give birth to a daughter, and enrol in graduate school – all by the end of 1947.[75]

---

73. Griesse and Stites, 'Revolution and war', p. 68.
74. Tat'iana Sumarokova, *Proleti nado mnoi posle boia* (Fly Over Me After the Battle), 1st edn (Moscow, 1988), pp. 89–91.
75. *Ibid.*, pp. 94–5.

Gridnev noted several examples that indicate a plan to diminish the achievements of his regiment and relegate it to post-war obscurity. He believes that certain high-ranking officials in the air defence command pursued an ongoing vendetta against the women fighter pilots, and that women like Khomiakova, Beliaeva and Prokhorova were purposely sent into dangerous and unreasonable circumstances in order to hasten their deaths. Gridnev told me, 'I understood then, and so I understand now, they already had a plan to destroy [them]'.[76]

Smith noted that 'in striking contrast to the US and Britain, where women left the work force in great numbers after the end of the war, more Soviet women than ever started to work in the immediate post-war era'.[77] What was true in the civilian sector was not true in the military, however. Most Soviet women who had been mobilized or had volunteered for military duty were mustered out of military service immediately after the war. Indications are that this was the intention of the Soviet government from the start. The rapid demobilization of women from active duty after the war, and the exclusion of women from service academies since that time, indicate that the Soviets never intended to create an ongoing tradition of military women.

In Stalin's speech of 6 November 1944, when nearly a million women had served at the front, he noted the contribution of Soviet women to the war effort, but did not mention the fact that women had actually participated in combat. On the contrary, he stressed the role of women as supporting the men who did the fighting:

> The matchless labor exploits of the Soviet women . . . will go down forever
> in history; for it is they that have borne the brunt of the work in the
> factories and mills and on the collective and state farms . . . They have
> shown themselves worthy of their fathers and sons, husbands and brothers,
> who are defending their homeland against the German fascist fiends.[78]

The women fliers and other women combatants were also virtually ignored in the writings of the most famous Soviet war correspondents, such as Konstantin Simonov, Vasili Grossman and Ilya Ehrenburg.[79]

In July 1945, President Kalinin spoke to a gathering of recently demobilized women soldiers. Although he acknowledged their strength and heroism,

---

76. Alexander Gridnev, personal interview, 12 May 1993.
77. Smith, 'Impact of World War II', p. 333.
78. Joseph Stalin, *The Great Patriotic War of the Soviet Union* (New York, 1945), pp. 134–5.
79. I examined wartime issues of newspapers such as *Pravda* and *Krasnaia Zvezda*, as well as a large selection of of wartime works and/or memoirs, and found no references to the women aviators (and few, if any, to women in combat).

he made no mention of continued military careers; his main concern was that they quickly find civilian jobs. His final advice to them was:

> Apart from everything else, there is one more thing you have done. Equality for women has existed in our country since the very first day of the October Revolution. But you have won equality for women in yet another sphere: in the defence of your country arms in hand. You have won equal rights for women in a field in which they hitherto have not taken such a direct part. But allow me, as one grown wise with years, to say to you: do not give yourself airs in your future practical work. Do not speak of the services you rendered, let others do it for you. That will be better.[80]

Kalinin's speech is revealing. He claimed the women had 'won equal rights' as soldiers, which implied that the military had become a potential career for women. Yet Kalinin urged the women to forget their combat service as soon as possible. The same man who had pinned the gold star of the HSU on Raskova in 1938 now urged women not even to talk about their combat achievements.[81] It seems unlikely that the same sort of speech was made to male war veterans.

The overwhelming message of Soviet propaganda was that although women could fulfil combat roles when duty called, they were not to expect a permanent career in the military. Their achievements were acknowledged during the war but quickly forgotten or even obscured. Griesse noted that 'what women accomplished earned them credit from other women or in women's journals, and in a once-a-year splash on International Communist Women's Day'. According to Tatyana Mamonova, former editor of the *samizdat* (underground) publication *Woman and Russia*, 'the heroism of Soviet women in World War II, when they distinguished themselves as snipers, fliers, and parachutists, is forgotten'.[82] In a study of Soviet education, a Western scholar confirmed the fact that the Soviets no longer discuss the role of women in combat, or even remember their women heroes. 'Most of the "celebration of women" is essentially a eulogizing of motherhood . . . female heroes are, in large measure, absent . . . One is led to suspect that the failure to honor female heroes . . . is not an oversight but a deliberate policy.'[83]

---

80. M.I. Kalinin, *On Communist Education: Selected Speeches and Articles* (Moscow, 1953), p. 428.

81. Marina Raskova and Ekaterina Migunova, *Zapiski shturmana/Prodolzheniie podviga* (Notes of a Navigator / Continuation of a Brave Deed) (Moscow, 1976); see photo of Raskova and Kalinin, p. 238.

82. Anne E. Griesse, 'Soviet Women and World War II: Mobilization and Combat Policies' (unpublished M.A., University of Georgetown, 1980), p. 81; Tatyana Mamonova, *Russian Women's Studies: Essays on Sexism in Soviet Culture* (New York, 1989), p. 150.

83. Mollie Schwartz Rosenhan, 'Images of male and female in children's readers', in Atkinson *et al.*, eds, *Women in Russia*, pp. 302–3.

Conclusion

Women were never received as part of the Soviet military elite. It is clear that the Soviets regarded the use of women in combat as a temporary measure; even while women were at the front, the Soviets instituted gender segregation in the educational system and the exclusion of women from the newly created Suvorov cadet schools. In 1943, the groundwork was already laid for exclusion of women from the post-war military. It seems apparent that no matter how well women performed in non-traditional combat roles, they could not change ingrained societal ideas of gender roles. Not only was their performance irrelevant to Soviet decision-making about whether to allow women to remain in military service; there is also strong evidence that during the post-war period, the Soviet government deliberately obscured women's wartime achievements.

Nancy Goldman believes that this is 'a phenomenon that was almost universal in the twentieth-century utilization of women'. She draws attention to 'the willingness of the military to use women for the most dangerous missions in the emergency of a desperate struggle and then to demobilize them after the emergency is over'. However, 'even maximum participation in quantity and quality in a combat war situation does not guarantee equality in the service, in other walks of life, or in the postwar society'.[84] Although the Soviets were willing to use women in combat on a much wider scale than other countries when the situation demanded, they also reverted to traditional role models and behaviours as soon as the crisis ended.

Even if Soviet military women had not already been consigned to planned obscurity by the Soviet government, the fact that gender roles had not changed would almost certainly have forced a snapping back of their roles. Any image of the new Soviet woman as military officer and pilot that resulted from wartime experience was far outweighed by the overwhelming official emphasis on the Soviet woman as mother, wife, and builder of society. Where the Americans had Uncle Sam, the Soviets had Mother Russia. Soviet women were constantly reminded – and many believed – that their true place was on the homefront, not the battlefront.

---

84. Goldman, *Female Soldiers*, pp. 8–9.

PART TWO

Sexual Integration in the Military
since 1945

Ambiguity, Contradiction and Possibility

CORINNA PENISTON-BIRD

During the Second World War, Olivia Aykin, who served in the Auxiliary Territorial Services, was taught by a friendly sergeant to shoot. She was one of a very tiny minority of women who were allowed to learn to fire a weapon while serving in the British armed forces. Aykin termed it a 'worth while experience'. She would never be permitted to use her training, which had to be carried out with the utmost secrecy. Aykin was told that if Hitler learned that British women were being trained to use weapons, and especially if any pictures were taken of them doing so, he could use it as propaganda to show that Britain was so short of men that it was necessary to train women.[1] By implication, therefore, the only reason a country might allow its women to be trained killers was if men were scarce and the country was weak. Furthermore, the image of 'a woman and a soldier' was as powerful as the individual herself. Aykin's training was a weapon of war, not because she was learning how to shoot the enemy, but because any photographs shot of her could serve the enemy's cause.

Over 50 years later, the issue of the combatant woman remains topical. Despite the lesson reiterated in the Second World War that women could serve as effectively as men, women's presence in the armed forces often remained more dependent on whether females were required to supplement male numbers than on women's ability to serve. In the Vietnam War, as Karen Turner's chapter in this volume shows, Vietnamese women were only included in the armies after only sons and politically suspect males had been drafted. The case was not dissimilar in the United States. In 1963,

---

1. Olivia C. Aykin (E.O. Scovell), 'Live a little, die a little' (1978), Unpublished Memoir, Imperial War Museum, London, p. 320.

Edmund Fuchs and Charles Hammer published a paper on women's aptitudes for US Army jobs in *Personnel Psychology* which showed that women possessed the aptitude required for a far larger number of non-combat jobs than those to which they were being assigned.[2] In the 1990s the debate has widened to include combat roles. Currently, although American servicewomen can fly combat aircraft and serve on combat ships, they remain excluded from service on submarine duty and some small vessels, and from units that engage in direct ground combat. As the chapters in this volume show, the question of how and where women should best be deployed is still open to discussion.

The image of the woman as soldier also remains loaded. In China, as Susan Rigdon shows, the image of the female soldier was used to promote patriotism and to spur on the troops. As in the Israel Defence Forces, the implication may be that no man would wish to be outdone by a woman. However, the Chinese women singled out for respect – Madame Yang, the magistrate's wife who led troops into battle, for example – represent their role rather than their gender. Emphasis on these exceptional women implies that women largely contributed to service through their emulation of men's roles. Hence recognizing them does not necessitate re-evaluation of the position of women, because they could be viewed as exceptions to, not representatives of, their gender.

The combatant woman can also be relegated to an exceptional category because her role is often clearly defined as temporary. Turner, for example, concludes that Vietnamese legends of the active female participant in war underline that women 'can trespass the boundaries between the private domestic world and the public military realm only temporarily'.[3] The warrior remains an essentially male image, and pinpointing women who have successfully emulated their male counterparts serves to reinforce rather than dispel this image.

As Edward Rielly and Catherine Taylor show, it is not only the soldier but also the related images of the 'veteran' and the 'terrorist' which continue to be identified as male, despite the fact that women too can be found in these categories. In resistance, as in terrorism, the female can take advantage of this perception, gaining protection from the misconception that women are unlikely to be engaged in political violence. Kuwaiti women resisting the Iraqi occupation of their country in 1990–91 could exploit the fact that they were rarely searched at checkpoints and were seldom required to reveal their faces for identification, for example. In the Algerian struggle

---

2. Edmund F. Fuchs and Charles H. Hammer, 'A survey of women's aptitude for army jobs', *Personnel Psychology* 16, 2 (1963), pp. 151–5.
3. Karen Turner, 'Soldiers and symbols: North Vietnamese women and the American war', p. 187.

against the French, women could move more freely in public than men and gain access to the enemy by adopting a Western appearance. As it is their feminity which determines their value to the cause, women's contributions will not necessarily encourage re-examination of traditional gender roles.

As combat status is usually labelled as male, women's contributions in armed struggle have often been in more traditional female roles. Women in the Israel Defence Forces, as Dafna Izraeli argues, perform traditional clerical and personnel tasks, function as 'the personification of wife/mother/ sister' and provide status trophies for the men. In Algeria, women made their greatest contribution to the war of liberation through nursing, providing food and acting as couriers. As Nicole Ladewig emphasizes, the idea that they liberated themselves through active combat is a myth. Even where women have been active in the 'male sphere', this did not make them immune from expectations that they would also continue to perform more traditionally female roles, as Taylor reveals: Patty Hearst pointed out that female comrades in the Symbionese Liberation Army were also there to service the men's needs, while a female member of the Weather Underground could return home from a mission to find a note from a male colleague reminding her to clean the fridge. Even where their sex is not central to the role they are performing, women's activities can be relegated to a female sphere. It is no coincidence that the women's service in the North Vietnamese anti-aircraft defence system was described as weaving 'a fine hairnet of opposition'.[4]

The distinction between the combatant male and the non-combatant female is reinforced not only in terms of symbolism, but also in terms of ideology during war, which encourages a 'masculine' view of men as protectors and a 'feminine' view of women as the protected. In practice, however, the distinction has consistently been eroded. The instability generated by conflict creates opportunities to reform the social order, but the resultant change has often been superficial and easily reversed. In particular, societies have proved resistant to changed perceptions or practice of gender roles. Thus, for example, despite their service, the most respected role for Vietnamese women after the war against America was as mothers. Although the placement of the line between the home and the battle front has been increasingly arbitrary in the twentieth century, the identification of the male as the warrior and protector has proved resilient to re-interpretation. Furthermore, despite the importance (indeed, preponderance) of noncombatant contributions to military actions (scientific and medical research, logistical support etc.), those performing these supporting functions receive

---

4. *Ibid.*, p. 185.

little status through their work. Often this means that women's contributions within the military go unrecognized. The contribution of Vietnamese women labourers who transported supplies during the battles against the French at Dienbienphu in 1954, for example, was ignored in General Vo Nguyen Giap's subsequent accounts. Izraeli shows that, in Israel, women's military roles are perceived as secondary, 'inessential and expendable', while the combat soldier has heroic status.[5]

While the male in logistics may share the status of his fighting counterpart because of sharing his gender, women's contributions are often made within or are rewarded by relegation to the civilian sphere. In China, for example, large numbers of female Red Army veterans were assigned to civilian positions during the war with Korea, despite their pleas to remain on active duty. Even those women who do serve within the military are not accorded membership, despite the fact that, as Rigdon points out, 'it is hard to believe that anyone would refer to a conscripted man performing clerical or support services as not being "in the army" simply because of the duties he was assigned'.[6] Similarly, Turner argues that if, because of the functions they fulfilled, Vietnamese women do not constitute 'real' soldiers, then nearly 90 per cent of the American men who served in Vietnam were not real soldiers either. As Rielly shows, the American female veterans of the Vietnam War are denied entry into traditional support organizations because, as nurses rather than combat soldiers, they are not viewed as genuine veterans. Vietnamese veterans of the same war are trapped by equally restrictive preconceptions on gender, denied a role in post-war society if their service resulted in an inability to reproduce.

For propaganda reasons, it can be important to present the nation as united in opposition to the aggressive outsider. The presence of an external enemy can be used to justify the temporary inclusion of women in the battle against the oppressor, defending the homeland, but this is an inclusion which can lead to contradictory symbols. So in Vietnam, for example, village women were used as symbols of the unsullied spirit of Vietnam in the face of colonial oppression, but also presented as its most vulnerable victims. The distinction in status between the combatant male and the non-combatant female may survive even within an ideology of apparent equality, such as that found in Maoist China. It cannot be assumed that combat experience automatically grants status and equality, regardless of the gender of the combatant. As Kathryn Coughlin shows, for example, although Muslim

---

5. Dafna N. Izraeli, 'Gendering military service in the Israel Defence Forces', p. 256.
6. Susan M. Rigdon, 'Women in China's changing military ethic', p. 281.

women have served on the battlefield in Iran, Iraq, Syria, Indonesia and Nigeria, their field service has not resulted in their necessarily being granted the same political and economic rights as their male counterparts. But as the attempts to discredit Bill Clinton by labelling him a draft evader showed, military service, and more specifically service in the field, remains closely linked to the idea of earned and deserved membership in the nation. In China, no one could rise to the highest level of party leadership who had not served in the Red Army as a field commander or political commissar. In consequence, no women came close to being part of the centre of power. In Israel, again lacking field service, no woman regularly participates in the meetings of the General Staff. Although there were some Vietnamese women in leadership positions, there was fundamental resistance to women in decision-making roles, exemplified by the belief that 'women cannot lead but must be led'.

The combat taboo therefore has implications for professional, social and economic mobility, as well as for citizenship. In Israel, demands that combat experience should no longer hold the weight it does in appointment to senior positions are increasing, especially for positions which do not require such experience. As Lance Janda shows, one argument for opening the United States Military Academy to women was the fact that West Point graduates had an advantage in competing for promotions. It should not be assumed, however, that equal military service is necessarily a signifier of equal gender status. While in the West, equal military service has been seen as a way of achieving equality in other areas also, in other societies equal military service has not automatically translated into equal social or political status, as Coughlin, Ladewig, Izraeli and Turner show. Women in Libya, for example, appear to accept what would constitute a paradox in the West: 'an increasingly conservative Muslim society where women voluntarily veil but serve in the military and in paramilitary organizations'.[7]

In terms of feminist progress, equal rights can easily be equated with equal professional possibilities. Furthermore, it need not constitute a huge step for a woman who has served beside a man to start expecting that she should have the same rights and responsibilities. As Turner concludes, the greatest impact on gender perceptions could result from 'the evaluative gaze' which women directed at their male comrades-in-arms. Yet it is easy to query whether women gain from being integrated in an institution built on principles identified as masculine (competition, power, status) and dependent upon conformity, where they are more likely to be converted than

---

7.   Kathryn Coughlin, 'Women, war and the veil: Muslim women in resistance and combat', p. 233.

convert. As Izraeli argues, 'for men, military achievement enhances their masculinity, while for women it frequently involves a rejection of femininity'.[8] Service as a feminist issue is thus also complicated by the fact that in attempts to transcend the constraints of her gender and find personal fulfilment, a woman may adopt the characteristics of the opposite gender. A pivotal scene in *G.I. Jane* shows the protagonist cutting off her hair as a step towards integration into her unit: her physique increasingly mirrors that of her male peers. While the ritual of head shaving is usually intended to undermine the status of the individual or rob them of their sense of individuality, G.I. Jane seems to believe empowerment comes by *choosing* to conform. She shaves her head herself. Her action is nonetheless a response to her male environment: to empower herself, she must become one of the men. The emphasis in the military on physical equality (such as in the debate over gendered physical standards) underlines the fact that the standards set are male, and even alterations are defined in relation to the male base line. The female body is one which must be overcome for a woman to serve: G.I. Jane ceases to menstruate, the famous Vietnamese rebel Trieu Thi Trinh strapped her large breasts over her shoulder. The change is more than physical: as Izraeli shows, escape from the constraints of 'Israeli feminity' often involves adopting the misogynist attitudes of male counterparts. As the legend of Trieu Thi Trinh implies, women who do not lose their femininity will be betrayed by it: the heroine commits suicide when she finds herself in battle against unwashed ruffians.

The female protagonists in the films discussed in Chapter 18 all indicate in different ways that it is difficult, if not impossible, for a woman to serve beside men in the armed forces as an equal and not sacrifice her identity. In Joan Furey's moving poem 'Camouflage', quoted by Rielly, military fatigues symbolize a combat or veteran identity the poet can no longer reconcile with her post-war sense of self. In 'Vigil' she asks

> And when I leave
> What will I be?
> I can't be what I was before
> I can't be what I am during
> I must be something else.[9]

The 'phenomenon of absence' that Rielly identifies (that is, the absence of women veterans in published poetry) can partly be explained by the failure

---

8. Izraeli, 'Gendering military service', p. 260.
9. Edward Rielly, '"Dark Angel": Vietnam war poetry by American women veterans', in this volume, p. 217.

of the outside world to recognize that veterans can be women. However, it is also a consequence of the fact that the women themselves have difficulty reconciling these identities and understanding how to encompass all the roles they have played.

Conversely, as Turner shows in her discussion of Vietnamese women in the American war, it is possible for women to be far more comfortable with their feminine and martial roles than male observers or public officials are. Experience of service did not automatically lead women to reject a culture in which motherhood is still one of the primary defining roles of women. It is frequently the case that serving women who seek to express some sense of individuality against the conformity imposed within the armed forces have recourse to signifiers of their gender – cosmetics or feminine under-garments. Even within all-female platoons, Vietnamese fighting women would place flowers in their hair 'to try to look nice for a while'. Traditional female clothing can even bestow power, as Coughlin's tale of the Palestinian woman who used her full skirt to hide a man from Israeli soldiers indicates. Attempts to disempower women by robbing them of their clothing can backfire, as French colonial soldiers had to learn in Vietnam. When a female demonstrator's clothing was torn off in order to shame her publicly, her fellow activists tore off their clothes in solidarity and marched off to prison together, *déshabillé*.

The identification of the nation with the home can mean that for serving women, little contradiction is perceived between female roles in peace and at war. As one female Vietnamese veteran put it: 'I had to go out to fight. If my country and my home were destroyed, I would have had no safe place to raise the children I hoped to have someday.'[10] External perceptions are as likely to create the problems for the individual as self-inflicted identity crises: thus in 1965 Ngo Thi Tuyen successfully carried great weights of ammunition defending a strategically important bridge, but hurt her back reproducing her feat for sceptical journalists.

As the case of Shannon Faulkner also showed, there are dangers of identifying a cause with an individual. When Faulkner left the Citadel, the Military College of South Carolina, in August 1995, her withdrawal was presented by the media either as proof that her battle for entry into the all-male institution had resulted in significant damage to equal rights, or that she had been a pawn of feminist organizations. Either way, the central issue of whether both sexes should have the right to enter the Citadel was obscured. Conversely, in his discussion of the admission of women to West Point, the US Military Academy, Lance Janda shows that the 'simple matter

---

10.   Turner, 'Soldiers and symbols', p. 186.

of equality' was not so simple after all, as it had the potential of fundamentally altering the role of US women in the military. There are complex agendas behind the debate over the role women should play in the armed forces. The issue of which posts should be open to women can be interpreted in many different ways: as representing separate spheres, as denying or as supporting feminism, as relating to equality and citizenship. However, it must be remembered that many women seek to fulfil themselves, not to represent their sex.

If servicewomen are striving to express their membership of a collective identity, that identity is more often that of the nation, and informed by patriotism, than it is of their gender, and feminist principles. Ladewig points out that, although interpretations of female participation in the Algerian National Liberation Front have concentrated on a feminist impetus, the perception of the participant women was that they were freeing themselves from colonial oppression, not male dominance. Rather than trying to undermine Algerian traditions, they sought to defend them. It is not beyond governments to manipulate both national and gender identities in their populations. As Turner shows, for example, when Ho Chi Minh wished to mobilize the entire population against the foreign aggressor, he emphasized the poor treatment of women by the French and promised women would gain a better position in an independent socialist nation. However, gender and loyalty to national ideals can easily come into conflict, as the position in which Algerian women find themselves today testifies. As is apparent in many of the chapters here, religious, cultural, national and gender identities do not necessarily form a coherent whole, and individuals move between identities depending upon the context. The ambiguity of the symbolism of the veil is the perfect example of this phenomenon: worn by Algerian women as a symbol of solidarity with Algerian culture, but viewed by the French as a religious statement.

It is clear that gender integration in the military carries with it a host of problems. Explicitly physical, implicitly sexual, the armed forces frequently fail in their attempt to subordinate sexuality.[11] Many institutions have to find some way of encompassing the sexuality of their members, but the military has a particularly complex task because of being an environment in which physical prowess is emphasized. The sexual ramifications of this – for example, the debates over homosexuality in the armed forces, or the impact of gender integration on group cohesion – have proved difficult to resolve. The repeated scandals in the military – from sexual harassment at the 1991

---

11. Jeff Hearn and Wendy Parkin, *'Sex' at 'Work': The Power and Paradox of Organisational Sexuality* (Brighton, 1987), p. 70.

Tailhook Association Convention to the discharge of the first female B-52 pilot, Kelly Flinn, after the revelation of her affair with a married man – have attracted public attention and required the US military to address the related issues of unit cohesiveness and sexual harassment/fraternization through its justice system. While recent Hollywood films on women in the military would appear to imply that, in fiction, gendered standards in the armed forces are uncircumventable, Fred Borch's exploration of the issues involved in the scandal at the Aberdeen Proving Ground in the United States shows that issues which involve both genders need not necessarily be cast in gender terms. In the trial of drill sergeants who had abused their authority and power over female recruits, the application of the 1950 Uniform Code of Military Justice cast the scandal as a criminal offence, rather than a gender issue. This approach was not widely accepted by the general public, which saw this as an attempt by the army to cover up its treatment of women, and the trials showed that the law was not always adequate to cover the circumstances.

However, it is clear that the armed forces cannot afford to fail to adapt as they become gender-integrated, if they do not wish to sacrifice the basic principles upon which discipline and efficiency are predicated, such as unit cohesion. As Borch and Izraeli indicate, where efficacy is the central issue rather than equality, the armed forces can play a leading role in engendering social change. There is an interesting parallel here with Turner's discussion of sexual harassment in the Vietnamese army, which would also imply that when another factor comes into play – for example, morale or inter-dependence – gender divides can be overcome.

When the categories humans create begin to break down, the consequence is contradiction and ambiguity. This can provoke a counter-reaction to stabilize boundaries, but it can also create possibilities for redefinition and change. The chapters in this collection show that, on the one hand, there is considerable consistency and continuity across cultures and periods. Despite the fact that the Israeli military has the reputation of providing a model for emulation, the practice shows that women are not integrated as equals in the armed forces. Women soldiers face the same problems in countries as diverse as the USA, China, Vietnam and Algeria: their contributions are under-valued, the implications of their presence contained, and their possibilities for advancement stifled.

On the other hand, this volume warns against over-simplification. For example, the military is clearly an institution designed to uphold tradition. Essentially conservative, it is resistant to change. But it has also always played a significant part in instigating or contributing to social change – for example, in educating the population, or highlighting such issues as the poor diet of many potential recruits. As Janda and Borch show, military institutions can have a significant impact on gender relations when the law is used to ensure that the military spearheads social change. Another issue which should not be over-simplified is the attitude of the different sexes to the question of what roles women should play in the military. As Janda's chapter highlights, the debate over women's admission to West Point found women speaking out against the proposal, and men speaking for it. The question of women's roles in the military implicates many different identities, and involves an institution clearly associated with specific values. Therefore uniform attitudes within or between genders cannot be expected. As the chapters in this collection show, it is the presence of both consistency and diversity which makes the topic of the soldier woman such a rich area for discussion. The issue of the female soldier provokes discussion not only of military readiness and gender identities, but also of topics as diverse as perceptions of the body, power structures, gendered symbolism, personal and collective identities, the purpose of myths and the power of the media, the confusion of equality with conformity, as well as the consequences of change and resistance to change: ambiguity, contradiction and possibility.

CHAPTER TEN

Soldiers and Symbols: North Vietnamese Women and the American War

KAREN TURNER

Vietnam's veterans of the American War have a great deal to tell the world about women as fighters, leaders, heroes and peacemakers. Official accounts produced in Hanoi since the end of the war point to women's unstinting service, behind the lines and on the battlefields, as a major factor in tipping the balance between defeat and victory in 1975. Describing women's contributions to the American War, veteran and military historian Nguyen Quoc Dung in 1997 feminized the North's wartime anti-aircraft system: 'The American pilots never knew that beneath them, our Vietnamese women had woven a fine hairnet of opposition'. He repeated a common theme in post-war northern Vietnamese reconstructions of history – that women soldiers embodied the very spirit of Vietnam itself. It was the 'simple, modest activities of Vietnamese women . . . using their small guns to shoot and their delicate hands to defuse bombs' that defeated the 'well-fed American pilots in their big heavy planes'. But, despite their real and symbolic contributions to victory, and the admiration of the men who worked and fought alongside them during wartime, Vietnam's fighting women have not been successful in parlaying their extraordinary military service into post-war rights in the home and the workplace. Their choices, and the social pressures that work against them even in the renovation era after 1986, can be understood only in the context of women's roles in patriotic resistance movements throughout Vietnam's long history of struggle against outside aggressors and deeply entrenched beliefs about women's rights and duties to family and community.

I want to acknowledge my debt to my friend and colleague, Hanoi journalist and writer Phan Than Hao, without whom my work on women in Vietnam would never have been possible.

Written and oral sources from post-war Vietnam suggest that women themselves juggled their feminine and martial roles with far more ease than nervous public officials and male observers believed during the war. It is important for our understanding of the Vietnamese side of the American War, and of wartime human relations in general, that disillusionment about the human costs of war and ambivalence about women's proper roles in post-war Vietnam should not overshadow their real accomplishments during wartime.

Symbols

When hundreds of thousands of northern women took up arms to defend the homeland after American air raids began to strike their villages and neighbourhoods after 1966, they harkened not only to Ho Chi Minh's call for an all-out people's war but also to a long tradition of martial women who risked their lives to save the nation and secure their personal stake in the future. As one veteran recalled 30 years later, 'I had no choice. I had to go out to fight. If my country and my home were destroyed, I would have had no safe place to raise the children I hoped to have someday.'[1] Young women saw no contradiction in their decision to enter a masculine world of violence and death in order to realize their most fundamental rights as women.

The relatively high legal and ritual status that Vietnamese women have enjoyed throughout history suggests that a matriarchal kinship system had far deeper roots than the Confucian patriarchy that the Chinese exported to Vietnam in the first century AD.[2] Included among the goddesses whose sites of worship dot the Vietnamese landscape today are warriors who defended the nation against foreign invaders.[3] The most famous cult is devoted to the Trung Queens, two aristocratic sisters who mobilized local forces against the Chinese in AD 40.

---

1. Interview with the author in Hanoi, 1996, and recorded in Karen Turner with Phan Thanh Hao, *Even the Women Must Fight: Memories of War from North Vietnam* (New York, 1998). Unless stated otherwise, interview data comes from the author's three trips to Vietnam in 1993, 1996 and 1997. In some cases, names have been changed to protect informants.
2. For a Vietnamese view of the many forms of family relations see Rita Liljestrom and Tuong Lai, eds, *Sociological Studies on the Vietnamese Family* (Hanoi, 1991). See also John Whitmore, 'Social organization and Confucian thought in Vietnam', *Journal of Southeast Asia Studies* 60 (1984), pp. 296–306, and Ngo Vinh Long, *Vietnamese Women in Society and Revoluion*, Vol. 1 (Cambridge, MA, 1974).
3. See the special issue on religions and popular beliefs in Vietnam in *Vietnamese Studies* 3 (1996).

Interpretations of the Trung Queens' motives for fighting have changed to suit national priorities. For example, the reformer Phan Boi Chau (1867–1940), writing in support of a nationalist movement against the French, slanted the story to emphasize the sisters' devotion to a higher patriotic cause. In his representations, these heroines conveniently embody both feminine and martial sensibilities, for he has the elder, Trung Tac, crying over her husband's body in womanly fashion and her younger sister reprimanding her: 'Come now, we can't give way to ordinary female emotions. We've got to go out and take care of military matters.'[4] Whether these elite women took up arms out of familial duty to avenge the death of a husband, or whether they acted to safeguard personal property rights against Chinese attempts to place control of lands in the hands of men, their brave foray into public life ended tragically. After setting up a local court and abolishing Chinese regulations, they committed suicide in AD 43 when the Chinese returned and their own followers deserted them.

The cult that has grown up around these patriotic women and their female lieutenants and the messages that emerge from their story have left a far more lasting impression than has their short-lived regime. In the dominant narrative of the creation of the Vietnamese nation, war comes from outside forces rather than internal divisions. Women's participation in military resistance to these incursions makes sense because indigenous traditions protect their interests far better than foreign policies. These legends also warn women that they can cross the boundaries between the private domestic world and the public military realm only temporarily, and only when the very existence of the nation is threatened. Once a war ends, they must not expect permanent positions of authority but must retreat instead to their proper place within the patriarchal family.

Ambivalence about the martial woman is even more evident in the tales about the famous rebel Trieu Thi Trinh. According to one colourful account, she was an androgynous figure, so beautiful she captivated men, but endowed with exaggerated masculine qualities that frightened them. Nine feet tall, with breasts three feet long, she had a huge appetite and virile physical stamina. Around AD 240, she rode into battle against the Chinese, perched on an elephant, her huge breasts strapped over her shoulder. She killed a troublesome sister-in-law and when her brother ordered her to stay home and mind her own business, she retorted: 'I only want to ride the wind and walk the waves, slay the big whale of the Eastern sea [China], clean up our frontiers and save the people from drowning. Why should I imitate others, bow my head, stoop over and be a slave? Why resign myself

---

4. See David Marr, *Vietnamese Anticolonialism: 1885–1925* (Berkeley, CA, 1971), pp. 153–4.

to menial housework?'[5] According to some stories, her fierce gaze unnerved her enemies but she so feared dirt and chaos that her enemies sent naked, yelling unwashed soldiers into the field to distract her. Her forces panicked, and Lady Trieu killed herself. But her image so haunted the dreams of the victorious Chinese commander that he blamed a pestilence on her, and ordered phallic images placed on doors in the region to mute her power.

When the French colonized Vietnam in the mid-eighteenth century, the Vietnamese faced a modern nation-state whose threat was more dangerous than any earlier Chinese encroachment. As Vietnamese intellectuals searched for the causes of Vietnam's weakness in the face of a Western power, they brought into the open the question of women's oppression as a sign of cultural backwardness. Discourse about women's issues was never, however, simply about women. As historian Hue-Tam Ho Tai argues, 'The Vietnamese woman stood like an emblematic figure against the canvas of tangled meanings and crumbling institutions that colonial society had become'.[6] She warns that mixed emotions about women, who stand for a multiplicity of coded meanings, can all too easily obscure the actual conditions of real women.

Anti-French Vietnamese intellectuals portrayed the autonomous villages and their women as representations of the pure untouched spirit of Vietnam, unsullied by their distance from colonial forces – visible signs that the state and the people were not one and the same entity. Or they viewed women as the most oppressed, sullied members of colonial rule, their bodies the objects of colonial atrocities. Ho Chi Minh described hideous acts of violence against women and children and promised better conditions for women in an independent, socialist nation.[7] The anti-colonial and anti-Japanese campaigns during the Second World War militarized large numbers of Vietnamese women, not just elite women as in the past, but ordinary women as well. A few flamboyant heroines appear, women like Duong Thi An, who donned a uniform and rode a horse in an army on its way to liberate Hanoi. She knew full well that her actions evoked a potent tradition, as her later reflections reveal: 'Maybe women along the road didn't see a Trung sister on an elephant; yet they were stunned and excited to see a woman handle a horse well'.[8] Most women worked collectively. David Marr describes the spirited defence put up by women in the Nghe-Tinh

---

5. David Marr, *Vietnamese Tradition on Trial: 1920–1945* (Berkeley, CA, 1981), pp. 198–9.
6. See Hue-Tam Ho Tai, *Radicalism and the Origins of the Vietnamese Revolution* (Cambridge, MA, 1992), pp. 90–1.
7. See, for example, 'Annamese Women and French Domination' (a speech made in 1922), in Bernard B. Fall, ed., *Ho Chi Minh on Revolution: Selected Writings, 1920–66* (New York, 1967).
8. Marr, *Vietnamese Tradition*, p. 248.

uprising of the 1930s: 'In one particular confrontation, colonial soldiers tried to break up a demonstration by tearing off the clothes of one female activist in front of her peers. To show that they would not be cowed in this way, other women proceeded to strip off their clothing in solidarity, then marched to jail with the first activist, chanting Communist party slogans en route.'[9] Women's skills as strategists were important in skirmishes against the Japanese. One young peasant woman, Nguyen Thi Hung, inspired in her youth by stories of Lady Trieu and the Trung Queens, described how women carefully planned their attack on a Japanese-controlled rice depot: 'We had to discuss in detail the whole field of battle: the morale of the people, the strength of the guard at the depot . . . then we prepared for the mobilization'.[10] Though women are missing from General Vo Nguyen Giap's accounts of the historic and final battles against the French at Dienbienphu in 1954, they made up a large number of the labourers who hauled supplies to the remote mountain fortress.[11] Not many women joined the regular Viet Minh armies, but the anti-colonial wars provided an ideological and strategic training ground for women.

In 1996, retired artillerywoman, movie star and director Duc Hoan recalled that it was the French who radicalized her:

> I left my home to join the anti-French resistance when I was ten. Bigger than other girls of my age, I was able to convince the authorities for a time that I was old enough. Why did I, a sheltered, bourgeois girl, take such a chance with my life? Because I hated the way that my French Catholic school teachers looked down on the Vietnamese students . . . Because when my mother died, home had no meaning for me anymore. You see, I was the youngest of six daughters and my father was a traditional Confucian man. In 1948, at age 60, he remarried and had a son, and after that, my sisters and I were pretty much on our own.

Raised by a father who expected women to submit their individual needs to the demands of the patriarchal family, Duc Hoan grew up with alternative visions dancing through her head. She remembers being inspired by Vietnam's female heroes. 'The stories of Vietnam's women heroes, the Trung sisters, Lady Trieu, were sung as lullabies by our mothers. We took the fact that women would fight for granted. Our heroines were not always successful in the long run – but they weren't sad, crazy figures like Joan of Arc!' She found the historic French maiden's male attire strange. 'Why would a

---

9. *Ibid.*, p. 245.
10. Mai Thi Lu and Le Thi Nham Tuyet, *Women in Vietnam* (Hanoi, 1978), p. 146.
11. See Vo Nguyen Giap, *Dien Bien Phu* (Hanoi, 1994).

woman want to dress up like a man?' Indeed, Vietnam's women fighters have not hidden their female side. In fact, the women's local guerrilla units that formed to fight the Diem regime in the south after 1960 were proudly named the 'Long Haired Army'.[12]

Duc Hoan's life trajectory would follow both martial and traditionally feminine paths. She served as an interpreter for the Vietnamese armies in China in the early 1950s (she was allowed to work so far from home 'because I didn't have family to worry about me'), learned to shoot a gun and handle combat situations with the E367 Artillery Unit in 1953, then became a movie star who used her extraordinary beauty to play a variety of roles in the service of nationalistic causes. During the American War, she used her talents as an entertainer to boost morale around the most danger-ous southern battlefields. And like women of her generation who played their part in the wars against colonial rule, Duc Hoan served as a role model for younger women: 'I wasn't surprised when my teenaged daughter put on a straw hat and carried a gun'.

Guardians

'The French ate away at our souls', Duc Hoan recalled, 'but the Americans threatened to destroy the very body of our country. During the French wars women could choose to resist, and many did. But during the American war, women had no choice.' As the feminist scholar Cynthia Enloe has noted, 'It takes a lot of power to turn a man into a soldier and a woman into the wife or mother of a martyr'.[13] It takes even more power to militarize a woman, especially in a conservative society that places a woman's ultimate power and well-being squarely within the domestic arena. But when Ho Chi Minh urged the entire population of the North to fight the Americans in 1966, most of his people needed little convincing that they had to play their part if they wanted to save their neighbourhoods and villages from obliteration. The bulk of Vietnamese women contributed to the war effort by taking on men's roles at home. Women kept agricultural and industrial production at pre-war levels and took their turn in the militia and anti-aircraft defence teams. Even though an estimated 1.5 million women never left home, the war profoundly altered their conceptions of gender and work and their future place in society.

---

12. See Tu and Tuyet, *Women in Vietnam*, pp. 180–91.
13. Constance Sullivan, ed., *Feminism, Nationalism, and Militarism* (Washington, DC, 1979), p. 73.

It is difficult to capture accurately the spirit that prevailed in North Vietnam during the early years of the American War, since the requirements of socialist realism dictate the form of so many wartime narratives. Yet oral histories taken from the late 1960s yield clues to how women linked their wartime service with their future hopes. Gerard Chaliand's encounters with farmers in North Vietnam in 1967 aimed to tell the world of the patriotic vigour of the Vietnamese. He recorded several women's stories. A militia woman, for example, noted that she and her teammates felt physically small in the face of big clumsy guns, but, after five days of training, they managed to bring down a US plane. A nurse, who was put in charge of a heavy machine gun team, expressed disdain for the old men 'who don't measure up to us. They can't see well and they aren't agile. So it is the young girls who are in charge of the heavy 37mm anti-aircraft guns.' Another young woman boasted that her team of women shot down four US aircraft and predicted that their expertise will surely liberate them from traditional social constraints:

> There is certainly complete equality between men and women today. I'm not married, but when I do get married I shall choose my own husband. True, men and women were officially equal even before the attacks started. But the spirit which women have shown under fire has won them far more respect than they enjoyed before. Men's attitudes have changed.[14]

This youthful enthusiasm makes sense in light of the responsibilities young women assumed; they not only took charge of defence but village government and production teams as well. But their hopes that war work would bring them equality in the future seem almost tragic in light of later disappointments. Yet remnants of the very real patriotic feeling and youthful energy that took over when everyone pulled together to serve the endangered nation linger on in Vietnam. For example, the many stories that revolve around one of northern Vietnam's most beloved heroes, Ngo Thi Tuyen, a militia woman, show how a personal history becomes tangled up with political agendas. But oral histories taken after the war reveal that she understands that her story serves a purpose, and that she can separate out the propaganda from her real accomplishments even if others cannot. She won fame in 1965 for shouldering 95 kilogrammes of ammunition to supply artillery defending the strategic Dragon's Jaw Bridge, located in her hamlet outside Thanh Hoa city. The bridge itself, the target of continuous American air attacks from 1965 until 1972, stood as a powerful symbol of resistance. Residents of Hanoi today remember how they listened to their radios to

---

14. Gerard Chaliand, *The Peasants of North Vietnam* (Middlesex, 1969), pp. 215, 232, 240.

learn the fate of the bridge, how they felt that as long as the Dragon stood fast, the country would prevail and how the young peasant woman Ngo Thi Tuyen became a symbol of stoic, persistent resistance. But when she was invited to Hanoi to receive her medals, Hanoi leaders tried to play up her feminine charms rather than her accomplishments. She recalled to a Hanoi-based reporter her exploits and her reaction to fame with a mix of pride and embarrassment:

> In 1965, just a few hours after our marriage, my husband was sent to area B [the southern battlefields]. As a militiawoman, I was in charge of transporting ammunition to the regular forces. That very night, the American planes poured bombs into the area and 22 of my comrades in arms were killed. But we had to defend the Dragon's Jaw Bridge at all costs on that terrible night – and we had to keep the trucks going over it on their way to the south. I don't know why I was able to carry those big boxes of ammunition that time. More than once, my strength came from anger and the need to avenge my dead comrades. Later I was interviewed by many journalists. I had to pose for their photos. I was young then and proud of myself. I was even invited to Hanoi to make a speech. It was so nice to be there. But they made me wear the traditional Vietnamese long dress, the *ao dai*, and it was too complicated for me and the high heeled shoes tortured my feet. So I had to hold up my dress to keep it from flopping around and walk barefoot when I finally retreated back to my room in the guest house. And I didn't know how to talk to people in Hanoi – I did not have a high level of education, you know.
>
> [Interview with Phan Thanh Hao, 1991]

Ironically, she was harmed as much by her role as a post-war icon as by her wartime burdens. 'Many foreign journalists from the socialist countries wanted to interview me, and one East German television team didn't believe that I had carried ammunition twice my weight. So to prove it, I had to repeat the feat for them, right in front of the provincial guest house. After that, my back felt funny.'

Today, Ngo Thi Tuyen is a lieutenant-colonel in the regular army, in charge of veterans' affairs for her area. She is disillusioned and angry about the treatment meted out to those who sacrificed so much to win the war. And she is childless, a result she thinks of her back-breaking exploits. Her importance to her countrymen and women has changed. Now it is her barren, broken body that compels pity, and her shoddy treatment at the hands of local party cadre that arouses anger. Yet, Lieutenant-Colonel Ngo Thi Tuyen reminds visitors to her hamlet, now the site of a museum commemorating the dead, that she and her team shot down their fair share of planes, not out of simple good luck, but because they were well-trained, disciplined fighters.

Fighters

Less is known, even in Hanoi intellectual circles, about the women who left their homes to join the volunteer youth corps (*thanh nien xung phong*), or the regular army of North Vietnam (PVN) as people's soldiers (*bo doi*), or the professional teams recruited for their special skills. The film director Duc Hoan said in 1996 that even the Vietnamese did not understand how terrible it had been for the women who worked on the Ho Chi Minh Trail until a documentary about them came out in the early 1990s. As the stories of these women who lived, fought and worked with men in the jungles and mountains for years at a time become better known, they should dispel any doubts about women's capabilities or their positive influence on men under fire.

Over 60,000 educated women worked as engineers, reporters, doctors and communications operators on the Ho Chi Minh Trail and the southern battlefields. The largest number entered the army through the volunteer youth corps, and most of them were recruited from the rural areas outside the North's major cities. The party's first appeal to northern youth came on 21 June 1965, when the government issued Directive 71 to establish an 'Anti-US National Salvation Assault Youth Unit'. Historians estimate that at least 50,000 young men and women signed on. It was Ho Chi Minh's personal appeal on 16 July 1966 (and the Christmas bombings in 1972), however, that brought young people into the war in large numbers.[15] When Ho declared in 1966 to his countrymen and women that Vietnam would fight to the end no matter what the odds, and that it would be the spiritual will of the Vietnamese that would win out, young people lied about their ages and signed pledges with their blood to join up. The number of young women who worked in the shock brigades sent to the most dangerous spots along the Ho Chi Minh Trail is a matter of dispute in Hanoi today, but, according to conservative estimates, at least 170,000 youth joined between 1965 and 1973, and at least 70 per cent were women.

Military commanders understood that women presented special problems, but they could not afford to keep them out of the army once only sons and politically suspect men had been drafted. Colonel Le Trong Tam, who directed personnel for Line 559, the military division in charge of the Ho Chi Minh Trail after 1959, regretted the wartime losses of the women he had loved:

---

15. Nguyen Van De, *Than Thanh nien xung phong: phuc vo giao thong van tai thoi chong my* (Hanoi, 1995) and Nguyen Thi Thap, ed., *Lich su phong trao phu nu viet nam*, Vol. 2 (Hanoi, 1981).

We had never planned to use women on the Trail, and we knew very well the risks and hardships for women. In fact, our late President, Ho Chi Minh, cautioned us to watch out for women's welfare and special health needs. But we couldn't spare our able-bodied men after the US expanded the land and air war after 1965.

The women who worked on the Trail became cogs in a huge conveyor belt with one goal only – to keep the supply trucks and marching soldiers on the move to the south. Most received only rudimentary training and signed on for two-year stints. But, in fact, most women stayed on as long as their health held out. Some eventually joined the regular army.

Why did these young women volunteer to leave the relative safety of their homes to enter an unknown world of violence and death? Their reasons for joining echo those expressed by young people anywhere. Some felt the pull of adventure; the lure of freedom from home and village super-vision was all the more attractive if they could save the nation as well. Some hoped that their families would be relieved of yet another mouth to feed in hard times, while others simply went because 'Uncle Ho' had asked for their help. Many young women who in normal times would have been dreaming of a husband and children figured that they had to leave home to save home. As one woman veteran recalled in 1996:

> I was born in Thai Binh Province. My family were farmers. In 1948 my father was killed in the French War. My mother was with child when he died and she raised us four children alone. In 1968, I volunteered to be a people's soldier [bo doi], and I spent five years in the field during the most terrible time of the war. Why? Four people in my family died when the Americans bombed the Hanoi suburbs. I was angry and I believed that what men could do, I could do too. Life was hard. In the jungle, we kept the telephone lines open, and at first, I was homesick and afraid. But I wanted to avenge my family, to kill Americans for what they did. I survived, and when the war was over, my spirits soared. But life was still not easy. My husband is a career military man who served in the south during the American War and then in Cambodia. He carries a bullet in his body and he is not well after so many years in the battlefields.

When assessing her life, however, she placed ultimate value on her family. 'We are lucky, because we have two children, a boy and a girl.' When asked whether it had been hard to return home to domestic life after so much independence during the war, she responded indignantly:

> Why would I not treasure my home? Sure my family would never be the same again. Some were dead, some wounded and sick. But the hope that I would one day raise children in a safe place kept me alive. It was what I

was fighting for. And I was lucky. I survived when so many others died. I have children, when so many stay alone.

It is well known that the US–Vietnam War was not waged in a conventional fashion, with a distinct battlefront where combat took place and a rear that remained safe. In a people's war fought on the homeland, everyone was both potential victim and combatant.[16] Moreover, if one were to argue that the women who lived in tunnels operating communication equipment, or tended the wounded in jungle hospitals, or defused bombs on the Ho Chi Minh Trail, did not really face combat and were therefore not 'real' soldiers, then we must accept that most American men who served were not combatants either. The Vietnamese nevertheless did have a distinct idea of the dangerous spots where fighting was most fierce – the area around the Dragon's Jaw Bridge, the 'southern battlefields' south of the Demilitarized Zone, the hotly contested choke points on the Ho Chi Minh Trail, for example. The men and women sent to these areas are recognized for their extraordinary courage.

When middle-aged veterans remember their journey from home to war, they narrate the experience as a time of transition. One farm woman from Hanoi remembered her passage 30 years earlier:

> We left from a place near here – it was farm land then – on July 17, 1966. We were provided with a knapsack, two sets of uniforms, a pot, and a tin can. When they gave me a shovel and a hoe, I knew we would be road builders. We took the train to Thanh Hoa and started marching from there. We rested by day and walked by night, to avoid the bombs. It was so dark that we had to hold on to the shirt tail of the one in front of us, just like the game we played as children, 'dragons and snakes make a ladder to the clouds'.

After 21 days, this troop of 200 teenaged girls and boys reached their destination in Quang Binh Province, their feet bloody and infected. And there they saw a side of war that was far more systematically destructive than the sporadic attacks on their northern villages.

> We cried. We were so frightened by the bombs, constantly falling down on us, everywhere. We came upon a woman about to give birth. We were all young girls, and we knew nothing about it. There was no one else to help her. When the baby came out the cord was wrapped around its neck. We cut it and the woman stood up, bleeding. The American flares helped us to see. We don't know what happened to her or the baby. As we got closer to

---

16.   See Miriam Cooke, *Women and the War Story* (Berkeley, CA, 1996); Cynthia Enloe, *The Morning After: Sexual Politics at the End of the Cold War* (Berkeley, CA, 1993).

the battlefields, sometimes we came upon dead women, still holding on to dead babies.

And so these young women passed from innocence to adulthood. Once they reached their destinations, they set about their work. Isolated in the jungles and highlands of the Truong Son mountain range that borders Laos, these young people learned quickly to place the needs of the truck drivers and the marching soldiers first, even if that meant skimping on their own food and supplies. Equipped only with the barest essentials, forced to forage for food and at times to manufacture their own shovels and hoes, women tried to maintain decent hygiene and appearance in the wilderness against all odds. Even simple ornaments could prove lethal, one woman remembered:

> When we worked in the daylight, we had to paint our hair ornaments black, because the gleaming metal could attract air fire. We couldn't even dry our white underwear for the same reason. We had to wear damp clothes in that wet jungle. We had no thread to mend our clothes and only two sets of clothing to begin with. When they had worn out, we got down to one set and the men gave us their clothes to wear when we washed our own in the streams.

A woman who chose the army over college described how her all-female platoon hated leeches and snakes, ate out of tin cans with branches for utensils, and yet tried to preserve a normal life: 'We carried books and we read. At night we would try to forget, and write home or read. Sometimes we would put flowers in our hair, to try to look nice for a while. We sang a lot, because we believed that our songs were louder than the bombs.' Mrs Linh, who spent almost ten years underground with a small team of men operating radio equipment, remembered her own efforts to keep sane and clean: 'I tried to maintain some feeling of order and routine in these conditions, which were terrible, especially for women. There were no sanitary supplies, but women's menstrual periods often stopped anyway, because of bad diet and stress.' She recalled that male–female relationships were based on mutual respect and pragmatic needs:

> I lived this way from the age of 18 to 24. The men did the harder physical work and they got sick more easily than the women. We made our own clothes and helped the men with their sewing. Some people couldn't live this way and went mad. Women seemed better able to endure because they are naturally more patient. We gave the men our best rations, because we felt sorry for them. The most terrible time came when two of my male comrades-in-arms starved to death. We couldn't take time out to cook rice because the smoke would attract the planes. Their diet of freshly picked grass wasn't enough to keep them alive.

Linh had a boyfriend at home, and said that she and her teammates would read the one letter he had sent over and over again, because it was the only token they had of the world outside.

When interviewed in 1997, military historian Nguyen Quoc dismissed questions about sexual tensions between men and women in the field as irrelevant to the Vietnamese situation. 'We had no comfort women like the Japanese. People were sick, tired, just trying to survive.' Colonel Le Trong Tam pointed out that, in the decade of peace after 1954 and before the Americans invaded, young people were able to get an education, to read literature and develop romantic ideas. He admitted that romance did happen and that some women did become pregnant. The commanders sent them home, with marriage certificates in some cases, to protect them and their children from ostracism by conservative villagers. When asked about sexual harassment, most people agreed that it did exist – usually behind the lines and almost always when a power differential existed – but rarely among equals in the armies. As one woman said, the morale of the armies and the people back home would have been endangered if young women were routinely harmed by men in the field, and morale was what the Vietnamese armies depended on above all.

The few pieces of evidence from the war that do deal with women as sexual objects show that some men were intrigued by the prospect of female bodies in unlikely places and others worried about the consequences of hard living on the women's health and fertility. More obviously erotic notions about women in war were more likely to be expressed by visitors to the battlefields than by the rank and file. Major-General Phan Trong Tue, during a visit from Hanoi to the Ho Chi Minh Trail, rhapsodized over the 'poetic sight' of the young volunteers' underwear and penned a poem celebrating their 'pink brassieres', 'frail heels' and 'sweet songs'.[17] A common image in memoirs and war literature is that of the young female liaison agent, guiding the truck drivers through difficult terrain by 'floating' through the jungle paths in her white blouse, encouraging the discouraged, tired drivers with her smiles.[18]

Accounts by male observers and veterans focus more often on the loss of women's female qualities than on their ornamental value. A journalist on the trail, for example, noted that young women volunteers who pushed heavily loaded pack bicycles up steep trails had to endure taunts from male

---

17.   Diary entry dated 1965. Translation taken from *Tap chi van nghe quan doi* (Military Literature and Art Review) (Hanoi, 1990). 'Memoirs' hereafter refers to to this version unless stated otherwise.

18.   See, for example, Cao Tien Le, 'The sound of night', in Kevin Bowen and Bruce Weigl, eds, *Writing between the Lines* (Amherst, MA, 1997), pp. 46–50.

soldiers like 'Be careful or you'll destroy your sex'. A male survivor of volunteer youth troop C 814, 200 men and women from the outskirts of Hanoi who enlisted in July 1966, recalled how he had worried about women's health in harsh conditions:

> We men felt sorry for the women. It was harder for them. Sometimes they had to work underwater, moving stones. I was in charge of logistics. I went to find the women one day. I had to be careful to warn them, so they wouldn't be surprised, because they had to take their clothes off to work. These long stretches underwater harmed their health and now they have women's diseases. I know, I am a married man. Some of these women got sick during the war and now they are old and still they have no medicine. Some couldn't marry later, like Mau here.

In the same interview, however, his female comrade Mau emphasized not her physical vulnerability but her endurance and competence with rifles and bombs:

> Most of us carried AK 47s. One time when a bridge had been bombed and there was no time to rebuild it, we used our bodies to hold the planks so the trucks could keep moving. Sometimes people drowned in the mountain streams and rivers. . . . We had different educational levels and we were young. A few had finished secondary school, but the majority was still in primary school. We were divided up along the same lines as the regular army, working in squads of fifteen to twenty people. We had to protect our 15 kilometres of road and that was it. The road came first. We had orders not to run for cover when the bombs came, but to keep on working and to stand up and shoot at the planes.

Mau had more schooling than the others and so was trained on the spot to defuse bombs and land mines. She described how hard it was to learn to deal with each new kind of bomb the USA developed, but that, like typical teenagers, the volunteers made a game out of this dangerous work. She was especially proud of her decision to join a squad of 30 people who volunteered to defuse particularly lethal bombs: 'We had a service, and we asked our comrades to tell our families we had done our duty if we were killed and couldn't tell them ourselves'. The women of volunteer youth troop C 814 wanted it to be known that they had performed men's work with competence. And although the men declared that women suffered because they were women, they did not remember their female comrades-in-arms as creating undue burdens or tensions under fire. In fact, working with women who handled weapons and danger with poise served to deepen the resolve of men to act with similar courage.

The most obviously admiring reports of women's stoic courage often came from soldiers who had just arrived at the hot spots where women worked, or from reporters on the lookout for heroic stories. Road 20 held a special appeal – the youths who worked on it were viewed as romantic, heroic figures. Constructed through rough mountain terrain in Quang Binh Province as an alternative route through the mountain passes on the borders of Laos, it was named for the average age of the youth who built it. A lore grew up around this site, which was one of the most fiercely contested along the Trail. It became a favourite stop for journalists in search of a story to inspire the people back home. Many of the visitors from the rear wrote about the women who fought there, mixing their stories with pity, admiration and anxiety. A reporter painted a vivid picture of young women working together, singing and standing fast as American planes fired rockets. One woman, who had defied orders that she remain behind because of illness, impressed him: 'Judging by the way she held her rifle and the look on her face, I imagined that she thought she could defend the whole . . . area with her small rifle'.[19] A newly arrived soldier reacted strongly to the presence of women in so dangerous a place. 'They were young maidens, and I felt a deep pity for them. Anyway, they are women, just out of seventh grade. They have been here only seven months. Their skin is still smooth and not yet tanned. How beautiful and how youthful they are.' Later, he began to admire them for more than their looks – as he witnessed how they worked with makeshift materials, laughing in the face of hardship. But he could not forget that they were women after all when he noted that they were beginning to look pale and ill and no longer menstruated.

Leaders

Many women worked in all-women squads and platoons, but others fought with men and sometimes took leadership positions. There is no hard data about how many women commanded these small units, but party documents and anecdotal evidence suggest that resistance to women as decision-makers was a serious problem. For example, an article in the Party organ, *Nhan Dan*, from 6 March 1966, exhorts male party members to overcome their belief that 'women cannot lead but must be led'.[20] A party notation on the life history of a woman guerrilla fighter who mobilized and commanded seven

---

19. Memoir of Do Vu, who travelled with the armies during the dry seasons after 1967.
20. The author is Vu Dung.

battles and taught school when not fighting admitted that she was 'brave and diligent', but that she was hot-tempered, quarrelsome and incapable of seeing the larger picture.[21] Some women overcame these prejudices through persistence and competence. A veteran of the regular army who enlisted in 1972 after Nixon renewed bombings in the North gave up her chance of a university education to join the army. Lieutenant Phan Ngoc Anh, now a military librarian and a war widow with a child to raise, was inspired not only by men who fought but also by the young women who had joined the armies and youth corps in 1965 and 1966 during the darkest years of the war. She maintained that she could never be considered a heroine by their standards. But she had no doubts about her own capabilities in the field:

> In all of the companies, there were women like me, between 17 and 18 years old. I thought I would fight. That was why I joined the army. But I was assigned to be a cook. I was angry and disappointed. But after a month, I became a sapper, working with dynamite, filling craters, and rebuilding bridges along Highways 9 and 14. I became the head of a company. There were twelve people under me, all in charge of explosives. We worked in teams of three and we did everything by hand. Most of the time I did not have trouble with the men.

Eventually, the teams worked so well that she did not have to give orders. Her recollections echo those of veterans everywhere, that soldiers in the field eventually work for each other rather than a distant ideal or policy. 'Each of us understood that our life depended on the actions of each and every one of us.' For the Vietnamese, good morale mattered more than physical strength and women's abilities as peacemakers were valued at times. A member of the Women's Union in Thanh Hoa Province laughed when she remembered how men in her platoon had been initially disgruntled when she was ordered to take command, but finally accepted her because she had the ability to get people to work together.

Women did not always succeed in gaining the respect their work merited, even though many had come to equate their ability to take on a man's job with a right to full citizenship. In a very telling account from the field in 1968, a newly arrived male commander revealed how his conception of women's place in war differed from the convictions of the young women in his charge. He met with resistance when he tried to convince a group of seasoned women volunteers to retreat to safer ground when the fighting grew close.

---

21. Document (1967) preserved in the Captured Documents Exploitation Centre (on microfilm in Healey Library, University of Massachusetts, Boston). This was taken from a 35-year-old woman.

I decided to keep only the fittest and to transfer the girls back to the second line. Girls could be good at bookkeeping, handling freight, or even manning anti-aircraft guns. But they would be no match for the Saigon infantry. Sometime earlier, in fact, areas south of Highway 9 had been declared off-limits to women. And several all-women units there had gone on strike against the decision.

The women in his area also refused to retreat, but in the end he forced them to leave. Most telling, however, are the terms in which they protested his decision: 'As human beings, we are not inferior to other people. We are members of the Youth Union. We want to know if you really have a bias against us.'

This story demonstrates how the dichotomy between the male warrior and the female 'protectee' blurs when women work with men as equal partners in war. When women discovered that they could do men's work, they began to believe that they should enjoy men's rights and responsibilities. Even more troubling for conservative men, these women lost their awe of male authority figures. More than one woman commented during interviews in 1996 that she would never be afraid of anything again after what they had endured during the war. The writer Le Minh Khue related how her feelings about stern, authoritarian military commanders changed when they called for their mothers as they died. The war turned traditional gender roles upside down. Men turned to women for support in their weakest moments. Women expressed vengeful threats and carried weapons with the intent of killing an enemy who thwarted their hopes for a peaceful domestic life. Indeed, evidence from the Vietnamese side of the American War suggests that the most dangerous threat to the conception of male valour was not the disruptive presence of women under fire but the evaluative gaze they directed to their male comrades-in-arms.

Mothers

Just after the end of the war, the Vietnamese Women's Union reassured readers in a tract called *Glorious Daughters of Vietnam* that the military authorities had not neglected their duty to socialize women in the field. One story, of a brigade named after Lady Trieu, is constructed to show how even the toughest women, who made their own shovels and hoes, and built a road by moving massive amounts of hard rock, paid attention to domestic skills. 'Classes are regularly held for brigade members, at which they can acquire a general education and learn sewing and embroidery. Brigade 609's idea of a good woman is one who works diligently, fights courageously, shows good morals and is likely to become a good wife and mother.'[22] Here, from the official organization that represented women to the state, we see the dilemma that would vex women veterans after the war.

As Cynthia Enloe has written so perceptively, 'Wars have their endings inside families'.[23] In Vietnam, veterans returned to decimated families and local communities to rebuild their lives in a nation politically unified but economically fragile, culturally divided and isolated from global events. As the focus of attention shifted from outside aggression to internal divisions, the notion of the ideal woman mutated as well. Women fighters had no place in this civilian society in which the unselfish mother, who will replenish the nation through her reproductive power and engender peace within family and community through her moral force, became paramount. This contemporary preoccupation with the moral mother is vividly displayed in the very shape of the museum constructed by the All Vietnam Women's Federation in Hanoi in 1995. In the vestibule, the Amazonian statue holding a baby that stands under a breast-shaped conical ceiling with an elaborate chandelier is described by a young Vietnamese guide as 'the mother of Vietnam, whose milk brings peace and unity to all of her people'.

This obsession with motherhood is not simply the product of an official propaganda effort. Discussions about how a woman must give birth to fulfil her natural function percolate through daily conversation with men and women alike. 'She might be crazy because she has never had a child', is a common observation of the childless woman. The problems faced by barren veterans is the topic of many television stories, fictional accounts and reportage. The brave woman who has lost her hair, her looks and her fertility after years of hard living and exposure to disease and chemical poisons, and the guilty male survivor who admires women veterans but in the end prefers a younger, healthier woman as a wife are stock figures in post-war media productions.[24] The volunteer youth who have never been officially recognized or recompensed for their war service have been taken up by writers who see them as living reminders of the human costs of war and the heartlessness of a corrupt bureaucracy. Some of the local areas that lost young women to the war are using their martyrdom to bargain for advantages from the central government. Women veterans today serve as symbols of the disenfranchised rather than the heroic spirit of the nation at war.

---

22. Vietnam Women's Union, *Glorious Daughters of Vietnam* (Hanoi, 1975).
23. Cynthia Enloe, 'Women after wars: puzzles and warnings', in Kathleen Barry, ed., *Vietnam's Women in Transition* (London, 1996), p. 306. Barry's compilation of short articles mostly by Vietnamese scholars is a very useful source for seeing the sorts of problems that concern Vietnamese women in the 1990s.
24. See, for example, Ngo Ngoc Boi, 'The blanket of scraps', in Rosemary Nguyen, ed. and trans., *Lac Viet* 16 (1997), pp. 96–123.

In the face of official and popular cultural icons and messages that glorify the mother, women veterans cannot forget that, no matter what their wartime accomplishments, in civilian society they will be measured by their reproductive success. These outside pressures often mirror their personal desires. But the terrible irony for so many of those who gave their youth and their most fertile years to the war is that they cannot realize their dream of forming a family in peacetime. It would be a mistake, however, to see women as passive respondents to social constructions of the ideal woman or popular messages about their limited choices. Some women have used the shared assumption that motherhood is a sacred right to fly in the face of government policies and conservative notions of family. Veterans in the countryside admit proudly to having more children than official population control policies dictate. Data is beginning to emerge that document large numbers of women, many of them veterans or childless war widows, who are opting to have children outside marriage. Sociologists who have studied the practice of 'asking for a child' write about single women who pay men with good genes to inseminate them and then sever ties with him once pregnant.[25] Some of these single mothers live in all-female communes in remote areas in conditions of extreme deprivation. Others, however, live within communities in which the fathers of their children are known. Married women view these aggressive single women in search of a child with pity, empathy and unease.[26] And the government has had to recognize the social problems the children in question will face. In fact, in 1986, the state passed a law guaranteeing that these children must be treated as legitimate, full citizens.

Vietnamese women fought the French and the Americans not only for personal security but also to purge their country of outside forces that harmed their well-being. It is especially galling for them to realize that Vietnam's market-oriented global economy has allowed trafficking in women and prostitution to increase. Vietnamese feminists today express disappointment that women are still treated poorly in the workplace and that domestic violence persists in so many families.[27] But they have not yet begun to press for full gender equality within the family – largely because the family still

---

25. See, for example, 'Remarks on women who live without husbands', in Barry, ed., *Vietnam's Women in Transition*, pp. 87–92.

26. Sociological studies by conservative women academics, for example, are remarkably tolerant. Interview data confirm the impression that a general feeling that childless women veterans are owed a debt that can be partially repaid by allowing them to have children out of wedlock prevails in the North. Harriet Phinney, a University of Washington doctoral student, is writing a dissertation based on extensive fieldwork on this phenomenon.

27. See, for example, Le Thi Quy, 'Domestic violence in Vietnam and efforts to curb it', in Barry, ed., *Vietnam's Women in Transition*, pp. 263–74.

stands as their only bulwark in a very uncertain political and economic system, but also because the effects of half a century of almost continuous war have not been erased. Western feminists might well express disappointment that Vietnam's women warriors have not claimed their rights to full equality with vigour, but their choices must be respected in the context of a culture that still views the experience of motherhood as an essential rite of passage to adulthood, a country still so poor that a child is a woman's only security, and a culture that values a woman's sacrifices far more than her personal accomplishments. We can only watch with empathy and respect as women in post-war Vietnam develop their own strategies to find a measure of personal satisfaction just as they so effectively put their ingenuity and quiet courage to work during the war.

CHAPTER ELEVEN

'Dark Angel': Vietnam War Poetry by American Women Veterans

EDWARD J. RIELLY

Women veterans of the Vietnam War are an important if yet largely hidden component of the ever-expanding universe of literature written about the war. To understand their poetic accomplishments, however, requires consideration not only of the poetry but also of the way women veterans have been perceived since the Vietnam War.

Women served in large numbers and in many roles during the war. The numbers remain inexact due to imperfect, if not careless, documentation. The United States Department of Defense, for example, reported that about 7,500 American women were on active military duty in Vietnam during the peak years of American involvement (1962–73); while the Veterans' Administration put the figure at in excess of 11,000. Overall, between 33,000 and 55,000 American women, including both military and civilian, worked in Vietnam during the war years.[1]

Approximately 80 per cent of the military women in Vietnam were nurses, with the vast majority in the army. Army nurses served in hospitals from Quang Tri, within 35 kilometres of the Demilitarized Zone, to the Mekong Delta in the south. Although not directly engaged in combat, nurses in fact experienced the war in very vivid ways as they cared for wounded and dying soldiers. In addition, direct attacks on hospital facilities all too often brought nurses under enemy fire. United States military women,

---

1. Kathryn Marshall, ed., *In the Combat Zone: Vivid Personal Reflections of the Vietnam War from the Women Who Served There* (1987; New York, 1988), p. 4. For another collection of first-person accounts of war experiences by women, see Keith Walker, ed., *A Piece of My Heart: The Stories of Twenty-Six American Women Who Served in Vietnam* (Novato, CA, 1985).

of course, also worked in a variety of support and tactical roles, as secretaries, clerks, air traffic controllers, photographers and decoders.[2]

Other women went to Vietnam as civilians to work for the American Red Cross, the US embassy, and other government offices. Red Cross employees helped to facilitate emergency leaves for soldiers and, within the Red Cross Supplemental Recreational Activities Overseas programme, operated canteens in rear areas and conducted coffee and doughnut runs to the front. Women also worked as journalists and helped to provide church-sponsored educational and social services to Vietnamese. Some even worked secretly for the Central Intelligence Agency.[3]

It would be expected that from such large numbers of American women and their varied experiences during the Vietnam War would come a considerable body of published poetry to rival the rich and ever-growing array of literature written by male veterans of the war. That, however, has not been the case. Although women veterans appear to have written much poetry, they have been consistently reluctant to seek publication. A major exception is the important anthology *Visions of War, Dreams of Peace: Writings of Women in the Vietnam War*, edited by Lynda Van Devanter and Joan A. Furey.[4] Yet, even several years after the publication of this pioneering work, the poetry world remains strikingly short on women veterans. Both the reasons for this phenomenon of absence and the quality of the poetry that has been published deserve serious consideration.

The unfair reality is that women returning from Vietnam were usually not viewed as genuine veterans because they were not combat soldiers. Norma J. Griffiths, who was an emergency room and triage nurse in Qui Nhon, confronts this perception in her poem 'The Vietnam "Vet"':

> *The 'Vietnam Vet'*
> *people instantly conjure*
> *their own picture*
> *in their mind*
>
> *Is it ever of*
> *a woman?*
> *Huddled . . . somewhere . . .*
> *alone*

---

2. Marshall, *In the Combat Zone*, pp. 4–7. Elizabeth Norman, *Women at War: The Story of Fifty Military Nurses Who Served in Vietnam* (Philadelphia, 1990) is a useful study of personal and professional aspects of nurses' Vietnam War experiences.
3. Marshall, *In the Combat Zone*, pp. 8–9.
4. Lynda Van Devanter and Joan A. Furey, eds, *Visions of War, Dreams of Peace* (New York, 1991), hereafter referred to as *Visions*.

sleeping
trying desperately to shut out the world
that shut her out
or
that disappeared
as she reached out to trust it

Is it ever
that vision?
that woman?[5]

The answer to the questions raised in this poem, of course, is no. Almost universally, both male veterans and civilians of both sexes saw a man when they imagined a veteran. The result of this identification of veteran with male was to deny not only an important role played by women during the Vietnam War but also the woman veteran's very identity. If she did not exist as a veteran, what had she been doing in Vietnam? How could she lay claim to perhaps the most vividly felt year (or years) of her life?[6]

The woman veteran therefore was forced to deny a vital part of herself. Where there had been a person struggling to hold back death, to ease suffering, and to make whole again the lacerated bodies of her patients, the nurse returned to a world that failed not only to value the extraordinary nursing experience that she had gained while often funtioning more as doctor than nurse, but also denied her entry into the traditional veterans' organizations. The Veterans' Administration, for example, was very slow to provide medical services unique to women veterans, such as gynaecological care. A report from the General Accounting Office in 1983 finally gave public utterance to the problem in VA hospitals by citing the Veterans' Administration for failing to extend its services adequately to women.[7] Even the anti-war organization Vietnam Veterans Against the War maintained for years an exclusively male vision of the veteran, an attitude vividly described by Lynda Van Devanter in her memoir *Home Before Morning*.[8]

With the civilian nursing profession, the United States government, the Veterans' Administration, and an array of veterans' organizations in effect denying the reality of women's military service, and faced with the often hostile reaction to service in Vietnam that confronted both women and men upon returning to the United States, it was natural that women would

5. *Ibid.*, p. 94.
6. For an excellent examination of psychological dimensions of the woman veteran, see Myra MacPherson, *Long Time Passing: Vietnam and the Haunted Generation* (Garden City, NY, 1984), pp. 438–55.
7. *Ibid.*, p. 446.
8. Lynda Van Devanter, *Home Before Morning* (1983; New York, 1984).

deny even to themselves their identity as veterans. This rejection left a void in the woman veteran that for large numbers of women would not be filled for years, if ever. Diane C. Jaeger, an army nurse at Long Binh, describes the woman veteran's rediscovery of this long-denied portion of herself in the poem 'Reunited':

> *I came upon the veteran, about two years ago.*
> *She probably was in there, though, long before 'Hello.'*
> *I don't know where she came from, nor where she hopes to go.*
> *I only know I've missed her – the memories now aglow.*

Jaeger's nurse explains that she had not always liked this veteran, that she had ignored her for years because of her pain and anger, and 'the bitterness, the feeling used, the grief'. Now, though, the speaker in the poem acknowledges that 'it's good to have her back again' and welcomes discussions with this veteran of what they had feared and 'the talk of the distant Vietnam Wall they built'. Later, after the speaker's reunification with her veteran self, they go to Washington, sit on the Wall, and share stories and memories. The poem ends with a commitment to a unified self:

> *I really do believe she'll stay – the veteran in me.*
> *She says she's really weary and it's good to be let free.*
> *I don't know how we'll co-exist, with values all askew,*
> *But one thing is for certain, that we'll find one way, not two!*[9]

The general ignoring of the woman veteran was evidenced in many ways, not least of which included national monuments to the Vietnam veteran. The initial Vietnam Veterans Memorial in Washington, DC, consisted of the black granite wall, usually known simply as the Wall, a moving recitation in etched starkness of the names of the approximately 58,000 Americans who died in Vietnam during the war. Seven of the names on the Wall are of women, but the maleness of this commemoration of America's war dead was emphasized by the accompanying bronze statue of three infantrymen staring in the direction of the Wall. The granite and bronze presence is powerful, and visitors find it almost impossible not to be deeply moved by the experience of visiting these momuments. Nonetheless, the continued absence of proper recognition of the woman veteran perpetuated her suffering in isolation.[10]

---

9. *Visions*, pp. 152–3.
10. For a visual account of the Vietnam Veterans Memorial, see Sal Lopes with intro. by Michael Norman, *The Wall: Images and Offerings from the Vietnam Veterans Memorial* (New York, 1987).

Today, visitors to the Wall also see a statue of three nurses, one cradling a wounded male soldier, another gazing downward at a helmet, and a third staring skyward as if watching for an incoming helicopter. The person most responsible for this addition is Diane Carlson Evans, who began her efforts to elicit support for a memorial to women veterans in 1983, approximately one year after the other Vietnam War memorials were completed. After ten years of lobbying, raising money, giving speeches and organizing, she saw her dream realized in 1993.

Evans, a former nurse in Vietnam, gave up nursing after her return to the United States because she grew unable to stand being around blood. Suffering from horrifying nightmares, she sought counselling, and found herself the only woman in her therapy circle. Her healing was facilitated by her determined efforts to create the memorial to the women who served in Vietnam.[11] Also a poet, she writes in the poem 'Left Behind' of her effort to reclaim that part of her left behind in Vietnam:

> *I search my soul*
> *And memories of war*
> *To find that lost space*
> *That part of me that's gone*
> *Left in Vietnam so many*
> *Years ago and hoping*
> *Someday to find it and*
> *Make me whole again*
> *I didn't leave behind*
> *A limb, an arm or a leg*
> *What is it then that's gone*
> *It can't be seen and*
> *Perhaps just as a lost*
> *Limb it can never be*
> *Retrieved*[12]

The statue that Evans brought into existence answers the dream of another poet already mentioned above, Norma J. Griffiths, who writes in 'The Statue' of how, when 'heroes dream of statues, they dream of men with guns'; but

> *I dream of a woman*
> *with only her heart, hands and mind*
> *her 'weapons'*
> *to deal with the world of carnage.*[13]

---

11. Sally Eauclaire, 'Sculpting a vision', *Vietnam* (December 1993), pp. 22–8.
12. *Visions*, p. 71.
13. *Ibid.*, p. 196.

The reluctance or inability to recognize women as veterans, and to assume that women who were in Vietnam were surely tucked away in a nice safe place, is represented, with the frustration and anger attendant on this consistent rejection, in Sara J. McVicker's 'Saigon':

> *If one more guy*
> *asks me if I was in Saigon*
> *or DaNang*
> *I think I'll scream.*
> *Or maybe pop him in the nose.*
> *That's what male vets do to get rid of their frustration.*

The solution for this former army nurse ultimately is not to imitate the male soldier. Instead, the poem concludes with the plaintive wish:

> *I've read so much about them.*
> *Couldn't they learn something*
> *About me?*[14]

Among the insights that others could, and should, have gained about women veterans was that many of them, like male soldiers, came home badly scarred by their war experiences. Post-traumatic stress disorder (PTSD) has affected large numbers of American servicemen and women, numbers no one can precisely calculate. A National Vietnam Veterans Readjustment Study in 1990 found that 15 per cent of the 3.1 million men and women in combat situations in Vietnam suffer from PTSD.[15] Myra MacPherson, in her ground-breaking book *Long Time Passing: Vietnam and the Haunted Generation*, offers a sobering account of PTSD among Vietnam War nurses, based on a 1982 survey:

> Approximately one third of post-traumatic stress symptoms were identified by 25 percent or more of them as presently occurring between ten and thirty times a month. Some 27.6 percent reported having suicidal thoughts between one and nine times a month, 19.2 percent reported feeling depressed between fifteen and thirty times a month, 16.1 percent reported feeling an inability to be close to someone they care about between fifteen and thirty times a month. And 70 percent of those who reported having experienced stress symptoms stated that those symptoms are still present today.[16]

---

14. *Ibid.*, p. 130.
15. Margaret Benshoof-Holler, 'Post traumatic stress disorder', *Vietnam* (December 1993), pp. 38–44.
16. MacPherson, *Long Time Passing*, p. 450. For an in-depth discussion of the causes and symptoms of PTSD, see Jonathan Shay, *Achilles in Vietnam: Combat Trauma and the Undoing of Character* (New York, 1995).

Regrettably, women's difficulty in being recognized as legitimate veterans meant that they also found little receptivity to the possibility (now known as a certainty) that they, like their male counterparts in the Vietnam War, carried the war home with them, sometimes into deeply troubled lives in the form of PTSD.[17] Lynda Van Devanter in *Home Before Morning* offers perhaps the most comprehensive account by any woman of the slow and agonizing struggle to understand her own problems as manifestations of PTSD and to begin the long road towards health.[18]

This ignoring of women veterans as PTSD sufferers continues with recent otherwise profound studies of the illness. Jonathan Shay considers women in *Achilles in Vietnam: Combat Trauma and the Undoing of Character*, but only as civilian victims of war, that is, women who lose spouses to combat, are taken prisoner, suffer rape, and so forth.[19] Similarly, Eric T. Dean in *Shook Over Hell: Post-Traumatic Stress, Vietnam, and the Civil War* largely confines his account of women victims to civilians who may indeed suffer serious psychological effects from war, but from loss of husband or the effects of enemy soldiers foraging for supplies at their homes.[20]

It is perhaps unrealistic to expect men to focus on women as veterans suffering from PTSD when women writing about women at war often also ignore that possibility. In such books as *Women and War*, by Jean Bethke Elshtain, and *Images of Women in Peace and War: Cross-Cultural and Historical Perspectives*, edited by Sharon MacDonald, Pat Holden and Shirley Ardener, the reader searches in vain for any recognition of women as potential PTSD victims.[21] Is it any wonder then that women veterans themselves were slow to come to an understanding of the cause of their own suffering?

Faced with the almost omnipresent denial of their veteran status, including their own self-rejection, women who served in Vietnam understandably were as reluctant to offer their poetry to the world as they were to present themselves in their old uniforms. They were no more likely to identify themselves as poets than they were to see themselves as PTSD sufferers. The poetry they wrote remained (and still remains) largely unpublished and unshared, as if it were not quite real. Joan Furey could as well be writing of

---

17. For an extended examination of women veterans, including their problems with PTSD, see June A. Willenz, *Women Veterans: America's Forgotten Heroines* (New York, 1983).
18. Van Devanter, *Home Before Morning*, especially the last few chapters, pp. 245–375.
19. Shay, *Achilles in Vietnam*, pp. 131–5.
20. Eric T. Dean, Jr., *Shook Over Hell: Post-Traumatic Stress, Vietnam, and the Civil War* (Cambridge, MA, 1997), pp. 62, 96, 124.
21. Jean Bethke Elshtain, *Women and War* (New York, 1987); Sharon MacDonald, Pat Holden and Shirley Ardener, eds, *Images of Women in Peace and War: Cross-Cultural and Historical Perspectives* (Madison, WI, 1987).

her poetry as of her military fatigues in 'Camouflage' when she recalls seeing green fatigues everywhere – on television, in malls, at the Wall – but, for her, only

> *one piece remains*
> *hanging in my closet*
> *near the back.*
> *I can no longer don it*
> *and parade*
> *Nor can I discard it.*[22]

She keeps the piece of clothing but cannot bring it forward to illustrate herself as veteran any more than she and other women veterans have been able to offer their self-revealing, self-defining poetry to a world that defines veteran in male combat terms.

Fortunately, however, Furey and a large number of other women veterans finally donned their poetry in public. That the primary source of published poetry by women veterans remains Van Devanter and Furey's *Visions of War, Dreams of Peace* in no way diminishes the importance of presenting a close examination of that poetry.[23] On the contrary, the continuing shortage of published poetry by women veterans calls for a close analysis of the poetry they have published so that readers will recognize this poetic dimension to the woman veteran, and so that women poets who served in the Vietnam War may finally become more willing to exhibit their poetry in the public forum.

Leaving home for war service, for women as well as men, was a matter of both detail and uncertainty, of packing away the things of youth for safekeeping and wondering what the future would bring. The film *Platoon* opens with a quotation from Ecclesiastes: 'Rejoice, oh young man, in thy youth'.[24] The quotation is poignant because many young men, even among those returning home with healthy bodies, left their youth forever behind. The same can be said for women, and Dana Shuster, who served two tours of duty in the 1960s as an army nurse, working in emergency rooms, operating rooms and intensive-care units, reflects that reality in her poem 'Dried Corsages'. Packing away what she wants to keep from her youth is the easier part of her preparations:

---

22. *Visions*, p. 184.
23. For another examination of this volume, see Vince Gotera, *Radical Visions: Poetry by Vietnam Veterans* (Athens, GA, 1994), pp. 228–45.
24. Ecclesiastes, 11.9.

Dried corsages
tissue-shrouded
the last thing laid
into the crate
atop the diaries
atop the poems
atop the yearbooks
the detritus of adolescence.

It is, she knows, her 'last day of childhood', but what she should pack for her trip overseas is unclear. 'What do you pack', she wonders, 'to take to a war?'[25]

The unforeseen revelations of war, for which one cannot adequately pack or prepare, float slowly into view in Marilyn McMahon's 'In this Land'. McMahon, who was with the Navy Nurse Corps at Da Nang Naval Hospital from 1969 to 1970, is one of the finest poets among women veterans of the Vietnam War; and this poem shows her skill at using colours and sounds, warmth and cold, and gradual movement against a static and seemingly peaceful setting: a patio looking out on a beautiful sandy beach. A woman is having a drink with a colonel, ignoring the distant sounds of helicopters, jets and jeeps, seemingly forgetful of the previous night's explosions. The young woman in the yellow lawn chair, warmed by the sun, wearing a 'sleeveless, short, sunflower yellow' dress, can see beyond the colonel to the beach. The colonel, back to the water, watches her as she hangs on his narration, 'responding to his rank and masculinity', the woman carrying out her role of listener, 'the assigned role of her sex for hundreds of years'. Between sips of her gin and tonic, she begins to become aware of something moving gradually into her field of vision on the waves:

Her stomach begins to chill. She knows.
She asks: look, what is it? She is afraid
to say what she knows.

The colonel continues his self-important account of his work as a military lawyer, while the silent woman watches the scene behind him unfold:

The object — she cannot
say its name yet — floats closer on the tide.
Finally others see it — but now there are
two — they launch a boat, row out to retrieve
the body. Another body. A third.
In flight suits, swollen with three days
submersion. White. Blue. Black. Khaki.

---

25. *Visions*, p. 3.

> *She remains silent. Ice cold. Unable to*
> *see the white of the sun or the blue of the*
> *waves, only the black of the shadows.*[26]

The scene vividly represents, not just for the young woman in the yellow sun dress, but for all women veterans, that moment when the innocence of youth (those dried corsages of Shuster's poem) and the certainty of fixed traditions (McMahon's assigned roles) gave way to the suffering and death experienced and often carried home by women veterans – and written about in the poems that constitute *Visions of War, Dreams of Peace*.

There are moments, of course, when the individual tries to shut out the war and return to a realm of pre-war normality. It is 'Saturday Night' in Dana Shuster's poem by that title. The initial scene could almost be a college residence hall on a slow weekend:

> *Saturday night*
> *Oldies night*
> *on AFVN*
> *Letter-writing night*
> *Toenail-painting night*
> *fantasy-spinning night*

But the comforting setting is first disturbed by small reminders of the real locale: geckos on the wall, the smell of mildew. Then the war intrudes:

> *Silence shattered*
> *by artillery boys*
> *across the road*
> *playing with guns*
> *No dates tonight*
> *for these teen warriors*
> *firing H & I*
> *'Harassment and Inderdiction' –*
> *harassing only my rest*
> *interdicting only my dreams*[27]

The 'artillery boys' are just that – boys, the 'teen warriors' – in actual years, but their playing with guns is far removed from cowboys and Indians; and they may, after all, have dates with those young women listening to the artillery sounds, but as patient and nurse.

---

26. *Ibid.*, pp. 10–12. Also see McMahon's *Works in Progress* (Seattle, 1988) and *Works in Progress II* (Seattle, 1990) for her poetry.
27. *Visions*, pp. 27–8.

Given the large percentage of American military women who worked as nurses, it is to be expected that much of the poetry by women veterans of the Vietnam War would depict the nurse's war experiences. The crucial relationship for a nurse, of course, is with her patients, most of whom in a war in which the average age of the soldier was about 19 (compared with almost 26 for Second World War combatants) were younger than the nurses.[28] An army nurse writing under the pseudonym 'Dusty' notes that 'there is nothing more intimate than sharing someone's dying with them'.[29]

As the poems indicate, nurses in Vietnam also served as comforter, letter-writer, priest, reminder of the soldier's girlfriend back home, and surrogate mother. It was almost impossible not to become emotionally involved, especially given the youth of the wounded and dying soldiers and the many roles that nurses were forced to play. Lily Lee Adams, who worked as a nurse at Cu Chi, conveys several of these roles in 'The Friendship Only Lasted a Few Seconds', a refrain in the poem as well as the title:

> He said 'Mom,'
> And I responded
> And became her.
>
> . . .
>
> But the friendship
> Only lasted a few seconds.
>
> And he called me Mary.
> I wished she could
> Be there for him.
>
> . . .
>
> But I did the
> Best I could
> And the friendship
> Only lasted a few seconds.
>
> And he told me,
> 'I don't believe this,
> I'm dying for nothing.'
> Then he died.
> Again, the friendship
> Only lasted a few seconds.[30]

---

28. See MacPherson, *Long Time Passing*, pp. 52–3, for a discussion of sending youth into combat.
29. *Visions*, p. 121.
30. *Ibid.*, p. 38. For autobiographical accounts by Adams, see Marshall, *In the Combat Zone*, pp. 206–29; and Walker, *A Piece of My Heart*, pp. 313–35.

In 'Hello, David', Dusty assures the patient that she will stay with him, that she will write to his mother and 'bratty kid sister', that she will stay beside him and hold his hand until he dies:

I am the last person
who will love you.

The poem builds powerfully through its sequence of assurances, passes beyond David's death, and concludes with a lingering question:

So long, David – my name is Dusty.
David – who will give me something for my pain?[31]

The poem 'Cheated', by Mary Lu Ostergren Brunner, appears more futile hope than achieved goal as the the poet speaks of trying to maintain an emotional distance from her patient. The former operating-room nurse at Pleiku writes at the end of the poem:

I must not allow myself
To get too close
The distance
Is better for me.

Nothing earlier in the poem, though, supports that conclusion, even as the speaker talks of neither knowing nor trying to know the patient's name or hometown. She tries to think of him as a body rather than a person. Yet she admits:

I want to follow you
From the OR to the ward
Did you make it home OK?
Did you survive?
Who are you?[32]

Like the previous poem, 'Dark Angel' by Joan Arrington Craigwell, an air force nurse, demonstrates that knowing the tortured body parts can be a knowledge far more profound than the stuff of small talk, such as a person's name or hometown. The nurse in the poem knows her patient only as a Mexican. At first, she is his 'dark madonna'; after he wakes up she will be 'the bitch/who cut off the best part of him'. There is also 'a white boy/crying in the darkness', for whom she is his 'mama tonight', not caring

---

31. *Visions*, pp. 43–4.
32. *Ibid.*, pp. 45–6.

that her 'skin is black/cause he'll die/before dawn's early light'. There is an Indian with no eyes left and a black boy without legs. For all of these nameless soldiers missing various parts of their earlier wholeness, this African-American nurse is their 'dark angel'.[33]

Joan A. Furey, who worked as an army nurse at Pleiku from 1969 to 1970, contributes several poems to *Visions of War, Dreams of Peace*, along with co-editing the book. In 'Vigil', she also focuses on bodies no longer whole:

> Day after day, week after week
> A parade.
> What about his family,
> his girlfriend — his wife and kids.
> He's maimed, stumps where once
> there was a leg and arm. A face even
> adults will hide from.
>
> . . .
>
> He's one, look at them all
> those who died, those who left,
> blind, deformed, paralyzed.
> Young men,
> bright, handsome, funny.
> Now sad and confused and wondering
> Why me?

The speaker cannot answer that question either; nor can she answer questions about herself:

> And when I leave
> What will I be?
> I can't be what I was before
> I can't be what I am during
> I must be something else

As a nurse, she knows that she should be able to put aside personal feelings and simply move ahead with her caregiving, but that is difficult for her, and for most of the nurses who worked with the wounded and the dying:

> I'm sorry, it got to me today
> I'm a nurse and maybe it shouldn't.
> but it does, And I ask also
> Why God? Why?[34]

---

33. *Ibid.*, pp. 75–6.
34. *Ibid.*, pp. 35–6.

When the nurse was able not to react emotionally to the carnage confronting her, it was as likely to be the result of emotional exhaustion resulting from a surfeit of emotion than from a rational decision to retain an emotional distance and objectivity. Such is the case in 'The Coffee Room Soldier' by Penny Kettlewell, who served two tours of duty as an army nurse in the late 1960s and early 1970s at hospitals in Qui Nhon and Long Binh. The nurse in the poem enters the coffee room for a short respite

> *to re-group*
> *for the next assault on our forces*
> *and on my senses.*

As she moves forward for a cup of coffee, she steps over a dead soldier 'laid out, unbagged, on the coffee room floor'. Her reaction is a casual thought concerning 'where would I find them next:/in my bed?' She dispassionately examines his chest wall, which was blown open to reveal the internal organs, much like an 'anatomical drawing'. She sips from her cup as she studies the corpse at her feet and comes to a frightening realization:

> *I then saw his face*
> *that of a child in terror*
> *and only hours ago*
> *alive as I*
> *or maybe I was dead as he,*
> *because with another sip, a cigarette and a detached analysis*
> *I knew I could no longer even feel.*

After she mops the floor, puts supplies away, and bags up the coffee room soldier, she goes 'outside to watch the sunrise,/alone and destitute of tears'.[35]

The Vietnam War has had such a lasting effect on veterans because many of them have been unable to leave the war behind in the jungles, rice paddies and hospitals of Vietnam. They carry the war with them through their personal and professional lives, often without being able to acknowledge that part of themselves. This is as true for the woman veteran as for the male soldier. Sharon Grant, an operating room nurse for the army, writes of frightening dreams, one of the most common symptoms of post-traumatic stress disorder. In an unrhymed villanelle entitled 'Dreams that Blister Sleep', Grant uses the following refrains:

> *You try to repress them because you know.*
> *You are probably going to come back.*

---

35. *Ibid.*, p. 47.

These lines reflect two continuing characteristics of PTSD-caused dreams. They recur again and again, bringing the dreamer back to her war experiences; and, because this return is so horrifying, she tries to repress the dreams. But the dreams keep returning, and the speaker keeps returning – strip-searching a mama-san, trying to keep a friend named Barry alive, sudden gunfire during a play.[36]

Mary O'Brien Tyrrell writes in 'Saving Lives' about a teenage medic a few years younger than her own 22. His platoon called him 'Doc', and he 'learned in months' what she spent years to learn in college. When the medic is transferred, the nurse and his other friends throw a party for him. Then,

> *Yesterday, I went to the 'Wall'*
> *Dear God –*
> *I found you there!*[37]

What is especially striking about this poem is the common experience of making friends, being separated from them (first in Vietnam, and later by the passage of years), and not knowing what happened to them. Reading the names on the Wall, especially for anyone who had served in Vietnam, is a frightening act, for the person never knows whose name might appear – that instant when death becomes real, chiselled into the black granite, as real as if one were staring at a corpse in a coffin. 'Saving Lives' ends in the dramatic and horrible moment when the name of a former friend on the memorial comes into view.

A constant in these poems is the dead. 'My Dead are not Silent', Dana Shuster writes, in the poem by that title:

> *They scream in my dreams.*
> *My dead are not still.*
> *They reach for their mothers.*
>
> *My dead are young soldiers*
> *spent, wasted discarded.*
> . . .
> *Their blood yet drips through my soul*
> *Their moans still echo through my heart.*[38]

Penny Kettlewell remembers the dead in 'Cordwood' as bodies 'stacked up high'. Like the dark plastic bags in which the bodies are 'zipped up tight', the veterans have followed their lost patients: 'For safety's sake, we've zipped our shells'.[39]

---

36. *Ibid.*, p. 59.
37. *Ibid.*, p. 60.
38. *Ibid.*, p. 168.
39. *Ibid.*, p. 170.

More than the dead, however, follows the survivor. Marilyn McMahon, in the powerful poem 'Knowing', remembers the practice of defoliation, the use of Agent Orange to kill vegetation that might give cover to the enemy. Unfortunately, the defoliant, named after the orange-striped drums in which it was stored, contained dioxin, believed by many scientists and veterans to cause chloracne, personality changes, insomnia, birth defects, and several types of cancer.[40] As the speaker in the poem recalls women friends exposed to Agent Orange who have borne children with various health problems, and several who have suffered multiple miscarriages, she conveys her resolution not to give birth to a child of her own. This decision is accompanied with much pain in the knowledge of what she will never know:

> *I knew more*
> *when I watched my parents*
> *celebrate their fortieth*
> *wedding anniversary,*
> *four children, three grandchildren*
> *sitting in the pews.*
> *I knew what I would never know,*
> *what the poisons and my fears*
> *have removed forever from my knowing.*
> *The conceiving, the carrying of a child,*
> *the stretching of my womb, my breasts.*
> *The pain of labor.*
> *The bringing forth from my body a new life.*

The poem ends with a withering metaphor that both returns the speaker to Vietnam and reinforces the continuing presence of the war within her most elemental core of being:

> *I choose not to know*
> *if my eggs are*
> *misshapen and withered*
> *as the trees along the river.*
> *If snipers are hidden*
> *in the coils of my DNA.*[41]

---

40.   A class action suit filed by Vietnam War veterans against the United States government and seven chemical companies resulted in a judgment of $180 million against the companies. For further reading on Agent Orange, consult Fred A. Wilcox, *Waiting for an Army to Die: Tragedy of Agent Orange* (New York, 1983); William A. Buckingham, *Operation Ranch Hand: The United States Air Force and Herbicides in Southeast Asia* (Washington, DC, 1982); and Michael Gough, *Dioxin, Agent Orange: The Facts* (New York, 1986).

41.   *Visions*, pp. 187–9.

The 'Wounds of War', another poem by Marilyn McMahon, testifies to the common reality for Vietnam veterans, including women veterans, that for many of them their wounds remain unhealed. The memories, the anguish of not knowing what has happened to friends and patients, the continuing alienation from parts of one's own identity, a society still insufficiently recognizing the role of the woman veteran, the multiple manifestations of post-traumatic stress disorder – all these wounds, and more, require healing. Often the wound can be healed only by being laid more open. As a refrain in the poem states:

> *Wounds heal from the bottom up*
> *and from the outside in.*
> *Each must be kept open,*
> *must be probed*
> *and exposed to light.*
> *Must be inspected*
> *and known.*[42]

Casting light on these wounds, both from without and within, can take various forms. Some veterans undergo counselling, which often includes 'walking through Vietnam', that is, reliving their war experiences under professional supervision. This therapy usually includes reconstruction of a personal narrative, which, as Jonathan Shay explains, 'can transform involuntary reexperiencing of traumatic events into memory of the events, thereby reestablishing authority over memory'.[43] Some veterans return to Vietnam, as Lynda Van Devanter describes her return, to see a different Vietnam and separate the country from the war.[44]

Recognition and appreciation also contribute to the healing process. Diane Carlson Evans describes a personal moment at the Wall in 'Thanks, Nurse'. Wearing her old jungle hat with 'Pleiku' written on it, she is confronted by a soldier who throws his arms around her and thanks her: 'You nurses saved our lives, you know'.[45] The story of another Vietnam War nurse, Saralee McGoran, is told in MacPherson's *Long Time Passing*. For her, as for many, there was uncertainty regarding how much good she did, and whether in some cases keeping badly disabled soldiers alive to return to the United States was more cruel than letting them die would have been. She 'had to know what the men felt about what we did'. Her answers came at a national reunion of Vietnam veterans in Washington, DC, in November 1982.

---

42. *Ibid.*, p. 85.
43. Shay, *Achilles in Vietnam*, pp. 183–94.
44. Van Devanter, *Home Before Morning*, pp. 361–75.
45. *Visions*, p. 146.

As if on cue, a crippled veteran sees McGoran's hat with 12th Evac. on it. He sobs and grabs her. 'You saved my life. I was there, in Cu Chi. Thank the rest of the girls.' McGoran tells of searching for the redemptive key to dissolve those years of anguish. 'I needed to know that I did a good job. Needed to know it from the guys who were there.

'In the 25th Division reunion suite, everyone was coming up and saying "thank you." For fourteen years, I needed to know that.'[46]

Perhaps it is not too much also to recogize what women veterans have accomplished in their poetry. What they present in these very personal, deeply emotional, and often quite aesthetically successful poems is their status as veterans, which neither they nor others can deny without denying an important part of who they were and are. Their poetry deserves recognition. So do they.

---

46. MacPherson, *Long Time Passing*, pp. 439–42. McGoran also tells her story in Marshall, *In the Combat Zone*, pp. 243–57.

CHAPTER TWELVE

Women, War and the Veil:
Muslim Women in Resistance and Combat

KATHRYN M. COUGHLIN

Although significant numbers of women have served in military units and resistance forces throughout history, most cultures still hold that men are the warriors and protectors. On occasion, this hegemonic social discourse has given way to the exigencies of war and resistance; under these circumstances, women have stepped into the traditional boots of their male compatriots and served alongside them. In the West, breaches of social convention followed a model of gendered behaviour until the middle of the twentieth century. War (or armed conflict) and its concomitant social disorder relaxed relatively well-defined social conventions in gender relations. Due to the diversion of men from the 'public' spheres of society to front lines, women assumed roles ordinarily performed by men. Initially, in addition to providing moral support, these women assisted the male fighting forces in areas like transportation, communication and administration. In response to the attendant disruption in education and social welfare services, women taught, organized charities and cared for the orphaned and widowed. Owing to a lack of sufficient medical care, they often cared for the wounded and even performed emergency surgery. In addition, because traditional social conventions have generally protected women from physical searches, they have often been critical in intelligence gathering and in smuggling small items through checkpoints and in and out of prisons. On occasion, defensive strategies required more troops than were available or needed an operative who was above suspicion for a delicate mission. Here, women took up arms and fought alongside their male partisans. When peace was restored, the women returned to their homes in largely traditional gender-segregated societies.

The post-world war era experienced a disruption in the centuries-old model outlined above and the lives of women in most industrialized nations in the West changed. They began to enter the 'public' sphere of society in ever-increasing numbers. Today, Western women have full legal parity with men in virtually all facets of political, social and economic life, though social reality might paint a different picture. A 200-year legacy of developing social consciousness and feminist thought, combined with the quite substantial defence contributions of women during the First and Second World Wars in Europe, Canada and the United States, transformed gender relations in the West.

In the Middle East and the greater Islamic world, the experiences of women after 1945 differed sharply from those of their Western sisters. For Muslims, the end of the Second World War did not bring peace and rising prosperity as it did in the West. Instead, throughout the world, Muslims were fighting for independence from colonial rulers, foreign intervention and imperialistic aspirations.[1] After achieving independence, many of these newly formed nation-states wrote constitutions and legal codes based on an amalgam of colonial administrative practice, Western constitutional law and Islamic codes. An awkward, unwieldy body of jurisprudence emerged in countries as divergent as Egypt, Iran and Tunisia; Islamic law tended to dominate in the area of family and criminal law, while secular legal codes were culturally modified to suit Muslim needs. The battle for cultural authenticity was often fought in the arena of gender relations, and though women's rights were protected by law in most Muslim countries, asserting them became an increasingly complicated challenge. The integration of women into the armed forces was certainly not on the agenda of most Muslim suffragists.

Muslim feminists argue for women's political, social and economic rights from *at least* three different positions. The first we might call an Islamicist perspective: proponents hold that the gender-based roles of men and women are outlined in and sanctioned by the Qur'an. A second, revisionist, Islamic perspective posits that Islam upholds the equality of men and women spiritually, socially, politically and economically; centuries of interaction with other cultures eventually corrupted the 'true' Islam. A third group, secular feminists, accept Western feminist thought as a basis for Muslim women's rights. Of course, these classifications tend to reduce the incredibly sophisticated and nuanced feminisms found in the Muslim and developing worlds to mere generalizations (in reality, there are potentially as many theoretical bases for feminist thought in the Islamic world as there are in the West). Whatever the perspective, however, it is extremely difficult to find Muslim feminists

---

1. Most Middle Eastern and North African countries did not achieve independence until the 1950s and 1960s. Jordan and Syria were two exceptions, their independence coming in 1946. Some argue that Palestine has not yet achieved independence.

who argue that women should play a combat role (or even an active role) in the military: economic rights, political rights and social equality are far more pressing issues. But Muslim women do play varied roles in the militaries and armed resistance forces of the Muslim world. To understand that seeming paradox, we look to the scholarship on women in the Islamic world.

Scholarship on women in the Middle East and the Muslim world

Throughout history, women have been largely excluded from civilizational endeavours such as exploration and settlement, the making of war, wealth, laws and governments and the accomplishments of art, science and 'high' culture. When men recorded their history, they inevitably emphasized these aspects of civilization; consequently, by the end of the nineteenth century, the broad field of Western historiography had subdivided into diplomatic, military, economic, constitutional and political histories. Women appeared primarily as exceptions in these male-dominated narratives: women such as the Queen of Sheba, Joan of Arc, Catherine the Great and Elizabeth I, who were 'as smart as', 'as powerful as' or 'as rich as' any ruling man on earth, merited attention. When feminist historians sought to introduce women to history, they rejected military and political history and looked to the historical development of society and culture, spaces traditionally dominated by women.

Influenced by the birth of social and cultural histories, feminist historians of the Islamic world began to examine the history of women in Islam. Some were mildly surprised to find that throughout history many Muslim women owned businesses, were involved in overseas trade, negotiated their own marriage contracts and often appeared in court to protect their economic interests.[2] At a time when most married, upper-class European women were unable to see a physician without the permission of their husbands, Muslim women sued their husbands for breach of marriage contract and sought monetary damages in court.[3] Many of these feminist historians ignored 'elite' male-dominated military or political history; when examining the

2. Please see Leila Ahmed, *Women and Gender in Islam* (New Haven, CT, 1992); Deniz Kandiyoti, ed., *Women, Islam and the State* (Philadelphia, 1991); Nikki R. Keddie and Beth Baron, *Women in Middle Eastern History: Shifting Boundaries in Sex and Gender* (New Haven, CT, 1991); and Judith Tucker, *Arab Women: Old Boundaries, New Frontiers* (Bloomington, IN, 1993).

3. See for example Judith Tucker, *In the House of the Law: Gender and Islamic Law in Ottoman Syria and Palestine* (Berkeley, CA, 1998).

interaction of women and warfare, these scholars analysed the very real consequence of war on the more marginalized sectors of society: the elderly, women and children. Women as violent actors in armed conflict rarely appear on the pages of their histories, which are largely framed by the dominant narrative of bellicose men/pacifistic women.

To assume that the lack of scholarship on Muslim women in combat corresponds to their physical absence on a battlefield is to err. Iran, Iraq, Syria, Indonesia and Nigeria are some of the nations in which Muslim women serve in single-sex or mixed-sex military units. Some are assigned to combat positions (Iran) or internal security posts (Pakistan), while other militaries assign women support roles (Indonesia and Palestine). Elsewhere, Muslim women have been notably involved in anti-colonial resistance movements, 'terrorist' or 'freedom-fighter' operations and rebel armies. Algerian women were instrumental in intelligence-gathering and terrorist activities against the colonial French government in the 1950s and early 1960s. In northern Afghanistan, Shi'a women have engaged in battle against the Kabul-based Taliban, who are predominantly Sunni extremists. In Asia, Philippine women served in the Moro National Liberation Front, a group of Muslim rebels who sought political autonomy from Manila. The Iranian Mujahidin employs all-female units in its bid to unseat the Islamic government in Tehran. How is it that, in societies that do not grant meaningful political and economic rights to women, they are accepted in the bastion of male exclusivity – the military? How do we understand their roles in the armed forces and resistance groups of these countries? In part, we can look to the general paradigm of wartime gender behaviour as outlined above. The Muslim world, however, stretches across the massive Afro-Asian land mass and includes incredibly heterogeneous and complex societies. It is only in examining the historical contexts of these Muslim women in combat that we can assess their wartime behaviour against the paradigm and attempt to come to grips with the paradox of 'veiled' women in combat. And, faced with a dearth of scholarship on Muslim women as actors in war, we look to sources on women's discursive strategies in informal power structures such as resistance movements and anti-colonial rebel forces for information about female Muslim combatants.

Women and combat in the Muslim world

Like their sisters in the American Revolution, Muslim women fought in resistance groups against colonial powers in a bid to secure their sovereignty. One of the most celebrated women resistance fighters is the legendary Algerian hero Jamilah Buhrayd. Captured, shot and tortured by the French Army in the late 1950s, Jamilah recalled the numerous men and women imprisoned for terrorist activities during the Algerian War of Independence: 'There were thousands of us in that prison, men and women. We would be arrested, put in the cells, and taken out now and then and tortured. Some died under torture.'[4] As the object of nationalist poetry by the renowned Syrian/ Lebanese poet Nizar Qabbani, Jamilah was bemused by her notoriety.

> You know, my friend, there were thousands of Jamilahs, just like me. They all moved, like me, from the Qasbah to the French Quarter. Carrying bombs in their handbags and throwing them into cafés. I'm not really sure why all the publicity ended up centering on me. For there were many women in the prison with me, subjected to worse kinds of torture, and they didn't betray their friends either. . . . Individuals don't make a cause, you know. It's the principle you believe in. Our aim was revolution, our aim was independence. We won both![5]

Jamilah was initially involved in collecting donations and distributing leaflets. Soon, however, the Algerians realized that women were near-perfect covert operatives. Dressed in European clothes, sporting heavily applied make-up and French-style handbags, Algerian women by the dozens entered cafés frequented by French soldiers and dropped bombs under tables or tossed them into club doorways. First and foremost, their aspirations, like those of the mobilized Palestinian women, were not feminist but nationalist.

Much has been written about Palestinian women and their lives as both refugees and freedom fighters. As early as 1884, Muslim and Christian Palestinian women struggled against colonization of their land by both the British and the Zionists, and by the 1920s, urban, educated Palestinian women had organized committees in response to British colonization to address their social and political concerns.[6] During the 1936–39 revolts, women provided food and medical care for the wounded men, and as the armed revolt escalated, peasant women undertook increasingly dangerous political activities: smuggling weapons, hiding fighters and taking up arms. Fatmeh Ghazzal, the first known Palestinian women killed in combat, died on 26 June 1936 in the Battle of Wadi Azzam.[7]

---

4. Khawlah Qal'aji, 'Interview with Jamilah Buhrayd', *Al-Hawadith*, 22 January 1971.
5. Walid 'Awad, 'Interview with Jamilah Buhrayd', *Al-Hawadith*, 15 January 1971.
6. Souad Dajani, 'Palestinian women under Israeli occupation: implications for development', in Tucker, ed., *Arab Women*, p. 115.
7. Julie Peteet, *Gender in Crisis: Women and the Palestinian Resistance Movement* (New York, 1991), pp. 52–5.

In response to the announcement of the United Nations Partition Plan, Palestinian women peacefully demonstrated and distributed leaflets, but with the war of 1948, the role of women quickly changed from quasi-political to social. Faced with massive numbers of refugees and displaced Palestinians, women established social organizations to care for the orphaned, disabled, wounded and needy; these Muslim and Christian women administered programmes to further literacy, address health and sanitation concerns, and preserve Palestinian culture and heritage.[8] The subsequent 1967 Israeli occupation of the West Bank and Gaza Strip perhaps trebled the work of Palestinian women: confronted with thousands of refugees, especially widows, orphans and the wounded, a sharp decrease in food and commodities, and the horror of separated families, the women again stepped into social and welfare roles.[9]

By the late 1960s, scores of Palestinian women had also become actively involved in 'terrorist activities'. Palestinian women such as Rashida Obeida and Leila Khalid underwent rigorous military and guerrilla training. Leaving behind family and friends, they endured harsh commando training in Lebanon and Syria, where they were inculcated with revolutionary ideology and taught to make explosives. On 18 February 1969, Amina Dhahbour and several male commandos attacked an Israeli El-Al jet in Zurich.[10] Leila Khalid was one of two Palestinians who hijacked TWA 840 from Rome to Athens on 29 August 1969. Scores of planes were commandeered between 1968 and 1970 under the directions of three unnamed Palestinian female 'captains of the revolution'.[11] In the West Bank and Gaza, Lebanon and Jordan, the roles of women in the refugee camps increasingly transgressed traditional gender boundaries: as elsewhere in times of crisis, the role of women in public life increased dramatically, raising consciousness about the role of women in 'post-occupied' Palestinian society.[12]

The Israeli occupation of the West Bank and Gaza continued. In December 1987 the *Intifada* erupted and, alongside their male relatives and neighbours, Palestinian women joined in throwing stones and Molotov cocktails at Israeli soldiers.[13] As a rule, the involvement of Palestinian women in

---

8. Laurie Brand, 'Palestinians in Syria: the politics of integration', *Middle East Journal* 42, 4 (1988), p. 635.

9. *Ibid.*

10. Leila Khalid, *My People Shall Live: The Autobiography of a Revolutionary*, ed. George Hajjar (London, 1973), p. 116.

11. *Ibid.*, chs 5 and 6.

12. Rosemary Sayigh, 'Palestinian women and politics in Lebanon', in Tucker, ed., *Arab Women*, pp. 175–194; and Brand, 'Palestinians in Syria'. See also Dajani, 'Palestinian women under Israeli occupation', pp. 102–28.

13. The *Intifada* is a civil uprising which, in Arabic, literally means 'to shake off' the Israeli occupation.

the *Intifada* mirrors the characteristic quasi-political or paramilitary activities of women involved in resistance efforts. But a glance at some 'legendary' narrative regarding gender relations during this period demonstrates that the normal social parameters of gendered behaviour were suspended as women became active agents in the fight to regain their homeland. In one such anecdote, an unarmed Palestinian woman bests an Israeli soldier in a vivid display of courage:

> A woman was participating in a demonstration in Jenin when she got into a shouting argument with an Israeli soldier. The woman shouted to the soldier that if he was to put his gun aside, she would show him who was the more courageous of the two. The soldier accepted the challenge and put his gun aside. The woman attacked him and with one blow knocked him down on the ground, sat on him, and continued to beat him until the other soldiers came and saved him.[14]

In an interesting twist on the use of traditional dress in subterfuge, a young woman hides a wanted young man from Israeli soldiers:

> One time, a young *shab* [young man] threw a Molotov cocktail at the soldiers and ran into Shifa Hospital, and the soldiers followed him into the hospital. He ran into the reception room. He was so scared that he became confused and did not know where to hide. There was a woman there from Khan Yunis [a Gazan refugee camp] with a *dayer* [a long, flowing black skirt]. She called to him and hid him between her legs under the *dayer*. And she said to him, 'Stay there, you are like a son of mine.' The soldiers came after him to the reception room but couldn't find him. When they left, he came out.[15]

By the end of the twentieth century women are serving in the Palestinian National Authority's (PNA), Preventive Security Services (PSS) and the Civil Police (CP). These are not strictly speaking military units, but in the fledgling Palestinian quasi-state, the PSS serves as both internal and 'state' security. As they are admitted into the security services based on their involvement in the *Intifada*, most of the PSS female officers are older, married (some with children) and more established than their CP counterparts; quite a few have been jailed by the Israelis for 'terrorist' or insurrectionist

---

14. Sharif Kanaana, 'Women in legends of the *Intifada*', in Suha Sabbagh, ed., *Palestinian Women of Gaza and the West Bank* (Bloomington IN, 1998), p. 122.
15. *Ibid.*, pp. 123–4. Though the author discusses these stories as 'legends', both anecdotes are similar to ones I heard while researching in the West Bank (December 1992 to August 1993).

activities.[16] As is the case in so many modern 'militaries', Palestinian women are generally assigned secretarial positions, though at least one woman has worked on the 'strike team' (an immediate response team of trained fighters).[17]

Politically as well as 'militarily', Palestinian women are more visible in public space; they are enfranchised and serve in some political and legislative offices. The nascent Palestinian Legislative Council boasts several women representatives, and Intisar al-Wazir currently serves as Minister of Social Affairs.[18] After over 50 years of struggle, Palestinian women are beginning to focus more on gender issues and questions of their status in the new Palestinian state, though stalled peace process negotiations effectively mute any significant discourse on the role of women in society. As long as nationalist concerns dominate public debate, the feminist concerns of Palestinian women (whether they be Islamist, secular or other) will remain sidelined.

In another war of armed resistance, Kuwaiti women fought against Iraqi occupation during the Gulf War in roughly the same ways as Algerian and Palestinian women. In the first few days after the invasion of 2 August 1990, between 400 and 500 women assembled in mass demonstration at the 'Adailiyah Mosque, chanting anti-Iraq slogans and demanding that the army withdraw.[19] At subsequent peaceful demonstrations, Iraqi soldiers fired without provocation at the women, killing and wounding dozens.[20] In response, the Kuwaiti women became more pro-active, printing and circulating flyers announcing Iraqi defections to demoralize the occupying forces.

Women who had never worn the Islamic covering donned full black 'abayas and took to the streets to demonstrate, collect intelligence and move weapons and ammunition. Unlike the Algerian and Iranian women who veiled themselves during their revolutionary wars, Kuwaiti women assumed Islamic garb for purposes of anonymity. 'The 'abaya had no religious or cultural significance but became a weapon in the defense of the women and the nation.'[21] Men's clothing also took on strategic meaning. In order to hide their identity from the Iraqi soldiers, Kuwaiti men discarded the traditional

16. Interview with Sarah Meyers, 23 October 1998 (London).
17. For more information on the role of Palestinian women in the state security forces, please see Sarah Meyers, 'Police, state and society: the Palestinian police and security forces and the maintenance of public order' (Ph.D. thesis, University of Durham, 2000).
18. Dr Hanan Ashrawi recently resigned from the Cabinet, leaving al-Wazir the sole female cabinet member charged with a portfolio.
19. Margot Badran, 'Gender, Islam and the state: Kuwaiti women in struggle, pre-invasion to postliberation', in Yvonne Yazbeck Haddad and John Esposito, eds, *Islam, Gender and Social Change* (New York, 1998), p. 194.
20. 'The conduct of Iraqi troops in Kuwait towards Kuwaitis and non-Westerners', *News from Middle East Watch*, September 1990, p. 5. Also see 'Kuwait: deteriorating human rights conditions since the early occupation', *News from Middle East Watch*, November 1990, p. 19.
21. Badran, 'Gender, Islam and the state', pp. 194–5.

dishdasha for Western trousers and shirts worn by the Arab and Indian guest workers to disguise their nationality. As they were wanted by the Iraqi military, most of the men fled the country or hid underground in basement storage spaces while women organized and ran the resistance effort. In a complete reversal of gender roles, women occupied 'public' space while men were relegated to 'private' space.

In addition to conventional activities such as food distribution, education and health and social welfare services, Kuwaiti women were involved in armed resistance as well. Organized into cells along the lines of the Algerian National Liberation Front (FLN), women transported arms, ammunition and intelligence. Like their Muslim sisters in Palestine and the Philippines, the Kuwaiti women took full advantage of the protection that the Islamic dress afforded. Women were rarely searched at checkpoints and seldom were required to reveal their faces for identification. As the war escalated, women assumed more dangerous duties, tracking explosives and hiding weapons beneath car seats.[22] Kuwaiti women in the armed resistance died while defending their country.

Margot Badran tells of Asrar Qabandi, a computer specialist who worked in the Ministry of Foreign Affairs:

> Putting on a sari to pose as an Indian, [Asrar] retrieved computer disks from the government's central record office in Jabriya. She routinely passed messages to the Kuwaiti government in exile and the international media, and clandestinely crossed the desert to Saudi Arabia smuggling money and ammunition for the armed resistance. In early November 1991, she was arrested while carrying a large sum of money through a checkpoint. [Asrar] was imprisoned at Meshatil, an agricultural experimental station that the Iraqis had turned into a 'rape farm'. She was later killed, and her mutilated body was thrown in front of her house.[23]

At the end of the war, Kuwaiti women reasserted their demands, which had begun in the 1960s, for full political and social rights. As first-class citizens, women had been granted full rights to political participation, but subsequent electoral laws restricted the vote to only some male citizens. Naturalized citizens, children of Kuwaiti women and non-Kuwaiti men, and desert nomads were denied political participatory rights. In post-liberation Kuwait, women still await full social, political and economic integration into their society; while the sultan has voiced sympathy for their cause, it remains to be seen whether and when their demands will be met.

---

22. *Ibid.*, pp. 197–8.
23. *Ibid.*, p. 198.

Little statistical information is available about the military in Libya and even less about women, although it is generally agreed that women in Libya enjoy far greater political rights and social participation than do any other Arab women.[24] This perception is based in good part on Colonel Muammar Qaddafi's positions on women as recorded in *The Green Book*, the 'official' primer of the Libyan revolution. A strange amalgam of ideas and attitudes, confused constitutional principles and bizarre economic theories, Qaddafi's *Green Book* sets forth relatively advanced notions on personal freedom, women's rights and individual involvement in a participatory democracy. Perhaps most notable is the section on women and women's rights: loosely based on biological determinism, Qaddafi contends that men and women should enjoy equal status in all things before the law, albeit their roles in society may be different.[25]

Either as evidence of his commitment to women or as a brilliant propagandistic move, Qaddafi's Republican Guard and his personal body-guards are all highly trained women.[26] On 1 September 1981, Qaddafi delivered a graduation speech to mark the anniversary of the revolution and the graduation of the first Libyan women from the nation's all-female military academy.[27] In a highly charged speech, the colonel condemned the status of women in Arab society, calling it 'un-Islamic':

> Inside the Arab nation, women have been dominated by forces of oppression, feudalism and profit. We call for the outbreak of a revolution for the liberation of women in the Arab nation. . . . What goes on at present does not agree with the true constitution of any Islamic society. . . . We would like to announce that Libyan military colleges and Libyan military schools are wide open not only for Libyan Arab girls but for all the girls of the Arab nation and Africa.[28]

From the early 1980s, the Libyan government has required that every citizen, male and female, undertake continuous military training, provided he or she is physically capable.[29] Military science is mandated for all students above the primary school level; they are required to wear a standard-issue military

24. Amal S.M. Obeidi, 'Changing attitudes to the role of women in Libyan society', unpublished paper.
25. Muammar al-Qadhafi, *The Green Book*, Vol. 3 (Tripoli, 1979), pp. 92–106.
26. George Tremlett, *Qaddafi: The Desert Mystic* (New York, 1993), p. 193.
27. *Ibid.*, pp. 232–3.
28. *Ibid.*, p. 233.
29. 'Mada 2, Qanun Raqam 3, Lisant 1984 Bisha'n al-Sha'ab al-Musalah', *Al-Mawsu'a al-Qanuniya: al-Mara'a fi al-Tashriy'at al-Libiya* (Tripoli, 1994), p. 35 ('Article 2, Law No. 3 of 1984: People's Army', in *The Encyclopedia of Law: Women in Libyan Legislation*).

uniform and attend weekly military exercises. At the university level, students attend training camps but are not required to wear military uniforms during their studies. And all Libyans must serve in the military a minimum of one year after graduation.[30] As of 1998, female graduates from the military academy have been promoted to the rank of lieutenant.[31]

Despite (or perhaps because of) the revolutionary ideology of the regime, Libyan society has become more conservative, self-segregating along gender lines and turning to 'traditional' mores.[32] By the mid-1980s, Islamist practice had become commonplace and although the government had implemented different programmes to counter their growing influence, Islamists and their values became increasingly attractive to young women. Where veiling had been reserved for women of the pre-revolution generation, it has now become more commonplace.[33] It is interesting to note that, of 500 university students surveyed in 1994, only 43 per cent of the male students favoured women's participation in the armed forces as compared with 70 per cent of the women.[34] When asked whether they thought that Libyan women currently possessed adequate civil, political and social rights, almost 70 per cent of the men and women responded in the affirmative.[35] Here we are confronted with another paradox: an increasingly conservative Muslim society where women voluntarily veil but serve in the military and in paramilitary organizations. Libya, as with so many Muslim societies, defies easy categorization.

Like many armed forces in the Middle East, there are no available statistics on women in the Syrian military; the Syrian military attaché to the United States denied a request for an interview. But in an informal discussion in July 1994, a senior military officer confirmed that women were serving as fighter pilots and in some limited combat positions in the Syrian Army.[36] Though not subject to conscription or eligible to serve as enlisted soldiers, select Syrian women were being trained for combat, primarily in the Syrian Air Force and Medical Corps.

Outside the Arab world, Muslim women occupy relatively high profiles in the Turkish and Iranian militaries. Mustafa Kemal Atatürk, the founder of the Republic of Turkey, raised his adopted daughters according to strict Kemalist (secular) principles. One of his daughters, Sabiha Gökçen, bombed Kurdish rebels in the 1937 rebellion during her career as an air force

---

30. See Maria Graef-Wassink, *Women at Arms: Is Ghadafi a Feminist?* (Edinburgh, 1993), ch. 3.
31. *Ibid.*
32. Interview, Zaynab 'Binhamid, 25 June 1998 (Washington, DC).
33. Obeidi, 'Changing attitudes to the role of women in Libyan society', n.p.
34. *Ibid.*
35. *Ibid.*
36. The name and rank of this officer are withheld to protect his identity. Discussions July 1994 (Damascus and Latakia, Syria).

pilot.[37] Today, women can enter the Turkish military as officers through post-secondary military training, though they are not subject to compulsory service as are Turkish males.[38] After comprehensive written and rigorous physical exams, the female matriculates learn all facets of military science and participate in mock manoeuvres. Formerly, Turkish women were employed solely in the support branches of the armed forces but today they serve in field, infantry, artillery, armoured, transport and engineer branches of the army. Demographic statistics broken down along gender lines are not available.[39]

When picturing Iranian women, most Westerners see huddled masses in black *chador*, women covered from head to toe. To most people, this is Islam. But before the Iranian revolution in 1979, the streets of Tehran were filled with unveiled young Muslim women wearing the short skirts of the 1970s; men and women comingled in the open. The sunny café-lined boulevards and trendy restaurants masked a wholly unpopular, repressive regime. In February 1979 and to the utter amazement of the rest of the world, the Ayatollah Khomeini led a massive, grass-roots revolution, over-threw the Shah and installed a strict Islamic theocratic government. Women found themselves to be the central focus of a culture war, in which Iranians attempted to define themselves in juxtaposition to 'corrupt' Western values. Forced to cover in public, women began to disappear from the streets; husbands and fathers called women home from work and demanded they spend their energies and time on the family and in the home.

Not all women rejected this call to islamicization. In the summer of 1984, female supporters of Khomeini from throughout the Muslim world gathered in Tehran at a conference. Zahra Rahnavard, the wife of the Prime Minister, addressed the audience: 'The oppressors of the world have conspired together to denigrate the wearing of the veil'. She challenged 'all oppressed women in Islamic countries to express their resistance to the cultures of heretics and atheists by wearing the Islamic veil and going into war'.[40] Her posture was not a sudden break from typically docile, timid, veiled Muslims: rather, Rahnavard's call to arms was the most recent in a long tradition of radical Shi'a women fighters.[41] One enduring image of the American Embassy attack in Tehran (1979) was of veiled, armed female commandos holding hostages at gunpoint.[42]

---

37. Feroz Ahmad, *The Making of Modern Turkey* (London, 1993), p. 87.
38. Interview, Mehmet Öztürky, Turkish military and defence attaché to the United States, 14 November 1998 (Washington, DC).
39. *Ibid.*
40. Minou Reeves, *Female Warriors of Allah: Women and the Islamic Revolution* (New York, 1989), pp. 19–20.
41. *Ibid.*, ch. 6.
42. *Ibid.*, p. 188.

Law precludes women, however, from serving in combat-related positions in the Iranian military or the revolutionary guards; most women employed by the armed forces work in support capacities such as secretarial work and transport.[43] Despite legal strictures forbidding women in combat, both men and women were recruited for the *Baseeji* militia, formed during the Iran–Iraq war (1980–89) to provide supplementary forces for the army and revolutionary guard. After the war, this rag-tag group of irregulars and trained guerrillas had no real purpose in the armed forces. Operating under a loose command structure, many of the *Baseejis* are involved today in some internal security functions. On occasion, highly trained female commandos perform martial arts demonstrations and display some hand-to-hand combat techniques learned in their militia training.[44]

Outside the traditionally defined Middle East, Muslim women have engaged in numerous armed struggles. In December 1997, Hazara[45] women rebels in northern Afghanistan re-took a Shi'a stronghold which had been occupied by the Islamic extremist Sunni Taliban. In response, the Taliban stormed and captured Mazar-n-Sherif on 9 August 1998, an area held by the anti-Taliban alliance of Uzbek and Shi'a Hazara. According to Amnesty International and UN sources, over 2,000 Hazara were massacred.[46] In Pakistan, Muslim women serve in the paramilitary 'Women's Guard' in administrative, nursing and clerical positions. While the Police Service of Pakistan is overwhelmingly male, former Prime Minister Benazir Bhutto commissioned the first all-female police station in 1994.[47] About 50 female officers of the Rawalapindi police station supplement Punjab's provisional police force of about 85,000 men. During her election campaign, Bhutto promised to appoint women to 10 per cent of the top police posts, but it is unclear whether she did so during her tenure.

The Nigerian Navy, the largest maritime force in West Africa, has approximately 500 officers and 4,500 enlisted men and women. Statistical

43. Interview, Dr Farideh Farhi, 30 September 1998 (Honolulu, HA).
44. *Ibid.*
45. The ethnic Hazara are predominantly Shi'a and number close to 870,000. D. Levinson, *Ethnic Groups Worldwide: A Ready Reference* (Phoenix, AZ, 1998), p. 196. They represent 19 per cent of the population, which numbers approximately 23,738,000 (1997). This includes Afghan refugees estimated to number about 1.2 million in Pakistan and about 1.4 million in Iran. *Britannica Online.* See 'Statistics: Afghanistan' *Britannica Online* <http://www.eb.com:180/cgi-bin/g?DocF=wld/K10000.html>
46. 'All Things Considered', National Public Radio broadcast, 10 December 1997; Ahmed Rashid, 'Islamic Face-Off', *Far Eastern Economic Review*, 17 September 1998.
47. Bhutto's initiative is not unusual in conservative Muslim societies. Women police officers or delegates are employed to investigate crimes against women – cultural conventions hold that women should interview female rape and assault victims and examine evidence in these cases. The Prime Minister's actions should not necessarily be read as inspired by feminist theory or a response to constituent demands.

information on the demographic distribution of Muslims and Christians, men and women in the armed forces is not available, but it is estimated that 70 per cent of senior officers come from the northern or middle regions, which are predominantly Muslim.[48] By 1984, the highest-ranking women served in the Medical Corps: one army colonel, one air force wing commander and one navy commander; the former two are Muslim.[49] In 1989, the Nigerian Navy announced that it was suspending recruitment of women except nurses until adequate and appropriate conditions of service had been devised such as accommodation, training and authorizations for marriages and pregnancies; whether the suspension has been lifted is unknown.[50]

Muslim women serve in the armed forces of Indonesia, where 87.2 per cent of the total population is Muslim.[51] Here, the army, navy, air force and police are collectively referred to as the Armed Forces of the Republic of Indonesia; each branch has an attached women's unit. According to Brigadier General Dadi Susanto, the Indonesian defence attaché to the United States, the all-female units are not assigned combat roles[52] but rather are 'set to work at places and in functions conform[ing] to their feminine disposition'.[53] This includes administrative work, nursing, health and nutrition, and the women police 'play an important role in solving problems [of] drug addicts and juvenile delinquents'.[54]

In perhaps their most visible role in Asia, Muslim women served in the Moro National Liberation Front (MNLF), the largest Muslim secession movement in the Philippines.[55] Formed in response to over 400 years of Spanish, American and Philippine interventionist policies against the indigenous Muslim minority,[56] the MNLF sought to establish an independent nation of Mindanao and the surrounding southern islands. Over almost three decades, revolutionary forces engaged in irregular hostilities with the

---

48.   The population of Nigeria totals 103,460,000 and religiously breaks down as follows: Muslim 50.0 per cent; Christian 40.0 per cent, of which Protestant 21.4 per cent, Roman Catholic 9.9 per cent, African indigenous 8.7 per cent; other 10.0 per cent. 'Statistics: Nigeria', *Britannica Online*. <http://www.eb.com:180/cgi-bin/g?DocF=wld/K10640.html>

49.   Interview, Capt. J. Odey, Nigerian defence attaché to the United States, 12 November 1998 (Washington, DC).

50.   *Ibid.*

51.   'Statistics: Indonesia', *Britannica Online* <http://www.eb.com:180/cgi-bin/g?DocF=wld/K10385.html>

52.   Interview, Brigadier General Dadi Susanto, 12 November 1998.

53.   William H. Frederick and Robert L. Worden, eds, *Indonesia, A Country Study*, 5th edn (Washington, 1993).

54.   *Ibid.*

55.   Vivienne S.M. Angeles, 'Philippine Muslim women: tradition and change', in Yazbeck Haddad and Esposito, eds, *Islam, Gender and Social Change*, pp. 210–15.

56.   Muslims form the largest single religious minority in the Philippines. See Samuel K. Tan, *The Filipino Muslim Armed Struggle*, 1900–1972 (Makati, Rizal, 1977).

Philippine military, reaching an unprecedented level of warfare by the early 1970s. A short-lived truce achieved through the Tripoli Agreement of 1976 provided 'autonomy . . . within the context of Philippine sovereignty',[57] but the MNLF and the Philippine government did not achieve a stable peace until 20 years later.[58]

Like their sisters-in-arms throughout the world, Moro women initially provided support for the guerrilla movement through recruitment, organization and consciousness-raising in the rural Muslim areas. But with President Ferdinand Marcos's declaration of martial law in September 1972, the women's involvement became more active. Quite a few Moro women were arrested, detained and questioned by the military, and some fled to guerrilla-held areas in fear of arrest or torture. Just as the Kuwaitis and Palestinians used traditional and Islamic dress to their advantage, Moro women were instrumental in moving weapons and information past checkpoints under their traditional full, blowsy skirts. And while the MNLF did not plan to send women to the more combat-active areas, scores of female guerrillas fought when necessary. 'Farouza' was killed by government forces in Jolo in 1974; in Basilan, the wife of an MNLF commander led 150 men in armed conflict after her husband died in combat.[59]

When the camps or villages were raided, women were often abused, and as violence intensified, the MNLF recognized the need for women to be formally trained in combat and self-defence. The Women's Auxiliary Forces were organized and in 1972 women began military training in Jolo. In addition to self-defence, these women learned how to fashion small crude weapons, home-made explosives and ammunition for delivery to men in the field. More often than not, however, the division of labour in the camps and villages fell largely along gender-segregated lines. Like women in the Palestinian Liberation Organization before 1970, Moro women offered moral support to the fighting men and nursed the wounded. Ongoing battles disrupted the education system, so Muslim women organized make-shift schools and tutored children in reading and writing. By selling some of their handicrafts, collecting contributions and engaging in money-lending, Moro women supported the MNLF financially.

---

57. Vivienne S.M. Angeles, 'Women and revolution: Philippine Muslim women's participation in the Moro National Liberation Front', *Muslim World* 86 (1996), p. 132.

58. A more militant break-away faction of the MNLF, the Moro Islamic Liberation Front (MILF), does not accept the 1996 peace agreement and continued violent attacks in the south until July 1997, when a ceasefire was declared. With the exception of a few breaches, the ceasefire has held, but a peace treaty between the government and the MILF is not expected in the very near future.

59. Angeles, 'Philippine Muslim women', p. 224. Also see Cesar Majul, *Contemporary Muslim Movements in the Philippines* (Berkeley, CA, 1985).

The extensive involvement of Philippine women in resistance activities raised social consciousness regarding their normal status. By the 1980s, Muslim women had assumed responsibilities in the organizational structure of the MNLF. Operating at municipal, provincial and national levels, numerous committees directed finance, foreign and economic affairs, transportation and communication, intelligence and information, and social welfare and women. While women were involved in all levels of committee work, initially a woman chaired only one national committee: the Women's Committee.[60] In 1994, Chairman Nur Misuari appointed women to chair the Social Welfare, Health and Sanitation Committees.[61] And while women were involved in the peace negotiations of 1986 and 1996, they primarily provided support through secretarial work and information-gathering.

Since the peace agreement has been reached, the question remains whether and in what ways women will be more fully integrated into non-traditional spheres of power. In a 1995 interview, Chairman Misuari acknowledged the substantial contributions of women in their struggle for self-determination. At the same time, however, the leader of the MNLF also 'pointed out the complementary roles of men and women in Islam, with women usually controlling matters relevant to the home, and men dealing with matters outside the home'.[62]

Conclusion

All across Islamic societies, the behaviour of women during wartime and resistance loosely follows the paradigm outlined above. In response to the demands of national crises, Muslim women contributed to the efforts of war or armed resistance, whether through combat or support roles. In all of the countries and movements surveyed above, Muslim women provided moral support and promoted their causes by raising social consciousness and financial support, and assuming duties in society ordinarily performed by men. Perhaps the most striking example of this occurred during the 1990–91 Gulf War; Kuwaiti women organized and ran the resistance movement as most of the men had fled or were in hiding. When fighting suspended educational and social services, Palestinian women (like many Muslim women in other countries) stepped into the breach and made sanitation arrangements,

---

60. See 'Role of women in the Bangsa Moro revolution', *Mahardika* 9 (1982), pp. 1–3, and Angeles, 'Women and revolution', pp. 140–1.
61. Angeles, 'Women and revolution', p. 140.
62. *Ibid.*, p. 146.

taught children and organized food distribution. And, when necessary, women throughout the Muslim world took up arms and defended their families, homes and countries – sometimes losing their lives.

In the Muslim world and elsewhere, wartime typically suspends cultural norms, including those of gender. But more than merely assuming the tasks typically performed by men, these women astutely used normally strict social conventions to their advantage. Women who are often seen simply in terms of the veil or *chador* demonstrate this through the politics of dress. Algerian women in short skirts, Kuwaitis anonymous in full, black *'abaya* or disguised as Indians in saris, Palestinian women hiding wanted men beneath their skirts and Philippine women smuggling arms and ammunition under long billowy skirts – all successfully used the cultural norms of conservative garb to further their covert interests. Beguiling French soldiers with short skirts and artfully applied make-up, Algerian women gathered intelligence and planted bombs in their war of independence.

In the West, the service of women in the world wars, coupled with an evolving tradition of feminist thought, was followed by an ever-increasing female participation in the public sphere. But it would be faulty to assume that Muslim societies will necessarily follow this 'trajectory' of historical development. While involvement in the defence of the nation has led to heightened awareness of the status of women in Muslim society, one cannot easily explain away the rising mass conservatism of Libyan society or the calls for *jihad* from veiled women in Iran. Just as the peoples of the developing and Muslim world are heterogeneous, so are the feminist voices. Not all Muslim feminists are interested in adopting the Western model of gender relations; and neither are they interested in adopting a rigid code of quasi-religious law. We need to understand the seeming paradox of Muslim women in combat rooted in its historical and cultural context, while appreciating that 'their' feminist issues may not be 'ours'.

Muslim women throughout the twentieth century – and indeed, throughout history – are no less involved in the defence of their homes and countries than are Western women. In striking gender role reversals, public and private space is redefined as Muslim women respond to national crises. Functioning as more than wives and mothers – they are nurses, farmers, artisans, teachers, intelligence operatives and fighters – Muslim women defy easy categorization or simple explanation.

CHAPTER THIRTEEN

Between Worlds:
Algerian Women in Conflict

NICOLE F. LADEWIG

Histories written according to the framework of gender often depend upon the dichotomy between the oppressor and the oppressed. Distinguishing enemies and allies along gender lines implies the historical goal of unified empowerment for uniformly oppressed women. The integrity of such gendered histories relies upon these rigid definitions and presumes that they transcend cultural and political contexts. The modern Algerian women's struggle to participate in an Islamic, patriarchal society that has become defined by war, itself viewed as a masculine endeavour, appears to fit seamlessly with this model. However, understanding the evolution of Algerian national identity requires recognition of complex processes that defy oppositional absolutes based upon gender distinctions. Algerian society from colonial times to the present has witnessed violence predicated on economic, political and social upheavals in which identity roles, whether national, male or female, conformed to the exigencies of the time. Wars of both words and weapons have been fought continually since 1830, and the accompanying social, cultural and political transformations have necessitated a profound series of identity changes for Algerian women. The women mediated these historical changes from Berber clans to Algerian nationhood; and they will shepherd the Algerian future, and the future of Algerian women, by assuming and blending roles of active agency and passive silence.

The women of North Africa have historically reconciled opposing forces within complex social relationships that encompassed the Maghreb. The Berbers' indigenous matrilineal societies, complete with legends of female warriors, faced Islamic expansion and incorporated the associated Arabic patrilineal societies in which women held an inferior status to men. The incomplete, and relatively contested, process of social arabization affected all North African societies well into the latter half of the nineteenth century.

240

The arrival of European colonial administrations rapidly added further complications to the Maghrebi societies. The colonial territory defined by French administrators as Algeria experienced a uniquely complex and wrenching transformation as the French government of 1830 created a settlement colony, encouraging French citizens to relocate to the North African coast. In addition to the network of colonial administrators, this new wave of foreigners assumed a proprietary role over all that was Berber and Arab. Women and their roles, often solely defined by social structures such as marriage and family, were acutely affected by these social transformations. Algerian women, recalling the social reformation subsequent to Arabic invasion, created additional layers of identity for themselves in reaction to the altered social hierarchy now dominated by the French. Nonetheless, these women also tried to preserve pre-colonial social traditions. The multifaceted roles that modern Algerian women occupy find their lineage in both subservient and dominant historical identities. The images of both veiled and unveiled women in Algeria provide the clearest symbols of these imbricated roles. Women continue to define their identities, and subsequently the identities of Algeria as a whole, in the context of new, often opposing, cultural and social forces.

These social and cultural transformations and the mediating role of women obviously and significantly impacted upon Algerian women's interpretations of themselves, and such processes certainly continue to inform the evolving gender identity of Maghrebi women. The roles women play influence society and are simultaneously influenced by society as the female gender occupies a focal position in Algerians' understanding of their national identity. Alya Baffoun most concisely captures this touchstone quality of Algerian women, defining them as 'the ultimate reference matrix bear[ing] within [their] deepest being those very notions through which societies identify and by which they name themselves'.[1] However, such centrality does not necessarily translate into control over the development of identity and status; thus, '[b]eing the guardian [of society's identity] is being a potential traitor who should therefore be closely watched'.[2] Indeed, Algerian women's participation in society from the war for liberation through independence into today's civil strife needs to be examined in order to comprehend fully the roots of both agency of action and silence of passivity among women in Algeria.

---

1. Alya Baffoun, 'Feminism and Muslim fundamentalism: the Tunisian and Algerian cases', in Valentine M. Moghadem, ed., *Identity Politics and Women: Cultural Reassertions and Feminisms in International Perspective* (Boulder CO, 1994), p. 168.
2. Marie-Aimee Helie-Lucas, 'The preferential symbol for Islamic identity: women in Muslim personal laws', in Moghadem, ed., *Identity Politics and Women*, p. 394.

Prior to European colonialism, Algerians, and particularly Algerian women, understood their identities in terms of immediate family, a network of kinship and clan ties, followed by a wider regional connection. The introduction of the Islamic faith and its subsequent reinforcement through waves of Arabic and Islamic overlords served to unify North Africans religiously. Due to this blanket of religious conformity, identity was only peripherally understood in terms of being Muslim; family and region rather than religion differentiated Algerians internally. The appearance of French colonials radically changed, arguably forever, this hierarchical order of identity (family primarily, religion secondarily). Sociologist Marnia Lazreg claims that the French authorities' nearly singular focus on the Islamic religion as a basis of Algerian identity rendered this social aspect the most significant.[3] This alteration of identity, reflected in the consistent colonial dialogue in Muslim and European terms rather than Muslim and Christian terms, powerfully impacted women. Traditions which reflected culture and faith became immediately political and had imposed upon them significance not warranted by faith alone.

The tradition among some Algerian women, particularly those fully arabized, of wearing a face-covering veil was transformed into 'a social practice and a powerful symbol – [playing] a central role in producing and maintaining both Algeria's difference from its colonial oppressor, and the uneasy coalition of *heterogeneous* and *conflicting interests* under a single national banner'.[4] The veil, shorn of religious meaning and uniformly associated with all Algerian women, served as a recurring symbol for the 'woman question' during times of social and political unrest. Its absence or presence provided the most striking physical sign of which social faction or political party controlled Algerian life. In the context of colonial Algeria, women's lives, regardless of their pre-colonial practices, became the instruments of social reorganization under French colonial rule. Alf A. Heggoy posits that this new form of Muslim identity cemented women's social subservience during the colonial period. In reality, Algerian women saw nothing become constant or cemented in their lives as the Europeans interpreted them as 'the key[s] to breaking down resistance to colonial domination'.[5]

Algerian women, in image only, gained political importance as tools of mediation between the French, initially hesitant to involve themselves in Islamic practices, and the Algerians, obviously resistant to French colonial domination. Although the colonial administrators promised to leave the Algerian Islamic religious practices unaltered, actions and circumstances proved

3. Marnia Lazreg, 'Gender and politics in Algeria: unravelling the religious paradigm', *Signs* 15, 4 (1990), p. 758.
4. Winifred Woodhull, 'Unveiling Algeria', *Genders* 10 (1991), p. 114, emphasis mine.
5. Lazreg, 'Gender and politics in Algeria', p. 767.

their promises to be hollow. Beyond the central mosque in Algiers being converted into a Catholic church, the presence alone of French military, administrators and settlers unavoidably polarized interaction around the Islamic faith and its followers. Participation in Algerian society, as conceived of by the French nationals, was accessible only by adoption of and assimilation to the French culture. However, this assimilation 'obliged [Algerians] to renounce Islamic law and their self-perception as Algerian Muslims and accept the application of French law to themselves'.[6] Beyond religious faithfulness, the new unifying distinction and politicization of the Muslim identity, created by the French presence, made this an impossible option. For the majority of male Algerians, this exclusion from participation, power and prestige left them with few avenues to express authority, 'and thus [they] turned inward to their families. . . . The superiority of the male, already well entrenched through historic and religious developments, became almost absolute.'[7] The two cultures had formed their terms of interaction by reconfiguring women's lives to express and demonstrate power, either French or Algerian, but always male.

Economic subjugation required all Algerian family members to contribute to the welfare of the household in ways not traditionally pursued. Women had historically contributed to the economic welfare of the family through household management and, most importantly, cultivation of family land. The French effectively closed this avenue for many families by seizing or buying control over most of the productive land. Women had to turn outside the confines of the home to meet the needs of their families. Consequently, they sought menial service work from French or Westernized Algerian employers. They shuttled between two very different cultures. Doria Cherifati-Merabtine poignantly acknowledges that 'they were battling with two worlds, the cramped and poor Muslim districts, and luxurious and comfortable European suburbs. The first world denied her because she had transgressed the forbidden; the second denied her identity and integrity in so far as it had placed her in a non-world.'[8]

These economic and social experiences of Algerian women illustrated the repression experienced by the majority of Algerians. Increasing discontent and evaporating economic participation under colonial rule spurred segments

---

6. Alf A. Heggoy, 'Algerian women and the right to vote: some colonial anomalies', *Muslim World* 64, 3 (1974), p. 230.
7. Alf A. Heggoy, 'Cultural disrespect: European and Algerian views on women in colonial and independent Algeria', *Muslim World* 62, 4 (1972), p. 330.
8. Doria Cherifati-Merabtine, 'Algeria at a crossroads: national liberation, Islamization and women', in Valentine M. Moghadam, ed., *Gender and National Identity: Women and Politics in Muslim Societies* (London and Karachi, 1994), p. 44.

of Algerian society to revolt in 1954, demanding the liberation of their land under a tenuously unified resistance movement called the National Liberation Front (FLN). The role of women became integral to the success of the resistance as national freedom for *all* Algerians defined the war's purpose. However, women's participation perpetuated their complex role as surviving between competing forces rather than constituting a force in and of itself. Importantly, not a single woman held a significant role of influence in the FLN; Algerian males directed the war and devised its strategies. The FLN leaders realized that women would necessarily play essential roles in the reconstruction of a free Algeria, although it assiduously avoided engaging in discourse that addressed the potential assertion of women's rights. The rights that concerned the leaders of this war encompassed national rights, not necessarily male or female. The resistance, precariously held together by FLN leaders, consisted of several competing political ideological factions; therefore, leaders necessarily avoided additional sources of contention among Algerians. Because women's participation in the war effort proved vital to the success of the resistance, leaders appropriated an ambiguous stance towards women soldiers that recognized their contributions, but avoided guaranteeing particular rewards as a consequence. Lazreg points out that FLN leaders preferred to let actions suffice for promises: 'Initially the FLN argued that women's less-than-equal status was the result of years of colonial neglect of the Algerian people. . . . The FLN further pointed out that by participating in the war women had essentially freed themselves of the fetters of colonial oppression.'[9]

This position of liberation through participation in the war gained support through the publications of Frantz Fanon, who, writing during the war, associated women's involvement with modern roles for their liberated status, free from colonial oppression. He felt women had shorn themselves of cultural and political repression through their active participation in the men's game of war, exemplified by unveiling and travelling in public without male companions. An important distinction must be made between what Fanon interpreted as a distinctly feminist impetus for women's participation and the motives expressed by those who participated. Rather than undertaking the bold steps of selective use of the veil, unchaperoned excursions from the home, and defiance of familial male authorities for the purpose of creating a new and independent *feminine* role in their society free from colonial rule, women soldiers sought a new *national* role of freedom from the French administration. Women sought the reassertion of Algerian traditions and culture, not their dismantling. Houria, who participated in the war for independence in the countryside, states: 'We talked about getting

---

9. Lazreg, 'Gender and politics in Algeria', p. 765.

the French out, that is all'.[10] This is supported by Djamila Bouhired, one of the three Djamilas that captured the public image of female militants, who stated when reflecting upon her arrest by the French: 'I realized that nothing worth while could be achieved until we had seen to our country's needs'.[11] The goal had always been to reassert the Algerian culture, not to assert the liberated nature of women. Accepting the lack of feminist rhetoric and the absence of assurances for feminist reforms in an independent Algeria, women tacitly approved the *national* agenda, not a *feminist* agenda. Anessa Benamour supports this position as she writes, 'To be Algerian was all – and we neglected to ask what that might mean, in terms of rights and responsibilities and social and political relations'.[12]

The nature of the nationalist cause allowed little challenge of its motives; the support which female participants have acknowledged demonstrated this focus on a goal exclusive of gender equality. Success of the resistance depended upon gathering and sustaining substantial support among the people. But some factions of Algerians chose to support the maintenance of French rule, and the resistance movement with FLN at the forefront possessed relatively weak cohesive powers over nationalist factions. Dedication to the cause of the nation was of utmost importance and '[o]bedience, morality and conformity were necessary conditions to be part of the revolution'.[13] The demand by women for a newly defined role of equality would have harmfully diverted Algerian attention and endangered the unification of resistors. In fact, women did not conceive of such questions, even in reaction to the continuing connotation of female status through the use of the veil. In the throes of a war 'how was one to take up the issue of the veil as oppressive to women? How could [women] do it without betraying both the *Nation* and the *Revolution*.'[14] Furthermore, the issue of the veil proved to be a moot point during the war; the French had made the veil an ideological instrument of utility, hence the Algerian women reappropriated the veil as a tool and used it for the nationalistic cause. The women seized upon and effectively used a tool created by the French, who never assumed Algerian women possessed the capacity to do so.

---

10. Cherifa Boutta, 'Feminine militancy: Moudjahidates during and after the Algerian War', in Moghadem, ed., *Gender and National Identity*, p. 29.
11. Nora Benallgue, 'Algerian women in the struggle for independence and reconstruction', *International Social Science Journal* 35, 4 (1983), p. 704.
12. Anessa Benamour, 'Women as targets', *Freedom Review* 26, 5 (1995), p. 33.
13. Marie-Aimee Helie-Lucas, 'The role of women during the Algerian liberation struggle and after: nationalism as a concept and as a practice towards both the power of the army and the militarization of the people', in Eva Isakson, ed., *Women and the Military System* (New York, 1988), p. 178.
14. *Ibid.*, p. 177.

The French realized that the participation of women in the war kept alive an organizationally and militarily overwhelmed resistance movement. Colonial officials staged elaborately designed events to show Algerian men that, should Algerian women choose to align with the French, the liberation movement would be lost. The purported goals of liberating Algerian women were nothing more than a thinly disguised divide-and-conquer strategy. In effect, both the French and the Algerians realized the women were the linchpin. Algerians needed their support and active participation; the French needed their passivity and renunciation of an Islamic, patriarchal society. As a hallmark of this 'liberation' policy, the events of 13 May 1958 demonstrated that the French continued to hold women and their cause as the most decisive factor in overpowering the nationals. By this date, key army officers and administrators felt 'neither aided, nor encouraged, nor supported in the battle for a French Algeria'.[15] Explosively protesting this state of affairs, they revolted against the French government and demanded that General Charles de Gaulle assume control, believing he would ensure a French Algeria. To bolster their claims that a French victory was certain, and in an effort to demoralize any Algerian feelings of success, the officers' wives 'presided over the public unveiling of Algerian women whose slogan was "Let's be like the French woman"'.[16] While this strategy eventually backfired, serving to coalesce Algerian women into more fervid support of the liberation movement, it demonstrated that the women remained 'the best tools the French could use to break down traditional society', the essential ingredient for dominating a culture and a nation.[17] The French clearly misunderstood two key facets of this event's impact. First, the audience consisted largely of French supporters of the generals in revolt. Few press accounts made it to the Algerians, of whom only a small percentage could read French. Second, Algerian women never envisioned female liberation as being a necessary component of national liberation. The French had chosen an issue they believed to be significant to female participants in the war, and therefore antagonistic and divisive for Algerian males. However, the issue remained irrelevant compared with the larger goal of Algerian freedom.

As the war progressed unabatedly, Algerian women used the veil in its new utilitarian role. Women realized that alternately donning and shedding the veil provided them with unique abilities to play their roles without question, particularly during the Battle of Algiers in 1957. The urban setting of this battle proved women indispensable. Algerian men operated

---

15. Alistair Horne, *A Savage War of Peace* (New York, 1977), p. 269.
16. Winifred Woodhull, 'Unveiling Algeria', *Genders* 10 (1991), p. 118.
17. Heggoy, 'Cultural disrespect', p. 324.

underground, avoiding interrogation and detention by French authorities. However, women moved relatively freely and unharassed either by assuming a European appearance, thus seeming to adopt and support the French ways, or by wearing a veil, which the French, despite interference with other religious practices, viewed as a religious expression beyond suspicion. Women dismissed the French overtures of 'liberation' from the traditions and culture of Algeria; rather they *actively* sought to liberate themselves from *French* subjugation, which meant reaffirming a solidarity towards their own culture, of which the veil was a part.

The actual participation and roles undertaken by women demonstrate their pursuit of a liberating and equalizing agenda for the *nation* of Algeria as a whole. Two avenues of participation in the war existed for women: joining the civilian ranks of the FLN or enlisting in the soldier ranks of the National Liberation Army (ALN), the armed branch of the FLN. Becoming a member of the ALN entitled women to a uniform, which proved nearly the only distinction between branches. Women's participation in both the FLN and the ALN incorporated armed manoeuvres which directly targeted enemies, as well as staffing and operating 'auxiliary services such as nursing, communications . . . [and] underground networks of sanctuaries'.[18] Despite the avenue of military enlistment, and its remarkable similarity to civilian roles, the vast majority (over 85 per cent) of women joined the civilian ranks of the FLN. Marnia Lazreg comments that, although any participation in war proved dangerous, 'the bulk of women's work was less spectacular, perhaps even tedious'.[19] Nevertheless, the tedious tasks provided vitally necessary services; women kept the network of male soldiers mobile, alive and protected.

Neither branch of the resistance consistently provided wages or benefits for participants, regardless of their sex. Nationalists launched their resistance to provide exactly those social resources for its people, and no network existed for such formalized operations within the underground movement. Recognition and remuneration of veterans would be the benefits of success. Approximately 11,000 women registered as veterans of the Algerian Independence War, a misleadingly low official figure as veteran registration required some basic level of literacy and provision of testimonial evidence. Such requirements often barred those women who even bothered to attempt the bureaucratic maze. Out of the officially registered female veterans, less than 0.05 per cent served in any leadership position and less than 70 veterans directly worked with explosives or carried arms.[20] This fact destroys the

---

18. Marnia Lazreg, *The Eloquence of Silence: Algerian Women in Question* (New York, 1994), p. 124.
19. *Ibid.*, p. 124.
20. *Ibid.*, pp. 124–125.

important female myths surrounding Algerian female soldiers and 'gives a blow to Fanon's mythology (and followers) of the liberated Algerian woman', who created her liberation by participating in the war on equal grounds with the men.[21] According to the research of veteran Djamila Amrane, the majority of women functioned in largely feminine roles, such as caring for the wounded, providing supplies and food, delivering messages and hiding men sought by French authorities. These participatory roles reflect women's pre-war status; none reflected an egalitarian atmosphere of war in which women assumed the same roles as men. In an ironic twist, the French gave equal credence to Algerian women's roles and demonstrated that belief by imprisoning, torturing and murdering those who participated. Women had the equality they did not yet seek in this realm of war.

After six years of war, the FLN finally had what it sought, agreement from the French government that the colonial administration would disband and Algeria would be an independent nation with an Algerian administration. In the initial days of victory, the new political leaders overcame their dearth of future political planning and drafted a National Charter and Constitution which granted full equality and equal participatory rights to women. But R. Tlemcani notes, 'this goal [of women's full and equal status] was more rhetorical than attainable because the Algerian political leadership . . . is fundamentally conservative when it comes to the issue of women's rights and status'.[22] The goal certainly sounded legitimate, but the actions of the independent government back Tlemcani's claim: women became profoundly insignificant to the male political leadership, other than being the means by which a campaign of national growth, i.e. childbearing, commenced.

Inclusion of women in the improvement programmes, such as education, furthered the appearance of liberation, but this was a double-edged sword for most women. Schools developed curricula that emphasized modernization tempered by the importance of recapturing traditions necessary to rebuild a culture seriously injured by 132 years of French rule. Textbooks included women in home-oriented roles, modernized through the use of new efficiencies in home economics and raising children in an Algerian culture and faith. The social improvement programmes effectively eliminated women from any role of political influence in the independent government. The organization of the National Union of Algerian Women (UNFA) bestowed positions of figurehead spokeswomen. Cherifa Boutta notes that 'the UNFA [was] under the guardianship of the single political party: the FLN. The role

---

21. Helie-Lucas, 'The role of women during the Algerian liberation struggle and after', p. 175.
22. R. Tlemcani, 'The rise of Algerian women: cultural dualism and multi-party politics', *Journal of Developing Societies* 8, 1 (1992), p. 70.

of the UNFA was insignificant . . . The social eclipse of women [soldiers] after independence is a fact', and the utility of these spokeswomen is question-able.[23] Their overwhelming position of political minority effectively silenced opposition to implemented programmes as well as any suggestions of altern-ative agendas such as women's rights.

The contradictions in Algerian rebirth and the roles given to women are striking. The Algerian national goals of socialist modernization and recon-struction of a pre-colonial society were fundamentally incompatible; the tension between these two pivoted on women's roles. Women, in their social roles, mediated the expectations of cultural restoration and the creation of socialism, serving in a role familiar to their foremothers. They willingly followed the overarching pursuit of a more egalitarian economic and polit-ical society yet found their specific roles not only restrictive but also sub-missive in nature. The expectation of total commitment to both aspects of independent Algeria existed due to the nationalistic sentiments still gripping the new nation. This position of 'betweenness' stems from the larger un-resolved reality of the war for independence; a revolution was fought for the restoration of an Algerian culture, yet the women's involvement proved crucial not only for the military defence of their nation, but also for the defence of Algerian society's self-definition. The contradictions between national goals and the roles assigned to women remained unrecognized by the women themselves for years, and thus no impetus for a resolution existed.

Compounding this ill-defined role of women, the entire Algerian nation began to endure the economic difficulties that ravaged so many African nations during the 1980s. Years of autocratic rule and economic misman-agement had taken their toll on the Algerian citizens, and the dissatisfaction of the younger generations began to surface in a variety of expressions dur-ing the early 1980s. The economic depression felt by the bulk of Algerians very visibly exempted society's privileged elite. The tension and dissension created by this situation produced new political and economic ideologies among the masses. The compulsory education plans had an unintended consequence of creating a generation of young, reasonably educated people who found their fair expectations of employment and a comfortable life impossible to achieve. F.Z. Karadja, in examining this 'lost generation', writes: 'The young unemployed were looking, not for real jobs, but for ones that do not even exist . . . their grudge against the state [had] crystallized into a plan of action.'[24]

The plan of action was formulated in the mosques, which often provided the only opportunities for free expression, albeit under a religious umbrella.

---

23. Boutta, 'Feminine militancy', pp. 23, 35.
24. F.Z. Karadja, 'Young Algerians: a lost generation', *Freedom Review* 26, 5 (1995), p. 34.

This setting, coupled with a desire to revolt against the secular and modern government viewed as the cause of their distress, led to political strategies built on top of a revitalized religious faith. A return to the perceived traditions of Islam would further the reclamation of an Algerian culture that the dissenting youth believed had not been salvaged from Western and colonial influences. For this generation of revolutionaries, the nationality of political leaders caused no problem, but the source of their economic and social practices did. The solution for Algeria was found in a 'fundamentalist' interpretation of the Muslim faith. The term 'fundamentalism' is in itself a complex negotiation of culture, society and politics in the Algerian context. A female university student in Algiers defines the situation: 'You have to distinguish between true Islam and what it has been saddled with. People were deprived of cultural resources during colonization, and as they emerge from ignorance, they often have a superficial or distorted idea of Islam.'[25] Karima Bennoune distils fundamentalism into 'specific political movements', thus distinguishing between secular and religious doctrines.[26] The crisis in Algeria focuses on precisely how religious doctrines can, or should, inform political ideologies. In a remarkable continuance of Algerian habits, the status of women has become the focal point for the mediation of secular and religious, social and political forces. Despite the intention of the reactionary movement to bury the image of female soldiers crucial to the success of the war for independence, the fundamentalists failed to realize that their discourse relies upon the very symbolic heart of the war of independence: Algerian women. Just as the French and Algerians recognized the importance of women's alliance, the fractious Algerians return to the same group to demonstrate either success or failure of national goals. Women again become the bellwether for the country's strife.

Active fundamentalists 'obstreperously demand "purification" measures . . . and above all, wearing the hidjab for women', making women the visible instrument for social conversion to the fundamentalist political cause.[27] Borrowing from Islamic cultural practices, particularly those of Iran and Saudi Arabia, the idea of the hidjab – a full-length, cloak-like covering worn over the clothing in combination with a headscarf or a face-veil is an alien imposition on Algerian women. Traditionally, women only wore a face-veil, and some Berber clans chose not to assume that aspect of Islamic culture. The full-length cloaking, while selectively in use during the colonial

25. Fatiha Akeb and Malika Abdelaziz, 'Algerian women discuss the need for change', trans. Adele Fath, in Elizabeth Warnock Fernea, ed., *Women and the Family in the Middle East: New Voices of Change* (Austin, TX, 1985), p. 15.
26. Karima E. Bennoune, 'The war against women in Algeria' in *Ms* (September 1995), p. 24.
27. Tlemcani, 'The rise of Algerian women', p. 78.

period, was not a uniformly adopted practice. Hence, the fundamentalist movement seeks to 're-establish' a practice on the grounds that it is traditional to Algerian culture when in fact it has little historical precedent in Algeria.

In light of the economic woes of the country, the Algerian government selectively picked opportunities to compromise with the ever-increasing voices of discontent. Marnia Lazreg summarizes the government's accommodation of the early fundamentalists as 'an attempt to retain its power in the face of a dysfunctioning economic program and mounting political opposition'.[28] This alliance, or accommodation, focused on the interpretation of women's social and familial roles in Algeria. To acquiesce in the definition of women in society was perhaps the most logical point for the male FLN government, allowing new gender social prescriptions to reflect the fundamentalists' desire to purify Algerian society against the influence of Western cultures. This acquiescence served a purely political role of 'mut[ing] economic conflict between men, and also forestall[ing] violent struggle between the fundamentalist groups . . . and "progressive" nationalist factions, [thus] fix[ing] upon "the Arab and Muslim Algerian women" as the indispensable unifying force'.[29] The cooperation of these competing forces expressed itself in terms beyond merely the clothing of women. The sides collectively produced legislation, the Family Code of 1984, to codify women as subservient to men, which included granting each man the right to cast ballots in the name of up to three women in his household. This legislative milestone serves as the turning point in the women's movement of Algeria.

After years of silence, and an apparent loss of agency on their own behalf, the issue of the Family Code sparked the active voice of the independent woman, this time in support of herself rather than her nation, as an entity. In response to the fundamentalists' desire to shed the legacy of the war for independence, the women turned directly to the veterans of that war for legitimacy and foundational support for their newly feminist movement. Reinterpreting female participation in the war for independence as evidence of gender equality, Algerian women touched on the very issue that had long been buried. Women's social and political subservience was antithetical to the integral nature of their presence in society, including warfare. Interestingly enough, the female soldier of independence rejected her previous claims of nationalism's primacy and claimed a new role for herself 20 years after she helped cement her nation's freedom.

The only official representation of women, the UNFA, saw the issue of the Family Code as the impetus to 'come out of its lethargy' and to begin

---

28. Lazreg, 'Gender and politics in Algeria', p. 777.
29. Woodhull, 'Unveiling Algeria', p. 115.

building a stronger voice for the Algerian woman in her society, including publicly demonstrating in the streets of Algiers.[30] The women veterans of the war for independence recognized that their endeavours served as a logical foundation for feminist thought. Fully capable of assuming tradition-ally male roles (breadwinner for a family) and integrally participating in the game of war, female veterans had demonstrated that the doctrine of inferiority did not fit with their own history. They began to see the claims for equality they could have pressed forward but had failed to identify in the context of their time. The divorce of national liberation and female liberation, viewed in the modern context of the 1980s, recalled the pain of coloniza-tion. As veteran Houria states, 'What hurts me, what I cannot get into my head, is the women colonized by men. . . . The woman accepts this, she does nothing to change her situation. It is her fault.'[31] Women veterans, as well as the younger generations, began to realize the impact of their own silence and the necessity of examining what an independent Algerian woman could be.

Before a thorough campaign for feminine equality can begin, Algerian women face the task of defining the terms of their argument, as well as their legitimacy in making the argument for an independent, liberated woman. Malika Abdelaziz quotes Najet, an educator in Algeria, as acknowledging this task of definition by stating: 'emancipation has become suspect and is associated with renunciation of one's cultural and religious identity and is basically associated with the myth of Western influence; this usage obstructs women's aspirations'.[32] The fundamentalists' association of emancipatory or modernizing goals for women as imposed Western concepts, and there-fore morally bankrupt, requires that 'instead of going straight to the point, women first try to demonstrate that they are truly and genuinely rooted in their own culture . . . that they do not side with external enemies . . . [thus] they expend considerable time and energy trying to distinguish themselves from "Western feminists"'.[33]

The problem of asserting themselves as part of Algerian culture, yet pursuing goals of equality, became increasingly difficult as the overall polit-ical and social atmosphere of Algeria continued to disintegrate into unrest as the unabated economic woes drew heavier and sharper criticism upon the FLN-based government. The unrest eventually bubbled over into action as the Algerian youth and the disenfranchised erupted into riots during October 1988. After a modicum of order had been restored, the government

---

30. Tlemcani, 'The rise of Algerian women', p. 77.
31. Boutta, 'Feminine militancy', p. 31.
32. Akeb and Abdelaziz, 'Algerian women discuss the need for change', p. 22.
33. Helie-Lucas, 'The preferential symbol for Islamic identity', p. 399.

relaxed several of its traditionally autocratic practices and allowed for the organization of opposition parties. As the most cohesively organized movement, the fundamentalists gained official status as the Islamic Front of Salvation (FIS). FIS popularity and activism led to significant electoral victories in the elections of 1990 and they continued to centre many of their suggested reforms on the status of women. The solution to high unemployment amounted to remanding women to the home, thus creating employment vacancies for men. This suggestion gained momentum despite the decline since 1987 of women workforce participants to a low of approximately 4 per cent and the increase of overall unemployment statistics to roughly 25 per cent of the labour force. Above all else, fundamentalists viewed the 'polluted' Algerian society as the consequence of adopting or permitting Western ideologies to invade the perceived traditional and Islamic Algerian culture. Algerian women who dared to express alternative, modern interpretations of gender roles symbolize the 'symptoms of colonization, impiety, the destruction of the family, dissolute morals, and economic crisis'.[34] Hence, Algerian feminists 'are caught between two legitimacies: belonging to their people and/or identifying with oppressed women'.[35]

In 1992, the choice between these legitimacies turned into a choice regarding personal safety. The general elections of December 1991 indicated that the FIS would assume control over Algerian politics, a turn of events that the military deemed unacceptable. The elections were cancelled, the governing parliament dissolved, and the President was forced to resign. The military seated a new President and created a High Committee of Governance, all tailored along the original FLN political platform. The fundamentalists not jailed or executed exploded into violence and splintered along various lines of belief and levels of activism. Algerian citizens have since suffered through a bloody civil war with nebulous alliances and multiple factions of both government and fundamentalist forces. Estimates of civilian deaths alone number close to 80,000, and the casualties, dislocation and social dysfunction place the ultimate cost of this continuing civil war nearly beyond comprehension. Unsurprisingly, the women maintain their role as a reference matrix for the social and political life of Algeria during this new social conflagration.

The fundamentalists have continued to emphasize the importance of women in determining the health of an Islamic society. As the military government officially disbanded the opposition parties, the political conflict dissolved into a street war, the most symbolic target of which is the women.

---

34. Elizabeth Schemla, 'A battle of sexes in Algiers', *World Press Review* 42, 1 (1995), p. 20.
35. Helie-Lucas, 'The role of women during the Algerian liberation struggle and after', p. 186.

This symbol is reduced to the simple dichotomy of veiled women (believed to indicate support for the fundamentalist movement) and unveiled women (believed to indicate Westernization and thus support for FLN–military rule). In such an environment, feminists in Algeria are waging a dangerous war against not only the tradition of Algerian society but also the superimposed war of political fundamentalism versus political secularism. The women who choose to express views of feminine equality, to adopt freely public clothing styles of their choice and to demand social change are engaged in far more than political dialogue; they actively participate in a civil war, and thus make statements and decisions that translate into life or death. Khalida Messaoudi, a feminist activist on the FIS list of condemned people, illustrates the difficulty of pushing forward a feminist agenda in the context of this civil war as she comments on the ever-present symbol of the veil:

> We wear it because we do not realize what it means and because we are scared, very scared of men's laws. But that is not an adequate explanation. The [government] destroyed all the traditional settings in which women acquired self-esteem [when opposition organizations were disbanded in 1988] but did not put anything in their place. . . . But, if women consent to wear the veil, the FIS opens up all the 'extramural' settings to them, such as the mosque . . . and this gives women the impression of having acquired a degree of power.[36]

Furthermore, even those women not actively participating in this political war of ideology cannot escape involvement simply because of their gender. Women who remain veiled not as a form of political expression but in accordance with religious belief are not exempt from attack. Citizen 'militias' in support of the FLN–military government have responded to the fundamentalists' tactic of slaughtering unveiled women by targeting and killing veiled women. It is further suspected by Algerian citizens and international observers that the Algerian military has created elusive bands of soldiers that murder unveiled women in order to spur the Algerian citizens to reject the extremism of the fundamentalists, assuming that they are the culprits. In either case, Algerian women continue to find themselves as the point of mediation between factions in their country. While the female soldiers of the war for independence fought for national equality and the restoration of their culture, modern women fight for both the ideology of feminine equality and the right to participate in their culture regardless of their ideology; each war has distinctly different agendas but finds the agency of women necessarily vital to the outcome.

---

36.   Schemla, 'A battle of sexes in Algiers', pp. 20–1.

The future of Algeria lies in the resolution of a conflict that the 'woman question', more than any other single issue, epitomizes. At the heart of the fundamentalist versus secularist debate lies what James Ciment refers to as a 'schizophrenic attitude toward the West, at once embracing its mass consumer culture and rejecting its influence as inimical to Muslim society'.[37] The mediation framework that Algerian women have used to define themselves has altered itself radically in the last ten years by acquiring and modifying the global issue of women's rights to suit a unique Algerian culture, creating a new role for women on the foundation of the female soldiers of the war for independence. However, the process of defining the role of women in this social and political context has been difficult at best and life-threatening at worst, and this process has been little altered. Marnia Lazreg comments on this consistency: 'The French fought the Algerians through women. The Algerians fought the French through women. It's a tragic thing, but it's continuing to the present.'[38] As women maintain this centrality to Algerian identity, it is ironic that they are the members with the least significant voice in the dialogue of politics and society, relegated to the lowest rank; yet they are the people with the most significant impact, the people without whom Algeria could not create a social identity. The history of Algerian women since the colonial era encompasses the actions of women bolstered by the power of their agency and demeaned by the passivity of silence through which women 'feel [themselves] isolated and believe [themselves] lost whenever there is a problem'.[39] It is this multifaceted role women have played in Algerian society, in conjunction with the fluid manner in which gender identity mutates to fit opposing purposes, that defies the simple explanations offered by feminist theory. It has not been an experience of uniform oppression, and the goal has not always been unified empowerment. As Algeria struggles to find its national identity and establish political and economic viability as an independent nation, women will remain the hallmark of national dialogue and stratagems with or without their consent.

---

37. James Ciment, *Algeria: The Fundamentalist Challenge* (New York, 1997), p. 12.
38. *Ibid.*, p. 37.
39. Akeb and Abdelaziz, 'Algerian women discuss the need for change', p. 13.

CHAPTER FOURTEEN

Gendering Military Service in the Israel Defence Forces

DAFNA N. IZRAELI

There is a paradoxical aspect to women's military service in Israel. In a nation that prides itself on being the only country in the world where women, like men, are conscripted – seemingly a mark of gender equality – the military emerges as a major force for the production and reproduction of men's domination in society. The institution designated to symbolize and exemplify women's partnership in the national collective is, in effect, an agent of their marginalization. Another paradox is that although a significant proportion of women conscripts perform a variety of highly important, responsible and sensitive roles, their military service is widely perceived as secondary, and by some as even inessential and expendable. This discounting of their contribution is sustained by the high value attributed to combat roles and to reserve service, from both of which women are excluded. These paradoxes are the basis for internal pressures, and occasional disruptions which also provide the potential for resistance and change.

Gender dynamics are a major force constructing the military, both in the historical creation of military structures and in contemporary policies and practices. Gender is not something external which individuals bring with them to the military. It is rather embedded within the very logic of the military. To paraphrase Robert Connell, 'We need to appraise the . . . [military] from the start as having a specific location within gender relations and as

---

I wish to express my gratitude to my colleagues whose comments at various stages of this chapter's development enriched my understanding and spared me from embarrassing errors: Delila Amir, Rivka Bar-Yosef, Orly Benjamin, Hadass Ben Eliyahu, Deborah Bernstein, Nomi Chazan, Hanna Herzog, Neri Horowitz, Baruch Kimmerling, Molly Levine and Yisraela Oron. I thank the IDF for its cooperation in this project and for providing the data reported in the tables and elsewhere.

having a history shaped by a gender dynamic'. In other words, historically, the military developed within the context of an existing system of gender relations. 'Each empirical . . . [military] has a definable "gender regime" that is the precipitate of social struggles and is linked to – though not a simple reflection of – the wider gender order of society.'[1] A regime, as Foucault suggests, refers to the capacity to structure the situation in which others find themselves so as to limit their autonomy and life chances. The gender regime refers to the institutional arrangements that produce inequality in the positions men and women occupy and to their interactions, as these are structured by institutionalized gender relations. The gender regime, the historically produced state of play in gender relations within an institution, can be analysed by taking a structural inventory. Connell identifies three structures of gender relations: a gendered division of labour, a structure of power and a structure of cathexis. The latter refers to the gender patterning of emotional attachments.[2]

The main argument of this chapter is that the gender system or social order of the military, which is based on a gendered division of labour and a gendered structure of power, both formal and informal, constitutes and sustains the proverbial, taken-for-granted role of women in society as helpmates to men. As a structure of power and as one of the important agencies that organize the power relations of gender, the military intensifies gender distinctions and then uses them as justifications for both their construction in the first place and for sustaining gender inequality.[3]

The impact of gender occurs through a number of interacting processes identified by Joan Acker, including 'the construction of divisions along lines of gender; . . . the construction of symbols and images that explain, express, and reinforce these divisions; . . . the daily interactions between women and men, including all those patterns of dominance and submission that produce and reproduce the gendered meanings and structure. . . . The divisions and distinctions constructed then provide the justifications for their maintenance.'[4]

The military provides Jewish men with advantages in accumulating what Pierre Bourdieu calls forms of 'capital' or valued resources that are at stake in the field.[5] These advantages in social capital (referring to varied kinds of valued relations with significant others) and symbolic capital (referring to prestige, celebrity and reputation) are then used for accumulating more

---

1. Robert W. Connell, 'The state gender and sexual politics: theory and appraisal', *Theory and Society* 19 (1990), pp. 519, 523. For a fuller discussion see pp. 506–44.
2. *Ibid.*, p. 526.
3. See Joan Acker, 'Hierarchies, jobs and bodies: a theory of gendered organizations', *Gender & Society* 4 (1990), pp. 139–58; and Judith Lorber, *Paradoxes of Gender* (New Haven, CT, 1994).
4. Acker, 'Hierarchies, jobs and bodies', pp. 146–7.
5. R. Jenkins, *Pierre Bourdieu* (London, 1992), p. 85.

advantage in civilian life. The capital that women accumulate in the military provides significantly fewer advantages for them in civilian life both because of the nature of the capital attainable and the discounted rate at which it is converted in the civilian arena. This chapter identifies and analyses the processes and social practices that construct gender inequality in the Israeli military as well as the implications of these processes for gender inequality in civilian life.

The significance of the military for the production of gender

From the beginning of Jewish resettlement in Palestine at the end of the nineteenth century, women participated in guarding the settlements from attack by neighbouring Arabs. They were members, although only a small minority, in the various Jewish defence and underground organizations in the pre-state period and played a significant role in the War of Independence (1948–49). The Jewish women from Palestine who served in the British Auxiliary Territorial Service forces during the Second World War returned and set up the Women's Corps of the Israel Defence Forces (IDF). In 1993–94, approximately 70 per cent of the cohort of 18-year-old women compared with 83 per cent of the men were conscripted.[6] Since women serve less than two years, while men serve three, they constitute only 32 per cent of those in compulsory service. Women comprise 13 per cent of the professional military.[7]

A unique feature of Israeli society is the broad scope of military involvement in every sector of society and the privileged position enjoyed by the military in the national ethos. The military-industrial complex is the largest single employer. Until the late 1980s, approximately one-quarter of Israel's labour force received its salary from the defence sector, a proportion which

---

6. Alon Pinkas, '17 per cent of eligible males are exempted from military service', *Jerusalem Post*, 30 March 1995. The figures do not include Arabs, who are legally eligible but, except for Druze men, are exempted from military service. Approximately 25 per cent of Jewish women receive automatic exemption on the basis of a declaration of religious belief and conscience; approximately 5 per cent of Jewish men are exempted because of devotion to religious study. The exemptions on the basis of religion date back to the establishment of the IDF. For women they are automatic upon declaration, for men they require proof of enrolment in a religious school for higher learning.
7. Ami Liberman, 'The utilization of women soldiers' service in the IDF 1983–1993', Women and IDF Service: – Reality, wish and vision – Proceedings of a seminar held at Tel Aviv University, 21 January 1995, sponsored by the Israel Women's Network, p. 14 (Hebrew).

has declined due to recent defence cuts. Similarly, approximately one-quarter of the national budget was spent on the military until the early 1990s, but that declined to approximately 16 per cent in 1996.[8] The military has been used as a major vehicle for nation-building, and there is hardly an area of civilian life on which the hand of the military has not left its imprint.

The close relationship between the military and civil society is reflected in popular descriptions of Israel as 'a nation in uniform' or of the military as 'the people's army'.[9] Referring to the heavy reliance of the military on the reserves, these phrases incorporate the myth that every citizen is also a soldier and that the burden of service is shared by all – a myth that has important legitimating functions for the military's centrality in Israeli society.[10]

Military service is laden with symbolic meanings. It is equated with service to the Jewish collective and as such is constructed to be the basis for entitlement to full citizenship in the Jewish state, and in a sense even for consideration as a normal human being. The importance of military service as 'a key citizenship-certification process' is reflected in a genre of newspaper stories about young men and women who, after being exempted from service because of some personal disability, struggle with the military to accept them.[11] In an interview on the eve of the formation of his political party, Nathan Scharansky, the former Russian dissident, listed the marks of his entitlement to be considered a true Israeli: 'I am 100 per cent Israeli. I serve in the reserves, pay more than 40 per cent income tax, I got into a mess with my contractor, I have two mortgages and my car was stolen. How can one be more Israeli than that?'[12] Scharansky had emigrated to Israel as an older adult and consequently was exempt from compulsory military service. Nonetheless, his service in the reserves opens the list of the marks of his entitlement.

The fact that women, like men, are conscripted makes the military an important context for the enactment and reproduction of gender relations. Away from home, women also have the opportunity to experiment with alternative possible selves from among the multiple femininities within the military. For some women, especially those in traditionally male roles, the military provides an opportunity to free themselves from the constraints of 'Israeli femininity'. Research suggests, however, that these women soldiers

8. Baruch Kimmerling, 'Militarism in Israeli society', *Theory and Criticism: An Israeli Forum* 4 (1993) pp. 123–140 (Hebrew).
9. Dan Horowitz and Moshe Lissak, *Out of Utopia* (Albany, NY, 1989), p. 4.
10. Uri Ben-Eliezer, 'A nation-in-arms: state, nation and militarism in Israel's first years', *Comparative Studies in Society and History* 37 (1995), pp. 264–85.
11. Nitza Berkovitch, 'Motherhood as a national mission: the construction of womanhood in the legal discourse in Israel', *Women's Studies International Forum* (1998).
12. Lili Galilee, 'They are interpreting my life for me', *Ha'aretz*, 9 June 1995 (Hebrew).

often pay a price for their new-found freedom and empowerment. In identifying with men they tend to adopt the same disparaging attitude that men have towards other women. Thus, women pay for their new-found empowerment and self-confidence by, as Orna Sasson-Levy suggests, becoming misogynous.[13]

The gendered processes of incorporation

Gender is among the most important and pervasive signifiers for distinguishing between categories of people in the military. The differential impact of the military on men and women begins long before conscription. In a very real sense, it begins at birth. Society sends very different messages to boys and girls about who they will be in the military, and what significance their service will have for them as a rite of initiation into adult life. If for men military service resonates with masculinity, for women the relationship between the military and gender identity is more complex and contradictory. For men military achievement enhances their masculinity, while for women, especially those in the most prestigious positions, it frequently involves a rejection of femininity. By associating achievement with activities men do, the military intensifies the contradiction between femininity and achievement.

Within the military most men and women are treated so differently that one might say that they experience very different militaries. Through an elaborate system of gender divisions and distinctions, the military intensifies the salience of gender and constructs and reinforces gender differences, which in turn legitimate gender inequalities.

Legal distinctions

According to David Ben Gurion, architect of the state of Israel and its first Prime Minister, national security could not be defended only by the military. It required also the development and settlement of new residential-agricultural communities, especially along the borders. Women played an important role in this scheme as farmers, mothers, wives, and protectors of the borders.[14] This broad definition of national security made it possible to

---

13. Orna Sasson-Levy, 'They walk upright and proud: the power and the price of military service for women soldiers in men's jobs', *NOGA – a Feminist Journal* 32 (1997) pp. 21–30 (Hebrew).
14. Berkovitch, 'Motherhood as a national mission'.

incorporate both women and men into the hallowed project of securing the state in the name of gender equality, while assigning them different roles in the name of national security. As was reflected in the legal framework that Ben Gurion was so instrumental in forging, both men and women as citizens contributed to the security of the nation through compulsory military service. As biological beings, however, they were assumed to be different. Women also contributed to the security of the nation by bearing children and raising the family and, as Ben Gurion insisted, the military must not interfere with this important function, which men are unable to fulfil. In the security discourse child-bearing and child-rearing were linked by association, making the latter appear as biologically natural as the former. Until the mid-1990s the contradictions and tensions inherent in the 'different but equal thesis' were not considered problematic. Thus, women contributed to security by remaining with the family and securing the home front. They required military training for self-defence. Men contributed to security by leaving home in order to guard the collective and fight the enemy.

The Security Service Law, passed in 1949 and amended over the years, defines eligibility for compulsory military service in universal terms as applying to 'a citizen of Israel or permanent resident'. The law, furthermore, makes no gender distinctions with regard to the roles that men and women can fill in the military. Military policy, however, defines combat positions as closed to women.

The law does make gender distinctions with regard to the scope of compulsory service: its duration and exemptions, and the duration of eligibility for reserve duty. According to law, women serve for fewer months and are eligible for reserve duty for fewer years, and, in addition to the exemptions applicable to men, married women are exempt from compulsory military service, but not from reserve service, whereas pregnant women and mothers are exempt from both.[15] In other words, the law grants priority to women's family role over their obligations to military service. Since most women in Israel get married and have children, the law builds in the structure by which women are excluded from continued participation in the military, unless they choose the military as a career.

The legal gender differentiation in scope of service provides an additional disincentive for the IDF to treat women equally. Where the law made no gender distinctions, such as in type of service, a rigidly differentiated division of labour was institutionalized by the military (see next section). Where the law treated men and women the same, military regulations and practice treated them differently. For example, whereas the law does not exclude

---

15. Security Service Law, Article 39.

women, even married women, from reserve service, and women are eligible for service until the age of 38, the number of women called to reserve service is negligible.

Where the law treated men and women differently, the military increased the gap. For example, whereas the law specifies 30 months service for men and 24 for women, men in fact serve 36 months (the additional 6 months with pay). In 1992 the mandatory 24 months for women's service was cut to 22 months, in 1993 to 21 and at the beginning of 1994 to less than 21 months.[16] In fact, about a third of women currently serve less than 20 months.

The differentiation argument is circular, as we have already seen. The socially constructed gendered practices of assignment restrict the military's flexibility in its utilization of women. This constraint in turn limits women's usefulness to the military, which, in the face of budget cuts, becomes the justification for shortening women's military service. Women's shorter military service then means it is not cost-effective to invest in women's training, which reduces their usefulness even further. The end result is that women, at least the great majority of them, begin to appear increasingly dispensable.

Administrative distinctions

All women belong formally to the Women's Corps but almost all are assigned to serve in functional units. It is perhaps significant that the acronym for the Women's Corps – 'CHEN' – in Hebrew also means 'charm'. Until 1997, the Women's Corps had formal responsibility for all women soldiers with regard to military training (including officer training), job assignments, discipline and judicial matters, as well as welfare and well-being, including protection from sexual harassment. Protective policies underlined women's difference; they undermined the immediate commander's authority over the female soldier and consequently his sense of responsibility for her and thus proved dysfunctional for her status within her unit.[17] Since 1997, the emerging policy is to limit the intervention of the CHEN to matters that are 'relevant to the differences between men and women' or where the Women's Corps has 'a relative advantage', such as in matters of sexual harassment.[18]

---

16. Protocol of the Knesset Committee on the Status of Women (Jerusalem), 8 February 1994; 19 July 1994; 18 October 1994 (Hebrew).
17. Granted, the commander might also be a woman, but the effect is the same.
18. Shlomit Binyamin, 'Redesigning feminism: interview with the C.O. of the Women's Corps', *Status: The Monthly for Managerial Thought* 64 (October,1996), p. 64 (Hebrew).

The new policy, at least formally, has narrowed the sphere in which gender is salient. The military recently announced its intention to integrate basic training for women and men who are not in combat positions, beginning in the year 2000.

No woman is of high enough rank to participate in the meetings of the General Staff on a regular basis. The closure of senior positions to women thus also excludes their participation in making the policies that institutionalize their secondary status in the military. The Commanding Officer (CO) of the Women's Corps (raised to the rank of brigadier-general in 1988) reports to the Chief of Personnel and may advise the Chief of Staff on matters of specific relevance to women. In fact, until very recently, the CO of the Woman's Corps was rarely consulted on matters of general relevance to women. For example, she was not party to the decisions to cut the duration of women's military service.

The Women's Corps never emerged as a collective voice for women. Whether because of the CHEN's lack of clout or its symbolic representation of women's marginality, women officers serving in the 'men's army' have tended to view the CHEN as an impediment to women's integration in the military. The intense competition among women for the limited opportunities at each higher rank was a deterrent to their organizing to press their claims.

Masculine privilege, symbolic capital, and the gendered division of labour

The combat soldier – brave, self-sacrificing and tough – incarnates hegemonic masculinity in the military. Only activities coded as combat bequeath heroism and glory and are perceived as having greater entitlements than others, including those that other non-combat male soldiers enjoy. Masculine privilege in the military is premised on the preservation of gender divisions in the work men and women do. Jobs are generally assigned first by gender and then within gender by aptitudes, competencies and other considerations. The gender distinction overlaps with the distinction between combat units and non-combat units and between combat roles and non-combat roles. The most exclusionary category is the combat role. While increasingly the military assigns women to combat units, roles defined as combat and jobs performed in combat areas are, with only rare exception, closed to women.

The exclusion of women from combat roles is the dominant mechanism for maintaining masculine privilege. In the security discourse, the combat experience is the unique tempering fire that turns a person (man) into a real

Table 1 Percentage of women officers among all officers by service (1998)[19]

Service	Conscripts and professionals	Professionals only
Total IDF	23.7	14.5
1. Armour/tank	0.9	1.3
2. Artillery	1.9	0.3
3. Engineering	2.5	2.1
4. Ammunition/ordnance	6.8	5.2
5. Field command	12.7	3.6
6. Navy	12.1	8.9
7. Air force	14.1	9.9
8. Military police	18.1	6.9
9. Intelligence	16.9	12.7
10. Maintenance	23.5	15.9
11. Signal	23.2	14.5
12. Medical	32.9	32.1
13. General Staff	38.8	27.4
14. Rear command	39.7	25.7
15. Field	43.0	18.7
16. Adjutancy (human resources)	68.0	50.9
17. Education	83.3	59.5

soldier. Formal prerequisites for virtually all of the most senior positions and the majority of those below the senior levels include a period of service 'in the field'. Thus, women are first prevented from getting 'experience in the field' and then their lack of such experience becomes the justification for not promoting them to more senior positions. Table 1 reveals a gender division of labour with women highly under-represented in services with the greatest proportion of combat soldiers (1–8) and over-represented in services with the greatest proportion of soldiers in white-collar, semi-professional and administrative positions (12–17). In every service, the proportion of women among the officers in compulsory service is considerably greater than that in the professional army, reflecting both the greater proportion of women in compulsory service as well as the concentration of women officers at the lowest rank of the command hierarchy.

---

19. Source: IDF spokesperson.

Table 2 Percentage of women among officers by rank (column 1) and distribution of officers by gender and rank (columns 2 and 3) 1999

Rank	1	2	3
	women	women	men
Major-General	§	0.0	0.1
Brigadier-General	§	0.1	1.0
Colonel	§	1.0	3.0
Lieutenant-Colonel	1	4.0	14.0
Major	18	25.0	31.0
Captain	19	22.0	25.0
Lieutenant	32	48.0	26.0
Total		100.1	100.0

Note: § represents a total of 1 per cent for the combined number of major-generals, brigadier-generals and colonels).

As is the case with all occupational data, aggregated categories veil the true extent of segregation. A more detailed analysis would reveal, as was mentioned earlier, that there are relatively few jobs that are performed interchangeably by men and women. Where men are assigned to the same locale and do the same or similar jobs as women, the men usually have a lower quality-profile. The data in Tables 1 and 2 reflect what J. Grant and Peta Tancred call 'the dual structure of unequal representation'.[20] Women are unequally distributed through the hierarchy of the military as a whole. At the same time, those organizational units where women are well-represented and where they exert a greater measure of authority are peripheral in the internal organization of the military. Column 1 of Table 2 presents the proportion of women among all the officers in each rank. At the top there is only one major-general – the Chief of Staff. Clearly, women are very under-represented in the next three ranks. The appearance of a woman brigadier-general reflects the upgrading of the rank of the CO of the Women's Corps in 1988.[21] There were only eight women with the rank of colonel in 1985 and only nine in 1999. Between 1985 and 1999 there was a significant increase in the proportion of women officers up to and including the rank

20. J. Grant and Peta Tancred, 'A feminist perspective on state bureaucracy' in A.J. Mills and P. Tancred, eds, *Gendering Organizational Analysis* (Newbury Park, CA, 1992), pp. 117ff.

21. Bloom, 'Women in the Defence Forces', in B. Swirski and M. Safir, eds, *Calling the Equality Bluff* (New York, 1991).

of lieutenant-colonel, the result of pressure from women wishing to move up the hierarchy, progress which was supported by the COs of the CHEN and was reinforced by the military's greater recognition of women's competence. This progress has a mild ripple effect upwards. In 1995 only 2.7 per cent of the women officers were in the top four ranks, while in 1999 the figure had risen to 5.1 per cent.

There are two types of demand heard increasingly by women within and outside the military in recent years. The first is the demand for the military to open more job categories to women. This was voiced initially by the Commission on the Status of Women in 1978 and raised repeatedly by the media ever since. The second argument is that combat experience should cease to be a prerequisite for many senior positions, which, it is claimed, do not require such experience. It is argued that a policy based on the belief that those who have not crawled under barbed wire or have not stormed some fortified target cannot be successful commanders is anachronistic and blocks the promotion of capable women. Advocates for change have, for instance, highlighted those positions at the rank of colonel and above – including chief educational officer, CO of intelligence, CO of personnel, military spokesperson, chief medical officer, chief mental health officer, chief military prosecutor and president of the appeals court – as unwarrantedly closed to women. The women also argue that, if the military command were to perceive it to be in the interest of the military, it could provide promising women with the equivalent of combat experience in the field.

By refusing to open more senior positions to women, the military limits competition for those positions. The privileged accounting given to combat experience facilitates giving priority to men derailed from the combat career route perhaps as a result of injury, a drop in fitness or a lack of openings. In such cases the derailed incumbent is 'cooled out' by being granted access to an alternative career line normally accessed from a different route, on the basis of entitlement created by previous combat experience. This practice permits promotion up an alternative career path faster than normally expected and, not infrequently, gives the man priority over a more qualified woman in line for promotion. It enables the military to retain valued individuals who might otherwise leave the military for employment in the civil market.

What women do in and for the military

Women perform three major functions in the military. The first includes all those jobs that the military regularly assigns to women soldiers, among which various forms of clerical and personnel work are the most obvious and prominent. The second is that they provide a reservoir of labour for regulating human resource utilization, particularly in 'men-replaceable' jobs. The third function women fill comes in serving as 'women' and, as such, in reinforcing the glorification of the masculine in general and of hegemonic masculinity in particular.

Women's jobs: Public discourse on women's roles in the military has focused less on the issue of gender equality than on increasing the range of job categories open to women and especially jobs that are interesting and prestigious. Whereas the assignment of women to jobs has been dictated primarily by the changing needs of the military, it has also been influenced by the attitudes of senior commanding officers and by the pressure of women's organizations.[22] In 1976, according to the Commission on the Status of Women (1978), 210 out of 709 jobs were technically open to women, but women actually served in only about half of them. Approximately 70 per cent were in clerical positions. In 1988 women served in 234 of the approximately 500 jobs then open to them.[23] In 1999 they served in 330 of the 551 jobs open to them; 187 were closed to women for reasons of their association with either combat or religious service.

'Men-replaceable' jobs: Since the establishment of the IDF, women's participation in the military has been talked about and justified in terms of their 'freeing men for combat'.[24] This phrase is a metaphor for the asymmetry of status ascribed to each gender and for the differential nature of men's and women's incorporation in the military. Women not only free men for combat jobs but also for technical jobs, jobs that require physical strength and those that are performed under dangerous conditions. In the 1980s, in response to budget cuts, women were used to replace men in the standing army as well as in the reserves. Between 1983 and 1993, the number called for reserve duty (virtually all men) declined by 47 per cent and the number serving in the career army (mostly men) declined by 17.7 per cent. During the same period, the number of men in compulsory service increased by 32 per cent and women by 43 per cent. (The sex difference is a consequence of men's longer service, so that a growth in the same absolute number has a different effect on the proportionate growth of the population.) Sometimes women replaced male conscripts, who in turn replaced reservists.[25]

---

22. Dafna N. Izraeli, 'Sex structure of occupations', *Sociology of Work and Occupations* 6 (1979), pp. 404–29; Reuven Gal, 'The Israeli female soldier: myth and reality', research report for the Israel Institute for Military Studies (1986).
23. Bloom, 'Women in the defence forces', p. 35.
24. The recent COs of the CHEN have attempted to alter the terms of the discourse from that of 'freeing men for combat' to that of 'realizing women's potential', but with limited success.
25. Liberman, 'The utilization of women soldiers' service in the IDF'.

In the 1980s, women were used as instructors for training men in various field soldiering and combat skills including driving tanks, artillery and target shooting. Women's representation among instructors, while still very small, grew by over 400 per cent between 1983 and 1993, and was about 2000 in 1994.[26] Serving as an instructor for men-only units is among the most prestigious jobs open to women. It is the closest they come to a combat role. Jobs previously done by men were often redefined, made narrower and more specialized so that they could be learnt in a shorter period of time, and did not include a combat experience requirement. This redefinition preserves the distinction between what women do and what men do – even when it seems that the divisions are being dropped. For example, men usually become instructors after a period of combat training, while women are sent directly to instructor training.

Women instructors are confined to the classroom. They usually do not accompany the men during a military drill in the field and certainly never in real-life situations. As the deputy CO of Personnel recently pointed out, there is a big difference between being an instructor in the classroom and having to manoeuvre a tank on the battlefield. 'I think we are still far away from taking a tank instructor from the Armored Corps training school and putting her now on a tank to make a fighting reconnaissance in South Lebanon.'[27] Women's lack of experience under real-life conditions makes them less credible as instructors. What works in the books, the soldiers say, may not work in practice.

Once women enter a job and perform it successfully, it tends to be re-designated as a woman's job. Speaking of the 'progress' made by women in recent years, the CO of the Personnel Corps pointed out proudly: 'Instructor occupations are closed to boys in many places – including the most attractive places, the most combat like places – there, only girls are instructors . . . Only women train our pilots, the combat pilots, on the simulation machines.'[28] What he failed to appreciate is that the re-designation of these jobs into women's occupations, while improving female job opportunities, also pre-serves the gendered division of labour upon which the gender structure of power rests.

The glorification of masculinity: Women who serve with all-male units are perceived as bringing a touch of home to the otherwise cold, military world of boot camp. They become the personification of the collective wife/mother/sister. They function as morale boosters, symbolically personifying for the men some of the rewards of home – bestowed by women on men.

---

26. *Ibid.*; Protocol of the Knesset Committee on the Status of Women.
27. *Ibid.*
28. *Ibid.*

Gail Hareven thinks that the company clerk role in particular reveals the gender dynamics of the Israeli military:

> The company clerk – the miserable dream of too many serious girls, the closest a young woman can get to the field, to the fighters, to the real thing. They march 80 km with the company, bake a cake at home, and don't forget the birthday of anyone. The Company Clerk is a symbol . . . of what men and women learn about themselves and about each other in the military. They, [the men] are the warriors, they [the women] are always, always the 'helpmate unto him'. To be helpmates they are recruited to the military and that is what most of them learn there.[29]

Women are also trophies for heroes. A popular adage loosely translated says that 'the best men to the air force, the best women to the airmen'. The best women are, in this case, those with movie star femininity – tall, slim and beautiful. Their beauty is commodified and allocated to the most worthy. For some jobs – those close to senior officers – physical appearance is an important qualification. The most beautiful women are the prize as well as the mark of military achievement. The commander's access to this scarce resource says something about his status. Their feminine qualities, in turn, reflect upon his manliness, validate and bolster it.

A journalist who recently investigated the way female clerical staff are assigned to senior officers on the basis of their good looks concluded:

> All the models and the beauty queens, the prettiest girls in the IDF, serve as clerical staff in the office of the major generals. The most beautiful serve in the office of the Chief of Staff, or the CO of the Absorption and Classification Base. There is no paragraph in the orders of the Chief of Staff regarding the assignment of pretty women soldiers as clerical staff for senior officers. There is also no such verbal instruction. But, like the zubor [slang term for hazing routines performed on new recruits] and like the coffee served to the commander, this custom is deeply rooted in the system and is transmitted from generation to generation.[30]

The top brass siphons off the most desirable women. Officers further down the pecking order exert what influence they can to get the prettiest from the remainder assigned to them, as indicated in the following story:

> When I was a young officer, we were stationed in Sharm-el-Sheik [south Sinai Peninsula] where all the girls assigned to Sharm-el-Sheik as well as to

29. Gail Hareven, *Maariv*, 29 January 1995, p. 3 (Hebrew).
30. Kineret Rosenblum, 'How do you want your secretary, officer?', *Zman Tel Aviv*, 24 November 1995, pp. 26–9 (Hebrew).

the secondary bases in the outlying areas, were sent. We used to sit, all the young officers, and mark each for the person who sorted the girls. Thumbs up meant pretty soldier, leave her in Sharm. Thumbs down – send her to the outlying bases. Later when I was commander of one of the secondary bases, I called that same sorter and told him: 'Don't you dare send me anymore of those who get the thumbs down'.[31]

In some cases, the presence of women poses a challenge to masculinity that the military sees as beneficial to the training process. Referring to the outstanding success of women in their new role as platoon sergeants for male soldiers in basic training programmes, an army public relations pamphlet explains: 'New recruits do not dare complain of muscle aches and pains or drop out of a long distance run when it is being led by a female sergeant'.[32] Why they dare not complain is not explained – it is supposed to be obvious to the reader. No man, who considers himself a man, would wish to be outdone by a woman. The implication is, furthermore, that men are motivated to prove that they can do better than women, or that to demonstrate their superior toughness is an important performance incentive. This military publication, which is presumably intended to praise women's accomplishments, subtly reconstitutes their taken-for-granted inferiority.

Cashing in on the capital – moving from the military to civilian life and the reproduction of gender inequality

The military provides an important opportunity to develop social capital – the social networks so important for access to information and support, as well as to people, places and jobs in civilian society. Both women and men use those ties to get jobs and other advantages, but men have more of them. Men, who serve for a longer period of time than women, and more often in different jobs and locations, have opportunities to meet more and varied people. The reserves bring together people from many different walks of life who might otherwise not meet one another. Serving together creates social bonds of mutual obligation that bypass status differences in civilian life and often extend beyond the service. For example, in her study of civilian–military relations in Israel, Eva Etzioni-Halevy found that senior officers meet

---

31. *Ibid.*
32. Gal, 'The Israeli female soldier: myth and reality', p. 8.

civilian elites and prepare their second careers while still in the military.[33] Nineteen of the 26 officers in her study who had moved from the military to the political elite reported having had very close or fairly close informal social contacts with politicians while still on active duty.

The civilian employer views the military as a valuable training ground for general attributes as well as specific skills. In some occupations the link between the military and the civilian is institutionalized – most noticeably in high-tech industries. In an investigative article, Roni Aloni cites a manager who compared the burgeoning growth in start-up companies in Israel in the mid-1990s with what occurred in Silicon Valley in the early 1980s: 'In contrast to the entrepreneurs of Palo Alto, Israeli entrepreneurs have technological experience and prefer teams that already worked together in the army or the defence industry'. Or quoting another manager: 'All our workers served in the same unit and that is how it will be in the near future . . . We are in touch with other companies that have graduates of the Intelligence Corps . . . where a large part of their people came from our unit. In general, the high-tech market in Israel is very tightly networked. People know one another and that is very helpful.'[34] Aloni concludes: 'The uniqueness of the Israeli high-tech success lies in these army grounded networks and not in "the Israeli brain" as is commonly thought'.[35]

In some occupational fields, such as security-related jobs, a specific type of military experience is a condition for entry. For example, El-Al, Israel's national airline, recruits its pilots exclusively from the military. This policy was recently challenged in the Labour Court on the basis of the Equal Opportunity in Employment Law (1988). According to the El-Al Chief Executive, the reason for the preference was strictly professional. 'One doesn't have to be a man to fly a passenger aircraft but if I can select for El-Al the best pilots, those who are better equipped to cope with stressful situations because of their military training, there is no reason that I should forgo this advantage. If the air force will train women, I will accept women. If my board decides otherwise, I will fight them like a lion.'[36] After almost 50 years of discrimination, El-Al's policy was declared discriminatory. When two women members of the Knesset (Israeli parliament) petitioned the Supreme Court, El-Al backed down and agreed to hire women.

When senior officers enter civilian organizations, they frequently bring with them other officers who were their colleagues or subordinates in the

---

33. Eva Etzioni-Halevy, 'Civil–military relations and democracy: the case of the military-political elites' connection in Israel', *Armed Forces and Society* 22 (1996), pp. 401–17.
34. Roni Aloni, 'The good years of the entrepreneurs', *Ha'ir*, 24 February 1994, p. 16 (Hebrew).
35. *Ibid.*, p. 18.
36. Orit Schochat, 'The last masculine occupation', *Ha'aretz*, 31 July 1995, p. 1 (Hebrew).

military. For example, the following headline appeared in a Tel Aviv news-paper in September 1988: 'One more than in the general staff: 22 senior reserve officers fill senior positions in the municipality. Lahat [then mayor of Tel Aviv and senior reserve officer] chooses most of them.'[37] One senior officer hired as General Director of an important museum complex replaced the existing staff from top to bottom with military retirees from his unit, even bringing in his personal 'ralashit' (the military term for the female office manager of a senior officer).

Men reap greater value from the symbolic capital they accrue from serving in the military than do women. As has already been explained, they benefit from association with the glory of service and from access to the highest ranks – both of which are closed to women. Despite the fact that such resources are available to only a relatively small proportion of men, however, they reflect on all men in a way that they do not reflect on women. This differential symbolic effect of the military is exemplified in a recent study of gender bias in the Israeli courtroom, which found that military service is among the reasons judges give for leniency in sentencing a defendant.[38] The reference to military service as a consideration, however, applied only to male defendants – both those who had actually served and those who would, presumably, serve in the future. Military service, however, was never mentioned in relation to a woman defendant. This raises the question of whether Israelis think of women's military service as actual soldiering.

The relationship between the military and women's status in Israeli society is circular. A feedback loop dynamic leads from women's marginalization in the military to women's disadvantage in civilian life and back again. First, the gendered processes by which women and men are incorporated into the military intensify the perceived differences between them and marginalize women. Second, the differential treatment of men and women in the military and women's marginalization produce differential opportunities for mobility both within the military and in civilian life that privilege men. Third, the advantages men derive from military service are converted into advantages in civilian life.[39] Military elites slip into roles in civilian elites where they contribute to the reproduction of gender inequality and to the perpetuation of gendered processes within the military.

---

37. Anat Avnielli, 'One more than in the general staff', *Ha'ir*, 16 September 1988, p. 15 (Hebrew).

38. Bryna Bogosh and Rochelle Don-Yichiya, *The Gender of Justice: Bias against Women in Israeli Courts*, Jerusalem Institute for Israel Studies (1999) (Hebrew).

39. To say that men are advantaged is not to ignore the problem senior officers currently face in finding jobs of equivalent status to those they had in the military.

Patterns of resistance

Despite its importance as a context for gender reproduction, the military had not been the focus of interest-group formation and mobilization in sexual politics. The brilliant military victory of 1967 was an affirmation of the hegemony of the military, raising it to almost sacred proportions. After the 1973 war, in which the military seemed not adequately prepared, the symbolic wall that had protected it from public criticism weakened, creating a social climate more receptive to a critical reconsideration of women's status within it. The emergence of a feminist movement in the 1970s created the consciousness that there was a gender problem, and the Commission on the Status of Women provided a mechanism for gathering systematic data and a forum for discussing the issue.

Women's resistance to the gender regime of the military intensified in the 1990s and reached new heights in the Supreme Court decision in the case of *Alice Miller* v. *Minister of Defence* (1995). A feminist organization had petitioned the Supreme Court in the name of Alice Miller following the military's refusal to allow her – a new immigrant to Israel who possessed a degree in aeronautical engineering and a pilot's licence – to take the entry examinations that determine qualification for the most prestigious pilot training course.

This case was the first time the Supreme Court intervened in a matter of gender discrimination in the military. By instructing the military to invite Miller to be tested for admission to pilot training and, if successful, to admit her to the course, the court redefined the grounds for acceptable gender distinctions. The court rejected the military's claim that its differential treatment of men and women was merely a ramification of gender distinctions embedded in the law and that, given these *a priori* legal distinctions, the principle of gender-equal treatment did not apply to the military. It also rejected the military's claim that its differential treatment of men and women rested on relevant differences between them and, therefore, constituted a permissible and not invidious distinction. Finally, the court rejected the military's argument that the high financial cost of adjusting the conditions of pilot training to women's needs, as well as the difficulties involved in personnel planning caused by women's reproductive and mothering roles, were legitimate reasons for unequal treatment. In the words of Supreme Court Justice Eliyahu Matza:

> Declarations of equality are not enough; because the real test of equality is its realization in practice as a social norm that determines outcomes. This normative obligation applies to the IDF as well. The tremendous influence of the ways of the military on the way we live our lives is well known. The

IDF cannot stand outside the process of entrenching the consciousness of the importance of basic laws. It too must contribute its share.

Supreme Court Justice Dalia Dorner acknowledged differences in the law as making gender a relevant basis for differentiation, but then placed the obligation for correcting or neutralizing the effects of relevant differences on the military. The differences in the service of men and women, as defined in the law, is a factor that the IDF must take into consideration in its planning but cannot be a cause for permitting discriminatory practice in relation to the woman soldier. As it turned out, Alice Miller was found to be unqualified to take the course. Continued military resistance to women's full integration may be gleaned by the fact that after the completion of five pilot training course cycles, to date only one woman has graduated successfully.

The military argues that it will not change its policy regarding women in combat roles until instructed to do so by the Knesset. In January 2000, the Knesset approved a law that opens all military jobs, including combat roles, to women and men alike, except where gender is deemed to be a relevant consideration.

Some Israelis favour eliminating compulsory military service for women. Radical feminists argue that, as an instrument of violence, the military is an inherently masculine organization oppressive of women which violates women's value of life. Liberal feminists (including many men) contend that releasing women from compulsory service would give them a head start relative to men in higher education, and thus compensate them somewhat for the cost that motherhood exacts from their careers. The majority of Israelis, however, oppose differential treatment, both on principle and in recognition of the symbolic importance of military service for civilian life.

A greater measure of equality within the military could be achieved if universal compulsory military service were to be replaced by voluntary service and greater professionalization. This is more likely to occur if and when Israel achieves a more stable peace agreement with its neighbours. The culture of professionalism is less intensely gendered than the macho culture of military heroism. Furthermore, the need for employers to compete in an open labour market for educated personnel has historically worked in women's favour.[40] And if, in consequence, the military were to become a less powerful force in shaping the ideologies and practices of everyday life, gender inequality within the military would have a less significant impact on gender relations in society.

---

40. Barbara F. Reskin and Patricia A. Roos, *Job Queues, Gender Queues: Explaining Women's Inroads into Male Occupations* (Philadelphia, PA, 1990).

CHAPTER FIFTEEN

Women in China's Changing Military Ethic

SUSAN M. RIGDON

> *Little baby, hush your cries,*
> *It's for you that Mama tries,*
> *Mama trains to defend the motherland,*
> *So you'll live a happy life more grand.*[1]

In her comprehensive overview of Chinese women in the military from ancient to modern times, Li Xiaolin claims that their 'history of . . . involvement . . . is probably longer and more continuous than that of [women in] any other country in the world'.[2] That women's participation began early seems certain from the cache of 60 terracotta sword-carrying women soldiers dressed in wooden armour unearthed in 1990 by Chinese archaeologists who were excavating Western Han (206 BC – AD 8) imperial tombs near Xian.[3] An announcement of the finding was not made until three years later, and its full historical significance is still being debated. In fact the role of women in the regular military, and in combat, prior to the nineteenth century is not well-documented, although certainly in exceptional circumstances – civil war, revolution, the Taiping Rebellion and other large-scale revolts or uprisings – women have been militarily active.

Whatever the historical role, the symbolic woman soldier has been an important factor in arousing patriotism and rallying the troops. Some of

---

1. A song written by local militia women and quoted in 'The militia women of the Yellow Sea', *Women of China* 2 (1966), pp. 39–41.
2. Li Xiaolin, 'The role of women in the Chinese Army' (unpublished Ph.D. dissertation, University of Maryland, 1995), p. 22. The section on women in the PLA is based on a survey of 230 women serving in the air force, army and navy in the Beijing area.
3. Reported on the electronic news service *China News Digest*, 22 July 1993.

China's best-known plays, operas, ballets and films are built around themes of women as military heroines.[4] They draw on figures of legend like Hua Mulan, the creation of a fifth-century poet; Fu Hao, the martial arts heroine and imperial concubine who lived more than 3,000 years ago and who is sometimes called China's first female general; or Madame Yang, the Shang era magistrate's wife who led her husband's troops in battle to defend the city against invaders, as well as the lives of twentieth-century militiawomen, Red Guards, and veterans of the wars of resistance and liberation. The portraits rendered in *Red Detachment of Women* (ballet and film), *The Red Lantern* (opera and film), and numerous other works for stage and film have left an indelible image of the Chinese woman militant.

The symbolic use of fighting women was so prevalent in the first 40 years of the People's Republic that it came as something of a surprise to hear one veteran encouraging me to interview her colleagues because 'no one ever writes about women' in China's armed forces. Yet her point is well-taken when one considers that it is heroic prototypes on which most public attention has been focused. The real everyday, indispensable contributions of rank-and-file women soldiers in medicine, science, transport, aviation and communications are little noted except on International Women's Day and in publications that target women readers. When it comes to rallying patriotic fervour, army posters of women with stethoscopes, sextants and Bunsen burners are no match for those of the iconic young militiawomen with braided hair, red bandanas and raised rifles whose images radiated from murals, posters and billboards across China before the 1980s. In some sense, then, rank-and-file Chinese servicewomen have been upstaged less by male infantry and Red Army marshals than they have been by the portrayals in stage, film and popular art of women of legend and of those real-life revolutionaries who went to the front, served in the underground, or were martyred for the cause.

Service in the pre-1949 army

An official history of Chinese servicewomen dates the presence of women in the regular armed services in the contemporary era from 1927.[5] In that

---

4. For two good discussions of women and military heroics see Chang-Tai Hung, 'Female symbols of resistance in Chinese wartime spoken drama', *Modern China* 15 (April 1989), pp. 149–77; and John H. Weakland, 'Film images of invasion and resistance', *China Quarterly* 47 (July/September 1971), pp. 439–70.
5. Jiang Lin, *Ershi Shiji Zhongguo Nubing* (Twentieth-century Chinese Servicewomen) (Beijing, 1995), p. 141.

year the Huangpo Military Academy (jointly founded by the National and Communist Parties in their brief pre-war united front period) admitted 130 women with the academy's sixth entering class. One of the new recruits reportedly came to enlist carrying her baby, and was admitted only after putting the child in foster care. Though these cadets were not sent into battle after graduation, they were considered regular army and received the same training and took the same course work as their male classmates. After the violent break between the Nationalist and Communist Parties, some of the Huangpo graduates joined up with the new military arm of the Communist Party.

The Chinese Red Army, precursor of today's People's Liberation Army (PLA), was founded by Mao Zedong and Zhu De in 1927 and over the next two decades recruited thousands of women into the Women Guards, the militia units that served in local defence.[6] From the establishment of the first soviet government in China in 1931 (the Jiangxi Soviet) until liberation in 1949, there were women's militia units throughout Red Army-controlled territories.[7] In addition thousands served in support units of the Red Army: making shoes and clothing for the troops, feeding the men in combat units, serving in hospitals, participating in cultural units that entertained the troops, recruiting men into the army, and educating the general population about the goals of revolution.

Under conditions of guerrilla warfare, there was a fine line between civilian and soldier for both men and women. Women may not have been sent to the front, but the front frequently came to them. This was also true of women who did intelligence work and served in the Communist underground. According to one revolutionary heroine, more than one thousand 'radical' women leaders were killed in 1927 alone.[8] Over the past two decades, women's organizations have made a concerted effort to seek out and publish the stories of these veterans, especially those who survived the Long March.[9]

---

6. See Helen Young's article 'Women at work: Chinese soldiers on the Long March', pp. 83–99 and her forthcoming volume *Choosing Revolution: Chinese Women Soldiers on the Long March* (Urbana, IL).

7. Delia Davin, *Women-Work* (New York, 1968), pp. 14–15.

8. Cai Chang quoted in Norma Diamond, 'Women under Kuomintang rule: variations on the feminine mystique', *Modern China* 1 (January 1975), p. 6.

9. *Women of China* did a series of stories on these veterans, including Cai Chang (January 1983), pp. 8–10; a two-parter on Kang Keqing, wife of the Red Army's co-founder Zhu De (March 1983), pp. 37–30, and (April 1983), pp. 16–18; the actress Tian Hua (December 1983), pp. 40–3; Li Wenying (December 1983), pp. 14–16; and in 1986 a three-part overview of women on the Long March, including General Li Zhen (October), pp. 26–9; (November), pp. 40–2; and (December), pp. 18–20. Helen Young's 'Women at work' is based on interviews with some of the above and other Long March veterans.

Service in the PLA: 1949–1965

In the early years of the People's Republic, the prevailing military ethic was still rooted in Mao Zedong's strategy for fighting protracted guerrilla warfare. Perhaps no writing of Mao's is as well known as that on the conduct of war and the organization of military forces, and perhaps few of his sentences more often quoted than 'All power comes from the barrel of a gun'.[10] The Maoist concept of 'people's war' called for the militarization of the populace, the politicization of the military, and a commitment of military resources to civilian construction and development. Soldiers and the general population intermingled, each supporting the other in armed resistance to the enemy.

Although to a Maoist it is a heretical comparison, Mao's thinking on national defence was in line with Trotsky's concept of a people's militia, which devalued a professionalized corps in favour of the people armed. Whereas Trotsky, having helped found Russia's Red Army, was soon driven into exile, and the idea of a people's militia (a concept almost certainly terrifying to Stalin) with him, the Chinese Red Army continued under its founders' command after the consolidation of the state. The Russian Red Army was shaped as a professional force and trained to defend borders and airspace with conventional warfare; strategic and tactical thinking and military training moved with the times into the atomic age. Under Mao's chairmanship of the party's Military Affairs Commission, the PLA did have a competitive research and development programme, specifically for nuclear weapons and delivery systems, but this commitment was little known to rank-and-file soldiers and did not influence their training. High technology continued to be labelled a 'paper tiger' when pitted against the strength of the people armed, and military doctrine remained rooted, until Mao's death, in the ethic that brought it to power: a rankless corps in which being red took precedence over being expert.

Although not drafted or actively recruited, women were enlisted in all branches of the armed forces when the People's Republic of China was founded in 1949. This included service in the newly established navy, albeit as clerical and communications workers, not as sailors. And while the air force began training women pilots in 1951, it was to fly small transport, not fighter, aircraft. Despite its restricted nature, women's military role was important to the fundamental nature of the new political system, specifically to its emphasis on inclusiveness and equalitarianism. In addition, in a country

---

10. Mao Zedong, *Selected Military Writings* (Peking, 1966).

that was poor and Marxist, labour power was the most important resource in both practice and theory.

The laws of the People's Republic stress the equality of rights and duties for both sexes, while implicitly excusing women from some obligations through the extension of special protections.[11] To understand the significance of this, one must grasp that the primary emphasis, for all citizens, falls on 'duties'. China became and remained, until the reform era of the 1980s, a full integration/mobilization society, for which the discipline and regimen associated with military life was viewed as the appropriate work model for the population at large. It was not an option for women to work only in the home, or for them – or for men – to choose where they would apply their talents. Rights were not held as inalienable, but as granted by the state under party tutelage and therefore subject to revocation by the state. And there was no concept of full citizenship that did not entail participation. Rights were earned through fulfilment of one's civic duties, and in Mao's China defence of the homeland was the duty of every citizen.

Soon after the founding of the People's Republic, the PLA found itself engaged in the Korean War, and women's support role became essential once more. But even Red Army veterans were refused permission to serve at the front. A reported '150,000 women cadre (8% of the total cadre corps) were assigned to civilian positions' while the war was in progress in spite of the many requests by women veterans to stay on active duty.[12] Female medical personnel in field hospitals were close to the front, but service in combat units or zones continued to be forbidden.

The experience of fighting a ground war against UN troops prompted revisions in the prevailing military ethic and a brief period of flirtation with professionalization, including greater emphasis on training for conventional warfare and the reinstitution of ranks. At this time the Red Army veteran and political commissar Li Zhen became the first woman in modern times to hold the rank of general.[13] But the recognition of women's contributions to war efforts was offset by the reassignment of another 764,000 women cadres, some of whom had served during the anti-Japanese and Korean wars, to civilian positions.[14]

The post-war changes in military organization did, however, explicitly address the issue of women's obligation to do military service. 'With regard

---

11. 'Law of the People's Republic of China on the protection of rights and interests of women', *Women of China* (August 1992), pp. 29–32.
12. Mady Wechsler Segal, Xiaolin Li and David R. Segal, 'The role of women in the Chinese Peoples's Liberation Army', *Minerva* 10 (Spring 1992), p. 52.
13. See Young, 'Women at work'.
14. Segal, Li and Segal, 'The role of women', p. 52; Li, 'The role of women', p. 350.

to female citizens who have received medical, veterinary, or other training in specialized skills, the Ministry of Defence has the authority to promote reserve service registration, and can when necessary call upon those registered to participate in group training.' Within the reserve forces all-women squads, platoons and companies were organized, and eligible women between the ages of 18 and 40 who were registered for reserve service could be called into active military service during their five years of obligation. Orders were given to actively cultivate women cadres to lead these units.[15] But the policy of not allowing women to serve in combat units within the regular army was retained.

Service in the PLA: 1965–1978

The purge of the legendary Red Army commander Marshall Peng Dehuai as Defence Minister in 1959 for criticizing the economic policies of the Great Leap Forward and Mao's overall development strategy brought a tightening of Mao's authority over the PLA and a shift back to a rankless non-professionalized military. In the early 1960s this policy hardened when, as part of an intensive national programme to re-educate the public in socialist values, the party launched the 'Learn from Lei Feng' campaign. Lei Feng was a PLA soldier who, after dying young, was made a unisex model of the ideal citizen/soldier: an egoless, self-sacrificing, never-tiring servant of the party's will.

Mao's policy of 'forging the entire populace into a trained fighting force' hit its peak during the years of the Great Proletarian Cultural Revolution (1965–76; an unprecedentedly intense mass education campaign combined with a violent attack on party and state bureaucracy). During this period great emphasis was placed on the militia and reserve troops, and, as the 'everyone-a-soldier' concept implies, defence became the work of the population at large. The ordinary militia, under PLA control, was ordered to enrol all able-bodied citizens of both sexes between the ages of 15 and 50. A smaller number of those between 16 and 30 were assigned to the hard core or 'basic-level backbone' units, and supplemented by demobilized servicemen and veterans.[16] By the mid-1960s there were an estimated 225 million militia 'men'.[17]

Younger women especially were recruited into the militia and many, especially students, lived in quasi-military conditions, dressing in ersatz

---

15. Ch'iu Shih-tung, 'The role of women in Chinese communist armed units', *Issues and Studies* 10 (September 1974), pp. 54–5.
16. John Gittings, *The Role of the Chinese Military* (New York, 1967), p. 213.
17. Samuel Griffith, *The Chinese People's Liberation Army* (New York, 1967), pp. 268–9.

military uniforms, doing militia drills, and working and studying in units with joint military–civilian leadership. Youth sent down to the countryside often worked on civilian construction projects as part of the PLA's Production and Construction Corps (est. 1954), where all members received basic military training.[18] In 1967, the PLA began recruiting women into active-duty units.

Throughout the Cultural Revolution imagery of women fighters saturated popular culture. At the time cultural policy was largely in the hands of the former actress and estranged wife of Mao Zedong, Jiang Qing, whose maxim for state theatrical troupes, 'To act is to fight', was reinforced by sending actors to live with army units.[19] Most of the small number of theatrical works approved for public performance, such as *The Red Lantern*, *Red Detachment of Women* and *Women Fliers* (a play written by the air force's Political Department to celebrate the revolutionary zeal of its women pilots), had women soldiers or militiawomen as leading characters.[20]

Despite popular culture's paeans to women warriors, Western studies of the PLA published in the 1960s rarely acknowledged the existence of women soldiers.[21] Even the PLA's internal military bulletin *Gongzuo Tungxun*, 29 issues of which were released to the public by the US State Department in 1966, made no reference to women except as visiting wives of soldiers.[22] Gender segregation within the armed forces was sufficient to make women invisible even to those foreign observers who were looking for them. As late as 1974 the feminist writer Julia Kristeva found it credible to write – while acknowledging their presence in the militia – 'there are no women in the People's Army of China: they serve only in liaison, administrative, or medical capacities'.[23] The characterization of duties was factual for the majority of servicewomen, albeit with notable exceptions (the air force had been training women pilots for more than two decades at that time), yet it is hard to believe that anyone would refer to a conscripted man performing clerical or support services as not being 'in the army' simply because of the duties he was assigned.

Mao himself, the principal proponent of drawing women into defence work, told US Secretary of State Henry Kissinger in 1973 that 'Too many

18. Yitzhak Shichor, 'Demobilization: the dialectics of PLA troop reduction', *China Quarterly* 146 (June 1996), pp. 353–4.
19. Quoted in Ross Terrill, *The White Boned-Demon: A Biography of Madame Mao Zedong* (New York, 1967), p. 247.
20. Hsu Wei, 'Women fliers', *Women of China* 4 (1965), pp. 41–5.
21. See, for example, Gittings, *Role of the Chinese Military*; Griffith, *Chinese People's Liberation Army*; and J. Chester Cheng, *The Politics of the Chinese Red Army: A Translation of the Bulletin of Activities of the People's Liberation Army* (Stanford, CA, 1966).
22. Cheng, *Politics of the Chinese Red Army*.
23. Julia Kristeva, *About Chinese Women*, trans. Anita Bowers (New York, 1986), p. 149. (First published in French in 1974.)

women in China cannot fight', and that those who were in the PLA were only 'on stage' and would run for shelter if fighting broke out.[24] While this can be construed as consistent with Mao's thinking that all women *should* know how to fight, it confirms the leadership's lack of confidence in women in combat. It is also a manifestation of the kind of tautological thinking that puts women in the double bind: believing they cannot fight, the leadership does not assign them to combat positions, while their absence from combat positions is a sign that they cannot fight. Certainly it can be seen as a mitigating factor that in 1973 Mao was a very sick man who wandered unpredictably in and out of coherency. However, it is also true that no woman ever rose to a command position in the PLA or to any high-level policy position in the party during his years of leadership.

The PLA in the reform era

In 1978, two years after the death of Mao Zedong, the former party General Secretary and Red Army commissar Deng Xiaoping gained control of the government and instituted a programme of economic reform and opening to the West. One of the four areas Deng targeted for modernization was national defence.

In revising military regulations on compulsory service in 1984, the PLA acknowledged that the new army would be less dependent on the poorly educated but intensely politicized (red) conscript and more on the well-educated expert: 'compulsory . . . service . . . remains a basic part of our military service system. However, with the continued improvement and modernization of our Army's quality and its weaponry and equipment, it is required that a growing number of professional soldiers who have a good mastery of technology render long-term military service.'[25]

Under the current military service law national defence remains the legal obligation of every citizen. Treated as a supplemental conscript pool, Chinese women do not have to register for the draft in their eighteenth year as men do, but they are subject to call-up and, like men, they can be drafted into active service even before they turn 18 'according to the needs of military units'.[26]

---

24. William Burr, ed., *The Kissinger Transcripts: The Top Secret Talks with Moscow and Beijing* (New York, 1998), pp. 100–1.
25. 'The Military Service Law of 1984', reprinted from *Xinhua* in *Federal Broadcast Information Service-China*, 6 June 1984, p. K11.
26. *Ibid.*, p. K2.

In 1985, in accordance with the programme of modernization, the PLA began an extended period of downsizing its force strength of 4.2 million, upgrading personnel skills and introducing high-tech weaponry. To facilitate force reduction and ameliorate its impact, demobilized officers whose work was primarily of a professional rather than a military nature were absorbed into a newly created civilian officer corps. As civilian employees of the PLA, they are allowed to carry over seniority, pay and benefits, but they wear different uniforms and, instead of holding military rank, they are subject to a system of technical grades similar to the British or American civil service. One advantage for those transferred to the civilian officer corps is that they are no longer subject to the relatively low mandatory age limits that apply to officers in the regular force for retirement or for being in-rank.

During these years of downsizing, the PLA's annual conscription has fallen from 1,350,000 a year to just over 1 million, only 7,500 of whom are reported to be women. It was not until 1989 that *Military Balance* began to describe the PLA's force as being comprised of both men and women, and not until 1991 that the force was broken down by gender (presumably because that is when the PRC began reporting the information). In the eight years the government has been providing a gender breakdown of active-duty soldiers, the number of women, according to *Military Balance*, has held steady at 136,000.

Today's PLA is still the largest armed force in the world, divided between army (just over 2 million), navy (280,000) and air force (470,000).[27] The army ground forces are divided into rapid-deployment forces, or 'fist' units; combat, training and logistics support units; and service units that work in agriculture, construction and commerce (the PLA is said to own and control over 25,000 enterprises, apart from the state-owned defence industries that supply PLA weaponry).[28] Army women are found mainly in support and service units, working in logistics and communications and doing scientific, technical and medical research. Half of all PLA medical workers are women, and as has been true since the early days of the Red Army, they are well-represented in political education/propaganda and cultural (entertainment) units.

By 1994 the air force had trained 290 women, some of whom had learned to fly fighter aircraft even though not allowed to fly combat missions. Most women pilots have been assigned to airlift and disaster relief, other transport work or cloud seeding. However, a few have become training instructors for male bomber pilots.[29] The air force has also trained women paratroopers,

---

27. *Military Balance 1997–98*, pp. 176–8.
28. *Military Balance, 1995–96*, p. 270.
29. Peng Donghai, 'A navigator in the air force', *Women of China* (December 1987), pp. 40–1.

but their jumps may be limited to air shows and competitive meets.[30] Women have been in the navy since its founding and are said to be the backbone of its present communications system. They also have a strong presence in the navy's Art Troupe, entertaining the men at sea. But it was not until 1991 that the first group of 17 women were finally trained as sailors, albeit to serve on a medical not a warship.

In addition to the 2.8 million in the active-duty forces, China also has a militia of approximately 1.25 million troops and an 800,000-strong People's Armed Police (PAP) for internal security and border defence and to guard military installations and industries. The militia has been removed from direct PLA command and reorganized along provincial lines as reserve forces. While part of this reorganization may have to do with budgetary politics (concealing the size of defence expenditures), it can also be seen as part of the regularization process, one important aspect of which is to distance the armed forces from politics. The militia has always been highly politicized and during the end stages of the Cultural Revolution, Jiang Qing was accused of trying to gain control of the PLA by appointing her sympathizers, including women Red Guards, to cadre positions in the militia and the PLA's Production and Construction Corps (now also detached from direct PLA control).[31] There is no breakdown by gender of reserve troops, but with the end of a people's militia and the assignment of demobilized soldiers to militia reserves it is reasonable to assume that there are far fewer women in the militia than in earlier decades.

The PAP, formerly under the Public Security Bureau and now under the authority of the Defence Ministry and the PLA, has trained women for police work since the earliest days of the Republic. Women have long been important in border defence – mainly through service in the old militia – and it is still customary for women to be stationed at most border checkpoints in order to search and question women detained at border crossings.

Women have several routes to joining the PLA: qualifying for entrance to a PLA college or training school, of which there are more than 100; being part of the annual conscription; enlisting after graduation from a civilian undergraduate or graduate programme; or being selected during one of the talent searches conducted periodically to recruit youth gifted in sports, music, theatre or dance. Talented youth may move from middle school to one of the PLA's specialized training institutes. After basic training most regular conscripts are assigned to clerical jobs or to work as switchboard operators or medical orderlies. Unless they are among a small number who qualify

---

30. Ch'iu, 'The role of women', p. 59.
31. *Ibid.*, p. 61.

for higher training at a PLA school, they are discharged after meeting their basic term of service.[32]

For a woman to be admitted to one of the PLA's institutions of higher education requires exceptional performance on entrance examinations, with scores 20–30 points higher than those of qualifying male applicants.[33] If successful, these women enter one of the specialized PLA schools (such as for language or medicine) as cadets, and after graduation are commissioned as junior officers.[34] Women comprise around 25–30 per cent of the entrance classes in these schools but rarely are they admitted to the PLA's command and staff schools.[35]

Girls as young as 12 may be selected in the special talent recruitments and admitted to the PLA Art Institute or accepted for training by the August First Sports Team.[36] (1 August 1927 is the founding date of the Red Army.) Artists and athletes who excel can remain in the PLA for their entire performing or competitive careers. Among the highest-ranking women in the PLA are a nationally known actress who joined up in 1952 and an opera singer; both are graduates of the PLA Art Institute.

Men and women recruits and cadets attached to the same units or institutes undergo the same three months of basic training, although the training received by male and female cadets in a PLA language institute, for example, would not be the same as that for male conscripts, who would be assigned to the ground forces. However, all recruits and cadets participate in 'morning drills, military marches, field exercises, use of weapons and sometimes a little bit of military boxing'. For as long as women remain in the PLA they will be expected periodically to do morning drills and to take shooting practice at least once a year.[37] The same is true for women in the PLA's medical schools; male and female medical students take 'identical courses including shooting, grenade throwing, field nursing, and military topography'. One of their six years of training consists of 'practising military medicine and simulated war exercises'.[38] Nevertheless, since 1949 women doctors and nurses are known to have served in a combat zone only during the border conflicts with Vietnam.[39]

32. Col. Yao Yunzhu, 'Chinese women's role in the People's Liberation Army (part 1)', *Army Quarterly and Defence Journal* 125 (October 1995), pp. 415–16.
33. *Ibid.*, p. 415.
34. A complete list of all PLA officer training schools can be found in Lonnie D. Henley, 'Officer education in the Chinese PLA', *Problems of Communism* (May–June 1987), pp. 60–7.
35. Yao, 'Chinese women's role', p. 415; June Teufel Dreyer, 'The new officer corps: implications for the future', *China Quarterly* 146 (June 1996), p. 319.
36. Yao, 'Chinese women's role', p. 416.
37. *Ibid.*, part 2, p. 84.
38. 'Future women army doctors', *Women of China* (August 1984), p. 8.
39. Segal, Li and Segal, 'The role of women', pp. 52–3.

Enlisted men and women and cadets are not allowed to marry or to have sexual relations with one another. Male and female officers can marry, and according to one source over 90 per cent of women officers did marry male colleagues prior to 1990, under a policy that encouraged such unions.[40] Presumably this was a social convenience, economical and in some instances a security advantage. However, in an era of greater social freedom and more economic opportunity, officers are now less likely to marry within the armed forces.

Using the 136,000 figure given in each of the *Military Balance* annual reports for the 1990s, women appear to comprise about 4.8 per cent of the PLA's active-duty forces. However, in 1992 an official source set the total number of women involved in the military at 300,000.[41] No breakdown of this figure was provided but it apparently adds to 136,000 women on active duty in the regular army, those who now serve in the civilian officer corps, and perhaps women in the PAP and reserves as well.

Revisions in the Military Service Law adopted at the end of 1998 call for a further force reduction of 500,000 troops by the year 2000. The length of compulsory service is to be reduced to two years, regardless of service arm, and the percentage of the active force comprised of professionals increased from 18 to 35 per cent. The length of time volunteers (which includes most women) can stay in the army has been increased from 12 to 30 years.[42]

In this era of upgrading educational level and technical skills in the military, it follows that there would be greater job security for servicewomen. Most are well-educated, and necessarily so, because gender segregation has put many into jobs that require post-secondary education. According to the 1994 state report on the status of women, the work of servicewomen is concentrated in 'medical services, telecommunications, mapping, teaching, art, and scientific research'. Indeed women with science degrees, technical or professional training account for 93 per cent of all women holding officer rank.[43] In contrast, in the general labour pool the educational level of women is below that of men, with almost one-third of all women over age 15 illiterate or semi-literate (two and a half times the illiteracy rate for men).[44] During periods of layoffs in the civilian sector it is women who are

40. *Ibid.*, pp. 85–6.
41. Reported by *Xinhua* (the state-controlled New China News Agency) on 4 March 1992 (reprinted in *Federal Broadcast Information Service-China*, 12 March 1992, p. 30).
42. The text of the 1998 revision of the Military Service Law was released by *Xinhua* on 30 December 1998, and is available in translation from the Federal Broadcast Information Service (document FBIS-CHI 99-015).
43. 'Report of the People's Republic of China on the implementation of the Nairobi forward-looking strategies for the advancement of women', *Beijing Review*, 24–30 October 1994, p. 16.
44. *Ibid.*, p. 24.

the first to go. By comparison, servicewomen do have more job security, but it has not been enough to shield them from downsizing, paradoxically because of their high educational level. Because most servicewomen are in high-skill positions a disproportionate number are officers – the ratio to non-officers was extremely high at 3:1 when downsizing began in 1985 – and demobilization fell heaviest on the officer corps.

One woman I spoke with, the daughter of a general, had been recruited by the PLA while at middle school and assigned to a foreign language institute. After five years in the regular service she was offered admission to a PLA medical school, and jumped at the chance to further her education and to escape work she did not like. She is now a doctor working as a civilian employee in an urban military hospital. (Doctors in field hospitals are regular military.)

A breakdown by gender of all demobilized troops is not available, but many highly trained women veterans of 20 and more years, who had no interest in leaving the service, were released.[45] Of the 455,000 PLA officers demobilized between 1985 and 1998, virtually all were said to have been reassigned to civilian work in education, science and technology research, commerce and finance, cultural units, and public health departments. If this is true, women soldiers have fared far better than women in the civilian labour force who are laid off.[46] Even those enlisted women who are demobilized after their basic term of service have a far better chance at full-time employment than women in the civilian economy. If they return to their home towns or urban neighbourhoods they may be hired by local government or at least be given help in job placement.

Military reorganization during the reform era has seen a wave of promotions among high-ranking women officers. In 1986 five women were promoted to major-general, and after 1988, when a new ranking system was put in place, another eight women were elevated. At this time Nie Li, who had attained major-general rank in 1986, was promoted to lieutenant-general, another first for PLA women. In addition to the late Red Army commissar Li Zhen, 13 women had attained the rank of general by 1995. Of these, four are in medicine, two in science and technology, two in languages, two in art/culture (the opera singer and film actress), and one each in administration, political education/discipline, and military history. Unlike Li Zhen, none has a combat record.

---

45. Xiao Ming, 'From army women to civilian workers', *Women of China* (December 1987), pp. 20–2; 'In times of peace', *Women of China* (August 1987), pp. 4–6.
46. 'Demobilization', *China Quarterly* (March 1998), p. 347. Also see Xiao, 'From army women to civilian workers', *Women of China* (December 1987), pp. 20–2. For a comparison with civilian workers laid off see 'Female=unemployable, jobless Chinese learn', *New York Times*, 13 October 1998, pp. A1, A8.

Several of the generals are closely related to founding figures of the Chinese Communist Party and/or the Red Army. Nie Li, a Russian-trained engineer, is the daughter of the late Marshal Nie Rongzhen. Like her father, she oversaw – before her recent retirement – defence-related research and production in science, technology and industry. Deng Xianqun, who works in the field of civil–military relations, is the much younger half-sister of the late Deng Xiaoping (daughter of his father's fourth wife), one of the Red Army's most famous political commissars and later chair of the Central Military Commission as well as General Secretary of the party; Peng Gang, who serves in the PLA's General Political Department, is the daughter of revolutionary martyrs and also the niece/adopted daughter of Marshall Peng Dehuai; and He Jiesheng, a writer and military historian, is the daughter of Long March veterans Marshall He Long and Jian Xianren.[47]

Among these women generals, Li Zhen was the only one not to have a high level of professional or technical training or to be a nationally recognized performer. But like General Li, all have spent their adult lives in military service. Perhaps this is why there appears to be no hesitation in official publications to link several of these women (with the exception of Deng's half-sister) to their high-ranking relatives – something that in the past would almost certainly never have been officially acknowledged. It is not that unusual for children anywhere to adopt the profession of a parent, and a survey of PLA women stationed in the Beijing area found that 55.8 per cent of the respondents came from military families, while 63 per cent were married to military officers.[48] In addition, the PLA has a reputation for taking in and elevating relatives of the most highly placed. When the late Red Army veteran Yang Shangkun chaired the Military Affairs Commission, the PLA was sometimes referred to as the 'Yang Family Village'. And the lieutenant-colonel who allegedly funnelled illegal contributions to the 1996 Clinton re-election campaign was the daughter of China's highest-ranking military officer. Yet, despite these and other highly visible examples, studies show that only a small percentage of the PLA officer corps come from the families of high-ranking officials.[49] However, having relatives in the PLA command undoubtedly helped some of these now high-ranking women to avoid forced retirement during the recent and earlier demobilizations.

The presence of 13 generals and thousands of field-grade officers, including hundreds of senior colonels in the PLA, is offered as proof that women can rise to the top of the military hierarchy. But rank alone means little

---

47. General He was born just before her parents set out on the Long March. Her mother's experience on the March, as told to Helen Young, can be found in *Choosing Revolution*.
48. Li, 'The role of women', p. 427.
49. Dreyer, 'The new officer corps', p. 319.

without consideration of job assignment and unit placement, or without mention of where decision-making authority and real power lie within the armed services. Women doctors, entertainers, athletes, surveyors, clerks and communications specialists do not make contributions to security policy, or to strategic or tactical thinking. Women can have highly successful and productive careers in the military but no woman, including the highest-ranking women officers, is, or ever has been, anywhere near the centre of decision-making in the PLA – unless one speculates that a few may have had the ear of their well-placed relatives. But even Red Army veterans married to high-level cadres appear not to have been privy to any part of the decision-making process.[50]

This has special significance in China because in no other developed state has the military been more closely associated with the legitimate exercise of governmental and political power. During the Mao years political strategy was embedded in military doctrine, civic and military virtues were synonymous, and army and party leadership were merged. No one rose to the highest level of party leadership who had not served in the Red Army as a field commander or political commissar. Political alliances were formed around the field army in which veterans served prior to liberation. For women, this merging of party and army leadership was another barrier to mobility in both government and the army. A few like General Li Zhen did rise to prominence as political commissars, but no women came close to entering the central core of decision-makers.

PLA women are well-placed, however, to make contributions to the country at large through their research in military medicine, science and technology, as well as to develop and exercise individual talents in sports and the arts.[51] Although women researchers have been instrumental in advances in satellite and missile technology, for example, their major area of achievement – not surprisingly given that the majority of women soldiers work in some area of medicine – has been in military medicine.

Despite the fact that women are subject to conscription and have been officially described as 'an indispensable part of China's military force',[52] the State Council's 1998 report on national defence does not deal with any issue specific to the integration of women in the armed services.[53] Almost nothing has been written, for example, about sexual harassment in military

---

50. See the discussion of this in Young, 'Women at work' (forthcoming).
51. A list of some of their major achievements in science, technology, arts and sports can be found in *Twentieth Century Chinese Servicewomen*, pp. 185–92.
52. *Ibid.*
53. 'China's national defense', report prepared by the State Council of the People's Republic of China, reprinted in *Beijing Review*, 10–16 August 1998, pp. 12–34.

units, although if it has been a problem it is not likely that it would be reported in any periodical intended for public consumption. But given the level of job segregation with the PLA, enlisted men and women do not have the same level of daily contact that most American enlistees have after basic training. Also, all-female units typically have a woman as a commanding officer. There are several common-sense reasons why the recruitment, retention, promotion and integration of women soldiers go unmentioned in the 1998 defence report. The first and most obvious is that at this time the leadership does not see any need or feel any pressure to alter the role of women soldiers. Even if women want to expand their options in military service there is little opportunity for them to push for it. Women's rights, as is the case with the promotion of all other group rights in China, are the project of a state-founded mass organization: the All-China Federation of Women. Despite their seriousness of purpose in defending and promoting women's rights, Federation activists are not free to aggregate women's interests for the purpose of acting as a pressure group in support of an independent agenda. While mandated to serve as a women's interest group, their greatest charge is to change popular views in the direction of official policy. If the Federation's leadership's assessment of how change should be pursued is not in line with the nature and pace of changed sanctioned by the party, there is little opportunity to put forward a bolder agenda to the public.

Second, although China has the largest military establishment in the world, it is a tiny percentage of its population. In a country of limited opportunity and one where, until recently, people's geographical mobility was restricted by a household registration system, the army was a very important vehicle for physical, social and economic mobility. For many rural youths conscription was about their only chance to leave the countryside other than by passing university entrance exams (only about 1 per cent of China's population attends university). Today, even though there is far more opportunity, the army remains an important source of technical training for rural youth who have no chance at post-secondary education – training that may be converted to civilian employment on demobilization. With the downsizing of the military it is not likely that men are eager to lose positions by seeing women's share in them increase.

Third, minimum qualifications for conscripts have been raised, which gives men a further advantage over women in the draft since in the general labour pool women are less well educated than men. Given the size of the candidate pool in such a large population, however, there are more than enough qualified women available to fill the tiny number of slots available. But the PLA has tended to draw little on the general pool of women in the labour force, preferring instead to recruit women with high aptitude for university-level work as cadets for its own schools or to enlist graduates of civilian universities. Since university-educated women now have greater opportunity for finding higher-paying jobs in a civilian economy that will be much less restrictive of their freedom, military service may seem far less attractive than it did before the reform era.

In the end what does it matter if women are represented in any country's armed forces? In her study of the origins of the division of labour, the anthropologist Ernestine Friedl suggests that the role of warrior went to men in part because of women's irreplaceable function in sustaining a population: the necessary spacing of children, infant mortality, and the relatively short period of female fertility made the protection of women indispensable to the survival of any given society or culture. With their longer periods of fertility and the ability to impregnate many women, men were needed in fewer numbers to replicate or expand a population and hence they became the more dispensable sex and could be put at risk at lower social cost.[54] Whatever the validity of this explanation of its origins, the warrior role has evolved a quite different social and political significance in modern states, where military service has become inextricably linked with civic duty and rights of citizenship.

The coupling of rights and duties, in practice if not in theory, is common to all modern states, including the United States, where certain rights are said to be inalienable. This coupling can be seen in the implicitly exclusionist sentiments expressed at the founding of the American Republic: 'May all our Citizens be Soldiers, and all our Soldiers Citizens' and 'May only those Americans enjoy freedom who are ready to die for its defense'.[55] Because their competence was regarded as limited to the private sphere, eighteenth-century American women were seen as having no place in civic life or discourse, and hence no obligation to do military service. Women also had no political rights: without equal vulnerability to all the obligations and risks of citizenship, a person cannot demand the full rights and benefits of citizenship.

In China, a society where daughters have long been a 'little happiness' in comparison with the great joy of sons, gaining full rights of participation has been a long struggle. They have made their greatest progress, as have women in the West, in times when the need for women's labour in the public sector has been most needed – and recognized as needed by male leaders. During the years of war against the Nationalist government and the Japanese occupation, women in Red Army-controlled areas reportedly made their greatest political gains where their participation in military, political

---

54. Ernestine Friedl, *Women and Men: An Anthropological Survey* (New York, 1975), p. 59.
55. Linda K. Kerber, 'May all our citizens be soldiers and all our soldiers citizens: the ambiguities of female citizenship in the new nation', in Jean Bethke Elshtain and Sheila Tobias, eds, *Women, Militarism, and War* (Boston, 1990), pp. 93–4.

and economic work was absolutely essential to the survival of the movement. And where women saw combat or served in combat support units, the party is said to have acted most quickly and firmly in support of women's rights.[56]

In general the profound changes the PLA has experienced in the reform period have not greatly changed the role of women soldiers. Compared with women in the US armed services Chinese women are making slower progress in ending job segregation. Whereas in 1970 women were only 1.4 per cent of all active-duty US personnel, by 1998 they were 13.6 per cent (193,114) of the active force of 1.42 million. Some 80 per cent of all positions within the US armed forces were open to women, and women were beginning to move towards assumption of combat roles.[57] Women pilots have been trained in bombers and fighter aircraft and took part in the Persian Gulf War and the December 1998 bombing of Iraq. In addition policy issues involving integration of women in the military – co-ed basic training, sexual harassment, opening combat positions – have received extraordinary internal and public attention. Like Chinese women, however, American servicewomen are nowhere near the highest levels of decision-making. Still, the legal obligation of Chinese women to do military service remains greater than that of American women. American women have never been subject to conscription, and even if the draft were reinstated it is arguable that women would continue to be excluded, despite the military's now heavy reliance on their service.

It is no surprise that the expansion of the military role of American women occurred in conjunction with their struggle to gain full civil rights. In addition, the end of the draft, the introduction of high-tech weapons that make combat from a distance ever more possible, and record low unemployment levels have all contributed to the fuller integration of women in the armed forces. None of these yet applies in China. Nor does that other aspect of the American argument: the right of the individual to pursue his or her talents even if that means defying divisions of labour that have official sanction.

The policy of staffing PLA ground forces almost exclusively with men may be hardening. In the 1990s, along with yet another revival of the Lei Feng campaign (a role model long since regarded with deep cynicism among the general population), the army mounted two new campaigns to publicize military role models: the good military mother, Yao Cixian, and the good military wife, Han Suyun. Seen in the context of these camapigns the

---

56. Mark Selden, *The Yenan Way* (Cambridge, MA, 1971), p. 166 n. 81; Zhong Fu, 'Comrade Mao Zedong's investigations of women's conditions in the countryside', *Women of China* (December 1983), p. 6.

57. James Kitfield, 'Front and center', *National Journal*, 25 October 1997, pp. 2125–6.

essence of patriotism for women is standing by the men who fight. Military wives are asked to emulate Han Suyun, an exemplar of the Lei Feng spirit, in defending the country by supporting their husband's military careers.[58]

Today, most women in the PLA are professionals on a career track, not warriors. As the long process of introducing high-tech weaponry into the PLA continues, the number of positions in research and in logistical support work, which have often been filled by women, will increase.[59] But there are not yet signs that women are moving into combat positions, where they would operate new weaponry, even though the skills required are quite different from those associated with fighting conventional ground wars, a development that has been used to argue for the movement of women into combat positions in the American military.

---

58. Discussion of the Yao Cixian campaign can be found in *Federal Broadcast Information Service-China*, 5 July 1995, pp. 37–8; and of Han Suyun in *ibid.*, 18 January 1995, pp. 18–20.
59. Li, 'The role of women', p. 430.

CHAPTER SIXTEEN

'And Don't Forget to Clean the Fridge': Women in the Secret Sphere of Terrorism

CATHERINE TAYLOR

Terrorists operate in an unconventional world. They defy the rules of warfare, wear no uniforms, seldom confront their enemies and thrive on mystery and stealth. Within the secret sphere of paramilitary organizations, social convention would appear to have no utility. One would assume that, in consequence, such a sphere would offer opportunities for women, that obstacles based solely on gender would not impede their progress or prevent them from making a significant contribution to the cause. In fact, the opposite is true. Women encounter the same impediments to progress which characterize conventional military organizations. Moreover, the terrorist method of warfare utilizes in particular a thoroughly unmodern woman, namely the archetypal *femme fatale* who lures her prey with sex and then kills in cold blood. Thus, ironically, unconventional paramilitary organizations are often bastions of gender conventionality.

In 1977 an article in *The Economist* reported that over half of the German terrorists for whom an arrest warrant had been issued were women.[1] Nine years later, *The German Tribune* revealed that although women are responsible for only 10–15 per cent of crime in West Germany, 14 out of the 21 most wanted terrorists were women.[2] Nevertheless, though female terrorists clearly exist, public knowledge of them does not go much deeper than the stereotypes handed down by Hollywood films, in which, like the gangster's moll, the female terrorist offers the opportunity of combining sex and violence in thrilling combination. According to Deborah Galvin, there is 'terrorism and there is female involvement in it which is amorphous, scattered and has

---

1. 'German's dragon teeth', *The Economist*, 20 August 1977, pp. 12–13.
2. *The German Tribune*, 21 February 1986.

been subjected to little critical appraisal . . . the fragmentary nature of much of what we know about female terrorism, the lack of care and cohesiveness is quite striking.'[3] This may be because 'terrorism' as a subject for research is still dominated by male analysts studying predominantly male terrorists and writing predominantly for a male audience.

Another possible explanation for this gap in awareness is that the concept of a woman terrorist appears to be a contradiction in terms. Investigation of media coverage indicates a discrepancy between the self-perception of women terrorists and the manner in which they are discussed in public debate. A woman who turns to terrorism is a living contradiction – she has chosen to take life, not to give it. Her activities are therefore all the more aberrant, not only setting her apart from society, but also from her gender. Media coverage reflects the conceptual void that surrounds an issue which refuses to fit into a ready-made category. This brief exploration of the contrasts between the perceptions and practice of women terrorists provides some lateral insight into the broader issue of women who choose to bear arms, and highlights the taboo surrounding the notion that women can kill.

Motivations

Analyses of why women become terrorists have generally fallen into two categories of explanation: those based on the changing roles of women in society, such as their growing economic and political freedom; and explanations loosely based on biological or psychological analysis. In the former category, the logical argument is made that, as women have become more involved in politics, it is only to be expected that they should become more involved on the political fringes. As the head of a German anti-terrorist squad explained, 'women have thrown off the shackles of the traditional women in society and have realized that there is no reason why they should not be violent'.[4] Thus, equal opportunity is equated with equal opportunity to kill. In the latter category, pseudo-science has usually been moulded to fit a preconceived conclusion.[5] For instance, Anne Jones, in *Women Who Kill*, tries to explain violent women in terms of the purely physical structure of the woman's body. She maintains that violent women 'approximate more to males . . . than to normal women, especially in the superciliary arches in the

---

3. Deborah Galvin, 'The female terrorist: a socio-psychological perspective', *Behavioural Sciences and the Law* 1, 2 (1983), p. 20.
4. Mark Thornton, 'The cruelty of women', http://www.daily.umn.edu
5. RAND Database, University of St Andrews, Scotland.

seam of the sutures, in the lower jaw bones and in the occipital region'.[6] This is an interesting theory but unfortunately one which reveals more about Jones's own obsessions than those of female terrorists. The image of masculine-looking women in any case contradicts the widely held (but equally spurious) view that female terrorists are often strikingly beautiful. The latter theme was evident in an article published in *Top Security* in 1976, which united the above two categories. It suggested that a hormonal imbalance in women terrorists, caused by excessive sexual freedom, might explain their motivation to violence.[7]

The psychologist Carol Gilligan feels that men and women think differently – women have an 'injunction to care whilst with men there is a drive to respect the rights of others, protecting from interference the rights of life and self-fulfilment'.[8] Taken to its logical conclusion, this suggests that female terrorists are even more of an aberration than males are, because the former quite clearly fail to fulfil their predetermined social roles. However, a gendered debate of motivational factors can obscure more than it illuminates. Konrad Kellen insists that 'the external conditions of life and the psychological factors that lead women into terrorism are very similar to those of men'.[9] As in conventional war, so too in terrorism: a gendered explanation for violence suggests too many contradictions to be of any serious use.

The evidence seems to buttress Kellen's assertion that differences between male and female terrorists are contrived. Female terrorists, like their male comrades, often have a clear view of their commitment to the cause. Silveria Russo, an Italian terrorist, for example, joined Prima Linea because 'it was a personal decision: a responsibility to be taken on'. She wanted to be a modern day 'Robin Hood'.[10] Bernadine Dohrn, of the Weather Underground, once explained that she 'did not choose to live in a time of war'. She and her comrades 'chose only to become guerrillas and to urge our people to prepare for war rather than become accomplices in the genocide of our sisters and brothers'.[11] In her mind, the important thing was that a choice had been made; she had not followed the aimless collective.

Testimony from Astrid Proll, a former member of the Baader–Meinhof Gang, underlines the fact that issues surrounding gender equality pervade the world of terrorism, or that the decision to join a terrorist movement can

---

6. Anne Jones, *Women Who Kill* (New York, 1980), p. 7.
7. 'The female terrorist and her impact on policing', *Top Security* 2 (1976).
8. Carol Gilligan, *In a Different Voice* (Cambridge, MA, 1993), p. 100.
9. Konrad Kellen, *On Terrorists and Terrorism* (Santa Monica, CA, 1982), p. 24.
10. Luisella de Cataldo Neuburger and Tiziana Valentini, *Women and Terrorism* (London, 1996), p. 120.
11. Peter Collier and David Horowitz, *Destructive Generation* (New York, 1989).

be affected by a sense of injustice with a patriarchal world. At a visit to a photographic exhibition, Proll saw many examples of men in uniform, but no women. She concluded 'that is one of the reasons why so many women joined the RAF [Red Army Faction] . . . German revolutionary women were convinced that if they had had a voice during Hitler's time many of the atrocities would have not happened.'[12] Likewise, 'Marta', one of the first women revolutionaries of the Tigrayan People's Liberation Front (TPLF), equated the ability to bear arms with gender equality in one of her revolutionary songs:

> *Women, Get up off your knees.*
> *We knelt beneath the feudal's rule.*
> *We were only speaking tools.*
> *Now we as well as men have guns.*
> *And one day we'll be free.*[13]

Perceptions

Clearly, women who have turned to terrorism have made a choice to move from political activism to political violence. This choice is the result of a process begun in their personal background or of circumstances which have developed over time and which lead them to turn to arms. There should be no surprise in this conclusion, however misguided the individual motivation to terrorism might seem. Nevertheless, it is clear from media analyses of female terrorists that commentators are reluctant to credit women with the same serious political commitment which is generally attributed to men. Various contradictory approaches have been taken to pigeonhole the female terrorist into a convenient conceptual category.

When female terrorists are covered in the media it is often in such a way as to emphasize their womanhood in a manner which trivializes and marginalizes their activities. For instance, one finds an inordinate emphasis on their physical appearance. Nalan Gurates, who served in the Turkish Liberation Front, was often described as not very good-looking, while it is difficult to find a media treatment of Gudrun Ensslin, a German terrorist, which does not mention the fact that she once acted in *Das Abonnement*, a pornographic film.[14] Articles about Fusako Shigenbou, a Japanese terrorist, and Susan Stem of the Weather Underground, usually make mention of the

---

12.   Eileen MacDonald, *Shoot the Women First* (London, 1991), p. 201.
13.   Jenny Hammond, *Sweeter than Honey: Testimonies of Tigrayan Women* (London, 1989), p. 44.
14.   RAND Database, University of St Andrews, Scotland, Rosemary File.

fact that they worked as dancers in night clubs.[15] According to one commentator, Dohrn's 'strong-jawed sensuality and look of sultry defiance . . . made her into something like a radical pinup'.[16] The advantage of this approach is that it provides titillating copy, places the women on the margins of respectable society, and simultaneously avoids awkward discussions of ideologies. As in so many other contexts, one of the easiest ways of denying women professional credibility is to concentrate on their sexual behaviour or physical appearance.

Female terrorists are, on the other hand, often also described as 'girls'. Mairead Farrell, the Irish Republican Army (IRA) terrorist killed by the security forces in Gibraltar for the part she may have played in a proposed bombing, was often described as a 'girl'. After her death *The Times* ran a headline, 'How schoolgirl chose a career in terrorism'.[17] In another paper the headline ran 'A girl who turned to terror'.[18] The fact that Farrell was over 30 at the time of the incident made no difference, nor were her two male colleagues ever called 'boys'. Similarly, Susanna Albrecht, a German terrorist, was described by the British Press as a 'gun girl',[19] and more recently a *Daily Mail* headline asked of Roisin McAliskey, supposedly a member of the IRA, 'Is Devlin girl a terrorist?'.[20] The epithet 'girl' serves two purposes. It emphasizes the terrorists' youth, denying them political maturity. It also desexualizes them, making the contradiction between their gender and their actions less overt.

If not 'girl', then 'girlfriend'. In *The Good Terrorist* by Doris Lessing, Alice is a 30-year-old British woman who decides to dedicate her life to a left-wing political movement called the Communist Centre Union (CCU). She is motivated by antipathy to her middle-class upbringing, and is drawn in by her boyfriend Jasper. The stereotype of the unthinking woman who, like Alice, is drawn into the world of terrorism through a boyfriend is common in media coverage of female terrorists. Farrell, for instance, was often assigned the girlfriend tag. The *Sunday Times* attributed her IRA affiliation to a man rather than to her own family ties with the Republican movement.[21] As with the 'girl' tag, this approach denies women a mind of their own, or personal ideological commitment. The responsibility is given to the male, who is permitted both independence and the ability to make personal political decisions. The

15. Jillian Becker, *Hitler's Children: The Story of the Baader Meinhof Terrorist Gang* (London, 1977), p. 72.
16. Collier and Horowitz, *Destructive Generation*, p. 68.
17. Richard Ford, 'How schoolgirl chose a career in terrorism', *The Times*, 8 March 1988.
18. 'A girl who turned to terror', *Sunday Times*, 13 March 1988.
19. MacDonald, *Shoot*, p. 209.
20. David Williams, 'Is Devlin girl a terrorist?', *Daily Mail*, 26 November 1996.
21. *Sunday Times*, 13 March 1988.

female terrorist, like the gangster's moll, becomes involved out of a naive attraction to excitement, danger and the thrill of being near a dominant male.

In practice, entry into terrorism through a partner and a personal commitment to a cause are not necessarily incompatible. Nalan Gurates (or 'Scorpion Nalan' as she was known) appears at first glance to fit the 'girlfriend' label. She confessed that 'Only one person thought I was pretty and I married him . . . I fell in love with him and became close to him. At that time, I wasn't aware of the fact that he was a militant member of a terrorist organisation. By the time I learned this, it was too late.'[22] But, after her husband was killed in a shoot-out with police during a bank robbery in 1978, instead of denouncing violence, Nalan assumed the leadership of a small faction of the Turkish Liberation Front and played an active part in a series of terrorist incidents.[23] Although her husband brought her into the movement, it was her choice to continue in it, to assume a leadership position and ultimately to use violence.

The assumption that women cannot make an independent decision to turn to violence contrasts dramatically with the fact that many women terrorists are highly educated, independent women. Ulrike Meinhof and Gudrun Ensslin of the Baader–Meinhof Gang, Silveria Russo and Susanna Ronconi of the Red Brigades and Rita O'Hare of the IRA all had some university education.[24] Dohrn was a qualified attorney. Meinhof, a journalist by training and one of the founders of the Baader–Meinhof Gang, intellectualized her gradual move towards violence. She was aggrieved by the hypocrisy of large conglomerates, which criticized stone-throwing and arson attacks by student protesters, yet supported the bombing of Vietnam and the terror in Iran. She felt their commitment to non-violence was hypocritical and reacted against the inconsistency of rejecting student revolt but supporting state terror.[25] However misguided her actions might seem, one has to accept that her views were both deeply felt and intellectually logical – not those of a mere girl or lovestruck girlfriend.

Sexual dynamics

Margarethe Mitscherlich-Nielsen, a former Red Army Faction (RAF) member, rather optimistically felt that 'the harshness and tenacity of women

---

22. RAND Database, University of St Andrews, Scotland, Rosemary File, Turkish Female Terrorists, 12 April 1982.
23. *Ibid.*
24. 'Why terrorism attracts so many women', *German Tribune*, 21 December 1986.
25. Becker, *Hitler's Children*, p. 161.

terrorists was perhaps connected to the fact that they were now the dominant ones. Women terrorists now enjoyed a triumph to experience the reversal in dominance between men and women and to see men trembling from their acts.'[26] In truth women have seldom been able to exercise this sort of assertiveness within terrorist organizations. However sincere and non-gender-specific the motivations of female terrorists might be, the fact remains that they find it difficult to escape gender stereotypes once they join a movement. Even Dohrn, who exerted enormous power within the Weather Underground, did so by exploiting her sexuality, not through more conventional modes of authority. Her male acolytes were tied to her in large part out of sheer lust and she would control them, for instance, by keeping her blouse unbuttoned and breasts exposed during strategy meetings.[27]

Terrorist organizations have been quick to exploit aspects of femininity in order to achieve a specific terrorist purpose. A woman trading upon the impression of being a mother, a non-violent figure, can, for instance, more easily pass by security forces than a male.[28] In an interesting turn on the 'girlfriend' tag, Basque terrorists confessed to using the excuse that they had been duped by a boyfriend in order to escape punishment if they were captured.[29] As in the French Resistance during the Second World War, terrorist organizations have often successfully used women as decoys, gun-runners and spies because they are more likely to be above suspicion. In other words, women are useful to terrorist organizations as *women*. This fact limits their power within the movement and their ability to break down gender barriers.

Female sexuality also has its uses. Like the character in the film *The Crying Game* who used her female guile to lure an American soldier to be captured by the IRA, female terrorists have used their attractiveness as women to entice their targets to capture or a violent death. According to one commentator, Maureen O'Hara, an IRA terrorist, 'relied on her outstanding figure, red hair and outstandingly pretty face to lure British soldiers to over drink, over reach, then die slowly and horribly'.[30] This rather overblown journalistic description of O'Hara illustrates two aspects of female terrorists: first, the stereotype discussed above which combines sex and violence in a titillatingly erotic mix, and second, the probably quite accurate description of the role which female terrorists often play.

---

26. Neuburger and Valentini, *Women and Terrorism*, p. 83.
27. Collier and Horowitz, *Destructive Generation*, p. 75.
28. *The German Tribune*, 21 December 1986.
29. Katherine Dunn, 'Just as fierce', http://www.ryu.com
30. David Truby, *Lady Killers: Affirmative Action Comes to the Assassins Guild* (London, 1990), p. 25.

While women have proved useful as sexual lures, they have also apparently served a purpose as sexual playthings. Patty Hearst gained an insight into underground life in the Symbionese Liberation Army (SLA). She found it ironic that although 'her female comrades believed in liberation, it was as if they were there to service the men's sexual needs'.[31] Stokely Carmichael, when asked what the position of women in the Black Power movement was, replied, not entirely facetiously, 'on their backs'.

Many a radical organization has advanced the line that women's liberation constitutes a pointless deviation from the shining path of revolution. True equality will come when the capitalist oppressor is crushed. In the meantime, apparently, women prove useful by providing sexual gratification to tired, anxious warriors, or as those to weep and wail when heroes die. Shortly after the First World War, the novelist Storm Jameson remarked:

> Why do not women know that in any war, the enemy is not on the other side? Their enemy is war itself – which robs them of their identity: and they cease to be clever, competent, intelligent, beautiful in their own right and become the nurses, the pretty joys and at last the mourners of their men.[32]

The same, apparently, holds true in paramilitary war.

From myth to reality

Though women are useful to terrorist organizations as sexual ornaments and *femmes fatales*, it seems that they are also occasionally valued because of an aptitude unrelated to gender. When given the opportunity, women can be just as competent as terrorists as their male counterparts, if not better. Women terrorists frequently show themselves as ruthless, dominant and cool.[33] Marion Coyle, the IRA activist, and her male accomplice kidnapped a Dutch industrialist and held him prisoner for 31 days. After his experience, the prisoner commented that whilst he developed a relationship with the male terrorist, the female terrorist was 'cold and aloof, removed emotionally from her actions, speaking not a word to him'.[34] The woman kept strictly to the terrorist role of not engaging with the victim.

---

31. Patty Hearst, *Every Secret Thing* (London, 1982), pp. 172–3.
32. Margaret Storm Jameson, *No Time Like the Present* (London, 1933), p. 211.
33. Kellen, *Terrorists*, p. 24.
34. Allison Jamieson, *The Heart Attacked: Terrorism and Conflict in the Italian State* (London, 1989), p. 64.

Leila Khalid, the former Palestine Liberation Organization (PLO) terrorist, commented that 'on some missions girls are better than men. We believe that women are more coldblooded than men. A girl can go for sabotage missions hijacking is one – or plant mines because women are not nervous. Of course both women and men don't show it.'[35] It is perhaps significant that some female terrorists have expressed a fearful respect of the capacity of women to be violent. One terrorist from the Basque group ETA complained that 'the maddest and most barbaric' torturers she had encountered were women. Likewise, Ronconi expressed a disgust with female prison warders who 'used violence neutrally, as a type of control, and the amount they used, just doing a normal job, showed what truly violent people they were'.[36] Needless to say, some commentators have delighted in sensationalizing the behaviour of women who use violence in the manner described by Khalid. 'The female of any species is generally the hard killer . . . beneath even the warmth of motherhood, there lurks the soul of a killer', writes David Truby.[37] The contrast is again drawn between the giver of life and the taker of life: a tension particularly fascinating to some commentators when found in the same individual.

As with conventional militaries, the opportunity to serve a cause has not always been open to women. Those groups which have accepted women into their movements have followed different paths. In left-wing movements in Germany and Italy, where women were involved from the start, equality amongst members was not in theory gender-dependent, though the day-to-day reality might have been very different. However, in nationalist separatist movements, such as the IRA and the TPLF, women were recruited pragmatically for reasons of survival. The IRA in fact first used women in a manner not unlike the auxiliary services which characterized Western militaries during the First and Second World Wars – they served the movement, but were not strictly part of it. For IRA women, their initial involvement was to support the work of their men. Their movement, Cumann na Mban, was specifically created to provide women with a role in the struggle.[38] Their role was an extension of the tasks they generally performed in the domestic sphere. As it stood, 'the males were responsible for the gun carrying and breadwinning' whilst 'the women promoted the Republican movement by being mothers to the family and supporters of the soldiers'.[39] Their most

35. Freda Adler, 'A criminologist's view of women terrorists', *New York Times*, 9 January 1978.
36. Thornton, 'The cruelty of women'.
37. Truby, *Lady Killers*, pp. 24–6.
38. Suzann Buckley and Pamela Lonergan, 'Women and the troubles, 1969–1980', in Yonah Alexander and Alan O'Day, eds, *Terrorism in Ireland* (Beckenham, 1980), p. 75.
39. *Ibid.*

active involvement came in intelligence collection, as couriers, nurses, medical aids and safe house keepers, all important roles, but still ones which did not upset the male hegemony.[40] Many women felt it was wrong that they were denied a part in the armed struggle. It was only in 1972 when the IRA formally accepted women as equals within its organization that women had the choice to become terrorists. With many men incarcerated or dead, the recruitment of women was vital for the IRA's survival. In other words, this change was motivated by desperation, rather like the decision in some countries during the Second World War to relax the combat taboo as it applied to women simply because the supply of male warriors was running thin.

This is similar to the experience of Lemiem, a Tigrayan revolutionary and member of the TPLF. When she first joined, women were not welcome as fighters but only as underground workers in towns. The excuse given for denying women the right to take up arms was simply the natural differences between men and women. It was only when the TPLF underground organization was being hounded in the towns that women were allowed to become armed revolutionaries. It is now common to see women fighters, in all positions from guards to high commanders and departmental heads.[41]

When given the opportunity to contribute, women have sometimes been able to demonstrate their worth. In recognition of their contribution, they have advanced up the ladder of authority within their movements. According to Kellen, while one-third of German terrorists were women, 36 per cent of them attained leadership positions compared with only 32 per cent of men.[42] In fact, in the second wave of German terrorists, the majority of those in leadership positions were women, ten women compared with six men.[43] The Italian Red Brigades' leadership was composed of twelve men and seven women. In eco-terrorism also, women figure large in leadership positions.

But no matter how high a woman might rise within a movement, she can still find herself performing traditional female roles. A member of the Weather Underground tells an anecdote which illustrates that sexual equality was no more to be found within terrorist movements than in broader society. On arriving home after a mission, it was not uncommon to find a note left by one of the men telling her to clean the fridge.[44] As a 1983 headline in *The Guardian* asked: 'Guess who does the dishes in the Red Brigade?' The answer

---

40. Cindy C. Combs, *Terrorism in the 21st Century* (New York, 1997), pp. 60–70.
41. Hammond, *Sweeter than Honey*, pp. 46–7.
42. Kellen, *Terrorists*, pp. 24–8.
43. Neuburger and Valentini, *Women and Terrorism*, pp. 8–9.
44. RAND Database, University of St Andrews, Rosemary File.

was boringly predictable. Women might be able to break out of gender stereotypes in the advancement of a terrorist cause, but the movement still demanded that they be women.

Conclusion

In *The Subjection of Women,* John Stuart Mill argued that 'Unnatural generally means only uncustomary and that which is usual appears natural. The subjection of women to men being universal custom, any departure from it quite naturally appears unnatural.'[45] Within terrorist organizations, the 'unnatural' presence of women has occasionally been used as an asset to be exploited, but more often has been used as a way to limit their participation and denigrate their contribution. In the public sphere, the unnatural quality of the female terrorist has contributed to a tendency to question her commitment and often to ignore her existence entirely. Women terrorists, like women soldiers, hit the wall of what is considered 'natural'. There are only girls or sluts in the terrorist world, or deluded women led astray by men.

---

45. John Stuart Mill, *The Subjection of Women* (1869), p. 12.

CHAPTER SEVENTEEN

'A Simple Matter of Equality': The Admission of Women to West Point

LANCE JANDA

When Congress established the United States Military Academy on the banks of the Hudson River in 1802, no one realized West Point might eventually become an agent of social change or dramatically alter the place of women in the American armed forces. Thomas Jefferson and other proponents of the Academy saw it as a potential source of trained officers for a nation striving to expand on a continental scale, as a place where the army could train engineers and artillery experts who would form a regular cadre in time of war. In the century and a half that followed its creation, the Academy performed this mission with admirable success, producing officers who won American wars and helped explore and develop the United States at an astonishing pace. So great was West Point's success that Congress created the United States Naval Academy in 1845, and the United States Air Force Academy in 1955, so that every branch of the armed forces would benefit from having an institution dedicated solely to producing career officers. By the latter half of the twentieth century these academies were among the premier officer training institutions in the world, and recognized as places where combat leaders were forged and prepared for future greatness.

Yet the service academies admitted only men, in obeisance to a pervasive assumption that men alone could lead and fight in combat. By the 1970s, however, almost all assumptions about women were under intense pressure on a national scale, and the rapid pace of cultural change led Congress to use the military, and ultimately the academies, to offer greater opportunities to American women. When legislators opened these institutions to women in 1976, they did so to advance the cause of equality, not because supporters of admitting women saw themselves as taking a decisive step towards fundamentally altering the role of American women in the military. Yet this revolutionary event *was* a critical step towards placing women in direct combat positions, and towards expanding the importance of military women to the point where the armed services could not go to war without them. The military and opponents of greater opportunity for women foresaw some of these developments but were unable to stop them. Their resistance shaped the debate, however, so that supporters of dropping the gender barrier were unwilling to discuss the full implications of their actions. By focusing exclusively on equality they allowed a historic opportunity to debate fully the role of women in the armed forces to slip away.

The long journey towards that dramatic moment began in 1954, when Senator Dennis Chavez (Democrat, New Mexico) first called for the creation of a 'West Point for Women'. His efforts were expanded on in the early 1960s, when Representative Robert B. Duncan (Republican, Oregon) nominated a woman to the Academy.[1] The nomination was rejected, and the issue remained moot until 1972, when New York Republican Senator Jacob K. Javits nominated a woman to the US Naval Academy only a week after the Equal Rights Amendment passed Congress.[2] The timing of these events shows how clearly the cultural pressures of the 1970s, especially the civil rights and women's movements, shaped national policy affecting the military. Javits also co-authored a resolution with Representative Jack H. McDonald (Republican, Michigan) calling for an end to gender discrimination at the service academies. Though the Senate passed the resolution, it quickly died in the House, and the matter did not come before Congress again until 1973, when Representative Pierre S. du Pont IV (Republican, Delaware) introduced the first bill mandating the admission of women. At the same time, California Representatives Jerome Waldie and Don Edwards, both Democrats, nominated women to the air force and naval academies and sued Secretary of Defense James Schlesinger on behalf of their nominees, moving the campaign into the courts.[3]

In December 1973 the Senate passed by voice vote an amendment to the Armed Forces Enlisted Personnel Bonus Revision Act, which stipulated women would not be ineligible for admission to the academies based on gender. The amendment was co-sponsored by Senators Javits, William D. Hathaway

---

1. 'Senator Chavez seeks establishment of women's armed services academy', *Army Navy Air Force Journal*, 26 February 1955, p. 754, and Judith Hicks Stiehm, *Bring Me Men and Women: Mandated Change at the U.S. Air Force Academy* (Berkeley, CA, 1981), p. 11. The information within brackets indicates political party affiliation and the state that person represented.

2. Applicants to each service academy required nomination from one of a variety of sources before their application for admission could be screened. See Major William G. Tobin, Memorandum for the Director of Military Personnel Management, 'Admission Process for Women at USMA', 29 August 1975.

3. Stiehm, *Bring Me Men and Women*, pp. 11–13.

(Democrat, Maine), Mike Mansfield (Democrat, Montana), Strom Thurmond (Republican, South Carolina) and John C. Stennis (Democrat, Mississippi), who chaired the Senate Armed Services Committee. With strong support in the Senate the measure seemed certain to pass. Instead, it was dropped by the House Armed Services Committee in a narrow 18–16 vote. Representative Samuel Stratton (Democrat, New York), who supported the admission of women, argued that the Senate amendment had very little to do with bonus pay and thus was hardly germane. It had to be considered separately, after hearings on the admission of women were held in the House that summer.[4]

The hearings were held during May, June and July of 1974, and saw the services close ranks to present a determined, unified front against advocates of co-education at the academies. The Secretaries of the Army, Air Force, and Navy each testified against the admission of women, as did each of the three academy superintendents. Department of Defense General Counsel Martin Hoffman joined them, along with the Deputy Assistant Secretary of Defense for Military Personnel, Lieutenant-General Leo Benade, the Vice-Chief of Naval Operations, Admiral Worth H. Bagley, Air Force Chief of Staff General George Brown, Army Vice-Chief of Staff General Fred Weyand, and Jacqueline Cochran, who directed the Women Airforce Service Pilots (WASPs) during the Second World War. The number of witnesses, to say nothing of their high rank and prestige, said volumes about the seriousness with which the military establishment viewed the idea of opening Academy doors to women.

Cochran argued 'a woman's primary function in life is to get married, maintain a home and raise a family' and that 'women are nuts if they want to go into combat'. Men, she suggested, had to go into combat. When asked why, she responded, 'Because they are men and we don't have to do it because we are women'. Cochran's statements were both compelling and mystifying because she was an extraordinarily experienced pilot who logged more than 15,000 hours in flight, flew experimental planes as a test pilot, and ferried virtually every type of American military aircraft between US bases and England during the Second World War. Her life seemed to validate the claims of those who advocated a larger role for women in the military, yet she maintained a steadfast opposition to expanded opportunities for women in the armed forces as long as she lived. She argued passionately that women might be called upon in time of emergency, but suggested they should never serve in combat and never attend the military academies.[5]

---

4. *Ibid.*, p. 14.
5. US Congress, House, Statement of Miss Jacqueline Cochran, 'Hearings on H.R. 9832, *et al.* before Subcommittee No. 2 of the House Committee on Armed Services', 93rd Congress, 2nd session, 1974, pp. 254–64.

Military witnesses were more subdued in tone, though still deeply pas-
sionate. Howard 'Bo' Callaway, Secretary of the Army and a West Point
class of 1949 graduate, dominated the presentation. He spoke against the
admission of women to all the service academies in general and protested
against their possible inclusion in the Corps of Cadets at West Point in
particular. Callaway argued that the presence of women would dilute the
'Spartan atmosphere' of the Academy, thus lowering standards and dulling
the combat-oriented training that made West Point so vital. The army
could hardly be accused of sexism, he continued, because women were
eligible to become officers through Officer Candidate School (OCS) and
Reserve Officer Training Corps (ROTC) programmes, where the majority
of army officers received their commissions.[6] The implication was that women
posed no threat to ROTC or OCS training, and it was fine to allow women
those forms of commissioning because they were inferior to the Academy.
This sort of elitism was prevalent among many Academy graduates, some
of whom genuinely considered themselves superior to officers who were not
'academy men'. As Ward Just wrote, 'The Army is as hierarchical as the
church and as class-conscious and snobbish as Great Britain, West Point its
Eton and the Army War College its Oxford'.[7]

Callaway insisted that the minority of officers from West Point were vital
because they received four years of total immersion in a military environment, advanced training, and after graduation were far more likely to enter
one of the army's combat arms than an ROTC or OCS graduate. He
feared creating 'two West Points', one for men who would enter combat
units and one for women, who were barred by law from ever serving in the
front lines.[8] His arguments remained the bedrock of opposition to the role
of women at West Point and the other service academies well into the
1990s, and had their roots in army discussions which took place in 1972.
Officers at West Point, charged with determining how the impending
passage of the Equal Rights Amendment might affect the Academy, began
discussing possible ways to oppose the admission of women. 'My feeling is
that we should come out with an "over my dead body" approach to girls at
West Point', said one Military Academy memo. 'The more we act like
we can do it the more likely we are to be told to do it. I believe we should

---

6. Statement of Howard H. Callaway, Secretary of the Army, 'Hearings on H.R. 9832',
   pp. 160–5.
7. David H. Hackworth and Julie Sherman, *About Face: The Odyssey of an American Warrior*, with
   an Introduction by Ward Just (New York, 1989), p. 14.
8. Callaway, 'Hearings on H.R. 9832', pp. 160–5.

hang our hat on "this society is not prepared to accept women as combat leaders yet." ["]9

Proponents of excluding women argued that there had to be a place where professional soldiers learned the tools of their vocation in a demanding, unforgiving environment which cultivated the talents of those few who might one day lead the nation's armies in a time of crisis. They argued that graduates of West Point and the Naval Academy had dominated senior leadership positions in every major American conflict since at least the Civil War, proving a hard core of dedicated career officers was invaluable even if their absolute numbers were relatively small. In short, they passionately insisted that in wartime experience and training mattered, and for military leaders the best of both were gained at the service academies.

The combat-oriented mission of these institutions was merely implied, rather than directly stated, however, and critics had long argued that since many Academy graduates entered non-combat-oriented branches of their service there was no reason to keep women from competing for admission as well. This, said Callaway, was not the point. Law students might not practise law and medical students might not practise medicine, he pointed out, but that did not eliminate the need for special schools to produce lawyers and doctors. West Point was a specialized school, he continued, and its graduates formed a core of highly trained officers to which the rest of the army looked for leadership, especially in times of crisis. He closed by alluding to the accomplishments of generations of West Point graduates, and inserted into the record Douglas MacArthur's stirring 1962 speech entitled 'Duty, Honor, Country'.[10]

Supporters of the legislation included seven members of the House, representatives of several women's groups, the American Civil Liberties Union, and Lieutenant-Colonel Grace King, who appeared as an individual rather than a military witness. Rooted in experience as an army officer, King's testimony was the most powerful and concise. She argued the main issue was whether women, if they were barred from West Point and the other service academies, would have the same opportunity as men within the military and whether the nation could afford to ignore a 'pool of talent and intelligence more critically needed than ever'. Since ROTC and OCS

---

9. Colonel Burke W. Lee to Brigadier-General Philip R. Feir, 18 December 1972, United States Military Academy (USMA) files.

10. Callaway, 'Hearings on H.R. 9832', pp. 160–5. West Pointers have served in senior command positions in every major American war since 1861. A shortlist of the most famous would include Ulysses S. Grant, Robert E. Lee, John J. Pershing, Dwight D. Eisenhower, Douglas MacArthur, William Westmoreland and Norman Schwarzkopf. Critics argue such lists say more about the 'old boy' network among West Pointers than they do about the fighting prowess of Academy graduates.

courses admitted women, she suggested the army's position was that those programmes were 'good enough for women, but not good enough for men'. King also pointed out that West Pointers had an advantage in competing for promotions. Some 39 per cent of recently promoted brigadier-generals were Academy graduates, she noted, though only 9 per cent of all army officers attended West Point. Those figures indicated women suffered serious professional disadvantages, according to King, because they could only compete for the restricted number of non-combat officer slots within the army.[11]

The most vocal supporter was Representative Stratton, who blasted military objections and suggested no real argument existed for keeping women out of America's service academies. 'I do not regard the official Department of Defense report on our bill . . . as a serious document or even as worthy of what should regularly and predictably be the intellectual level of the Department of Defense', he said. 'They have no official arguments, only excuses.'[12] Stratton went on to argue that the bulk of opposition to women in the service academies stemmed from 'inertia and resistance to change'. He pointed out that 162 graduates of the West Point class of 1973 were commissioned into non-combat branches of the army, and suggested that 'the services need qualified women today more than the women need the service academies'. For him, the combat-oriented mission of West Point was a smokescreen, as were arguments related to morale, cost, spartan living conditions, and Academy discipline, which he called 'Mickey Mouse'. 'These are the sophomoric, Neanderthal traditional practices that still apply at West Point', he said, and 'there is no excuse for these practices in the military academies anyway'.[13]

The hearings offered no final resolution on the question of admitting women to American service academies, though they were successful in the sense that they allowed all parties involved to air their points of view. They may have helped gain support for the admission of women from members of Congress who wanted more information before supporting such dramatic change, and probably helped legislators to modify future legislation in a way the military found easier to accept.[14]

No further Congressional action took place until Stratton outflanked the military with a bit of legislative forced-marching in the spring of 1975.

---

11. Statement of LTC Grace M. King, US Army Reserve, 'Hearings on H.R. 9832', pp. 226–37. The problem endures even in the 1990s, for officers without combat experience are second-class citizens in the army.

12. Statement of Samuel S. Stratton, Representative from New York, 'Hearings on H.R. 9832', p. 35.

13. *Ibid.*, pp. 36–9.

14. Stiehm, *Bring Me Men and Women*, p. 15.

In the past, chairmen of the Military Personnel Subcommittee had kept legislation aimed at opening the service academies to women pinned down within the committee. Stratton bypassed the committee quagmire by amending a military appropriations bill and bringing the issue to the floor of the House of Representatives. His amendment called for the secretaries of the three military departments to take action needed to ensure that 'female individuals shall be eligible for appointment and admission to the service academy concerned', and called for 'academic and other relevant standards' to be the same for women as for men.[15]

The amendment triggered a short but vigorous debate on the House floor. Stratton summarized his support for women at the academies by arguing, 'It is just a simple matter of equality'. He warned that opponents of his amendment would suggest that the academies trained officers exclusively for combat, that if women were allowed to attend the academies then they should be allowed to serve in combat situations. Stratton pre-empted these arguments by saying it was clearly not true that academy graduates only went into combat, and that the issue of women in combat was a 'red herring'. He suggested that the question of whether women should serve in combat could be addressed later, and that it had nothing to do with admitting them to any of the service academies.[16]

Stratton was supported by a number of representatives, each of whom placed equality at the forefront of their reasons for supporting the admission of women to the service academies. Representative Duncan said, 'It has never been right' that women in the armed forces were excluded from 'those institutions in the military which have trained the cream of the military'. Pierre Du Pont argued, 'Discrimination based upon sex is clearly wrong', and that it was unfair to ask American women to support with their tax dollars institutions which barred their admission. He said it was 'ridiculous, wasteful, and anachronistic to maintain that the best officer training our Nation has to offer should be limited to men only', and argued, 'The only way we can take advantage of the most talented young women is to open the service academies to them'.[17]

The most vocal opponent of the Stratton amendment was G.V. 'Sonny' Montgomery, a Democrat from Mississippi. He echoed the military position that the admission of women was tied inextricably to whether Americans were willing to commit their daughters to battle. 'I am concerned that if we

---

15. *Congressional Record: Proceedings and Debates of the 94th Congress – First Session – House* (Washington, DC, 1975), p. 15449.
16. *Ibid.*, p. 15449.
17. *Ibid.*, pp. 15450–1.

have the adoption of this amendment, this really is a foot in the door of putting women into combat', he said. Montgomery was joined by others who suggested it was 'nonsense to say that all distinctions based on sex amount to invidious discrimination', that opening the academies to women would allow men incapable of combat duty to apply for admission, and that women would inevitable drag down physical performance standards.[18]

The irony is that neither the supporters nor the opponents of admitting women to America's service academies seem to have believed women would ever serve in combat. Proponents dismissed the possibility for fear it would derail their efforts to promote equality, while detractors dismissed it as an impossibility inseparable from the question of breaking down academy gender walls. In the end, both sides were wrong. Congress *did* separate the question of academy admission from the question of whether women should serve in combat, and the opening of the academies *did* play a role in putting women into combat situations in the future.

When the time came for a vote, the forces pushing for the admission of women triumphed decisively, 303–96.[19] Few members of Congress saw the impending change as revolutionary. For most it was simply a question of equity, of extending another excellent educational opportunity to women for a career that through ROTC and OCS was already approved by each of the armed services.[20]

They may have also been influenced by the knowledge that the courts were closing in. The Waldie and Edwards case was defeated in United States District Court, but that decision was reversed by the US Court of Appeals and remanded for a full trial on its merits in November 1974. Given the tenor of the times, and the questionable constitutionality of the military's legal position, the courts might have forced open academy doors by 1976 even if Congress had not eventually acted, and senators and representatives may have seen themselves as simply bowing to popular and legal pressure rather than leading a gender revolution on their own.[21]

What is certain is that they did not see the move to admit women as a step towards a greater sharing of power over state-sanctioned violence between men and women, and they failed to appreciate how in the long run the issue of women in combat might one day be finessed by the presence of women at the service academies. What actually was being debated was large indeed, involving as it did the question of what kind of society was

---

18. *Ibid.*, pp. 15452–4.
19. Stiehm, *Bring Me Men and Women*, pp. 36–7.
20. *Ibid.*, p. 2.
21. *Ibid.*, pp. 36–7.

best for both the military and the nation, and how much opportunity should be shaped by gender. These issues, however, were too controversial and abstract for most politicians. It was easier to focus on equity on a small scale, to take whatever political and social gain was possible from supporting the opening of the academies to women and move on.

These gains frightened many military leaders. They saw the opening of the service academies as a threat to the nation. Coming as it did on the heels of the disastrous involvement in Southeast Asia and the anti-militarism of the 1960s, many officers feared the armed forces were suffering another devastating blow. Each branch suffered severe discipline and recruiting problems in the wake of Vietnam, and the end of the draft in 1973 seemed a portent of an even greater widening of the gulf between the American people and their armed forces. Senior officers generally viewed changes within the military, and certainly at the academies, in much the same way as Edmund Burke spoke of dramatic restructuring of government. It should be undertaken, he wrote, only with 'pious awe and trembling solicitude'.[22] Yet American policy leaders and cultural forces were changing the military at an astonishingly rapid pace, and the admission of women to the academies seemed the capstone to one of the most turbulent periods in American military history.

The House vote also came as a surprise to many in the military, who believed Congress would never actually force them to admit women to their service academies. This surprise came despite the fact all three academies had been developing contingency plans for admitting women since the early 1970s. As West Point Superintendent Lieutenant-General Sidney B. Berry wrote, 'Right down to the day in May 1975 that Congressman Stratton took the issue to the floor of the House of Representatives, the senior people in Washington seemed confident that Congress would maintain the service academies as male institutions'.[23] Contingency plans existed, he said later, 'but nobody thought we would ever have to use them'.[24] Berry was a forceful advocate of keeping women out of West Point prior to the historic House vote, arguing that 'no modern country in the world . . . as a matter of policy permits its women to participate in ground combat'. The issue, as others in Congress and the military had argued, was thus whether women were ready for ground fighting. 'Those who would admit women to the

---

22. Edmund Burke, 'Reflections on the French Revolution', in William Elliott and Neil McDonald, eds, *Western Political Heritage* (New York, 1955), p. 684.
23. LTG Berry to Colonel E.H.B., 3 July 1975, p. 1, USMA files.
24. 'Address by Lieutenant General Sidney B. Berry, Superintendent, United States Military Academy, before the Defense Advisory Committee on Women in the Services', 16 November 1976, USMA files.

Military Academy should first openly and clearly decide that women should and will be combat soldier-leaders.'[25]

On 6 June 1975 the Senate followed the House of Representatives in calling for the admission of women to America's service academies, and on 7 October President Gerald Ford signed Public Law 94–106, which called for the admission of women in 1976.[26] Between those two events a vigorous debate ensued over the question of women at the academies on a national scale, and for critics to ask why women needed to be admitted to those elite institutions in the first place. One angry West Pointer summed up his feelings by saying, 'I do not intend to support the Academy in the future either financially or otherwise. If there is anything I will support now, it is the legislation to eliminate the service academies since they have been relegated to nothing more than coeducational trade schools.'[27] Another wrote, 'I am violently and unalterably opposed to females attending West Point. In my view it is an act on the part of an ultra liberal Congress to destroy the greatest military institution in the world.'[28] Their sentiments were echoed by a woman who wrote to Senator Barry Goldwater in June 1975. 'There has been, in the history of the world, only one successful female combat officer', she said. 'That was Jeanne D'Arc, and she was a Saint. Also she did not menstrate [sic]. Nature did not design women to be men, and even the honorable Congress and Senate of the United States cannot repeal the laws of nature.'[29] No less a figure than Matthew B. Ridgway added his voice to the debate, writing in a letter to Gerald Ford that opening the service academies to women would 'prove to be an ill-considered action inimical to the best interests of the nation'.[30]

Supporters included Columbia University Professor Sidney Forman, who noted in a letter to Lieutenant-General Berry that the admission of women to West Point was simply another occasion when the academy could adapt itself to the changing needs of the nation. Such adaptation was part of West Point's role, he said, and could be viewed as a positive good because 'resorting to an ideology of sexism, . . . neglecting any resource which may contribute to our military posture', in short, by continuing to keep women out, '[was] to disarm ourselves in the face of the enemy'. Further, the librarian and professor of education argued that the admission of women

---

25. MG Sidney B. Berry, Memorandum for Record, 'Thoughts on the Admission of Women to the United States Military Academy, 20 May 1975, pp. 2–3, USMA files.
26. Stiehm, *Bring Me Men and Women*, p. 10.
27. A.J.G. to LTG Berry, no date, USMA files.
28. J.R.R. to Captain P.P.H., 8 September 1975, USMA files.
29. Letter to the Honorable Barry Goldwater, 18 June 1975, author's name removed, USMA files.
30. M.B. Ridgway to President Gerald Ford, 9 June 1975, USMA files.

was a challenge well suited to the 'tradition of flexibility and responsiveness to national needs' that characterize the academy. 'This change', he wrote, 'which will bring all of our children into the officer corps is in the best tradition of West Point and our democratic society.'[31]

To understand the depth of these arguments over women attending America's service academies is to begin to understand the enormity of the steps Congress took in 1975. Breaking down academy gender barriers represented 'the pitting of an ancient and culturally embedded view of what it means to be a warrior against the irresistible force of democracy, in the sense of absolute equality'.[32] The admission of women was part of a larger social revolution which sought to redefine the roles women, and ultimately men, could play in American culture. By triggering debate over what it meant culturally and biologically to be male or female, and by forcing the armed services to adapt despite their reluctance, Congress did more than expand opportunities for women. It took a dramatic step towards sending women into combat and fundamentally altering their roles within the military.

This step was intimately tied to changes outside the armed forces. By the early 1970s political forces intent on expanding opportunities for women were in full stride and Congress, ever sensitive to public opinion, answered the clarion call issued by a resurgent feminist movement during the 1960s and passed the Equal Rights Amendment (ERA) in 1972.[33] Though the amendment was never ratified by enough states to become part of the Constitution, the high tide of 1972 convinced many Americans that even more radical advances were in store for women. During the ERA debate, and immediately after its passage, members of Congress even suggested women should be admitted to the various service academies, each of which had always barred them from admission.

Unlike so many other advances for women, this push to demolish the exclusive male hold on American service academies was not driven by mainstream feminist groups. They saw gender discrimination in the military as far less important than issues like equal pay and sexual harassment in the civilian workplace, which affected the majority of women. They were also divided as to whether military women were liberal-minded reformers attacking patriarchy or sell-outs to a male-dominated institution that practised violence and too often exploited women. As Representative Bella Abzug

---

31. S.F. to LTG Sidney B. Berry, 22 July 1975, p. 2, USMA files.
32. Richard Rayner, 'Women as Warriors', *New York Times Magazine*, 22 June 1997, p. 26. Rayner wrote about women as warriors in general, but his point is applicable to the academies as well.
33. Randy Shilts, *Conduct Unbecoming: Lesbians and Gays in the U.S. Military, Vietnam to the Persian Gulf* (New York, 1993), p. 161.

(Democrat, New York) put it, 'I do not regard women in the military as my first priority'.[34] In philosophical terms, the question was whether emancipation and equal access were the same thing, and whether women pushing to gain access to all-male societal enclaves risked imitating the groups they joined. This subtle debate was never concluded among feminists. Rather than pushing for the academies to open their doors to women, most were therefore silent on the issue until debate began in Congress, and even then their support was limited and often tied to the Equal Rights Amendment. Instead, it was average Americans and their representatives who pushed for the admission of women to the service academies, not because it was seen in their eyes as a step towards placing women in combat but simply because it seemed fair.

This commitment to fairness and equity had far-reaching social and military consequences, and the irony is that such a sweeping revolution was led by the military. In most countries the armed forces trail far behind civilian society when it comes to promoting social change. They wait, as conservative institutions often do, to take their cues from evolving cultural norms and adapt only when necessary. In the United States, however, the military is often forced by civilian leaders to launch social revolutions in behaviour. President Harry S Truman desegregated the armed forces far in advance of civilian America in 1948, and Congress and the courts (aided by the creation of the the All Volunteer Force) pushed the services to broaden opportunities for women during the 1970s in advance of mainstream society. These changes forced civilians to play catch-up rather than lead, and the pattern has held up to the present day. President William Jefferson Clinton's efforts to minimize discrimination against homosexuals in the armed forces may not have achieved complete success, but it was no accident he chose the armed forces as the venue in which to try.

The service academies were eventually asked to accomplish quickly and with a minimum of conflict a social revolution unprecedented in any military academy in the world. Nobody admitted women, and it was easy to ask why Congress chose a proud bastion of male dominance and patriarchy to lead the way rather than leaning on the private sector or even state and federal institutions to expand opportunities for women. It was as if the military became a sort of barometer for the kinds of changes society believed were right and just, even if it could not always bring those changes on itself.

Yet the military was not designed to be a tool for social re-engineering. It was a world with distinctive rules and rituals apart from civilian norms, one in which discipline and combat effectiveness under the most extreme

---

34. *Congressional Quarterly*, p. 15455.

conditions mattered most. Ironically, the hierarchical world of officers and enlisted personnel was also one of the most egalitarian. All soldiers had to believe their officers would share their risks, and that they had an equal chance for promotion and success if they excelled in their duties. This belief was imperative, for it was the one thing which could make distinctions like colour, ethnicity and religion fade away in the crucible of combat. This made the military as an institution far different from any other calling, and critics were quick to ask whether a value like equality had any place in determining military policy, whether the military should be concerned with anything besides winning wars.

The armed forces were thus torn between the relentless drive for equality in the civilian world and the need for equity within the ranks. As an ideal, the principle of equality meant women deserved equal access to the service academies. Once there, however, the military decided physiological differences demanded different physical standards for men and women so they would be fair or equitable. This is not what Stratton wanted. 'Mr. Chairman, I do not want any special concessions for women', he argued in 1975. 'I think they should be required to follow the same program, they should be required to meet the same standards.'[35] Yet in meetings with Congress during the summer of 1975, military concerns over whether women could meet the existing physical standards led to a change in the wording of the eventual legislation opening the academies to women. Rather than calling for equal standards, as the Stratton amendment had done, Public Law 94-106 mandated that

> academic and other relevant standards required for appointment,
> admission, training, graduation, and commissioning of female individuals
> shall be the same as those required for male individuals, except for those
> *minimum essential adjustments in such standards required because of physiological
> differences between male and female individuals.* (italics added)[36]

In the two decades which followed Congressional opening of the service academies to women, the single most controversial issue at each was different physical performance standards for men and women. Male cadets and midshipmen resented being held to a different benchmark for their performance and often blamed civilian officials for forcing academy doors open to women. Yet the military brought different standards upon itself, because it feared women would not graduate in sufficient numbers if the existing male standards were applied. It did not consider whether the standards

---

35. *Ibid.*, p. 15449.
36. Stiehm, *Bring Me Men and Women*, p. 10.

themselves needed modification. Did upper-body strength and running times really equate with combat prowess or leadership skill? Despite assumptions, no one really knew, and by not considering these questions the military joined Congress in missing a golden opportunity to consider the real potential of women in the armed forces. It also let slip away the chance to explain the differences between equity and equality throughout the military, and neither American society nor the military has effectively confronted them to this day.

Ultimately, gender integration at the academies did open the door to sending women farther into combat than previous regulations allowed. Once women were given advanced training and had graduated from the finest officer training institutions in America, it was impossible in the long run to argue that they should not be allowed into combat. Congress had the opportunity to make that decision deliberately, to consider whether new standards were necessary and what it might mean for America when women were taken prisoners of war or killed in large numbers. Rather than embrace that opportunity, however, they skirted it, primarily because it was too controversial. Instead, members allowed American military policy regarding women to advance one piecemeal, awkward step at a time, never realizing how deeply women might be committed in the event of war.

There have been other opportunities to have such a debate, of course, and it would be inaccurate to claim the lack of debate in the 1970s precluded more vigorous and frank discussions in the 1980s or 1990s. The fact remains, however, that there has never been a truly national debate regarding women in combat. This explains in part the powerful public reaction to the deployment of thousands of women during Operation Desert Storm in 1991. Most Americans had no idea how dependent the military had become on women, or how vulnerable those women were once the fighting began. This collective ignorance stems from a systemic refusal of American leaders to discuss the implications of trying to make the military more truly equal, and if opening the nation's service academies to women was not the only chance to bring such issues dramatically out into the open, it may have been one of the best.

Dropping the gender barrier at West Point, Annapolis and the Air Force Academy was, after all, hardly the only step in the revolution which made women more equal in the military. The admission of women to air force ROTC programmes in 1969 was important. So was the removal of ceilings on the number of women allowed to serve in each branch of the armed forces, and the expansion of job opportunities in the 1970s. Perhaps most important was the creation of the All Volunteer Force, which forced recruiters to realize there was no way to provide for the needs of the armed forces without relying more heavily on women than ever before.

In spite of those developments, however, it remains true that admitting women into the academies represents a watershed. Like the drop of rain that finally sends water flowing over a spillway, the arrival of women at the most elite officer training schools in America was the point beyond which there was no turning back. Once given the leadership skills those institutions impart and sent forth to prove their mettle, it was progressively more difficult to talk of what women could *not* do. Once they graduated from the citadels that produced Eisenhower, Patton, Nimitz and King, it was impossible not to talk of fuller equality. Instead, the success of women at these high-profile institutions was so great it had repercussions for civilian society as well, because photographs and news stories demonstrating the achievements of women at the academies made it harder for anyone to argue that women should not move even farther into formerly all-male domains. Congress sent the service academies to war with American culture in 1976, and did so without fully considering or ever realizing the dramatic consequences of their action. Perhaps they can be forgiven for not seeing the future clearly. It is a pity, however, that they failed to try and look farther down the road than they did.

By the autumn of 1975, most real national discussion focusing on the admission of women to the service academies was over. The major issues had been articulated prior to the critical House vote on 20 May, and most Americans seemed to support the idea that equity alone demanded that women be allowed entrance into West Point as well as the air force and naval academies. Like their Congressional representatives, they had little inkling of what such a change might bring. They believed they could allow women to receive academy rings and combat training while still somehow keeping them safe once any fighting began; that pushing equality of opportunity did not ultimately have to mean equality of responsibility or risk. They never realized that Representative Stratton's 'simple matter of equality' was not so simple after all.

319

CHAPTER EIGHTEEN

Delilah Shaves Her Hair: Women, the Military and Hollywood

CORINNA PENISTON-BIRD

The debate over women and the military is seeping into popular culture. Advertising hair products, the supermodel Kate Moss strides towards the camera declaring 'war on damaged hair and split ends'. Consumers are told that the Number Seventeen line of cosmetics is not make-up but ammunition, giving a different spin to the phrase 'getting your man'. Mainstream Hollywood films have introduced the debate to global audiences and play a significant part in raising the profile of the issue of women in combat. The fact that this debate is expressed in cinematic form is consistent with the tradition that the subject of women as combatants has as often been explored through images as through words. Furthermore, the media plays a highly significant role in creating, reflecting and confirming gender identities.

Edward Zwick, director of *Courage under Fire*,[1] was attracted to the controversy of women serving in combat after the Gulf War:

> I believe it's a theme that American society is getting ready to think about. What was revealed in the Gulf War, with the modern technologies, is that combat exists everywhere. Combat is behind the lines and in front of the lines. Combat is in rescue choppers or in Awac planes or behind in barracks, which are vulnerable to long-range missiles. And so women in the military are now, and will increasingly be, in peril.[2]

I am grateful to Jerry DeGroot, Jason Frowley, Ian Muth and Clare White for their insights on this chapter. I would also like to thank the students of the Open University, particularly those who worked with me at the A318 Summer School in 1998, for their enthusiasm and anticipation of the completion of this project.

1. *Courage Under Fire*, 1996, director: Edward Zwick; screenplay: Patrick Sheane Duncan.
2. Production Notes: http://www.hollywood.com/videoguide/movies/courage/text/3.html

The boundaries between the battle and the home front, the combatant and the non-combatant have consistently been eroded. The armed forces, and Hollywood, are struggling to come to terms with the implications this has for gender roles.

The war film has traditionally been a male preserve, featuring male protagonists, and aimed at a male audience. War films such as *Platoon, Full Metal Jacket* or *Apocalypse Now* depict war as an essentially male experience.[3] Many films have shown women taking an active part in warfare, as in *The Gentle Sex*. More often, however, women prove their patriotism by seeing their loved ones off to war (*Tomorrow is Forever*), waiting bravely for them (*Mrs Minniver*), or serving them (*Millions Like Us*). Nor are women always portrayed positively: the uniformed female nurses just make extra work for the men through their incompetence in *Ice Cold in Alex*; in *Swing Shift*, Goldie Hawn works in an aircraft factory, but she betrays her serving husband through her affair with a co-worker.[4] Women in the armed forces play traditional roles as foils for the male protagonists in *Down Periscope, A Few Good Men* and *Top Gun*.[5]

As a result of the current debate over the roles women should be permitted to play in the armed forces, the issue of women in uniform is being addressed on screen. *Private Benjamin, Courage under Fire, G.I. Jane* and *Mulan* all feature uniformed female protagonists.[6] These films illustrate the themes which permeate the debate over women in combat, including empowerment, women's mental or physical suitability for a career in the armed forces, and gender stereotypes. This analysis shows that opportunities to break out of gendered boundaries are limited, and that the alternative is equally restrictive. The media has consistently presented contradictory messages about women's roles and status: these films continue this tradition, despite their apparent message of emancipation.[7] It is important to emphasize that men are

---

3. *Platoon*, 1986, director and screenplay: Oliver Stone. Film details are taken from Derek Elley, ed., *Variety Movie Guide 1996* (London, 1995) and the website http://www.us.imdb.com

4. *Full Metal Jacket*, 1987, director: Stanley Kubrick. *Apocalypse Now*, 1979, director: Francis Coppola. *The Gentle Sex*, 1943, director: Leslie Howard. *Tomorrow is Forever*, 1946, director: Irving Pichel. *Mrs Minniver*, 1942, director: William Wyler. *Millions Like Us*, 1943, director and screenplay: Frank Launder, Sidney Gilliat. *Ice Cold in Alex*, 1958, director: J. Lee Thompson. *Swing Shift*, 1984, director: Jonathan Demme.

5. *Down Periscope*, 1996, director: David Ward; screenplay: Hugh Wilson, Andrew Kurtzman, Eliot Wald. *A Few Good Men*, 1992, director: Rob Reiner; screenplay: Aaron Sorkin. *Top Gun*, 1986, director: Tony Scott; screenplay: Jim Cash, Jack Epps Jr.

6. *Private Benjamin*, 1980, director: Howard Zieff; screenplay: Nancy Meyers, Charles Shyer, Harvey Miller. *G.I. Jane*, 1997, director: Ridley Scott; screenplay: David Twohy, Danielle Alexandra. *Mulan*, 1998, directors: Barry Cook and Tony Bancroft; screenplay: Robert D. Sans Souci, Rita Hsiao, Chris Sanders III, Philip La Zebnik, Raymond Singer, Eugenia Bostwick-Singer; original poem anonymous.

7. Susan J. Douglas: *Where the Girls Are; Growing Up Female with the Mass Media* (New York, 1994).

stereotyped as much as women in these films. In *Mulan*, they are gullible, if lovable, buffoons; in *G.I. Jane* they are competitive and sadistic players of status-games; in *Courage under Fire* they are macho; and in *Private Benjamin* they are sexual predators.

The first theme is that of self-fulfilment. *Private Benjamin*, for example, depicts a voyage of self-discovery in which Judy Benjamin (Goldie Hawn) develops from an airhead into an emancipated, independent woman. Benjamin's character is introduced in the opening seconds of the film. At eight years of age, the audience is informed, Benjamin confessed her life's desire: 'All I want', Judy whispered, 'is a big house, nice clothes, two closets, a live-in maid, and a professional man for a husband.' Benjamin always seeks a man to provide her with security, but the men in her life treat her with indulgence or sexual appreciation at best and disdain at worst. Unbalanced after her husband's death on their wedding night, Benjamin joins the army, believing it to be akin to a luxurious holiday. Although she initially does as badly at boot camp as could be expected, Benjamin starts to develop a sense of independence when her parents come to take her home. Objecting to her father's belief that she is obviously incapable of making her own decisions, she decides to stay. Benjamin's physical fitness improves, she bonds with the other female recruits, and she impresses some of her superiors. Nonetheless, forced to make a choice between her career and a French gynaecologist, Benjamin gives up the career she loves for the man she loves. However, in the weeks preceding the marriage, Henri becomes increasingly demanding and sexist, until he arrives late at the wedding ceremony having been with a former girlfriend. Benjamin punches him at the altar, and strides away down the road in her wedding dress, a liberated woman.

Over the course of the film, Benjamin finds independence and self-confidence. She punches Henri not when he confesses to further infidelities, but when he calls her stupid. The army provides the environment in which she can develop self-reliance because it encourages her to be fit; shows her that her actions have consequences for other people; provides opportunities for female bonding with the other recruits; makes her financially independent; and proves to her she can perform efficiently in a work context. The idea that the army can serve as a 'finishing school', helping soldiers to become mature individuals who are self-aware and who can take a responsible role in society, is not a new one. The twist to *Private Benjamin* is that in this case the soldier is a woman.

Courage Under Fire and *G.I. Jane* do not depict comparable development in their characters (Walden and O'Neil) – with the exception of O'Neil's muscles. The protagonists are both depicted as having clear goals and clear means for achieving them: the military provides them with professional identities, but reflects rather than moulds their personal identities. However, both of the comedies, *Private Benjamin* and the animated film *Mulan*, can be placed into the genre of 'rites of passage' films. Like Benjamin, Mulan (spoken by Ming-Na Wen) finds herself through service. At the beginning of the film, questioning her identity, Mulan sees only fractured or multiple images of herself (in her ancestors' gravestones, for example) until she sees a single reflection in a sword. Responding to a call to arms to defend China against the evil invading Hun, Shan-Yu, Mulan disguises herself as a man, Ping, to defend her family's honour. By the end of the film Mulan has saved the lives of her future husband, her fellow recruits and the Chinese emperor, as well as China itself. Service in the armed forces serves to make her adult and, above all, whole.

Mulan is struggling to express what she senses is her identity within the constraints imposed by the outside world. She finds it difficult to conform to her family's and society's expectations of 'ladylike' behaviour ('with good breeding and a tiny waist you'll bring honour to us all'), although she respects traditional values and responsibilities to the family and the state. However, *Courage under Fire* argues that identity is as much about perception as internal recognition. One strand of the plot centres around the character of Captain Karen Emma Walden (Meg Ryan), a Medevac pilot who served in the Persian Gulf. When Walden is under consideration for a posthumous medal of honour, Lieutenant-Colonel Nathaniel Serling (Denzel Washington) is sent to investigate the events surrounding her death in action. Serling has to sift through the different versions told him by survivors of the mission. Contradictory pictures emerge: Walden was a hero, Walden was a coward; Walden was competent, Walden was completely out of her depth; Walden could lead, Walden went to pieces under pressure. Meg Ryan was attracted to the role because of the alternative versions with which the audience is confronted:

> There's this macho person, which is the number one presentation. The second point of view is the fear, the cliché, or the expectation of what a woman would be like in that kind of stressful battle situation. And in the third version, her behaviour is made up of a combination of things. She's very human in the face of all this horror and making decisions despite the chaos.[8]

The third and final version shows that, in fact, Walden was betrayed by her men.

---

8. Production Notes for *Courage under Fire*, http://www.hollywood.com/videoguide/movies/courage/text/3.html

The second theme which is often addressed in films on women in the military is their influence on and approach to group dynamics. A major question in the debate over women serving with men in the military is whether group cohesion suffers. The plot of *Courage under Fire* hinges on Walden's relationship with her men and whether she has been part of the bonding which ensures that 'you never leave a man behind'. Experience of group cohesion is a central part of Private Benjamin's growing independence, although the emphasis is on female bonding. A successful training exercise is concluded with a dance in the barracks to the Pointer Sisters' 'We are family. I've got all my sisters with me.' Her first experience of a mixed unit is less than positive: her colonel attempts to force Benjamin to have sexual relations with him, which she avoids by jumping out of an aeroplane at 35,000 feet. Ironically this is a major step in her growing independence: initially too petrified to make the parachute jump, the colonel's actions precipitate her into new experiences she comes to enjoy.

Whether women can perform beside men in a man's world is the central question in *G.I. Jane*. Lieutenant Jordan O'Neil (Demi Moore) becomes the victim of a political exercise when she is the first woman to be permitted to train for the Navy SEALS, a job as a 'trained killer' denied Benjamin. When she does not, as expected, drop out, she is manoeuvred out on trumped up charges. O'Neil successfully defends her right to serve and completes a mission in Libya. *G.I. Jane*'s message is that women *can* serve side by side with men in the armed forces. As one character says, 'If women measure up to the men, they get the job'. The emphasis of the majority of the film is on whether O'Neil can compete on equal terms with the men physically. The opening scenes while she is still serving in the Naval Intelligence Centre establish her mental ability. Thereafter her physique is the focus as O'Neil fights to equal the male fitness standards. She argues against having special provision made for her, believing she will never 'fit in with the boys' if unequal standards are applied. It is partly through physical 'achievements' that she gains acceptance. She is told 'you're one of us now' when she gets jungle rot on her left foot.

In *Mulan*, the protagonist's attempts to disguise her sex and fit in with the men initially lead to internal fighting and military incompetence in her unit. Associating manliness with bravado and physicality, Mulan inadvertently causes brawls between the men. In time, however, she becomes close to three fellow recruits and gains the respect of her captain, Li Shang. Her sex means that the bonding can never be entirely complete: Mulan's suggestion, for example, that 'a girl worth fighting for' is not a woman with the right figure and domestic skills, but one who can think, finds little favour with her friends. But when Mulan is unmasked and she is left to fight the enemy Shan-Yu on her own, her three friends come to her aid. They even allow themselves to be persuaded to enter Mulan's feminine world, disguising themselves in women's clothing to gain access to the Huns.

The only film which takes as its premise that women and men will serve side by side as a matter of course is the science fiction film *Starship Troopers*.[9] Society is divided into citizens and civilians: to be a citizen, with concommitant rights, one has to have served in the military. Even here, however, females do not lose their traditional roles: when cadets are explaining their motivation for joining up, one female is there because service increases the likelihood she will be permitted to have a baby. Another, Dizzy Flores (Dina Meyer), has joined up to continue her pursuit of Johnny Rico (Casper Van Dien). Joint service was presumably also attractive to the director Paul Verhoeven because it offered the cinematic opportunity of a joint shower scene.[10] This is so self-consciously casual that, rather than showing gender divides can be successfully overcome, the scene underlines them.

Women's physical condition is of central concern in the debate over whether all military positions should be open to women, and is a theme in all four films under discussion here. It plays a minor part in establishing Meg Ryan's character: Walden is shown doing press-ups in a flashback while her parents discuss her dedication to her profession. In a different scene, Walden suffers a severe abdominal wound, but rejects help saying 'I gave birth to a nine pound baby, asshole, I think I can handle it'. Here the implication is that her female physique is actually superior to men's, making mockery of the concept of the 'weaker sex'. However, the emphasis is more on whether Walden has the mental stamina to be an officer.

Hampered not only by her sex but also by her youth, Mulan cannot initially compete physically with her fellow recruits, despite their being incompetent oafs. Discharged from training camp, she regains entry through completing a task which combines both physical and mental agility. Initially at a disadvantage to the men physically, the heroine outperforms them with wit and will. When under attack by the Huns, for example, Mulan saves her unit by firing the last charge not at Shan-Yu, as commanded, but at the snowy mountain peak behind him. The entire attacking army are buried under the resultant avalanche.

In *G.I. Jane* and *Private Benjamin*, the physical fitness of the recruit is integral to the plot. Private Benjamin's poor physical stamina is established by the fact she cannot perform one efficient press-up; O'Neil trains to perform single-arm press-ups. The battle with physical fitness is integral to

9. *Starship Troopers*, 1997, director: Paul Verhoeven; screenplay: Edward Neumeier; book: Robert A. Heinlein.
10. Supposedly this scene made some of his actors feel so uncomfortable, Verhoeven directed it naked. See http://www.u.s.imdb.com/Trivia?Starship+Troopers+(1997)

any film showing a training camp, frequently found in films about military service, and is not gender-specific. For instance, plot development in both *Full Metal Jacket* and *A Few Good Men* hinges upon the physical incapacity of a male soldier. In *Private Benjamin* it is intended to provide comedy – the protagonist expected training to 'be like exercise class. Leg lifts, a little stretching, maybe a disco class.' However, with effort she masters the obstacle course and gains the respect of a former adversary when she can no longer be beaten in hand-to-hand combat. Her greater physical prowess serves as a barometer of her developing self-confidence.

As women are joining a male hierarchy in the armed forces, the standards set are male standards. Walden 'had to be twice as good to become an officer'. The women are often defined in contrast to the male: G.I. Jane, for example, is described as a 'split tail'. The main method at the disposal of those attempting to break out of the constraints of their gender is to adopt the characteristics of the opposite. Of the four heroines, Mulan has the easiest task, in that she has to live up to male stereotypes rather than alter female ones. She pretends to be a man by burping and swaggering, but draws the line at not washing ('Just because I look like a man doesn't mean I have to smell like one'). O'Neil pays lip-service to both gender stereotypes as her success is attributed to the fact she unites intuition with physical stamina, but the consistent message is that she can become a stereotypical man.

G.I. Jane also supports the conclusion that to compete with men, women have to outperform them. In order to do so, they must often sacrifice being perceived as feminine. In both *Mulan* and *G.I. Jane*, the protagonists cut off their long hair. However, they have different motivations: Mulan is disguising herself as a man; O'Neil is endeavouring to become one. The agenda set is traditionally masculine: the emphasis is on physical prowess, male bonding, and status games. O'Neil shaves her head, smokes a cigar, drinks shots with the guys and wraps a towel *below* her waist after a shower, all in order to be equal to her male peers. When she tries to move into the same room as the men, a fellow recruit freaks out about 'tampons'. As we are told she has ceased to menstruate, this is presumably not so great a problem as he fears. In one shot showing O'Neil doing press-ups from behind, the camera is placed between her open legs. Her movements are reminiscent of those of the male in the missionary position; coupled with her muscle tone, this shot offers a curious blend of female and male imagery, a blend which reflects the O'Neil character.

It does little to progress the debate on equality or on women in the armed forces to emphasize their ability to emulate men. The men who possess the necessary physical and mental skills to serve in combat capacities constitute a minority; women who can fulfil that role constitute an even smaller one, but nonetheless exist. In its public statement about equal opportunities, the

British Army website argues that 'equal opportunities is NOT about pretending everyone is the same'.[11] *G.I. Jane* falls into this trap, confusing gender equality with gender conformity.

Despite conveying the very strong message that women can be equal to men, *G.I. Jane* is very conservative in what it permits its protagonist, and it is this which renders its message so contradictory. For example, O'Neil only uses violence once. Bent over a table with her hands tied behind her back, she hits back at the man who has cut off her trousers in a 'mock' rape. The female members of the cinema audience cheered at this point, in sympathy with a woman fighting back. But women using violence in defence of their virtue is hardly a huge stride in the battle for equality. Later O'Neil examines her bruises in front of a mirror in a public lavatory. A woman looks at her bruised face and says 'Ain't really none of my business, but I say leave the bastard'. The implication is that she has been a victim of male aggression, which, in a different context than that assumed, has indeed been the case. Although she does not accept victim status, we only see O'Neil involved in contact fighting in self-defence, not as part of her duties as a SEAL.

Women are seldom permitted to be violent on film. Fights with other women provide entertainment value, but fights with men tend to be defensive in nature. O'Neil would therefore lose the moral high ground by being violent, if it were not that she is defending herself against rape. At the climax of the film, O'Neil is hiding from a Libyan soldier whose throat she will have to cut if he finds her: as he approaches, a fellow SEAL spares her the ordeal by shooting him. The female senator (Anne Bancroft) argues that American families are not ready to let women come home in body bags. However, *G.I. Jane* seems to suggest that the issue is less whether women are killed, than whether they kill. Despite its apparent message of equality and anti-discrimination, *G.I. Jane* is not ready to permit women to be violent.

The same issue lies at the heart of the debate in the military on which posts should be open to women. Hence the posts which the recruiting officer says are not open to Private Benjamin in the army of the 1980s: 'You'd love it. All the ladies do. All 89,000 of them. Here, check out this list of jobs — over 300 offered to the ladies. Only a couple of jobs not offered to them: trained killers, stuff like that.'[12] Benjamin has no problem with that. In *G.I. Jane*, O'Neil may argue 'I want the choice', but we do not see her exercise it.

---

11. http://www.army.mod.uk/cgi/bin/netoutcome.exe?redeye_url=/army/recruit/equal/main.html, p. 5

12. About 50 per cent of military jobs are open to women in the US armed forces to date, with the percentage varying greatly by service. There is no law that prohibits women from serving in combat, just statutes that prevent women from serving on ships and aircraft engaged in combat missions, a term which is not defined. http://www.movies.com/gijane/history2.html

One reason why it is so difficult to reconcile ideas about femininity with effective service is that feminity is associated with vulnerability. O'Neil is aware that her sex is a threat to the unit, not because she is physically weaker, and not only because it can be used against her, but because it could be used against the men. The implication is that men will find it harder to stomach a woman being tortured, particularly sexually, than a fellow man. 'She's not the problem', says Master Chief John Urgayle, 'we are.' Captured in a training incident, a fellow male prisoner is beaten behind closed doors; O'Neil is tortured – nearly raped – in front of the men. The commander justifies his actions as proving to the men that 'her presence makes us vulnerable'.

The incident is also significant because O'Neil finally finds acceptance by the other SEALS when she refuses to be broken. They cheer when she tells the Lieutenant to 'suck my dick'. She has at last become one of them, constituting, and possessing, 'an honorary member'. She does not represent her gender, but has become an honorary male, a common phenomenon for serving women. O'Neil is accepted because she exhibits courage, but she has done so before. The difference is that this time she not only shows she will not let her gender be used against her, but she also swears publicly at a figure in authority. Profanity is, as any good girl can tell you, not ladylike. By using it, O'Neil joins the cool boys in the playground. Not only that, but the profanity involves the male organ: she could not choose an oath more symbolic of her identification with masculinity. In *Top Gun*, Maverick comments that the briefing on dogfighting 'gives me a hard on'; we know O'Neil has finally found acceptance when 'suck my dick' becomes a drinking oath.

If they do not become fully assimilated, women in what are traditionally seen as male roles face rejection from both sexes. Mulan is too independent to find favour with those of her gender in civilian life. Walden was disliked by her co-pilot's girlfriend, who complains 'she was so butch' (a description provoked more by her status as a female officer than by her appearance) and makes a derogatory comment about women who want to be officers. The implication here is that Walden is masculine not because of her profession, but because she holds authority. O'Neil attracts the sarcastic epithets 'Joan of Arc' and 'Supergirl', which permits the men around her to continue to see her as an aberration, and to distance themselves from the conclusions they would have to draw about women if she were categorized as a representative of her gender.

In the comedy *Down Periscope*, the men not only discriminate against the lone female on board because of her gender; they also use her gender to undermine her authority. They deliberately shrink her clothes, so that she appears at inspection extremely scantily clad. Arguably, these tactics could be intended to show up the men. In *Mulan*, for example, men's sexual urges are used against them when Mulan and her troops gain entry into the Forbidden City dressed as concubines. They are aided by their enemies' inability to consider a female presence a threat. But female sexuality is also exploited by scriptwriters as a way of undermining the status of the women. In an early analysis of military women in the media, Perry D. Luckett argues that women can seldom be both feminine and military, without sacrificing one to the other.[13] The most obvious example of this is the character Major Margaret Houlihan in *M*A*S*H*, who loses her authority by gaining the epithet 'Hot Lips' in a steamy sex session, despite the fact she has been seen to be an efficient nurse. In the military, the weapon of sexuality is an obvious one to wield against women. It requires no great leap of faulty logic to assume that a woman taking over traditionally male roles in one area of her life must be taking the male role in others: having sex with women, for example. Despite all of O'Neil's efforts to overcome the limitations imposed by her gender, it is her sexuality which is used against her when she proves more successful at SEALS training than had been assumed. Falsely accused of lesbianism, she is bumped off the programme.

In a study of sexuality in organizations, Jeff Hearn and Wendy Parkin argue that 'Men's sexuality tends to be associated with the properties of valued labour and hierarchy: control, activeness, physical power, freedom from constraint, intellectualism, coolness'.[14] The military uniform has a parallel symbolism, representing authority, status and order. This has an erotic potential exploited in cinema: the climax of *An Officer and a Gentleman*[15] is Richard Gere appearing in white dress uniform, and Tom Cruise is frequently seen in uniform (Navy Lawyer Lieutenant Kaffee in *A Few Good Men*; Maverick in *Top Gun*). But the uniform does more than bestow sexual attractiveness on its male wearer. In *Top Gun*, although Charlotte Blackwood (Kelly McGillis) is technically superior to Maverick, it is *his* status which is continually emphasized. (She is a 'civilian specialist tag rep PhD Astro Physics Civilian Contractor'; he is a lieutenant.) The beginning of their romance is a bet that Maverick can have carnal knowledge of Blackwood on the premises of the bar. Although she rejects him in his choice of venue – the female lavatories – when she leaves the bar, Blackwood says to his drinking companion 'Your friend was magnificent'. Much of the plot revolves around Maverick's daring (i.e. foolhardy) exploits with his $30 million plane.

13. Perry D. Luckett, 'Military women in contemporary film, television and media', *Minerva* 7, 2 (Summer 1989).

14. Jeff Hearn and Wendy Parkin, *'Sex' at 'Work': The Power and Paradox of Organisational Sexuality* (London, 1987), p. 92. Hereafter referred to as *'Sex' at 'Work'*.

15. *An Officer and a Gentleman*, 1982, director: Taylor Hackford; screenplay: Douglas Day Stewart.

Initially reprimanding him after one irresponsible act, Blackwood nonetheless tells him that his action was 'the guttsiest move I ever saw'.[16] Maverick is, therefore, a daring, fearless stud, a status reflected by his uniform; his uniform is a reflection of his identity. There is no *contradictory* tension between his masculinity and his uniform, just sexual tension resulting from the authority bestowed (or reflected) by the uniform.

In contrast, there is great tension in the image of a woman in uniform. On the one hand, as with men, there is an erotic potential. In *Down Periscope* when Lieutenant-Commander Thomas Dodge (Kelsey Grammer) meets Lieutenant Emily Lake (Lauren Holly), he assumes she is a stripper. In *Under Siege*[17] the only uniformed woman is a stripper. Under the regulation garb can lurk lace and silk. This is not merely the stuff of sexual fantasy. Serving women frequently refer to the importance of wearing feminine underwear under their uniforms. It is clear from memoirs of women serving in the armed forces in the Second World War that the issued underwear, dubbed 'passion killers', were cut up, embroidered, edged with lace, or replaced entirely.[18] Underwear still retains a symbolism beyond its function. A female police officer, Rachel Grazier, explained that her partner had been attracted by her uniform, but she felt that

> It's hard to express your individuality or feminity when you have it on, especially as I don't wear much make-up. The only way female officers can look different is with our bras. Our shirts are incredibly see-through, so while some go for cropped tops, I like to wear more feminine underwear – it makes me feel better.[19]

This choice serves to affirm a sense of individual identity. The irony is that the tools available to women attempting to circumvent enforced uniformity are signifiers of gender, an equally restrictive category.

There is an inherent tension between the control implied by the uniform, and the lack of control associated with female sexuality; the tension between the high status of the uniform and the low status of the woman. In *A Few*

---

16. The lengths gone to to give Maverick high status in *Top Gun* provoked the effective parody *Hot Shots*.

17. *Under Siege*, 1992, director: Andrew Davis; screenplay: J.F. Lawton.

18. Kelly Flinn, the first female bomber pilot, discharged for conduct unbecoming an officer, argued that the air force-issue underpants and the lack of time to shave legs could all be seen as 'an attempt to keep sex out of the ranks'. Kelly Flinn, *Sunday Times, News Review,* 11 January 1998, p. 1.

19. Interview with Rachel Grazier, in *Marie Claire* 121 (September 1998), p. 46. Bras have always attracted an inordinate amount of attention in discussions of feminity and emancipation, as the famous, but artificially created photograph of bra burning testifies. When pilot training for women commenced in 1989, the *Sun* headline read 'It's Biggles in a Bra!'.

Good Men, Jack Nicholson says to Tom Cruise, whom he believes to be having an affair with a female superior officer (Demi Moore),

> You're the luckiest man in the world. There is nothing on this earth sexier . . . than a woman you have to salute in the morning, promote them all, I say, 'cos this is true, if you haven't gotten a blow job from a superior officer, you're just letting the best in life pass you by. 'Course my problem is that I'm a colonel so I'll just have to go on taking cold showers until they elect some gal president.

A woman who is technically superior but who chooses to serve a man's sexual needs enhances the man's status even more, confirming that the masculine is always superior.

But when not erotic, the uniform on a woman can be profoundly disturbing. In *Courage under Fire*, Walden's problem stems from the fact that she is a woman in a man's world: her uniform gives her a status contradicted by her gender. Her main protagonist, Monfriez (played by Lou Diamond Phillips) cannot accept her:

> Monfriez is an infantry guy who has been battle trained and that's where the conflict comes in when we crash land. All of a sudden I figure that I should be in control, giving the orders because I know how to get out alive – regardless of the fact that she outranks me. Monfriez has a bit of difficulty handling the fact that Walden is a woman.[20]

He shoots her. It is the resulting cover-up that leads to the different images of Walden, until Serling arrives at the 'truth' and can establish that Walden did, indeed, deserve the Medal of Honour.

High-ranking females in uniform are seldom permitted simply to be good at their jobs: they are either made to look ridiculous by their inferiors; or are shown to be 'deviant' in some fashion. In *Private Benjamin*, Captain Doreen Lewis is both. As a result of a prank, Lewis showers in ink, dying her face blue; later it is implied that she is a lesbian, despite the fact she has previously been shown to be (ridiculously) love- and sex-starved in her interactions with her male counterpart. Benjamin has no role models to emulate in her superiors in the army, who are consistently presented as objects of ridicule. Lewis is depicted as sadistic, incompetent and vindictive. Women are repeatedly shown to be unworthy of the uniform, and without the characteristics it should represent.

---

20. Production Notes for *Courage under Fire*, http://www.hollywood.com/videoguide/movies/courage/text/3.html

Analysis of symbols in these films shows how easily established gender divides can be referred to in visual short-hand. The ambiguity of the uniform draws attention to the tensions which ensue when an object or individual cannot be clearly relegated to a distinct category. Other symbols serve as unambiguous signifiers of gender identities. They are used to permit quick and easy categorization of both the male and female characters. In *Courage under Fire*, the audience is encouraged to make certain deductions about the character of Monfriez when he is first seen boxing in a gym. Benjamin's character is established when she looks at her uniform in dismay and asks 'Is green the only colour they come in?'. When O'Neil revolts against being associated with 'pink petticoats', the audience can fill in the associations themselves.

Symbols are also used as indicators that identities are not as they might first appear. The viewer is encouraged to have a hint of sympathy for the sadistic drill sergeant Chief John Urgayle (Viggo Mortensen) in *G.I. Jane* because of his ability to quote poetry, although D.H. Lawrence is an interesting choice of poet in this context. In *Mulan* the audience is given an inkling of what is to come when a row of young women walk in single file to meet the match-maker. While the others hold their parasols demurely in front of them, Mulan slings hers over her shoulder like a rifle.

While here the symbols serve to underline the contradiction between the role and the individual, they can also be used to imply fusion. When Walden is shown chatting to her daughter while performing the ubiquitous press-ups, the mother and the soldier are brought together in one person. The most powerful use of symbolism to unify different positions is found in *Mulan*, but the genders return to their traditional roles. When his father dies defending a village, Li Shang (Ping's superior and Mulan's heartthrob) carefully places his father's sword upright in the snow as a makeshift memorial to the soldier and the man. Disguised as Ping, Mulan offers him her sympathy. She places at the base of the sword a ragdoll, used in the film previously to symbolize the village, and now, through the death of the girl to whom it must have belonged, a powerful symbol of the slaughtering of innocence, youth and females. While Li Shang commemorates the death of the warrior through a sword, Mulan puts the civilian victims of war back into the picture through the doll.[21]

As this final example shows, one factor these films have in common is that, while on the surface they appear to show that women can break out of traditional gender roles through serving in the military, in practice they

---

21. The frequency with which the theme of sons living up to fathers' reputations or expectations is found in films about the military also attracted satiricial treatment in *Hot Shots*.

show it is virtually impossible for an individual to break the confines of their gender roles. In *Purity and Danger*, the social anthropologist Mary Douglas shows that across time and cultures, that which defies categorization provokes counter-reaction and containment. To be out of place is to threaten the social order. Women in the military constitute precisely that kind of threat: they are not only out of place, but are also potentially acquiring power.[22] Human survival depends upon accurate categorization (safe/unsafe; poisonous/ nutritious; friend/foe). Women in the military do not fit into a 'category of non-contradiction'.[23] However, when an artificial order is imposed, the consequence is contradiction or hypocrisy. Hence, whatever the agenda of the films outlined, they all present contradictory messages of liberation and conformity. Non-conformist Mulan chooses to return home to her family rather than accept a public office offered to her by the Emperor, who instead rewards her by encouraging Li Shang to woo her. Benjamin cannot serve in the army and have a successful romantic relationship. A decent soldier, Walden is betrayed and killed. O'Neil cannot be both a woman and a soldier.

Lillian De Haven (Anne Bancroft), the US Senator whose political manoeuvrings permit O'Neil the opportunity to serve in the SEALS in the first place, cannot understand why she wants the choice to 'squat piss in some jungle, guys looking up your ass'. This hints at why gender equality and service in the armed forces constitute such a complicated issue. Gender definitions often simply serve to restrict, robbing the individual of choice. However, there are few methods available to the individual attempting to break out of gender constraints. As *G.I. Jane* shows, the main method is simply to adopt the traits associated with the alternative, particularly when that alternative is the dominant one. This has the advantage that the category remains clear as long as the aberration can assimilate: in this case, as long as the female can adopt male traits, she can be granted the status of a 'temporary gentleman'. But in so doing, one set of boundaries is simply replaced with another.

Feminists therefore question whether it constitutes progress for women to adopt characteristics associated with being male: 'One thing the women's movement is not all about is to adopt the most brutal, sadistic model of male machismo'.[24] The image of O'Neil shaving her head is a powerful one, but it is traditionally one of disempowerment. Women suspected of collaboration with the Nazi enemy in France had their heads shaved. In the

---

22. Mary Douglas, *Purity and Danger: An Analysis of the Concepts of Pollution and Taboo* (London, 1966), p. 161.
23. *Ibid.*, p. 162.
24. Betty Friedan, in *Newsday*, 19 August 1994. My thanks to Ilana Stanger for this reference and her thoughts on the relationship between feminism and militarism.

Old Testament tale, the mighty Samson tells Delilah, 'If my head were shaved, my strength would leave me, and I would become as weak as any other man'.[25] Individuals question whether by joining the army, women are merely becoming 'as any other man'. These doubts are not restricted to the women's movement: *G.I. Jane* is denounced by the cinema critic Michael Ollove because it means to stand for righteous feminism, but all it really is saying is, 'See, a woman can be every bit the sado-masochist as a man'. Ah, progress![26]

G.I. Jane's solution to gender equality is for everybody to become male. *Mulan*'s solution is to reconcile oneself to the rewards of conformity: by withdrawing from the public sphere, Mulan lands herself a hunk. *Mulan* shows that little has changed since Susan Faludi pointed out in 1992 that it is typical of 'post-feminist' fare to mouth sympathy for feminist aspirations, then promptly eat its words.[27] The original tale of Mulan concluded with the heroine returning home:

> *So swiftly comes off the warrior's vesture.*
> *And silently, I put on my old-time dress.*
> *Beside the window I dress up my hair,*
> *In front of a mirror, I rouge my face,*
> *And when I walk out to meet my compeers,*
> *They are perplexed and amazed.*
> *'For twelve years, we fought as comrades in arms,*
> *The Mulan we knew was not a lady of charm!'*[28]

The two identities cannot be reconciled. Private Benjamin cannot have both independence and a man because that would place her in the 'fuzzy' zone between categories. Not one of the heroines is able to survive in the army and be multi-dimensional.

There are strong parallels here with films which seek to depict men breaking out of their gendered constraints. In *The Adventures of Priscilla, Queen of the Desert*[29] or *To Wong Foo, Thanks for Everything, Julie Newmar*,[30] both films

---

25. Judges, 16: 17.
26. Michael Ollove: Review 'G.I. Pain', http://www.sunspot.net/our_town/movies/data/gijane.html
27. Susan Faludi, *Backlash: The Undeclared War Against Women* (London, 1992), p. 157.
28. According to the Disney publicity, Mulan was based on a Chinese folktale, translated on http://www.disney.com/Disney/Pictures/Mulan/garden/poem/poem_english-chinese.html. The character also appears as Fa Mu Lan in Maxine Hong Kingston's *The Woman Warrior: Memoirs of a Girlhood Among Ghosts* (London, 1989).
29. *The Adventures of Priscilla, Queen of the Desert*, 1994, director and screenplay: Stephen Elliott.
30. *To Wong Foo, Thanks for Everything, Julie Newmar*, 1995, director: Beeban Kidron; screenplay: Douglas Carter Beane. Its tagline was 'Attitude is Everything'.

about self-fulfilment and self-expression, the solution is to wear drag. This also has the advantage of cinematic potential, as *Some Like it Hot*,[31] *Tootsie*,[32] *Victor/Victoria*,[33] *La Cage aux Folles*[34] and now *Mulan* have shown. The use of clothing as a metaphor for transcending gender divisions, however, under-lines how superficial is the transformation which can actually take place. Furthermore, in defying social constructs, the protagonists ensure that they can never be fully integrated in society. The implication may be that this does not constitute a loss, with the drag artists of *Priscilla* and *Wong Foo* possessing insights and skills for living denied or lost by the more conventional characters. But they remain marginalized, exotic freaks, a description not wholly unapplicable to women in public and active spheres.

Courage under Fire plays most obviously with gender categories by portray-ing Walden first as traditionally male (brave and hard), then as traditionally female (weak and indecisive). It is the third version, however, (the one depicted as the 'truth') which is the most interesting. Zwick argues that *Courage under Fire* is not just a film about a woman in combat:

> The film examines the different facets of duty and courage. We also take a look at the notion of comradeship and sacrifice. *And how that immediately and absolutely crosses the lines of gender* [my emphasis] . . . I think there's the kind of courage that has to do with the explicit courage under fire and there's a very different kind of moral courage to overcome the demons in one's own life.[35]

There are terms, such as patriotism (despite its etymology), which should transcend gender. This is one of the arguments for why women should have the same responsibility to serve as men. Patriotism, rather than any feminist agenda, is clearly a motivation for many women who serve. *Mulan* goes furthest in making this a central theme of the plot because the idea can be rooted in the broader cultural context of the Chinese concept of honour. In *Courage under Fire*, however, it is clear that 'patriotism' is a gendered term too: we are told that as a patriot and a mother, Walden found it hard to leave her daughter to fight, but that it was important to her to do her duty.

---

31. *Some Like It Hot*, 1959, director: Billy Wilder; screenplay: Billy Wilder and I.A.L. Diamond.
32. *Tootsie*, 1982, director: Sydney Pollack; screenplay: Larry Gelbart, Murray Schisgal [Elaine May].
33. *Victor/Victoria*, 1982, director and screenplay: Blake Edwards.
34. *La Cage aux Folles*, 1978, director: Edouard Molinaro; screenplay: Francis Veber, Edouard Molinaro, Marcello Danon, Jean Pioret. The American remake was entitled *The Birdcage*, 1996, director: Mike Nichols; screenplay: Jean Pioret, Francis Veber.
35. Production Notes for *Courage under Fire*, http://www.hollywood.com/videoguide/movies/courage/text/6.html

These films, and the problems the armed forces are facing, indicate that neither the armed forces nor Hollywood have found a solution to the problem of how to progress in the battle of the sexes, and how to define equality within and between genders. There is a parallel moral at the end of the original Chinese tale on which *Mulan* was based:

> *They say to choose a hare*
> *you pick them up by the ears,*
> *There are telling signs to compare:*
> *In air the male will kick and strike,*
> *While females stare with bleary eyes*
> *But if both are set to the ground,*
> *And left to bounce in a flee,*
> *Who will be so wise as to observe,*
> *That the hare is a he or she?*[36]

To the historian, the current debate over women in the military is remarkably consistent with treatment of the issue throughout the ages. For women to serve beside men in the armed forces, there would have to be universal standards for members of either sex. This is not the case and, as Hollywood movies show, there are currently no solutions to overcoming gendered standards, even in fiction.

---

36. http://www.disney.com/Disney/Pictures/Mulan/garden/poem/poem_english-chinese.html

Military Law and the Treatment of Women Soldiers: Sexual Harassment and Fraternization in the US Army

FRED L. BORCH III

Until the early 1980s, most soldiers in the United States Army believed that aggressive masculine behaviour and explicit sexual banter strengthened personal bonds between them. They also believed that this male bonding resulted in better unit cohesion – an *esprit de corps* essential to battlefield success. Consequently, those leading this nearly all-male army condoned, and sometimes encouraged, sexually orientated jokes, graphic language and 'machismo' by men in uniform. In the 1970s, for example, each monthly issue of *Soldiers*, an official army magazine, published a photograph of a 'pin-up girl' on its inside backcover – a feature enjoyed by the young male readership. Similarly, it was not unusual for European-based male troops to take a respite from training by visiting nearby 'red light' districts, on trips organized by officers and non-commissioned officers (NCOs).

The end of the draft and the advent of an all-volunteer army in 1973, however, meant that there were simply not enough young men to meet manpower needs. This, combined with the disbanding of the Women's Army Corps in 1978, meant the end of the all-male force. Male and female soldiers now served together in one army, often working side by side, with many women in jobs which had been previously closed to them. By the late 1980s, women pilots and paratroopers were common in the new gender-integrated force. This revolutionary organizational transformation was, not surprisingly, accompanied by an equally dramatic increase in the percentage of women in the army, from about 2 per cent of personnel in 1973 to roughly 14 per cent today.

The views expressed in this article are those of the author alone, and do not represent any official view of the Department of the Army or any other US government agency.

This change in the composition of the army meant that old ways of promoting male bonding were no longer acceptable. While front-line infantry and armoured units remained exclusively male, the vast majority of other units – from engineer, medical and signal to transportation, ordnance and aviation – now comprised both men and women. Consequently, army leaders discovered that previously desirable male-oriented sexual behaviour now undermined military order and discipline. Many female soldiers took offence when sexually graphic language was used in the workplace, or when photographs of naked women in sexually suggestive poses were displayed in barracks. They also objected to unsolicited (and therefore unwelcome) sexual advances from male colleagues. As these and other forms of 'sexual harassment' disrupted good order and discipline, and thus undermined unit cohesiveness, they were now forbidden. Army leaders soon learned, however, that it was not easy to rid the army of a masculine military culture and the behaviour that culture implied. Many male soldiers did not accept, much less understand, why old standards needed changing. The fact that substantial elements of American society were comfortable with – or at least condoned – the masculine view of women as 'sex objects' exacerbated the problem. If American society could not agree on the status and treatment to be afforded women, it was not going to be easy for the army to set or enforce new standards for the treatment of female soldiers.

The huge influx of women into the army also brought with it a second sex-related problem: consensual sexual contact between men and women in uniform. While the army recognized that romance or sex, or both, naturally occurs in a force of both males and females, sexual contact between soldiers of different ranks may provoke jealousies among other soldiers, thereby undermining unit cohesiveness. As this is particularly true where sexual relations occur between an officer and an enlisted soldier – especially where the former supervises the latter – the army prohibited such 'fraternization'. This sex-related fraternization was also outlawed because it encouraged (or resulted in) undue personal familiarity between officers and enlisted personnel. As such overly familiar relationships had long been viewed as undermining a superior's authority in his dealings with subordinates ('familiarity breeds contempt'), sex-related fraternization had to be forbidden because it encouraged such familiarity and undermined the command process.

But if unit cohesiveness in a gender-integrated army required an end to sexual harassment and fraternization, how was this to be achieved? Educating and indoctrinating soldiers about the pernicious effects of such behaviour on the army was one method. Command influence, in the form of written rules, was another. But the ultimate command tool was military criminal law. This is because, while the American military legal system deters anti-social behaviour and punishes criminal conduct like any civilian criminal justice framework, it also promotes the 'good order and discipline' or unit cohesion necessary for military success. Having decided that achieving such cohesion in a gender-integrated army required an institutional climate in which all soldiers were treated with dignity and respect, and that sexual harassment and fraternization were detrimental to achieving that end, the army looked to criminal sanctions as the ultimate command tool for eradicating all forms of discrimination and harassment.

This chapter examines how the army has used its military justice system to deter sexual harassment and fraternization. It first defines the two terms as understood in the army, and explains how sexual harassment and fraternization are criminal offences in the military. Next, as an illustration of the application of military law in this context, the army's handling of sexual-related misconduct cases at Aberdeen Proving Ground from 1996 to 1997 is examined. While the army viewed events at Aberdeen as an aberration – and the accused sergeants as a criminal element whose misconduct did not reflect prevailing army values – many civilians saw things differently. It was widely felt that events at Aberdeen reflected the army's inability, or unwillingness, to eliminate a masculine-orientated military culture that tolerated sexual misconduct and harassment by those in authority. This essay explores the validity of both the army's perspective and that of the public. Finally, some observations about the army's success in using criminal law to combat sexual harassment and fraternization are offered, as well as some conclusions about future developments in the treatment of women soldiers.

Sexual harassment in military law

The army considers sexual harassment to be a common form of sexual misconduct and a manifestation of gender discrimination. It is defined as suggestive or blatantly sexual behaviour, which is unwelcome, and which creates a hostile or offensive work environment. Any sexual favours that are demanded, requested or suggested – especially as a condition of employment or career and job success – constitute sexual harassment.

While the army recognizes that sexual harassment is not confined to the work environment, it is nonetheless most concerned with workplace sexual harassment. Thus, an on-the-job soldier who tells sexually suggestive jokes or stories creates a hostile or offensive climate that interferes with the ability of other soldiers to get their work done. Depending on the individuals involved, this type of sexual harassment may seriously degrade work performance and mission success. Of greater concern, however, is the form of sexual harassment that involves a supervisor who explicitly, or implicitly, makes a subordinate's job, pay or career dependent on submitting to sexual relations, or to physical conduct of a sexual nature. This implies a lack of impartiality, and a personal self-interest that undermines the authority of the superior–subordinate relationship. First, the superior's actions are not compatible with the army's traditional beliefs in individual professionalism and respect for others; the army views sexual harassment as wrong *per se*. Second, his conduct creates a hostile work environment, interfering with the subordinate's work performance and, where submission or rejection of the sexual contact becomes a basis for career advancement, this abuse of power 'degrades mission readiness', which is devastating to the army's ability to work effectively as a team. For all these reasons, the army prohibits sexual harassment.[1]

Recognizing that effective suppression of sexual harassment requires clear delineation of prohibited behaviour, the army defines three broad categories of sexual harassment: verbal abuse, non-verbal abuse, and physical contact. Examples of verbal abuse include off-colour jokes, sexual comments, profanity, overt reactions to physical appearance (barking, growling, whistling), and applying terms of endearment to co-workers ('honey', 'baby', 'darling'). Non-verbal abuse includes leering, ogling, blowing kisses, licking lips, winking, provocatively posing or adjusting clothing in the presence of others, and giving or displaying sexually suggestive visual material. Examples of physical contact include stroking, patting, hugging, pinching, grabbing, kissing, giving unsolicited back or neck rubs, 'sliding up' to someone, 'cornering', blocking a passageway, adjusting someone's clothing (without permission), and making foot or knee contact (playing 'footsie-kneesie').[2]

Under military law, a soldier who sexually harasses another is subject to a variety of administrative sanctions. He may be given a letter of reprimand that, if filed in his official military personnel file, will have an adverse impact on promotion opportunities. His annual efficiency report may be annotated to reflect his inability to give women in uniform the dignity and respect required – a career terminator for a man who desires to be a professional soldier. In serious cases of sexual harassment, the perpetrator may also be administratively eliminated from the army, and given a discharge under 'general' or 'other than honourable' conditions. As both discharges are less than the 'honourable' discharge ordinarily received by a soldier leaving the

---

1. For an excellent discussion of the army view of sexual harassment, see Office of the Chief of Public Affairs, Department of the Army, Command Information Package, 'Sexual harassment: fixing the army's human relations environment', Spring 1998, p. 4.
2. Sexual harassment may be 'man on woman', 'man on man', 'woman on man' or 'woman on woman'. Given that almost all sexual harassment in the Army involves a male harasser and a female victim, however, this article focuses exclusively on that behaviour.

army, this may affect his ability to obtain future civilian employment since most employers are not willing to hire a man whose military service was less than satisfactory.

Recognizing, however, that administrative sanctions may be inadequate, the army looks to its military criminal law system as the ultimate tool for suppressing sexual harassment. The Uniform Code of Military Justice, Title 10, United States Code, Sections 801–946, was enacted by Congress in 1950. The Code applies to all soldiers, sailors, airmen and marines. Its more than 50 'punitive articles' cover offences ranging from murder, robbery, larceny, forgery and drug use to desertion, misbehaviour before the enemy, mutiny, disobedience of orders and drunkenness on duty. As a general rule, civilian authorities defer to the military when crimes are committed by men and women in uniform; this means that most serious crimes are tried by military courts-martial rather than before a civilian court.

Sexual harassment is deemed a criminal offence if it constitutes criminal sexual misconduct as set out in the Uniform Code. Thus, for example, a male superior who forces a female subordinate to have sexual intercourse is guilty of rape. While evidence that actual force was used by a man to overcome a non-consenting woman is usually necessary to secure a rape conviction in a civil trial, military law recognizes that threats, intimidation or the abuse of authority may constitute 'constructive' force. For example, where the actions of a superior involve an abuse of power that creates a reasonable belief in the subordinate's mind that she will be grievously injured if she resists him, the act of sexual intercourse is deemed to have been accomplished by force. Under Article 120 of the Uniform Code, the maximum penalty for rape is death, but no death sentence has been imposed for many years. Instead, the typical rape sentence ranges from 10 to 25 years imprisonment.

Similarly, sexual harassment that takes the form of unwanted oral or anal sodomy is punishable as a crime under Article 125 of the Code. As with rape, both force and a lack of consent are necessary to the offence of forcible sodomy. But, where intimidation or threats of injury make resistance futile, it is said that constructive force has been applied. The maximum penalty for forcible sodomy is life imprisonment. A life sentence, however, is rare; the typical punishment imposed at a court-martial ranges from one to ten years in jail.

Sexual harassment that takes the form of an assault or battery that is indecent, lewd or lascivious is also a criminal offence, punishable by a maximum of five years in jail. For example, a male soldier who fondles a female soldier's breast, or places his hand on her private parts, would be guilty of an indecent assault and battery if the contact came without consent. A related crime is 'indecent exposure', punishable by up to six months imprisonment. A soldier who wilfully shows his private body parts to another would be guilty of this offence provided the exposure was made in an indecent manner. Thus, sexual harassment in the form of 'flashing' (quickly revealing the genitals) or 'mooning' (lowering trousers to show one's buttocks) could be punished – particularly if it occurred during duty hours in the workplace, and was done in a grossly vulgar, obscene and repugnant manner.

Military criminal law does more than simply criminalize acts; using indecent words may also be a crime under the Uniform Code. Thus, a male soldier who said to a woman soldier 'I want to fuck you' or 'I want to eat you' may be jailed for up to six months if this is found to be indecent language. Under almost all circumstances, a court-martial would convict a soldier making unwelcome vulgar comments of this nature, based on the premise that they are grossly offensive to modesty, decency and propriety, and consequently prejudicial to good order and discipline.

One other criminal provision is available to combat sexual harassment: the offence of 'cruelty and maltreatment' under Article 93 of the Code. A soldier may be punished if he 'is guilty of cruelty toward, or oppression or maltreatment of, any person subject to his orders'. Thus, a senior NCO who threatens the career, pay or job of a subordinate in order to secure sexual favours, or who deliberately makes offensive comments or gestures of a sexual nature, is guilty of cruelty and maltreatment. This uniquely military offence (it has no counterpart in civilian law) is punishable by up to a year in prison.

Fraternization in military law

Sexual harassment and fraternization are both about sex, and both are proscribed because they have an adverse impact on order and discipline. But they are fundamentally different in one respect: sexual harassment involves *unwelcome* sexual contact, while most fraternization involves mutually *consensual* sexual relations.

The origins of the US Army's prohibition on fraternization stem from the class distinction between nobles and peasants that existed in feudal Europe, a distinction that, by the mid-1700s, was also firmly in place in British military forces. An aristocratic officer did not associate with his social 'inferiors' – the uneducated and poor men who were soldiers. An officer was expected to be a gentleman, and a gentleman did not 'fraternize', or act as he would towards his own brother, with a 'common' soldier who lacked 'good breeding' and had no 'social graces'.

While these class-based rules against fraternization did cross the Atlantic to the militias of colonial New England, the American military's current prohibition on fraternization has nothing to do with social class distinction. On the contrary, close personal relationships between officers and enlisted personnel are forbidden because of the well-founded notion that 'familiarity breeds contempt'. As an official army document stipulated in 1921:

> [U]ndue familiarity between officers and enlisted men is forbidden ... This requirement is not founded upon any difference in culture or mental attainments. It is founded solely upon the demands of discipline. Discipline requires an immediate, loyal, cheerful compliance with the lawful orders of the superior. Experience and human nature shows that these objects cannot be readily attained when there is undue familiarity between the officer and those under his command.[3]

In short, undue familiarity has an adverse impact on good order and discipline. Consequently, a superior may not be on overly friendly terms with his or her subordinates. Such fraternization is not permissable because it undermines the superior's authority. The army focuses almost exclusively on the sex aspect of fraternization, even though current rules against fraternization encompass much more than sex. In the gender-integrated army of the 1990s, fraternization in the form of mutually consensual sexual relations between superiors and subordinates is forbidden because, like sexual harassment, it undermines a unit's ability to function as a team.

While the army historically viewed fraternization as solely an officer–enlisted matter, today it considers improper 'officer–officer' and 'enlisted–enlisted' fraternization as equally damaging. Where a superior and subordinate have a close personal relationship, and there is an actual or perceived impact on good order and discipline, it is forbidden. Thus, for example, a colonel may not be romantically involved with a lieutenant in his unit. Similarly, the senior sergeant in a battalion may not have sexual relations with a subordinate who works for him. Nor may a drill sergeant date or otherwise socialize with trainees under his authority.[4] Again, these relationships are proscribed because of the belief that they will inevitably undermine that superior's authority.

As with sexual harassment, a variety of administrative measures are available to suppress improper relationships between military personnel of different

---

3. *A Comprehensive Course in Military Discipline and Courtesy*, US Army Pamphlet D-2 (Washington, DC, 1921), p. 5. For a historical examination of fraternization in the army, see Kevin W. Carter, 'Fraternization', *Military Law Review* 113 (Summer 1986), p. 61.
4. Thus, the enlisted–enlisted fraternization between drill sergeants and trainees at Aberdeen Proving Ground had a substantial adverse impact on good order and discipline because the NCO trainers were using their 'power, access and control' over trainees to obtain sexual favours.

ranks. Official records may be annotated to reflect a superior's inability to refrain from engaging in a sexual relationship with a subordinate. As these records are critical to continued professional success, the superior who is unwilling to refrain from fraternizing with a soldier who works for him will find his career curtailed. Again, elimination from the service – with a less than honourable discharge – may be used as a remedy in egregious instances of fraternization.

In addition to administrative remedies for combatting fraternization, the army, as with sexual harassment, has criminal remedies. Under the Uniform Code, officer–enlisted fraternization is an offence under Article 134 if the relationship compromised the superior–subordinate relationship (also called the 'chain of command'), if it resulted in the appearance of partiality, or if it otherwise undermined good order, discipline, authority or morale. A critical component of criminal fraternization is whether a reasonable person experienced in the problems of military leadership would conclude that the fraternization compromised the respect of enlisted persons for the professionalism, integrity and obligations of an officer. Under the definition of fraternization in Article 134, almost any sexual or romantic relationship between a superior officer and an enlisted subordinate would be a crime.

A catch-all punitive article in the Uniform Code makes criminal 'all disorders and neglects [that] prejudice good order and discipline'. Consequently, consensual sexual contact between the senior NCO in a unit and a soldier who works for him would be a criminal offence if their relationship undermines the NCO's authority in a unit, if it results in actual or perceived favouritism by the senior towards the junior, or otherwise has a demonstrably adverse affect on morale in that unit. For a number of legal reasons, however, the army prefers to prosecute enlisted–enlisted fraternization through the use of a so-called punitive regulation. This is a written order issued on the authority of the general officer in charge of an army organization or installation. If, for instance, a lawful punitive regulation states that dating or sexual relations between certain ranks of soldiers are prohibited, then any soldier violating that punitive regulation could be prosecuted for disobedience. As a practical matter, punitive regulations forbidding fraternization with trainees have been promulgated at all army installations where training occurs. Thus, for example, a drill sergeant responsible for training soldiers commits a criminal offence when he engages in sexual relations or otherwise socializes with raw recruits undergoing that training. Under the Code, a conviction for disobeying a lawful punitive regulation includes up to two years confinement.

In summary, conduct constituting the offence of fraternization may be prosecuted either as conduct prejudicial to good order and discipline, or as conduct violating a punitive regulation. But the same conduct might also violate other provisions of the Uniform Code: adultery, wrongful cohabitation, and indecent acts with another. If, for instance, one of the parties is married, then any sexual intercourse between them could be punished as adultery. Under current law, however, adultery is prosecuted only if there is a clearly demonstrated prejudicial impact on good order and discipline. A good example of criminal adultery would be one in which a married general officer was having an affair with his unmarried female enlisted aide-de-camp. A conviction may be punished with up to a year in jail. If the officer and enlisted person live together as husband and wife then they may be punished for 'wrongful cohabitation', which carries a maximum prison term of four months. Finally, if the fraternization involves indecent acts, this also may be punished under the Uniform Code. This covers sexual acts that tend to incite lust and are grossly vulgar, obscene, and repugnant to common propriety – for example, having sex in the presence of others. Although all parties might agree it is consensual, its public aspect makes it immoral, and therefore criminal. The maximum punishment would be five years in jail.

The Aberdeen Proving Ground experience

Given the existence of clear rules outlawing sexual harassment and fraternization, soldiers in the army were surprised about what happened at Aberdeen Proving Ground in the autumn of 1996. It certainly surprised, and shocked, the American people. As the story at Aberdeen unfolded, it appeared to some that efforts to stop sexual harassment and sex-related fraternization had fallen terribly short of the mark – if not failed.

Aberdeen Proving Ground, a small installation in northern Maryland, is the home of the Army's Ordnance Corps. While the testing of new vehicles, weapons and ammunition constitute the 'Proving Ground' aspect of Aberdeen, the major activity on the post is the 'Advanced Individual Training' of new soldiers. This is advanced training in a specific skill for men and women who have finished 'Basic Training' in fundamental soldier skills. At Aberdeen, for example, some soldiers learned to be wheeled vehicle mechanics while others were taught how to repair tanks and other tracked equipment.

Training at Aberdeen, like such training anywhere in the army, is supervised by 'drill sergeants'. By virtue of their proven abilities as leaders, these men and women are given the responsibility of ensuring that trainees in their care achieve their fullest potential while training, and successfully complete that training. Drill sergeants stand *in loco parentis* to trainees, over whom they have, in army parlance, 'power, access and control'. To some extent, they have even more authority than a parent; they decide when the trainee's day starts, what he or she will wear, eat, drink, and do during that day. This is because the army demands that drill sergeants transform raw civilians into loyal, capable and efficient soldiers. It is an awesome task, which implies phenomenal powers. The drill sergeant must teach young trainees quickly to obey and carry out orders, including the intentional killing of other human beings, with premeditation and without hesitation. Perhaps more importantly, the drill sergeant must teach these young soldiers that extraordinary conditions may require them intentionally to risk their own lives. To this end, the trainee must quickly and unquestioningly obey his or her drill sergeant. It is no wonder that trainees believe their drill sergeants have absolute and unbridled control over their lives, and will in large measure determine whether they succeed or fail.

Virtually all drill sergeants in the army are men and women of exceptional professional skill and personal integrity, who carefully exercise their awesome powers. At Aberdeen in 1996, however, a number of drill sergeants were discovered to be using their power for selfish sexual gratification. Some male drill sergeants used their status to obtain sexual favours from female trainees under their authority. Others used their 24-hour access to young women trainees to enter into sexual relationships with them. And at least one drill sergeant abused his authority by raping and indecently assaulting young trainees. This abuse of authority struck at the very heart of the army's rules concerning sexual harassment and fraternization.

From the beginning, the army did not view events at Aberdeen as being about sexual harassment or the status or treatment of female soldiers. It instead viewed these occurrences as purely criminal, with rape, sodomy and indecent assault among the most serious crimes. The American public and Congress, however, felt that the criminal conduct of the drill sergeants was a reflection of the army's failure to require soldiers to adhere to the new standards of behaviour outlawing sexual harassment and fraternization. This is an important point because, while the army pursued criminal action against criminals, it also had to answer a barrage of public criticism centring on the treatment of women, and the army's commitment to a role for female soldiers based on dignity and respect. On the other hand, because some of the sexual crimes at Aberdeen were consensual, the army also had to respond to those who questioned the need to punish those engaging in voluntary sexual activity. Thus, the case had immediate political importance far beyond the confines of the Aberdeen Proving Ground.

As the investigation unfolded, the army identified some 12 male drill sergeants involved in sexual misconduct. Most of the accused were guilty of unlawful fraternization, of a consensual nature, with trainees. Staff Sergeant Marvin C. Kelley, a 34-year-old drill sergeant, for example, was charged with having prohibited sexual intercourse, or 'social interaction', with three female trainees. Another instructor, 30-year-old Staff Sergeant Ronald Moffett, was charged with having consensual sexual intercourse with at least one 18-year-old woman soldier under his authority. Similarly, Sergeant First Class Tony Cross, who was 33 years old, was accused of having sexual intercourse with three different teenaged female trainees. Sergeant Wayne Gamble was accused of having prohibited sexual relations with three trainees, while Staff Sergeant Vernell Robinson, Jr., a 32-year-old soldier, was alleged to have had improper sexual relations with five female trainees ranging in age from 20 to 30.

The adverse impact on training at Aberdeen was self-evident. Gamble, for example, testified in court that he used male soldiers to set up meetings for him with female trainees. He also said that trainees who had sex with him were rewarded by being kept off duty rosters, having their Army Physical Fitness Test scorecards altered, or being exempted from bed check. Other drill sergeants followed a similar pattern. There also was evidence that some sergeants engaged in what was known as 'The Game'; they competed with each other to see who could have sexual relations with the most trainees. Gamble testified that he, Kelley and Robinson arranged meetings with potential sex partners for one another. They also 'covered' for the female trainees with whom they were having sex, and for each other. According to Gamble, '[i]f you're supposed to be in the game, you look out for each other . . . you basically cover each other's butts'. Gamble also quoted Robinson as bragging that '[t]he game is good, and I'm a gangster'.[5]

While some argued that the sexual fraternization between the drill sergeants and trainees reflected nothing more than poor judgement, the army insisted that a drill sergeant who had sexual relations with a trainee was using his access, power and control to take advantage of and manipulate young subordinates under his supervision, an abuse of power which seriously damaged the drill sergeant–trainee relationship. As Gamble disclosed in his testimony, trainees received preferential treatment in return for sex, clear proof that the fraternization impaired the effectiveness of training and undermined good order and discipline. Consequently, those drill sergeants discovered to have fraternized with trainees deserved to be punished.

---

5. Elaine Sciolino, 'Rape witnesses tell of base out of control', *New York Times*, 15 April 1997; Jackie Spinner, 'Aberdeen sergeant convicted of sexual misconduct', *Washington Post*, 30 May 1997; Lorrie Delk, 'Former drill sergeant receives 10 months', *Pentagram*, 7 November 1997; Jackie Spinner and Dana Priest, 'Drill sergeant kept sex lists, court is told', *Washington Post*, 15 April 1997; Jackie Spinner, 'Two ex-drill sergeants at Aberdeen charged', *Washington Post*, 26 March 1997.

The most highly publicized criminal case at Aberdeen, however, was not about fraternization or even sexual harassment. Rather, Staff Sergeant Delmar G. Simpson's court-martial involved non-consensual sex offences, the most serious being rape. An imposing 6′ 4″ man, 32-year-old Simpson had been a drill sergeant at Aberdeen's Ordnance Center and School since February 1995. Married and the father of four children, he had served in the army for 13 years, with stints in Somalia, Korea and Germany. A pre-trial investigation revealed that, over a 22-month period, Simpson had had improper sexual or social contacts with at least 30 female trainees, which led to 159 separate criminal charges, including rape, forcible sodomy, indecent assault, indecent acts, indecent language and communicating threats. Simpson also admitted to charges arising from consensual sexual relations with 11 different female soldiers. But these fraternization incidents paled in comparison with the non-consensual sex offences.

During the trial, Private First Class S.H. told how she had sexual intercourse with Simpson in exchange for a day off from training. Private K.G. reported that Simpson forcibly sodomized and raped her on two occasions. Similarly, Private First Class T.G. and Private First Class M.H. alleged that Simpson had raped and orally sodomized them. Private First Class P.R. described in graphic detail how Simpson raped her on nine separate occasions. Each time, she told Simpson that she did not want to have sex with him. But, as she said in her own words, when Simpson wanted her, he 'ordered her to his office or had another soldier send for her . . . I felt like I was a puppet, that I had strings attached to me . . . It got to a point I just gave up trying to resist . . . He was going to get what he wanted whether I resisted or not.' She further testified that some of the rapes occurred in a barracks storage room, while others took place in Simpson's office. P.R. also related how Simpson assaulted her by punching her in the arm and leg, and by pulling her by the hair. Other witnesses told similar stories of sexual abuse.[6]

By the time Simpson faced a jury at trial by court-martial, the 159 original charges had been reduced to 58. This occurred partly because the prosecution decided to eliminate those counts in which the evidence was conflicting or seemed inadequate to prove guilt beyond a reasonable doubt. But it also elected to dismiss those counts involving consensual sexual fraternization. As it was proceeding on a theory that Simpson had abused his power as a drill sergeant in having sexual relations with trainees, the prosecution wanted to focus its case on those trainees who had been raped

---

6. Jackie Spinner, 'Aberdeen case now in hands of army jury', *Washington Post*, 25 April, 1997; 'Aberdeen sergeant convicted of rape', *Washington Post*, 30 April 1997.

or otherwise forced into non-consensual sex. The fraternization counts, reflecting consensual sexual contact between him and the trainees, did not further the 'abuse of power' theme. On the contrary, to pursue the fraternization charges against Simpson would have diluted the impact of the rape and non-consensual sex offences, allowing his defence counsel to portray him as a 'lover' rather than a sexual predator and rapist.

But, even with 101 counts dismissed, the remaining 58 criminal offences against Simpson were an impressive demonstration of criminal behaviour; the prosecution still involved 21 different victims and 19 counts of rape. After a two-week trial by a jury of both men and women soldiers, Simpson was convicted of 18 counts of rape involving six trainees and 29 other offences, mostly involving sexual misconduct. In May 1997, he was sentenced to 25 years' confinement. He was further reduced to the rank of private, and dishonourably discharged from the army.[7] Within six months of the Simpson verdict, all remaining sexual misconduct cases involving drill sergeants were completed.

Sexual harassment and fraternization after Aberdeen Proving Ground

From the army's perspective, events at Aberdeen provided a number of lessons. Most importantly, it demonstrated that military law could be effective in punishing men in authority who abused women in their charge. Some commentators had questioned whether the military justice system was capable of handling sexual misconduct of this type. The guilty verdicts in more than five courts-martial, and the severe administrative sanctions meted out to more than ten other drill sergeants, proved that it was. This was a positive result, constituting a 'loud and clear' message that those who abuse their authority would be disciplined.

The criminal proceedings did, however, reveal at least one shortcoming with the Uniform Code of Military Justice. Some of the incidents of non-consensual sexual offences that should have been punishable as crimes could not be prosecuted under the Code because they did not satisfy the statutory definition of rape. Article 120 of the Code defines rape as sexual intercourse 'by force and without consent'. When enacted in 1950, this definition seemed adequate. As a matter of policy, military society wanted to punish any man

---

7. Gerry J. Gilmore, 'Simpson gets 25 years on rape convictions', *Pentagram*, 9 May 1997; Lorrie Delk, 'Simpson gets 25 years for rape, assault', *Aberdeen Proving Ground News*, 7 May 1997.

who had *forcible* non-consensual sexual intercourse with a woman. The element of force was thought to be important because requiring it would reduce the risk of a man being punished for rape when, in light of all the facts and circumstances, it was reasonable for him to believe that his partner was consenting. Forcible resistance by a woman, and the use of force by a man to overcome her, would constitute clear evidence that the intercourse was non-consensual, and therefore rape.

Events at Aberdeen indicated, however, that the requirement of force contained in the 1950 definition of rape made it difficult to punish certain non-consensual sexual misconduct. While the prevailing view continued to be that a female would not submit to unwelcome sexual advances without physically resisting her assailant, the reality was that a number of young women trainees at Aberdeen had submitted to sexual relations when merely threatened by their drill sergeants. Private First Class S.P., for example, insisted that she had not wanted to have intercourse with Simpson, yet she acquiesced when he threatened to declare her a 'training failure' if she did not. Forced to choose between submitting to sex or losing her job, she chose the former. As these threats did not constitute either the actual or constructive force required for rape, Simpson and any other drill sergeant who obtained sex through blackmail could not be charged with rape – or any similar offence.[8] The problematic nature of the rapes at Aberdeen went beyond legal issues. A number of the young victims (as is typical in cases of sexual assault) believed that they were partly 'responsible' for being raped. Thus, one young woman explained to an investigator that she did not think she had been raped because she had not been physically hurt; she believed that a woman must be beaten up for the sexual intercourse to constitute rape.

There were other troubling lessons. First, the Aberdeen events showed that the Ordnance Corps' training programmes lacked sufficient monitoring mechanisms to uncover the misconduct at an early stage. To a large extent, this institutional shortcoming had occurred because of personnel and budgetary reductions. The end of the Cold War had caused the army to lose more than 200,000 soldiers, meaning fewer personnel in supervisory roles, and fewer dollars for training programmes generally. As a result, only a few officers and senior NCOs were supervising drill sergeant activities. As long as the drill sergeants behaved properly, this lack of monitoring was harmless. But, as Simpson and his colleagues proved, insufficient supervision led to disaster when men of low moral character served as drill sergeants.

8. See Evan Thomas and Gregory L. Vistica, 'A question of consent', *Newsweek*, 28 April 1997; Thomas E. Ricks, 'Latest battle for the military is how best to deal with consensual sex', *Wall Street Journal*, 30 May 1997.

The failure to have 'checks and balances' in place explained how the misconduct of a dozen drill sergeants had gone unreported and uncorrected for so long.

Another lesson was that the morals and values of the young trainees made them susceptible to improper relationships. More than a few of the 19 and 20 year olds were very sexually experienced. Some young women were sexually attracted to their drill sergeants, and wanted to engage in relations with them for recreational or romantic reasons. Others desired to fraternize with drill sergeants because they thought that such a relationship would improve their chances of success, or make their service at Aberdeen less onerous. This 'sex-for-a-favour' mentality was evident in more than a few fraternization cases.

A common view of events at Aberdeen was that the drill sergeant–trainee relationships were that of a 'sexual predator' and 'victim', with male instructors the former and female trainees the latter. Given that a number of fraternization incidents were initiated by trainees, however, this was a myth. But, while these young women soldiers were not victims, it was hard to view them as criminals. Most recognized that consensual sex with their instructors constituted criminal fraternization under the Uniform Code, but they often simply did not *understand* why it was important to refrain from entering into these sexual relationships. They did not appreciate why good order and discipline required them to suppress their own desires for gratification. Convinced that the consensual nature of the sex meant that there was no real harm, these young trainees simply did not accept the army's need to forbid fraternization of this type. The army concluded that while these young women had not been soldiers long enough to understand and obey its rules, the drill sergeants had no such excuse. Having been entrusted with extraordinary powers and special responsibilities, these drill sergeants deserved punishment for violating that trust.

While some claimed that the guilty verdicts at Aberdeen were 'an indictment of a military system that aids and abets the abuse of power', the vast majority of commentators viewed the guilty verdicts at Aberdeen as 'a victory for the Army's efforts to punish men in authority who abuse women in their charge'.[9] The army, in any event, believed it had proved that a criminal element was to blame for the trainee abuse, and that it had fixed responsibility for that abuse. After all, had not the worst offender been sentenced to a quarter-century in prison?

---

9. Dana Priest, 'Verdict deepens divisions over women in uniform', *Washington Post*, 30 April 1997; Paul Richter, 'Drill sergeant guilty of 18 charges of rape', *Los Angeles Times*, 30 April 1997; Scott Wilson, 'Aberdeen sergeant convicted', *Baltimore Sun*, 30 April 1997; unsigned editorial: 'Women in the military', *Washington Post*, 1 May 1997.

The US Congress, influenced in part by news media and public interest in the courts-martial proceedings at Aberdeen, was not convinced that the army's policies on sexual misconduct had been vindicated. On the contrary, some elected officials claimed that Aberdeen was a symptom of a much bigger institutional problem. To discover whether their complaints had merit, and to learn if a systemic flaw needed fixing, senior army commanders commissioned two reports to review and assess policies on sexual harassment.

The first report, authored by the army's Inspector-General, reviewed sexual harassment policies and procedures at basic and advanced individual training sites throughout the army. It also evaluated sexual harassment training provided to men and women initially entering the army. The second report, by the 'Senior Review Panel on Sexual Harassment' (which included prominent men and women) was a comprehensive review of the army's human relations environment. Both reports were based on interviews with thousands of soldiers and civilians at over 50 army posts in the United States and overseas. Never had such a comprehensive examination of the treatment of women in the army been achieved.

Both reports reached the same conclusion: the army had serious problems in the area of the treatment of women soldiers. There was 'endemic sexual harassment crossing gender, rank, and racial lines [in the army] . . . and [the army] lacks the institutional commitment to treat men and women equally'. Both also opined that the army's system for reporting abuse was flawed. But, most importantly, both concluded that the root cause for these problems was that men and women soldiers did not trust their officer and NCO leaders to create a healthy, safe and secure environment for them, and consequently did not report sexual harassment or other sex-related misconduct to those in authority. As the Panel report put it, 'passive leadership has allowed sexual harassment to persist'. Taken together, the two reports were harsh criticism. Newspaper headlines loudly trumpeted that the army was 'rife with sexual discrimination', and that there was 'wide abuse of women'. Not surprisingly, both friends and foes of the army were alarmed at the seeming magnitude of the issue.[10]

Stung by this criticism, but also recognizing the need for a renewed institutional initiative towards ending sex-related discrimination, the army's senior leaders drafted a plan for correcting the leadership and training deficiencies identified. First, new procedures for selecting and training drill sergeants were implemented, and more officers and NCOs were added to

---

10. Associated Press, 'Report: army rife with sexual discrimination', *Daily Progress* (Charlottesville, VA), 12 September 1997; Dana Priest, 'Army finds wide abuse of women', *Washington Post*, 12 September 1997; Philip Shenon, 'Army's leadership blamed in report on sexual abuses', *New York Times*, 12 September 1997.

training programmes to ensure that there was an adequate leader presence in the training environment. Second, the army began an initiative aimed at strengthening the teaching and reinforcing of army values, specifically by adding an extra week to training during which raw recruits were indoctrinated in the values of loyalty, duty, respect, selfless service, honour, integrity and personal courage. Soldiers already on active duty also were to receive new training on the importance of these seven army values.[11] While the impetus for this new training was certainly a desire to end sex-related discrimination, and avoid any future Aberdeen Proving Ground scenarios, the new instruction has not focused on male–female relationships. On the contrary, because army values training emphasizes that all soldiers are entitled to be treated with dignity and respect, the training has not caused resentment among male soldiers, nor has it resulted in any hostility towards women soldiers.

By mid-1998, the army's plan had been fully implemented at its training centres, and soldiers who had long ago completed their basic and advanced training programmes were receiving additional instruction at their units. Left unsaid, but clear to all concerned, was that the ultimate tool for enforcing army standards regarding the treatment of women would continue to be criminal law.

Conclusion

Today, the army's leaders, if not all soldiers, agree that sexual harassment and fraternization corrode the military discipline needed in an effective fighting force.

Sexual harassment was the natural consequence of a traditional all-male army that viewed macho behaviour as good, reinforced by a similar point of view within wider society. A successful gender-integrated army, where every soldier must be treated with dignity and respect if the highest possible unit cohesiveness is to be achieved, requires an end to sexual harassment. Similarly, sexual relations between officers and enlisted personnel, or between enlisted superiors and their subordinates, must also be forbidden if a gender-integrated army is to succeed. To achieve these twin goals, commanders look to military criminal law as part of the solution for suppressing

---

11. Tom Bowman, 'Army panel expected to recommend tighter screening for drill sergeants', *Baltimore Sun*, 4 June 1997; Associated Press, 'Training emphasis on values', *Augusta Chronicle*, 25 October 1998.

sexual harassment and fraternization; the law will either deter unacceptable behaviour by causing individual soldiers to modify their behaviour, or it will result in their elimination from the army.

Events at Aberdeen showed conclusively that military law was effective in punishing those in authority who abuse female soldiers by engaging in coercive sexual relationships. But Aberdeen also demonstrated that the army's efforts to prevent sexual harassment and sex-related fraternization had been inadequate. New initiatives resulting from two reports commissioned in the aftermath of Aberdeen should invigorate the army's fight against sexual harassment and sex-related fraternization. It remains to be seen if these new initiatives will succeed. With women constituting about one-seventh of today's army, and serving in a variety of critical positions as both officers and enlisted soldiers, the army must eliminate sexual harassment and fraternization. There is no alternative if the gender-integrated force is to be truly effective.

Fred L. Borch III is a career army officer. A colonel in the Judge Advocate General's Corps, he has an A.B. (History), a J.D. (Law), LL.M. (International and Comparative Law), and LL.M. (Military Law). His speciality is military criminal law. He was in charge of the prosecution team in the recent high-exposure rape and sexual harassment trial involving personnel at the Aberdeen Proving Ground in Maryland. He recently completed a monograph entitled *Judge Advocates in Combat*, a history of army lawyers in military operations from Vietnam to Haiti.

Brian Crim is a Ph.D. candidate in modern European history at Rutgers University. Publications include articles on Geoffrey Parker, Alfred Vagts, and European expansion in the forthcoming volume of the Encyclopedia of Historians and Historical Writings, as well as several articles addressing the interaction between the military and society.

Gerard J. DeGroot is a senior lecturer and Chairman of the Modern History Department at the University of St Andrews. He has published seven books, including *Blighty: British Society in the Era of the Great War* (London, 1996), *Student Protest: The Sixties and After* (London, 1998) and *A Noble Cause?: America and the Vietnam War* (London, 1999). He has also written seven scholarly articles on the experiences of women in the military, which have been published in *History*, *War in History* and the *Army Quarterly and Defence Journal*. He is currently writing (along with Corinna Peniston-Bird) a monograph on women and war.

Kathryn M. Coughlin is a third-year Ph.D. candidate at Georgetown University in Washington, DC, in the Department of History, focusing on women and gender, and law and society in the Middle East. Her articles have appeared in the *Arab Studies Journal*, *Odyssey* and *Huguenot*. She has reviewed books for the *Arab Studies Journal*, *Middle East Studies Association Bulletin* (North America), *Islamic Law and Society*, *Periodica Islamica* and *Islam and Muslim–Christian Relations*; she is currently writing her dissertation on Islamic law on marriage in medieval North Africa and Spain.

Scott N. Hendrix received his B.A. in history and his M.A. in American history from Cleveland State University, in Cleveland, Ohio. He is currently a candidate for the Ph.D. in history at the University of Pittsburgh. He is preparing a dissertation entitled 'The spirit of the corps: the pan-European martial culture and the British Army in North America, 1754–1783'.

Dafna N. Izraeli is a professor in the Department of Sociology and Anthropology and is Chair of the Interdisciplinary Graduate Program in Gender Studies at Bar Ilan University in Israel. Her books include *Competitive Frontiers: Women Managers in a Global Economy* (Cambridge, MA, 1994, with Nancy Adler); *Women in Israel* (New Brunswick, NJ, 1993, with Yael Azmon) and *Dual Earner Families in International Perspective* (London, 1992, with Susan Lewis and Helen Hootsmans). Her current research addresses work and family.

Lance Janda received his Ph.D. from the University of Oklahoma in 1998. His dissertation was entitled 'Stronger than custom: West Point and the admission of women, 1972–1980', and has evolved into a manuscript now under consideration at a major university press. He is the author of 'Shutting the gates of mercy: the American origins of total war, 1860–1880', *Journal of Military History* 59 (January 1995). He is currently an Assistant Professor at Cameron University teaching 20th century American and military history.

Nicole F. Ladewig is currently a Masters student in History, with an emphasis in comparative world history, at the State University of New York, College at Brockport. Her undergraduate degree is in the field of economics and was conferred by Gordon College. She has spent two years working for an international comparative social database housed in Luxembourg and two years working for a marketing corporation in the field of corporate development.

Corinna Peniston-Bird is currently a research fellow at Lancaster University, working on gender and the Home Guard. She specializes in identity issues: her Ph.D. examined Austrian national identity and she has published an annotated bibliography on Vienna. She is currently exploring gender identities through the issue of women in the military and is writing a monograph on women and the military with Gerard DeGroot.

Reina Pennington is a former US Air Force officer and specialist on Soviet aviation. During her service she flew in a dozen different fighter aircraft, including the F-15 and F-16. She is currently completing a Ph.D. in history at the University of South Carolina, where she also teaches. She has published widely in academic and military journals and is the editor of the forthcoming *Military Women Worldwide: A Biographical Dictionary* (Westport, CT, forthcoming) and is also completing *Women and War: Soviet Women's Military Aviation Regiments in the Second World War* (Kansas, forthcoming).

Edward J. Rielly chairs the English Department and is director of the honours programme at Saint Joseph's College in Maine. His publications include seven books of poetry, a book on Jonathan Swift, and many short stories, articles and book reviews. His work on the Vietnam War includes several articles, a course on Literature of the Vietnam War that he teaches, and a book in progress on US poetry written about the war.

Susan M. Rigdon is a research associate in Anthropology and faculty associate in the Arms Control, Disarmament, and International Security Program at the University of Illinois. She is the author of a book on poverty and culture and co-author of five others, including a three-volume series on the Cuban Revolution, and (with Christina K. Gilmartin and Isabel Crook) the forthcoming *Surviving in Prosperity: Rural Reconstruction and Resistance in a Sichuan Township*.

Christopher Schmitz has lectured in the Department of Modern History at the University of St Andrews since 1979, teaching courses on social and economic history and late nineteenth-century British imperialism in Africa. He is the author of numerous books and articles, including *The Growth of Big Business in the United States and Western Europe 1850–1939* (Cambridge, 1995), and is currently writing a book on the experiences of nurses in the Anglo-Boer War of 1899–1902.

Laurie Stoff is a Ph.D. candidate in the Department of History at the University of Kansas. Her specialism is in Russian and East European History. Her dissertation focuses on the experiences of women soldiers in Russia during the First World War, both as individuals and as members of the all-female military units which were created by the Russian Provisional Government in 1917. She has also served as historical consultant for several television and film productions, advising producers on the experiences of Russian women soldiers of the First World War, including the Arts and Entertainment Network documentary series *Foot Soldier* and the PBS/BBC documentary series *The Great War*.

Penny Summerfield has been appointed to the Chair of Modern History at Manchester University. She was previously Professor of Women's History at the University of Lancaster. Her interests are in gender and history, focusing especially on women in the Second World War and the post-war period, and on the education of girls in the nineteenth and twentieth centuries. She has worked with oral history and is interested in the historical uses of autobiographical sources. She has published a large number of books and articles, most recently *Reconstructing Women's Wartime Lives: Discourse and Subjectivity in Oral Histories of the Second World War* (Manchester, 1998). She was guest editor of the 1997 special issue of *International History Review* devoted to women and war.

Catherine Taylor graduated from the University of St Andrews with a M.A. (Hons) in International Relations and Geography in 1996 and went on to earn an M.Litt. in International Security Studies in 1998. She was a member of the British Labour Party's National Executive Committee from 1995 to 1997 and stood as a parliamentary candidate in the 1997 general election. She is currently personal assistant to to Anne Begg MP (Aberdeen South), and a prospective candidate for the European Parliament.

Karen Turner is professor of History at Holy Cross College and a senior fellow in the East Asian Legal Studies Program at Harvard Law School. She earned her masters in Asian Studies from Yale University and her doctorate in Chinese history from the University of Michigan. Her research since 1979, when she first lived in China, has focused on law in early China and has been published in a variety of venues, including *The Limits of the Rule of Law in China* (Washington, DC, 2000). Since 1993, she has researched Vietnamese women veterans, and in 1998, with the assistance of a Hanoi journalist, Phan Thanh Hao, she published *Even the Women Must Fight: Memories of War from North Vietnam* (New York, 1998), based on interviews and writings from women of northern Vietnam.

Margaret Collins Weitz received her B.A. and M.A. from Ohio State University and her Ph.D. from Harvard University. In 1984 she was appointed chairman and professor in the Department of Humanities and Modern Languages at Suffolk University in Boston, Massachusetts. She has has won many awards and published extensively, including *Sisters in the French Resistance: How Women Fought to Free France, 1940–1945* (New York, 1986).

Helen Praeger Young is currently an Associate Scholar at the Center for East Asian Studies, Stanford University. After completing her graduate work at Stanford University in East Asian Studies, she taught at the Beijing Foreign Studies University for many years. Her publications include 'From soldier to doctor: a Chinese woman's story of the Long March', *Science and Society* 59 (Winter 1995–96); 'Why we joined the Revolution: voices of Chinese women soldiers', in Nicole Dombrowski, ed., *Women and War in the Twentieth Century: Enlisted With or Without Consent* (New York, 1999); and *Choosing Revolution: Chinese Women Soldiers on the Long March* (Urbana, IL, forthcoming).

(The place of publication is London, unless otherwise noted.)

General

For a single-volume introduction, Linda Grant De Pauw's *Battle Cries and Lullabies: Women in War from Prehistory to the Present* (Norman, OK, 1998) is an ambitious attempt to cover the roles women have played in warfare from the beginning of human history to the present day, in all areas of the world. Jean Bethke Elshtain, *Women and War* (New York, 1987) is a provocative and thought-provoking analysis of the myths surrounding men, women and war, which examines these themes in discourses on war and in conceptions of gender. A re-evaluation of conceptions of gender can also be found in Sharon Macdonald, Pat Holden and Shirley Ardener, eds, *Images of Women in Peace and War: Cross-cultural and Historical Perspectives* (1987), in which eleven essays explore the relationship between women and revolution and war, from the Amazons to the protesters at Greenham Common. The collection edited by Lois Ann Lorentzen and Jennifer Turpin, *The Women and War Reader* (New York, 1998), highlights the complexities within the gendering of warfare and addresses such issues as ethnicity, citizenship, motherhood, and policy and peacemaking. For articles specifically on the roles played by women in Europe and America in the two world wars, and the impact of those wars on gender relations, see Margaret Randolph Higonnet, Jane Jenson, Sonya Michel and Margaret Collins Weitz, eds, *Behind the Lines: Gender and the Two World Wars* (New Haven, CT, 1987).

Chapter One   Silent partners: women and warfare in early modern Europe

An introductory text on early modern warfare can be found in Michael Howard, *War in European History* (Oxford, 1976). The author, one of the founders of academic military history, provides a magnificent survey and useful background information, although little on women's roles. A foundation text for the issue of women and war is Jean Bethke Elshtain, *Women and War* (New York, 1987). More interested in philosophy and gender constructions than historical examples, Elshtain covers Antiquity to the modern era. Texts which cover the early modern era include Mary Erler and Maryanne Kowaleski, eds, *Women and Power in the Middle Ages* (Athens, GA, 1988), which delineates the division between the public and private spheres from the birth of feudal society to its decline. Both noblewomen and less prominent women are discussed in the various essays. An introductory study of gender in early modern Europe is also found in Merry E. Wiesner's *Women and Gender in Early Modern Europe* (New York, 1993), which offers a comprehensive treatment of the multiple ways in which gender influenced every aspect of society, including warfare. A text which specifically addresses women's involvement in the military is the collection edited by Helen M. Cooper, Adrienne Auslander Munich and Susan Merill Squier entitled *Arms and the Woman: War, Gender and Literary Representation* (Chapel Hill, NC, 1989). This collection of essays explores the ways in which women shaped the creation of literature related to war. It is cross-cultural, and several essays concern the early modern era. Finally, a textual analysis of Christine de Pisan's principal works set in the relevant historical background can be found in Marilynn Desmond's *Christine de Pizan and the Categories of Difference* (Minneanpolis, MN, 1998). This text reflects the recent explosion of interest in Pisan.

Chapter Two   In the army: women, camp followers and gender roles in the British Army in the French and Indian Wars, 1755–1765

Christopher Duffy is one of the acknowledged authorities in the field of eighteenth-century warfare. His *The Military Experience in the Age of Reason* (New York, 1988) is a general survey examining the eighteenth-century European military world. Victor Neuburg's *Gone for a Soldier: A History of Life in the British Ranks from 1642* (London, 1989) is not a scholarly work but it is an accessible, well-illustrated survey of the topic, which also discusses the lives of camp followers. Sylvia R. Frey, *The British Soldier in America: A Social History of Military Life in the Revolutionary Period* (Austin, TX, 1981) is, exactly as the title describes, a social history of the British Army in the Revolutionary War period, which also devotes some attention to camp followers. John R. Elting's *Swords Around a Throne: Napoleon's Grande Armée* (New York, 1988) is an in-depth study of Napoleon's army. It is also highly entertaining reading, and includes a chapter dealing with camp followers. Holly Mayer's *Belonging to the Army: Camp Followers and Community during the American Revolution* (Columbia, SC, 1996) offers a detailed examination of the entire non-combatant component, including women, of the Continental Line. Byron Farwell's *Mr Kipling's Army: All the Queen's Men* (New York, 1981), while not, strictly speaking, a scholarly work, is a readable account of life in the British Army in the Victorian era which includes a chapter on the lives of women who followed the army. Cynthia Enloe's *Does Khaki Become You? The Militarization of Women's Lives* (Boston, 1983) offers a feminist perspective on the subject of women and militarization. Its first chapter deals with women camp followers.

Chapter Three 'We too were soldiers': the experiences of British nurses in the Anglo-Boer War, 1899–1902

Thomas Pakenham's *The Boer War* (1979) is the standard history of the conflict. It is very detailed and highly readable, but tends to concentrate on political and military events. A stimulating and wide-ranging selection of essays on social, political and military aspects of the war is provided in Peter Warwick's edited collection *The South African War: The Anglo-Boer War 1899–1902* (1980). Particularly useful is its chapter on 'Women and the war', by S.B. Spies. The only readily available substantial account of the development of British military nursing before the First World War is *Angels and Citizens: British Women as Military Nurses, 1854–1914* (1988) by Anne Summers. It is essential reading for this topic. Juliet Piggott's *Queen Alexandra's Royal Army Nursing Corps* (1975) provides general background on the development of army nursing since the late nineteenth century, but with disappointingly little detail. Charlotte Searle's *The History of the Development of Nursing in South Africa 1652–1960* (Cape Town, 1965) is an authoritative and well-documented account, with a substantial chapter on the Anglo-Boer War. For the Australian experience, see Jan Bassett, *Guns and Brooches: Australian Army Nursing from the Boer War to the Gulf War* (Melbourne, 1992). It includes a vivid discussion of the mixed experiences of 'colonial' recruits to South African war nursing, with some evocative contemporary photographs.

Chapter Four   They fought for Russia: female soldiers of the First World War

The most authoritative and comprehensive study of the Russian Army during the First World War is Allen Wildman, *The End of the Russian Imperial Army, Vol. 1: The Old Army and the Soldiers' Revolt (March–April, 1917)* (Princeton, 1980) and *The End of the Russian Imperial Army, Vol. 2: The Road to Soviet Power and Peace* (Princeton, 1987), although the focus of both is on the collapse of the army in 1917. The second volume contains a sparse account of the women's units. Richard Stites covers both the individual women soldiers and all-female units only very briefly in his work *The Women's Liberation Movement in Russia: Feminism, Nihilism, and Bolshevism, 1860–1930* (Princeton, 1978), but it is a good starting point. For a broader perspective on the effects of the war on Russian women, Alfred G. Meyer's essay 'The impact of World War I on Russian women's lives', in Barbara Clements *et al.*, eds, *Russia's Women: Accommodation, Resistance, Transformation* (Berkeley, CA, 1991) is an excellent overview. Richard Abraham's essay 'Mariia L. Bochkareva and the Russian Amazons of 1917', in Linda Edmonson, ed., *Women and Society in Russia and the Soviet Union* (Cambridge, 1992) also contains useful information about the commander and her unit, but more closely resembles a literary review than a historical analysis. The most comprehensive published study of the women's units is Alexander Senin's 'Zhenskie batal'ony i voennye komandy v 1917 godu', *Voprosy Istorii* 10 (1987), though it is available only in Russian. Fuller coverage is given to both the individual women soldiers and the all-female combat units in Laurie Stoff's as yet unpublished dissertation 'Russian women in combat: female soldiers of the First World War' (University of Kansas M.A., 1995).

Chapter Five   Women at work: Chinese soldiers on the Long March 1934–1936

Edgar Snow's *Red Star over China* (New York, 1938) is the classic account of the Long March by a journalist and contains the only authorized biography of Mao Zedong, written from notes of interviews in Yan'an in 1936. Benjamin Yang's *From Revolution to Politics: Chinese Communists on the Long March* (Boulder, CO, 1990) is a political and military history which draws heavily on Chinese sources. For the role of women on the Long March, see Lin Jiang, ed., *Twentieth-Century Chinese Servicewomen* (*Ershi ji Zhongguo Funu*) (Beijing, 1995). The text is in both Chinese and English, and contains photographs of many of the women mentioned in this book. Helen Praeger Young's *Choosing Revolution: Chinese Women Soldiers on the Long March* (Urbana, IL, forthcoming), based on interviews with women soldiers, expands upon the experiences recounted in this book. For information about women in China generally, see Margery Wolf and Roxane Witke, eds, *Women in Chinese Society* (Stanford, CA, 1975), which provides useful insight into the complexity of the lives of Chinese women historically. Christina Kelley Gilmartin's *Engendering the Chinese Revolution: Radical Women, Communist Politics, and Mass Movements in the 1920s* (Berkeley, CA, 1995) is an excellent analysis of the work women did and their role in the Communist Party during the 1920s.

Chapter Six   Lipstick on her nipples, cordite in her hair: sex and romance among British servicewomen during the Second World War

The subject of sexual relations during the Second World War (and the eroticism of war) is covered, in somewhat sensationalist manner, in John Costello's *Love, Sex and War* (1985) and Paul Fussel's *Wartime* (1989). Relations (and love affairs) between British women and American servicemen are examined, with due seriousness but no consequent lack of fascination, in the excellent *Rich Relations* (1995) by David Reynolds. Penny Summerfield's recent study, *Reconstructing Women's Wartime Lives* (Manchester, 1998), provides a stimulating analysis of the way women's identity was shaped by their wartime experience and how that identity has evolved since. The phenomenon of the ATS mixed anti-aircraft batteries is examined in detail in Gerard DeGroot's ' "I love the scent of cordite in your hair": gender dynamics in mixed anti-aircraft batteries during the Second World War', *History* 82 (1997); and 'Whose finger on the trigger? Mixed anti-aircraft batteries and the female combat taboo', *War in History* 4 (1997). A personal memoir of the mixed batteries is provided by Vee Robinson in *On Target* (Wakefield, 1991). For a comparative study of women's combat experience, see D'Ann Campbell, 'Women in combat: the World War II experience in the United States, Great Britain, Germany and the Soviet Union', *Journal of Military History* 57 (1993).

Chapter Seven 'She wants a gun not a dishcloth!': gender, service and citizenship in Britain in the Second World War

The most authoritative recent history of the Home Guard is S.P. Mackenzie's *The Home Guard: A Military and Political History* (Oxford, 1995), although its coverage of the issue of women's membership is brief. More misogynist, and lightweight, is N. Longmate, *The Real Dad's Army: The Story of the Home Guard* (1974). Those interested in cultural representations of the Home Guard should see J. Richards, '"Dad's Army" and the politics of nostalgia', in J. Richards, ed., *Films and British National Identity, from Dickens to Dad's Army* (Manchester, 1997), although again this does not make more than a passing reference to gender issues. On feminist politics in wartime see A. Oram, '"Bombs don't discriminate!" Women's political activism in the Second World War', in C. Gledhill and G. Swanson, eds, *Nationalising Femininity: Culture, Sexuality and British Cinema in the Second World War* (Manchester, 1996). And for a discussion of women's memories of wartime experiences (including those of one woman who joined the Home Guard) see P. Summerfield, *Reconstructing Women's Wartime Lives: Discourse and Subjectivity in Oral Histories of the Second World War* (Manchester, 1998).

Chapter Eight Soldiers in the shadows: women of the French Resistance

Although the bibliography for the French Resistance is extensive, little focuses on women. Notable exceptions include Lucie Aubrac, *Outwitting the Gestapo* (Bozeman, MT, 1993) and Margaret Collins Weitz, *Sisters in the Resistance: How Women Fought to Free France 1940–1945* (New York, 1996, 1998), which offers an introduction into Vichy France and then examines the different areas in which women were active. Another text based on interviews is Margaret Rossiter, *Women in the Resistance* (New York, 1986). Useful background is also provided in Jean-Pierre Azéma, *From Munich to the Liberation* (Cambridge, 1984), which covers France from 1938 to 1944. Additional material can also be found in Marie-Madeleine Fourcade, *Noah's Arc* (1973) and the works of Roderick H. Kedward, including *Resistance in Vichy France* (Oxford, 1978). Readers of French could also examine the collection *Les Femmes dans la Résistance: Actes du colloque tenu à l'initiative de L'Union des Femmes*

Françaises (Monaco, 1977), Claude Bourdet, *L'Aventure incertaine* (Paris, 1975) and Henri Nogueres, *La Vie quotidienne des résistants:de l'armistice à la Libération* (Paris, 1984), which examines the daily life of the resisters. As a point of comparison, Maria de Blasio Wilhelm, *The Other Italy* (New York, 1988) examines the resistance in Italy from 1939 to 1945.

Chapter Nine   'Do not speak of the services you rendered': women veterans of aviation in the Soviet Union

The first scholarly history of Soviet women as military aviators during the Second World War is Reina Pennington, *Wings, Women and War: Soviet Women's Military Aviation Regiments in the Great Patriotic War* (Lawrence, KS, forthcoming). See also the author's article 'Offensive women: women in combat in the Red Army', in Paul Addison and Angus Calder, eds, *Time to Kill: The Soldier's Experience of War in the West 1939–1945* (1997). It provides an overview of women's experiences in the Red Army during the Second World War. A similarly scholarly overview which covers the combat experiences of women in many countries can be found in Nancy Loring Goldman's edited collection *Female Soldiers – Combatants or Noncombatants?: Historical and Contemporary Perspectives* (Westport, CT, 1982). This is an indispensable collection of essays for providing a comparative perspective. Published sources include Svetlana Alexiyevich, *War's Unwomanly Face* (U voiny – ne zhenskoe litso . . .) (Moscow, 1988), translated by Keith Hammond and Lyudmila Lezhneva. This is an invaluable collection of first-hand accounts based on the authors' interviews with more than 200 Soviet women veterans. Medics, snipers, partisans, and many other women soldiers tell their stories here for the first time in a book published in English. K. Jean Cottam's *Women in Air War: The Eastern Front of World War II* (Neapean, Ontario, 1997) is an edited translation of the second edition of a collection compiled by M.A. Kazarinova and A.A. Polyantseva entitled *V nebe frontovom. Sbornik vospominaniy Sovetskikh Letchits-Uchastnits Velikoy Otechestvenonoy Voyny* (In the Sky Above the Front: A Collection of Memoirs of Soviet Airwomen Participants in the Great Patriotic War) (Molodaya Gvardiya, 1971). An outstanding collection of interviews with the Soviet women who flew in the Second World War can be found in Anne Noggle's *A Dance with Death: Soviet Airwomen in World War II* (College Station, TX, 1994). This collection also includes photographs.

Chapter Ten   Soldiers and symbols: North Vietnamese women and the American war

The single most useful account of women's issues during the anti-colonial resistance movements is David Marr's *Vietnamese Tradition on Trial, 1920– 1945* (Berkeley, CA, 1981). For a very complete history of women in the resistance by female scholars in Vietnam, see Mai Thi Tu and Le Thi Nham Tuyet, *Women in Vietnam* (Hanoi, 1978); and Arlene Eisen, *Women and Revolution in Vietnam* (1984). Kathleen Barry's *Vietnam's Women in Transition* (1996), an edited collection of short articles mostly by Vietnamese scholars, is a very useful source for seeing the sorts of problems that concern Viet- namese women in the 1990s. For a Vietnamese view of the many forms of family relations see Rita Liljestrom and Tuong Lai, eds, *Sociological Studies on the Vietnamese Family* (Hanoi, 1991). Karen Turner's *Even the Women Must Fight: Memories of War from Vietnam* (New York, 1998) combines graphic interviews and original archival research in a book which allows the women veterans of the Vietnam wars to speak for themselves.

Chapter Eleven   'Dark Angel': Vietnam War poetry by women veterans

The most thorough examination of poetry about the Vietnam War is Vince Gotera's *Radical Visions: Poetry by Vietnam Veterans* (1994). Lynda Van Devanter's powerful memoir *Home Before Morning* (New York, 1984) is essential reading for anyone studying the effect of the Vietnam War on women who served. Her *Visions of War, Dreams of Peace* (New York, 1991) (written with Joan A. Furey) is the most important, and so far only substantial, anthology of poems by women veterans. Kathryn Marshall's edited collection *In the Com- bat Zone: Vivid Personal Reflections of the Vietnam War from the Women Who Served There* (New York, 1988) is, as the title suggests, a vivid description of the experiences of women who served and the effect of the war upon them. Marilyn McMahon's *Works in Progress* (Seattle, 1988) and *Works in Progress II* (Seattle, 1990) contain the work of perhaps the finest poet among women veterans of the Vietnam War. *Women Veterans: America's Forgotten Heroines* (New York, 1983), by June A. Willenz, is an important attempt to correct a long pattern of neglecting American women who have served in war. *Long Time Passing: Vietnam and the Haunted Generation* (Garden City, NY, 1984), by

Myra MacPherson, is a profound study of the emotional and psychological effects of the Vietnam War on military men and women who served there. The most perceptive exploration of the causes, symptoms and treatment of post-traumatic stress disorder can be found in *Achilles in Vietnam: Combat Trauma and the Undoing of Character* (New York, 1995) by Jonathan Shay, though it only touches lightly on women veterans. In *Waiting for an Army to Die: Tragedy of Agent Orange* (New York, 1983), Fred Wilcox provides a gripping and provocative study of the effect of Agent Orange on those contaminated by it.

Chapter Twelve   Women, war and the veil: Muslim women in resistance and combat

There is a dearth of scholarly literature on Muslim women in combat or armed resistance; on the other hand, a veritable flood of literature on women and Islam is available. The sole monograph on Muslim women as actors in war, Minou Reeves's *Female Warriors of Allah* (New York, 1989), is recommended with a caveat: this account is not a scholarly one and she tends towards sensationalism at times. Though a bit dated, Nikkie Keddie's and Beth Baron's edited volume *Women in Middle Eastern History* (New Haven, CT, 1991) offers a good overview of women and Islam from the classical period to the present; several chapters cover women and armed resistance. A more recent treatment of the subject is offered in Yvonne Haddad's and John Esposito's excellent volume *Islam, Gender, and Social Change* (New York, 1998). Eight case studies follow a solid introduction to the subject: Margot Badran's excellent research on Kuwaiti women and the Gulf War, Vivienne S.M. Angeles's article on Phillipine Moro women, and well-written articles on Muslim women in Iran, the Near East, the Gulf and Asia follow. For a historical foundation on women and Islam, Leila Ahmed's *Women and Gender in Islam* (New Haven, CT, 1992) offers a general background to the subject; the last third of the book deals with the modern period and the emergence of 'feminisms' in the Islamic world.

Chapter Thirteen   Between worlds: Algerian women in conflict

Alistair Horne's *A Savage War of Peace* (New York, 1977) remains the most detailed and reasonably balanced account of the Algerian War for Independence. For an excellent historiography of scholarship on Algeria, see Michael Brett, 'Anglo-Saxon attitudes: the Algerian war of independence in retrospect', *Journal of African History* 35 (1994). On the subject of Algerian women, Marnia Lazreg's *The Eloquence of Silence: Algerian Women in Question* (New York, 1994) offers a historical portrait of Algerian women which both frames and examines the ever-present 'women question' within the Algerian culture. Still immensely influential, particularly on the subject of women's liberation gained through active participation in the war for independence, is Frantz Fanon's *A Dying Colonialism* (New York, 1965), translated by Haakon Chevalier. Valetine M. Moghadam's edited collection *Gender and National Identity: Women and Politics in Muslim Societies* (1994) provides a comparative framework in which to place the stuggles of Algerian women. The recently published *Unbowed: An Algerian Woman Confronts Islamic Fundamentalism* (Philadelphia, PA, 1998), by Khalida Messaoudi and Elisabeth Schlema and translated by Anne C. Vila, provides a personal account of the current state of feminist movements within the turmoil of Islamic fundamentalism's resurgence in Algeria.

Chapter Fourteen   Gendering military service in the Israel Defence Forces

The extensive bibliography on the Israeli military only occasionally acknowledges women's presence with a passing reference to the exceptional fact that women are conscripted and totally ignores the issue of gender inequality. For a history of women in the Israeli military see Anne R. Bloom, 'Israel: the longest war', in Nancy L. Goldmann, ed., *Female Soldiers – Combatants or Non-Combatants? Theoretical and Contemporary Perspectives* (West Port, CT, 1982). For a discussion on compulsory service for women see Nitza Berkovitch, 'Motherhood as a national mission: the construction of womanhood in the legal discourse in Israel', *Women's Studies International Forum* (1998). Also useful are Rivka Bar-Yosef and Dorit Paden-Eisenstark, 'Role systems under stress: sex roles in war', *Social Problems* 25 (1977); Anne R. Bloom, 'Women in the Defence Forces', in B. Swirski and M. Safir, eds, *Calling the Equality Bluff* (New York, 1991), pp. 128–38; Anne R. Bloom and Rivka Bar-Yosef, 'Israeli women and military experience: a socialization experience', in M.P. Safir, M. Mednick, D.N. Izraeli and J. Bernard, eds, *Women's Worlds* (New York, 1983); Eva Eshkol, Amia Lieblich, Rivka Bar-Yosef and Hadas Wiseman, 'Some basic correlates of adjustment of Israel women soldiers to their military roles', in Dafna N. Izraeli (guest ed.) *Israel Social Science Research* 5 (1987).

For a critical appraisal of women's military service see Lesley Hazleton, *Israeli Women: The Reality Behind the Myth* (New York, 1977); Nira Yuval Davis, 'Israeli women and men: divisions behind the unity', *Change Report* 6 (1981) and 'Front and rear: the sexual division of labor in the Israeli Army', *Feminist Studies* 11 (1985). For a recent critical look at the impact of military experience on female identity see Orna Sasson-Levy, 'They walk upright and proud: the power and the price of military service for women soldiers in men's jobs', *NOGA – A Feminist Journal* 32 (1997), published in Hebrew.

Chapter Fifteen Women in China's changing military ethic

The most comprehensive English-language survey to date on the role of Chinese women's military activities from ancient to modern times is 'Women in the Chinese military' (unpublished dissertation, University of Maryland, 1995) by Li Xiaolin. The author is a former researcher in the PLA's General Political Department, whose mother was a veteran of the war against Japan. Coverage of the contemporary era is based in part on a survey of women soldiers in the Beijing area. Colonel Yao Yunzhu provides a concise summary of the current status of women in the Chinese armed forces in her 'Chinese women's role in the People's Liberation Army', published in the *Army Quarterly and Defence Journal* 25 and 26 (October 1995, January 1996). In a special issue of *China Quarterly* 146 (June 1996) entitled 'China's military in transition', some of the West's leading China scholars review professionalization, downsizing, administrative reorganization, and changes in weapons, strategy and tactics in the 1990s. But the minimal mention of women soldiers speaks volumes. Greater attention to women is given in Jiang Lin's *Ershi shiji zhongguo nubing* (Twentieth-Century Chinese Servicewomen) (Beijing, 1995), an official history released by Jiefang Chubanshe, the PLA's publishing house, in conjunction with the World Conference on Women held in Beijing in 1995. The writing style is socialist-heroic and the translation stilted, but this volume contains a good deal of useful information and a wonderful photographic survey of women soldiers. An official report on the status of women in China, including their role in China's national defence, is provided in the 'Report of the People's Republic of China on the implementation of the Nairobi forward-looking strategies for the advancement of women', in the *Beijing Review* (24–30 October 1994). Students of China's military must also familiarize themselves with Mao Zedong's *Selected Military Writings* (Beijing, 1967). These deal with strategy, tactics, the nature of warfare, and the supremacy of political over military doctrine.

Chapter Sixteen 'And don't forget to clean the fridge': women in the secret sphere of terrorism

As relevant background reading, Carol Gilligan's *In a Different Voice* (Cambridge, MA, 1993) provides a psychological analysis of men and women, showing how they think differently. A specific example of psychological analysis of female terrorists can be found in Luisella de Cataldo Neuburger's and Tiziana Valentini's *Women and Terrorism* (1996), which also outlines the motivations, roles and post-terrorism professions of Italian terrorists. A historical analysis of women in terrorism can also be found in Vera Braido's *Apostles into Terrorists* (1977), which is an account of Russian women terrorists at the turn of the century. An interesting contrast is provided by Jenny Hammond in *Sweeter than Honey: Testimonies of Tigrayan Women* (1989), which offers individual accounts of Tigrayan women who have turned to terrorism. A comprehensive volume of interviews with women terrorists from various movements and geographical locations can be found in Eileen MacDonald's *Shoot the Women First* (1991). For a fictional introduction to women in terrorism, see Doris Lessing's *The Good Terrorist* (1985), which, through the protagonist Alice, provides interesting insights into the motivations and experiences of a female terrorist.

Chapter Seventeen 'A simple matter of equality': the admission of women to West Point

The best secondary source on West Point is Rick Atkinson's *The Long Gray Line* (Boston, MA, 1989). It focuses on the class of 1966 and deals only briefly with the admission of women, but is invaluable to an understanding of the spirit, mentality and history of the institution. Judith Hicks Stiehm's *Bring Me Men and Women: Mandated Change at the US Air Force Academy* (Berkeley, CA, 1981) is easily the best scholarly treatment of the integration of women into the service academies. Stiehm, a sociologist, focuses on the Air Force Academy, but her themes and much of her writing touches on the other academies as well. Though not a scholarly work, Carol Barkalow's *In the Men's House: An Inside Account of Life in the Army by One of West Point's First Female Graduates* (New York, 1992) provides useful insight into the experiences of one of the first female graduates of West Point. Written with Andrea Raab, Barkalow's book also deals with her early years as an army officer. Donna Peterson, another graduate, recounts her experiences in *Dress Gray:*

A Woman at West Point (Austin, TX, 1990), and provides some interesting perspectives on the first women cadets. The recent experience of women in the US Navy is covered in *First Class: Women Join the Ranks at the Naval Academy* (Annapolis, MD, 1998) by Sharon Hanley Disher, a member of the academy's class of 1980. The Naval Academy was the most hidebound and antagonistic of all the service academies towards the admission of women. James Webb's 'Women can't fight', *The Washingtonian* (November 1979), encapsulates the arguments against women attending the academies and serving in combat, and sheds light on the views held by so many opponents of the integration of women into Annapolis, the Air Force Academy and West Point. Webb, a Naval Academy graduate, served with distinction in Vietnam, and later became Ronald Reagan's Secretary of the Navy. This article was very popular with male cadets and midshipmen when it was published.

Chapter Eighteen   Delilah shaves her hair: women, the military and Hollywood

Recommended reading falls into the three areas under debate: film, female identity, and the military. For the first, the excellent website: http://us.imdb.com provides information on actors, directors and screenwriters, as well as movie trivia. For a treatment of women in the media and the contradictory messages on gender identity, see the thought-provoking read provided by Susan J. Douglas, *Where the Girls Are: Growing Up Female with the Mass Media* (New York, 1994). For an introduction to gender and war in the twentieth century see Penny Summerfield's opening essay in the *International History Review* 19 (February 1997). For articles on various aspects of women and the military, including the gendering of the vocabulary of warfare, see Jean Bethke Elshtain and Sheila Tobias, *Women, Militarism and War: Essays in History, Politics and Social Theory* (Maryland, 1990).

Chapter Nineteen   Military law and the treatment of women soldiers: sexual harassment and fraternization in the US Army

On the modern American military, Jeanne Holm's *Women in the Military, An Unfinished Revolution* (Novato, CA, 1982) provides a comprehensive, if somewhat dated, treatment. The author, a retired general officer, supports a gender-integrated military. For the opposite viewpoint, see Brian Mitchell's *Weak Link: The Feminization of the American Military* (Washington, 1989). Mitchell, a former army officer who served in the 82nd Airborne Division, is outspokenly critical of the increased role for women in the US armed forces. On the subject of fraternization in the military, Kevin Carter's 'Fraternization' in *Military Law Review* 113 (1986) provides a comprehensive history of the problem. For a general discussion of sexual harassment, see Michele A. Paludi and Richard B. Barickman, *Academic and Workplace Sexual Harassment* (Albany, NY, 1991). Also of interest is Linda Francke's *Ground Zero: The Gender Wars in the Military* (1997), which offers a detailed study of the often bitter struggle to open combat positions to women and the unique problems women face in the military. Jean Zimmerman's *Tailspin* (New York, 1995) offers useful insight into how the US Navy dealt with the Tailhook scandal of 1991.

INDEX